DNA cloning
Volume III

a practical approach

TITLES PUBLISHED IN
THE
PRACTICAL APPROACH
SERIES

Series editors:
Dr D Rickwood
Department of Biology, University of Essex
Wivenhoe Park, Colchester, Essex CO4 3SQ, UK
Dr B D Hames
Department of Biochemistry, University of Leeds
Leeds LS2 9JT, UK

Affinity chromatography
Animal cell culture
Antibodies I & II
Biochemical toxicology
Biological membranes
Carbohydrate analysis
Cell growth and division
Centrifugation (2nd Edition)
Computers in microbiology
DNA cloning I, II & III
Drosophila
Electron microscopy
in molecular biology
Gel electrophoresis of nucleic acids
Gel electrophoresis of proteins
Genome analysis
HPLC of small molecules
HPLC of macromolecules
Human cytogenetics
Human genetic diseases
Immobilised cells and enzymes
Iodinated density gradient media
Light microscopy in biology
Lymphocytes
Lymphokines and interferons
Mammalian development
Medical bacteriology
Medical mycology

Microcomputers in biology
Microcomputers in physiology
Mitochondria
Mutagenicity testing
Neurochemistry
Nucleic acid and
protein sequence analysis
Nucleic acid hybridisation
Oligonucleotide synthesis
Photosynthesis:
energy transduction
Plant cell culture
Plant molecular biology
Plasmids
Prostaglandins
and related substances
Protein function
Protein sequencing
Protein structure
Proteolytic enzymes
Spectrophotometry
and spectrofluorimetry
Steroid hormones
Teratocarcinomas
and embryonic stem cells
Transcription and translation
Virology
Yeast

DNA cloning
Volume III

a practical approach

Edited by
D M Glover

Cancer Research Campaign, Eukaryotic Molecular Genetics
Research Group, Department of Biochemistry, Imperial College
of Science and Technology, London SW7 2AZ, UK

OXFORD · WASHINGTON DC

IRL Press
Eynsham
Oxford
England

First published 1987
Reprinted 1989

British Library Cataloguing in Publication Data

DNA cloning : a practical approach.—(Practical
  approach series)
  Vol.3
  1. Molecular cloning   2.   Recombinant DNA
  I.   Glover, David M.   II.   Series
  574.87′3282   QH442.2

ISBN 1-85221-049-4 (hardbound)
ISBN 1-85221-048-6 (softbound)

Cover illustration. The design for the cover was based on Figure 3 Chapter 4,
showing a phase contrast micrograph of *Escherichia coli* HB101 cells
producing prochymosin; Figure 10B Chapter 10, showing microinjection and
consequent swelling of the male pronucleus; and Figure 5A, Chapter 9,
showing a schematic representation for the generation of virus stocks.

Printed by Information Press Ltd, Oxford, England.

Preface

This is the third volume in this series describing DNA Cloning techniques, and as such is testimony to the pivotal position that these techniques now occupy in Molecular Biology. It was intended that the volumes complement and extend existing manuals describing the techniques of cloning DNA, especially the ubiquitous *Molecular Cloning* by Maniatis, Fritsch and Sambrook (Cold Spring Harbor Laboratory Press, New York, 1982). Their manual describes all basic cloning techniques and is referred to by most of the authors in this volume as it was in the first two volumes. The main theme of the first volume of *DNA Cloning* was the ongoing development of *Escherichia coli* as a host organism for a number of cloning systems. The second book looked at the diversity of other host/vector combinations that are used alongside *E. coli* to clone and express genes in prokaryotic and eukaryotic cells. The contents of this third volume are themselves diverse, and cover a variety of techniques for cloning and expressing DNA molecules. As with all laboratory oriented texts, some readers may well first require an introductory overview. As before, I recommend *Recombinant DNA: A Short Course* by Watson, Tooze and Kurtz (Scientific American Books, New York, 1983); *Principles of Gene Manipulation* by Old and Primrose (Blackwell, Oxford, 1985); and my book, *Gene Cloning: The Mechanics of DNA Manipulation* (Chapman and Hall, 1984).

The first chapter of the present volume covers the applications of plasmids containing promoters that are only recognized by RNA polymerases encoded by certain phages. These provide a means of synthesizing radiolabelled probes for several powerful types of analysis of nucleic acids. One set of cosmid vectors containing these promoters is examined in the second chapter. These vectors have been designed to facilitate walking along the chromosomes of higher eukaryotes. The phage promoters are positioned so that radiolabelled probes can be synthesized from the terminal regions of the inserted DNA, and subsequently be used to allow the isolation of overlapping cloned DNA segments. An alternative means of screening cosmid libraries appears in Chapter 3, which describes how cosmids can be selected genetically by homologous recombination with a probe plasmid *in vivo*. The latter half of the book focuses upon the expression of cloned genes. Many mammalian proteins have been expressed at high levels in *E. coli*, where they often form insoluble inclusion bodies, making the protein difficult to recover in a native form. Approaches to overcoming this and related problems are discussed in Chapter 4. The degradation of proteins of higher eukaryotes in *E. coli* can often be prevented by directing their synthesis as fusion proteins. These fusion proteins, in which the bacterial moiety is usually β-galactosidase, can be used as immunogens in order to raise antibodies against the eukaryotic segment. Two chapters describe how such fusion proteins can be used; one concentrating upon the production of antisera, and the other on monoclonal antibodies. Attention then turns to eukaryotic expression systems; first in a chapter devoted to the expression of foreign genes in yeast, and then in three chapters that examine mammalian cell systems. The first mammalian system that is described utilizes vectors which incorporate a gene that can be induced to amplify in order to overcome the toxic effects of a drug included in the culture medium. The cloned gene is also amplified and is consequently expressed at high levels. Retroviral vectors, described in the penultimate chapter, are finding widespread applications. Rather than dwelling upon the more specialized applications of these vectors, this Chapter describes the experimental principles of handling the vectors and their use as general purpose expression vectors. The final chapter in the book describes the approach that has so far had the most success as a means of introducing genes into the whole mouse; microinjection of the fertilized egg. This route is only one of several possibilities as a means of achieving this end, and perhaps these other approaches will be covered in other books in this series.

It can be seen from these three volumes that DNA Cloning techniques have made their impact upon most areas of biological research. Whilst the books reflect the current state of the technology, it is impossible to give definitive accounts of many of the techniques which are continuing to evolve over the years. I hope, nevertheless, that the essential experimental principles can be gleaned from this volume. The success of the book will be judged by whether it finds its way, tattered and torn, onto laboratory benches. I hope that it will and that the methods described in it will be useful to the Molecular Biology community. Finally, and most importantly, I would like to thank all the authors for their hard work.

David M.Glover

Contributors

C.R.Bebbington
Celltech Ltd, 244–250 Bath Road, Slough SL1 4DY, UK

A.M.C.Brown
Department of Cell Biology and Anatomy, Cornell University Medical Center, 1300 York Avenue, New York, NY 10021, USA

S.B.Carroll
Laboratory of Molecular Biology, University of Wisconsin–Madison, 1525 Linden Drive, Madison, WI 53706, USA

B.L.A.Carter
ZymoGenetics Inc., 2121 North 35th Street, Seattle, WA 98103, USA

J.Hanson
National Institute of Medical Research, The Ridgeway, Mill Hill, London NW7 1AA, UK

C.C.G.Hentschel
Celltech Ltd, 244–250 Bath Road, Slough SL1 4DY, UK

M.Irani
ZymoGenetics Inc., 2121 North 35th Street, Seattle, WA 98103, USA

I.Jackson
MRC Clinical and Population Cytogenetics Unit, Western General Hospital, Crewe Road, Edinburgh, UK

D.P.Lane
Imperial Cancer Research Fund, Clare Hall Laboratories, Blanche Lane, South Mimms, Potter's Bar, Herts EN6 3LD, UK

A.Laughon
Laboratory of Genetics, University of Wisconsin–Madison, 445 Henry Mall, Madison, WI 53706, USA

H.Lehrach
European Molecular Biology Laboratory, Postfach 10.2209, 69 Heidelberg, FRG

P.F.R.Little
Department of Biochemistry, Imperial College, London SW7 2AZ, UK

V.L.MacKay
ZymoGenetics Inc., 2121 North 35th Street, Seattle, WA 98103, USA

F.A.O.Marston
Celltech Ltd, 244–250 Bath Road, Slough SL1 4DY, UK

S.E.Mole
Imperial Cancer Research Fund, Clare Hall Laboratories, Blanche Lane, South Mimms, Potter's Bar, Herts EN6 3LD, UK

D.Murphy
National Institute of Medical Research, The Ridgeway, Mill Hill, London NW7 1AA, UK

A.Poustka
European Molecular Biology Laboratory, Postfach 10.2209, 69 Heidelberg, FRG

R.L.Seale
ZymoGenetics Inc., 2121 North 35th Street, Seattle, WA 98103, USA

M.R.D.Scott
Department of Microbiology and Immunology, HSE 407 University of California Medical Center, San Francisco, CA 94143, USA

A.V.Sledziewsky
ZymoGenetics Inc., 2121 North 35th Street, Seattle, WA 98103, USA

R.A.Smith
ZymoGenetics Inc., 2121 North 35th Street, Seattle, WA 98103, USA

Contents

3. GENETIC APPROACHES TO THE CLONING, MODIFICATION AND CHARACTERIZATION OF COSMID CLONES AND CLONE LIBRARIES 43

Annemarie Poustka and Hans Lehrach

8. THE USE OF VECTORS BASED ON GENE AMPLIFICATION FOR THE EXPRESSION OF CLONED GENES IN MAMMALIAN CELLS   163
Christopher R.Bebbington and Christopher C.G.Hentschel

9. RETROVIRAL VECTORS   189
Anthony M.C.Brown and Michael R.D.Scott

10. THE PRODUCTION OF TRANSGENIC MICE BY THE MICROINJECTION OF CLONED DNA INTO FERTILIZED ONE-CELL EGGS

David Murphy and Jennifer Hanson

Abbreviations

ADA	adenosine deaminase
AFP	alpha fetoprotein
AIDS	acquired immune deficiency syndrome
bGH	bovine growth hormone
BPV	bovine papilloma virus
BSA	bovine serum albumin
CAT	chloramphenicol acetyltransferase
CEA	anti-carcinoembryonic antigen
c.f.u.	colony forming units
CIP	calf intestinal phosphatase
dCF	deoxycoformycin
DEPC	diethyl pyrocarbonate
DHFR	dihydrofolate reductase
DIC	differential interference contrast
DMs	double minutes
DOC	deoxycholic acid
DPD	dimethyl-pimelimidate dihydrochloride
DTT	dithiothreitol
EDTA	ethylenediamine tetra-acetic acid
ELISA	enzyme linked immunosorbent assay
ES	embryonic stem cells
EtBr	ethidium bromide
FSH	follicle stimulating hormone
GS	glutamine synthetase
hCG	human chorionic gonadotrophin
HSRs	homogeneously staining regions
IGF	insulin-like growth factor
IPTG	isopropyl β-D-thiogalactosidase
KSCN	potassium thiocyanate
LPS	lipopolysaccharide
LTRs	long terminal repeats
2-ME	2-mercaptoethanol
MLP	major late protomer
MLV	murine leukaemia virus
Mo-MLV	Moloney murine leukaemia virus
Mo-MSV	Moloney sarcoma virus
MSX	methionine sulphoximine
ORF	open reading frame
PBS	phosphate-buffered saline
p.c.	post coitum
PDGF	platelet-derived growth factor
PEG	polyethylene glycol
PMSF	phenylmethylsulphonyl fluoride
RNAsin	ribonuclease inhibitor
RIA	radioimmunoassay
RSV	Rous sarcoma virus
SDS	sodium dodecyl sulphate

SDS-PAGE	polyacrylamide gel electrophoresis in the presence of SDS
SOD	superoxide dismutase
TBS	Tris-HCl, NaCl and EDTA
TCA	trichloroacetic acid
t-PA	tissue-type plasminogen activator
VNC	vanadyl nucleotide complex
xyl A	9-D xyloguanosyl adenine
YIp	yeast integrating vectors

CHAPTER 1

Application of plasmids containing promoters specific for phage-encoded RNA polymerases

PETER F.R.LITTLE and IAN J.JACKSON

1. SCOPE OF THE CHAPTER

This chapter provides methods for synthesizing and using RNA made *in vitro* with SP6, T7 and T3 phage-encoded RNA polymerases. We have concentrated primarily upon the use of radiolabelled probes for the routine analysis of nucleic acids and have not attempted to cover, in anything other than broad outline, more specialist uses such as *in situ* hybridization, anti-sense mRNA and translation of products. We have attempted to provide the key references in these areas that will allow a reasonable appreciation of technical possibilities.

2. BACTERIOPHAGE ENCODED RNA POLYMERASES

2.1 Background

It has been known for many years that a variety of *E. coli* bacteriophages encode RNA polymerases that are capable only of transcribing particular promoters contained on the phage DNA. T7 and T3 phages were early examples (1) and more recently the phage SP6 of *Salmonella typhimurium* was shown (2) to have a polymerase with similar properties.

Phage-encoded RNA polymerases differ in many respects from their host polymerases. They are generally small (90 – 100 000 daltons), monomeric and have very limited but none the less highly specific promoter requirements. In contrast, *E. coli* RNA polymerase is large, heteromultimeric and capable of initiating RNA synthesis from a wide range of promoter and promoter-like sequences (3). The practical consequence of these differences is that it is possible to use phage encoded RNA polymerases to initiate RNA synthesis *in vitro* and generate specific single stranded RNA molecules. This cannot easily be achieved with the *E. coli* enzyme.

The first enzyme to be systematically used for the preparation of RNA probes was SP6 RNA polymerase (4). This was primarily because the enzyme was exceptionally stable and could be isolated in high yield by simple procedures, in contrast to the enzymes from T7 or T3. These latter enzymes, because of a superior understanding of the genetic organization of T7 and T3, were subsequently made from cloned genes and are now readily available. The logic of use of the RNA polymerases is identical for

1

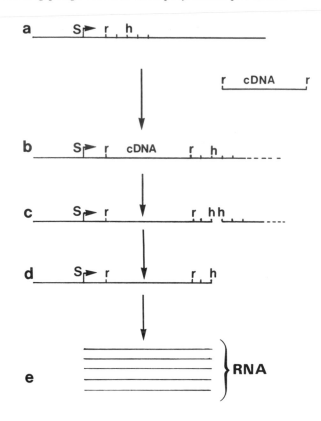

Figure 1. Principles of use of phage polymerase-containing vectors. **a.** The non-recombinant vector. The arrow head marked S is in this case the SP6 promoter, transcribing a multiple cloning site with cleavage positions of enzyme r and h indicated. **b.** A cDNA fragment (or any other DNA) with r sticky ends is cloned into the vector r site. **c.** The recombinant is cleaved at h, to generate a fragment that has promoter, cDNA and terminates at h. **d.** The template fragment, with h as the site at which the RNA polymerase will terminate by 'running-off. **e.** If template d is incubated with the appropriate RNA polymerase and NTP, RNA transcripts are generated that are co-linear with the DNA from the S promoter to the run off site, h. The transcripts can be separated from template by DNase digestion.

all three enzymes and is displayed in *Figure 1*. Usually the polymerases are used to run-off linear templates, but an alternative is to take advantage of the natural tendency of the enzymes to terminate prematurely in the presence of low concentration of nucleotide triphosphates. This has the advantage that no template linearization is required but the resulting probes are not of uniform length and so may not be applicable to some procedures detailed here.

2.2 **Why use RNA probes?**

RNA probes have all the advantages of single strand DNA probes — lack of competition of probe/probe hybridization, high specific activity compared to nick translation and readily defined length. They also have the added advantage over single strand DNA probes of great simplicity of preparation. Transcripts can be purified away from template by DNase digestion of templates and phenol extraction. This contrasts with the more laborious gel isolation required to obtain single-stranded DNA probes. However, RNA probes are more sensitive to degradation than equivalent DNA probes and this must not be overlooked. The commonest problem associated with RNA probes is the uncertainty of interpretation of a negative result.

2.2.1 *Unique properties of RNA probes*

RNA probes can substitute for DNA probes in all circumstances and generally with only minor modification of procedure. The greater stability of RNA:RNA duplexes can give rise to hybridization artifacts (hybridization to rRNA on Northerns can be a significant problem).

RNA probes used for RNase protection experiments have all the advantages enjoyed by single-stranded DNA probes (10) and nuclease S1 or Mung bean nuclease protection. RNA probes hybridized in solution will only protect from nuclease digestion sequences to which they are closely homologous and cleavage of some internal regions of mismatch may produce diagnostic fragment lengths. This enables specific sequences to be examined in the presence of other, closely related, sequences without interference. Thus, the product of one particular homeo-box sequence has been examined in the presence of others (11), transcripts of a human type II collagen gene were distinguished from the mouse homologue (12) and the human α1-antitrypsin mRNA was detected against a background of the mouse gene product (G.Kesley and R.Lovell-Badge, personal communication).

Sensitivity of detection of RNA by RNase protection is very high. Melton reports the detection of 0.5 pg of globin RNA in a simple model system (5). This is equivalent to detecting less than one transcript in 10^6 in a standard analysis of 40 μg of total RNA. Similar sensitivities are reported by Zinn *et al.* (13) using total cellular RNA to examine β-interferon transcription. Sensitivity enabling detection of one transcript in a million (or less than one transcript per cell) is about the same as the best Northern blot hybridization. O'Hare *et al.* (14) showed hybridization to the Drosophila *white* gene transcript, about 10 000-fold less abundant than actin. However, these Northern blots required 2 μg or more of polyA+ RNA equivalent to perhaps 100–200 μg total RNA, in contrast to 20–40 μg of total RNA in the protection experiments. Use of RNA probes in solution allows detection and quantitation of specific mRNAs from small amounts of material, and readily allows large numbers of samples to be processed quickly.

One significant advantage of RNase protection over any other method is that it allows an accurate quantitation of the level of RNA in the sample homologous to the probe. An explanation and an example of the method is given in Section 4.3. Note that the method gives an absolute figure (in terms of molecules per cell) rather than a value relative to some standard mRNA such as actin.

2.3 **Choice of vectors**

There are now a large number of vectors that contain promoters for SP6, T7 and T3 in a variety of contexts. Some of the most commonly used ones are detailed in *Figure 2*. Consideration of which vector to use is partly one of personal choice but a number of factors can be borne in mind.

RVIId7	SP6	250nt	H Bg P B R	
pSP62	SP6	42nt	H P S X B Sm Sa R	
pSP64	SP6	5nt	H P S X B Sm Sa	
pSP65	SP6	9nt	R Sa Sm B X S P H	
pSP64d1	SP6	2nt	S X B Sm Sa R	
pGEM3	SP6	7nt	H Sp P S X B Sm K Sa R	8nt T7
pT7-1	T7	6nt	R Sa Sm B X S P H	
BLUESCRIBE	T3	9nt	H Sp P S X B Sm K Sa R	5nt T7
BLUESCRIPT	T3	17nt	K A Xh S C H R5 R P Sm. . . . . . . .B Se Xb N E Sa2 Bx Sa	11nt T7

Figure 2. Cloning vectors contain SP6, T7 or T3 promoters. Only the useful cloning sites are shown for each vector and the distance between the initiation site and start of the polylinker cloning regions is given in nucleotides (nt). RV11d7 is detailed in reference 19, pSP62 in ref. 4, pSP64 and pSP65 in ref. 5. Ref. 6 contains details of eight additional plasmids, four of which contain SP6 and T7 promoters and many additional cloning sites. pSP64d1 is described in ref. 7. Transcripts from this plasmid have a very short 'leader' sequence. pGEM3 was constructed by and is available from Promega Biotech (Madison, USA), pT71 constructed by and is available from United States Biochemical Corp. (Cleveland, USA). Bluescribe and bluescript are both constructed and available from Stratagene (San Diego, USA). These latter plasmids have the significant advantage of having the α-complementation, lac Z color test for inserts, exactly as in the pUC series of plasmids. Bluescript can also be grown as a single-stranded DNA since it contains the M13 origin of DNA replication. Restriction site abbreviations A, *Apa*II; B, *Bam*HI; Bg, *Bgl*II; Bx, *Bst*XI; C, *Cla*I; E, *Eag*III; H, *Hin*dIII; K, *Kpn*I; N, *Not*I; P, *Pst*I; R, *Eco*RI; S, *Sal*I; Sa, *Sac*I; Sa2, *Sac*II; Sm, *Sma*I; Se, *Spe*I; Sp, *Sph*I; X, *Xma*I; Xb, *Xba*I; Xh, *Xho*I.

2.3.1 *Choice of cloning site*

This depends on the DNA sequence to be cloned but care should be taken to choose a cleavage site that is close to the site of initiation of RNA synthesis if little extraneous 'leader' RNA is required. On the other hand, if the probe is to be used for RNase protection (Section 4.3), it is undesirable to have the whole length of the transcribed probe protected, as the protected fragment would then be indistinguishable from the products of incomplete RNase digestion. If the sequence of the template is known, and introns or 5' or 3' non-transcribed flanking regions identified, enzymes cutting in these sequences should be preferred. Problems may still be encountered even in these cases, if alternative initiation or termination sites are used, or if there is a high level of unspliced RNA.

It is worth noting that cloning the template into a site distal to the promoter in the polylinker (e.g. *Hin*dIII in pSP65 or *Eco*RI in pSP64 or the appropriate choice depending on promoter used in the pGEM plasmids) will result in up to 55 base pairs of vector derived sequence at the 5' end of the probe. This will not hybridize to mRNA and upon RNase cleavage, if the full insert length is protected, will yield a fragment of detectable size difference from the full-length undigested probe, so allowing unambiguous differentiation of artifactually protected probe and probe protected by specific mRNA hybridization. Alternatively, there is a *Pvu*II site 180 bp downstream from the polylinker in pSP64 and pSP65, and downstream of the polylinker in the SP6 polymerase transcribed direction in the pGEM vectors. This is useful, as it can provide the probe with up to 180 bp of plasmid-derived sequence to enable monitoring of complete digestion (but note that *Pvu*II produces blunt ends, see Section 2.3.2).

Finally, most vectors are of known sequence and if the probes are to be used for hybridization to other plasmids, then care should be taken to ensure polylinker sequence do not cross-react with other plasmid sequences.

2.3.2 *Choice of run-off sites*

Virtually any restriction enzyme can be used to generate the required run-off fragment. All that is required is that the chosen enzyme does not cleave between promoter initiation site and inserted DNA. It does not matter if there is one or many fragments generated by cleavage − only the promoter containing fragment will be transcribed.

Artefactual initiation of transcription is observed from the 3'-overhanging termini and, to a lesser extent, from blunt ends (8). 'Back-transcription' results, generating a transcript complementary to the intended probe. For some uses this is not a problem since the level of 'back-transcript' is only a very small fraction of the promoter-driven transcript and it should not interfere if the probe is used for filter or *in situ* hybridization. However, if the probe is to be used for RNase protection experiments, there may be a background caused by the two strands hybridizing and being protected against RNase, resulting in specific, protected fragments in the absence of any test RNA. The amount of back-transcript may be in the same range as the assayed mRNA and significantly interfere with its detection.

If a detailed restriction map of the insert is known, a series of templates, linearized at different sites will produce a nested set of probes. These can be used to generate a transcription map of the inserted sequence.

2.4 **Choice of RNA polymerase**

The choice of RNA polymerase can be dictated by several considerations and may be defined by choice of the vector. However, the following points should be made. T7 and T3 are generally made from cloned genes and consequently are significantly cheaper than SP6 and it is, therefore, possible to use larger quantities of the enzymes. However, there is some cross-specificity of T7 and T3, particularly at low salt concentrations which can allow T7 to initiate on T3 promoters and *vice versa*. Thus, dual promoter vectors may direct the synthesis of self complementary RNA. This may not be a problem; for example, the templates used in run-off transcripts may make the cross-initiated RNA negligibly short. In our hands SP6 polymerase is always less efficient than T7 as judged by incorporation of available label. The reasons for this may relate to the limiting level of radiolabelled NTP used in transcription reactions. T7 and T3 polymerase will cease transcription if they are required to incorporate a nucleotide at low concentration within about the first 15 bases of initiation. The enzymes detach from the template and re-initiate producing abortive, short transcripts. The commonly used T7 and T3 vectors do not require UTP incorporation within this region and so are efficient at transcription even at low UTP concentrations (9 and W.F.McAllister, personal communication). It is not yet known if SP6 polymerase shows similar characteristics but it is to be expected that this will be the case. The commonly used SP6 promoter requires all four nucleotides within the first 15 bases and this probably reduces the efficiency with which SP6 transcribes templates in the presence of low UTP. Once the first 15 bases have been less successfully incorporated, termination and re-initiation are much reduced.

3. METHODS

Great care should be taken when working with RNA samples to avoid contamination of solution and reactions with RNase. All standard precautions should be taken to avoid this, including wearing gloves for all manipulations. Treatment of solutions with diethyl pyrocarbonate (DEPC) is very useful − add DEPC to 0.1% (v/v), leave for 1 h and then autoclave to destroy the DEPC. Note that Tris buffers cannot be effectively treated with DEPC and should be autoclaved. Heat sensitive reagents (such as nucleotides) should be made up in sterile, DEPC treated water and handled with sterile techniques.

Placental ribonuclease inhibitor (RNasin) can be used as an efficient inhibitor of RNase that still allows full RNA polymerase activity. Note that the commonly used vanadyl nucleotide complex (VNC) strongly inhibits RNA polymerase, by competitive inhibition, and should be avoided.

3.1 **Preparation of template DNA**

Plasmid DNAs for use in transcription reactions should ideally be prepared by CsCl/ethidium bromide (CsCl/EtBr) density gradient centrifugation. If a more rapid procedure is required, the rapid alkaline/SDS lysis procedure (15) followed by either polyethylene glycol (16) or spermidine precipitation (17) yields DNA which is an adequate template for SP6 or T7 reactions. In our hands these protocols never produce templates that are as good as the gradient purified material and wherever possible we would recommend the more elaborate CsCl/EtBr gradient purification.

The exact protocol for purifying DNA from the CsCl/EtBr gradient is a matter of individual choice. However, it is critical that all traces of EtBr are removed from the DNA since this can strongly inhibit RNA synthesis. The most satisfactory protocol for doing this is to follow steps 6 onward in Table 10 of Chapter 2 in this book. Details of a modified alkaline/SDS lysis procedure can also be found in Tables 9 and 10 of Chapter 2.

It is important that template DNA be cleaved to completion since super-coiled DNAs are efficient templates for all phage-encoded RNA polymerases and generate very long transcripts. These reduce the yield of run-off transcripts and also can create problems in the specificity of probes generated from reactions that contain mixtures of molecules.

Following restriction enzyme digestion, we routinely purify the DNA by phenol extraction, chloroform extraction, ethanol or propan-2-ol precipitation, wash with 70% ethanol and finally resuspend the DNA in 10 mM Tris pH 7.4, 1 mM EDTA (TE). These general procedures are referred to several times in this and the subsequent chapter and are given in *Table 1*. Many restriction enzyme preparations are not RNase free and considerable care should be taken. The DNA is required at a final concentration in the transcription reaction of about $20-40$ μg/ml so the template should for convenience be resuspended in TE to give a final concentration of greater than 200 μg/ml.

Table 1. General methods for extracting proteins from and concentrating nucleic acids.

1.	*Phenol extraction.* Add an equal volume of phenol saturated with TE[a] to the DNA or RNA solution. Mix by inversion until homogeneous. Separate the phases by centrifugation in a microcentrifuge for 5 min or in a bench-top centrifuge or Sorval HB4 rotor at 2000 r.p.m. for 10 min. Carefully remove the upper (aqueous) phase with a pipette or micropipette and place it in a clean tube.
2.	*Phenol:chloroform extraction.* Add an equal volume of phenol:chloroform (1:1 v/v) to the aqueous phase from step 1. Mix and separate the phases as described in step 1.
3.	*Chloroform extraction.* Extract the aqueous phase from step 2 with an equal volume of chloroform. Separate the phases as described in step 1.
4.	*Ethanol precipitation.* Take the aqueous phase from step 3 and add 1/10 volume of 3 M sodium acetate pH 5.4 and two volumes of ethanol. Chill to −70°C or on dry-ice. Pellet the nucleic acid by centrifugation in a microcentrifuge for 10 min, or in a Sorval HB4 rotor at 8000 r.p.m. for 10 min. Carefully pour off the supernatant. If required, wash the pellet at room temperature with 70% ethanol, and re-centrifuge as above. Remove the excess ethanol with a tissue and allow the pellet to dry in air. Resuspend in the required volume of TE.
5.	*Isopropanol precipitation.* This is a useful alternative to ethanol precipitation when it is necessary to keep the volume of precipitation material to a minimum. Add between 0.6 and 1 volume of propan-2-ol to the aqueous phase from step 3. Then treat exactly as described for the ethanol precipitation in step 4 (including the 70% ethanol wash).

[a]TE is 10 mM Tris-HCl pH 7.5, 1 mM EDTA.

3.2 Transcription reaction

A method for the production of high specific-activity, full-length RNA probes is given in *Table 2* and the method of assay of incorporation in *Table 3*.

SP6 and T7 polymerase transcription is sensitive to the concentration of ribonucleotide triphosphates. At low concentrations the polymerase reaction tends to terminate before the end of the template and transcripts of less than full length are formed. Transcripts are generally almost all full length when the nucleotide concentration is over 250 μM. When making radiolabelled probes the aim is to maximize the specific activity, by maximizing the specific activity of the radiolabelled precursor nucleotide triphosphate. It is obviously unrealistic to use high-specific activity labelled nucleotides at 250 μM; instead, 20−100 μCi of labelled nucleotide triphosphate are used, and the concentration of the same, unlabelled, nucleotide is reduced. This runs counter to the optimal conditions for full-length transcripts. Suboptimal probe length may not be a problem if it is to be used for hybridization to filters or *in situ*, but it is a severe drawback to the interpretation of RNase protection experiments. In practice a balance is struck between maximizing specific activity and minimizing premature termination.

The SP6-polymerase reaction appears to be most sensitive to low concentrations of ATP and UTP (5), and at least sensitive to CTP or GTP. GTP concentration is the least crucial with respect to full-length synthesis, but it is the first base of the transcript, and so reducing GTP concentration leads to a reduced yield through reduced initiation. Ideally then, the labelled ribonucleotide triphosphate should be CTP. Ironically many laboratories, our own included, use labelled UTP, which is the least desirable. The choice was governed by this being the first RNA precursor that Amersham International produced which was SP6-polymerase-tested.

The method in *Table 2* uses UTP at 25 μM, under which conditions usually more

Table 2. Synthesis of RNA probes.

A. *Materials*
    $10\times$ transcription buffer ($10\times$ TB):
      400 mM Tris-HCl pH 7.5
      60 mM $MgCl_2$
      10 mM spermidine
    $10\times$ ribonucleotide triphosphates ($10\times$ rNTPs)
      5 mM each of ATP, CTP and GTP
    250 μM UTP
    RNasin; placental ribonuclease inhibitor
    SP6 or T7 polymerase
    RNase-free DNase

B. *Method*

1. Mix the following at room temperature, *adding DNA after the $10\times$ TB has been diluted:*

$10\times$ TB	5 μl
100 mM dithiothreitol	5 μl
RNasin	1.5 μl ($\sim$80 units)
$10\times$ rNTPs	5 μl
water	26.5 μl
DNA template	1 μl ($\sim$0.1$-$1 μg)
[^{32}P]UTP	5 μl (50 μCi)

    Remove two 0.5 μl samples for TCA precipitation (see *Table 3*).
    Then add 1 μl of RNA polymerase (10$-$20 units).

2. Incubate at 37°C for 1 h.
3. Add 1 μl RNase-free DNase (1 unit)[a].
4. Add 5 μl of 10% SDS and 1 μl of 0.5 M EDTA.
5. Remove two 0.5 μl samples for TCA precipitation (*Table 3*).
6. Extract with an equal volume of phenol:chloroform (1:1 v/v) as described in *Table 1*. Remove the aqueous phase, re-extract the organic phase and pool the aqueous phases. It is optional at this stage to remove the unincorporated nucleotides by passing the reaction mixture over a Sephadex G50-medium column, equilibrated in 40 mM Tris, pH 7.5, 5 mM EDTA, 0.5% SDS. Collect the excluded material after the void volume.
7. Ethanol precipitate the RNA as described in step 4 of *Table 1* after first adding 5 μg yeast tRNA as carrier.

---

[a]This step is optional. See the text for details.

than 90% of the transcripts are full length. The amount of label in the reaction can be increased; doubling the amount of high-specific activity UTP will almost double the specific activity of the product. The reaction conditions of *Table 2* can be scaled down to allow more radiolabelled UTP to be economically added. For uses such as *in situ* or filter hybridization, when very high specific activity probes are required and full-length transcription is not vital, all the cold UTP can be omitted and the reaction volume reduced. 100 μCi of 400 Ci/mmol UTP in a 20 μl reaction has a concentration of 12.5 μM, which will give adequate probe lengths and maximal specific activity.

Gel-electrophoresis of labelled transcripts shows that templates differ in their production of full length transcripts. Even at nucleotide triphosphate concentrations as low as 4 μM, a mouse HPRT gene template produced a substantial amount of full-length probe, whereas a homeo-box gene template produced almost no full length transcripts at 15 μM (I.J.Jackson, unpublished observations).

The prematurely terminated products usually do not give observable, discrete, large

Table 3. TCA precipitation to estimate percentage incorporation of nucleotide triphosphate into RNA.

A.	*Materials*
	Whatman 540 filter paper
	5% trichloroacetic acid/1% sodium pyrophosphate (TCA solution)
B	*Methods*
1.	Spot 0.5 μl of the reaction onto a small (about 5 × 5 mm square) piece of Whatman 540 paper. These pieces can be labelled with pencil or ball point pen, so that a large number can be processed simultaneously.
2.	Measure the radioactivity on the filter by Cherenkov counting, so obtaining the total counts in the sample. (If ^{35}S or ^{3}H incorporation is being assayed, the filters should be dried before counting with scintillant and duplicate filters used for the TCA wash.)
3.	Wash the same filter in TCA solution by shaking in about 20 ml in a screw-capped disposable tube, or in a larger volume in a conical flask. Pour off the TCA solution and replace with fresh. Repeat the washes five times or more until no more radioactivity is washed off the filter. (If many filters are washed at the same time, the volume of TCA should be increased.)
4.	Blot the filter dry and again measure the radioactivity, by Cherenkov counting, to obtain the acid-insoluble counts.

fragments on gel electrophoresis. Some sequences, however, seem to contain leaky termination signals, resulting in bands of less than full length on the gel. These bands decrease in abundance relative to full-length transcripts at higher nucleotide concentrations, but they never disappear completely even at the highest concentrations. It is these discrete, prematurely terminated products which will cause the most problems in analysing RNase protection experiments. It is obviously prudent to analyse by gel electrophoresis the labelled probe before use, particularly if it is for RNase protection.

The following points should be noted about the method in *Table 2*.

(i) The DNA template (about $0.1-1$ μg per reaction) must be added after the transcription buffer has been diluted, as the 10× buffer contains spermidine at a concentration of 10 mM. Spermidine concentrations greater than 4 mM may cause the DNA to precipitate (17).

(ii) The presence of placental RNasin seems to be important to maximize full-length transcription.

(iii) The reaction is stopped and the template removed by treatment with RNase free DNase. It is not clear that this step is essential if the template is never denatured before the probe is used. Furthermore the possibility of nicking the probe with contaminating RNase activity exists. The presence of the DNA template might be a problem during solution hybridization if temperatures close to the T_m of DNA are used when the double-strands may 'breathe' and protect sufficient amounts of the probe from RNase to interfere with the assay.

(iv) At the end of the reaction period the yield of nucleotides incorporated into RNA can be measured by trichloroacetic acid (TCA) precipitation. A rapid method for TCA precipitation is given in *Table 3*. Duplicates are usually taken at each time point. The background of TCA insoluble counts is taken before enzyme is added. Incorporation into TCA insoluble RNA at the end of the reaction is usually $30-90\%$. Note that this assay method does not require an accurate volume of the reaction to be analysed since total and incorporated counts are measured from the same filter. However, for estimation of *total* counts incorporated into probe, an accurately known sample volume is required.

(v) Removal of unincorporated nucleotides by passing the reaction over Sephadex G-50 is not essential. Ethanol precipitation of the RNA will usually remove most of the nucleotides, particularly if incorporation is high.

3.3 Preparation of low specific activity or unlabelled RNA and alternative labels

The protocol for producing high yields of unlabelled or low specific activity RNA transcripts differs from that given in *Table 2* in only minor ways. All four nucleotides should be present at 500 µM and labelled nucleotide added to give the desired specific activity. Incubation conditions are as described and after 1 h a further aliquot of polymerase can be added. Using this protocol up to 10 moles of RNA can be synthesised per mole of DNA template. Note that reference (5) indicates that both template and enzyme are often limiting components of the reaction, implying that an increased template concentration may be desirable for highest yields.

Use of ^{35}S-α-labelled NTPs and of biotinylated nucleotides has been reported (6). Both these labelled nucleotides are incorporated less efficiently than the normal NTP, but yields are high enough to be usable. Detailed protocols are not published but are generally available from the manufacturers.

3.4 Problems

Problems are generally identified by either zero or low ($<5\%$) incorporation of counts upon analysis by TCA precipitation or by failure to generate full length transcripts. The following points need careful attention.

3.4.1 *NTPs*

Ribonucleotide triphosphates become less effective with age. Generally, be suspicious of reagents that are more than one or two months old. The radiolabelled nucleotides should be used within 1, or at most 2 weeks, for optimal activity and incorporation. Care should be taken to neutralize NTP solutions when making up reaction components.

3.4.2 *Template DNA*

Template DNA must be free of salts and EtBr. Always use a control sample, known to transcribe efficiently to check for problems with new solutions; this will help identify impure DNA. Carefully following the protocols in *Table 1* and also Table 10 of Chapter 2 should eliminate problems. Be sure to remove all phenol, by washing at room temperature with 70% ethanol after preparing linearized templates. Finally, be careful to avoid the DNA coming into contact with the high level of spermidine in the 10× transcription buffer − this can cause the DNA to precipitate.

3.4.3 *Failure to achieve full length transcripts*

The problems listed in Sections 3.4.1 and 3.4.2 above will often cause both low incorporation and also short transcripts, as will RNase contamination of the buffers. If these factors have been eliminated as a cause, then the template probably contains one or more transcription terminators. These can, in part, be overcome by increasing nucleotide concentrations. Should this fail or if it is not desirable for reasons of specific activity, it may be preferable to seek an alternative, shorter, run-off transcript. Krieg and Melton (6) also report that reduction of transcription temperatures from 40°C to 30°C increased the proportion of full length transcripts in one case. This would be worth trying. If none of these work, there is no alternative but to isolate some full length material from agarose or acrylamide gels.

4. THE USE OF RNA PROBES

This section covers the major uses of RNA probes for the analysis of nucleic acids in routine laboratory practice. It covers in detail protocols for the use of RNA as substitutes for DNA probes in Southerns and Northerns and RNase protection.

It should again be stressed that every precaution should be taken to eliminate RNase contamination of solutions and plasticware. Methods for this are given in Section 3 and the routine use of solutions containing 10 mM VNC is recommended after RNA synthesis is complete. Once sufficient familiarity with working with RNA has been achieved, some precautions can be relaxed, but they are certainly useful when work is first started.

4.1 **Southern hybridization**

Conditions of gel fractionation and transfer of DNA to nitrocellulose or nylon membranes do not require modification for RNA probe use.

Table 4. Conditions for Southern hybridization.

1.	Standard conditions are used for making Southern transfers and producing DNA immobilized on filters (see for example reference 28). However, take great care not to handle the filters with bare hands.
2.	Wash the filter in 5 × SSC for a few minutes to remove excess salt.
3.	Pre-hybridize the filter in:-
	0.1% (w/v) Ficoll 400
	0.1% (w/v) BSA
	0.1% (w/v) polyvinylpyrolidone
	50 mM sodium phosphate buffer pH 6.5
	0.1% (w/v) SDS
	250 µg/m salmon sperm DNA sonicated and denatured
	10 µg/ml PolyC
	10 µg/ml PolyA
	50% (v/v) deionized formamide
	10 mM Vanadyl nucleotide complex
	Leave at 50°C for at least 1 h. There is no harm or advantage in leaving it longer. Use 10−20 ml per 15 × 20 cm filter.
4.	Set up the hybridization reaction in 10 ml per 15 × 20 cm filter of the same solution as used for pre-hybridization supplemented with 10^6 c.p.m. per ml of ^{32}P-labelled probe RNA. Leave at 50°C for 17 h (overnight) or longer.
5.	After hybridization, wash the filter at 65°C for 3 × 30 min with 500 ml of 2 × SSC, 0.1% (w/v) SDS and then once in 0.1 × SSC, 0.1% SDS. This last stringent wash can be varied according to specific probe requirements. It is often a good idea to vary the temperature or salt concentration.
6.	It has not been routinely necessary in our hands to treat the filters after washing with RNase, although this may clear up background. This is most conveniently carried out at 37°C in 2 × SSC supplemented with 10−100 µg RNase A which has been heat treated prior to use.

Table 5. Northern analysis.

1.	Use standard protocols for gel separation of RNAs (28). Formaldehyde agarose is most convenient and the procedures described in reference (28) are suitable for transfer and filter analysis. We have good results with nylon Hybond filters (Amersham International) following the manufacturers instructions.
2.	Pre-hybridize filters exactly as detailed in *Table 4*.
3.	Hybridize filters exactly as detailed in *Table 4*. However, the optimum temperature for hybridization is 55−60°C depending on probe used (GC content, homology and length). Hybridize for 17 h.
4.	Wash the filters in three changes of 500 ml of 2 × SSC, 0.1% SDS and then in 0.1 × SSC, 0.1% SDS at 65°C, each wash for 20−30 min. The final wash can be varied by either increasing or decreasing the temperature to best accentuate the band patterns relative to the background.

A variety of hybridization solutions have been suggested and in *Table 4* we detail a method that is simple and uses the same solutions as are used for conventional DNA probe hybridizations. It is certain that most components of this hybridization mixture are not required for success and we use this method purely for convenience.

The use of RNA probes in Southern blot hybridizations appears to increase sensitivity, primarily because there is no probe/probe hybridization to compete with probe/target hybridization (similar sensitivity can be achieved with cDNA or other single strand DNA probes, but these are generally more complex to make).

An alternative protocol for detection of DNA on Southerns was developed by Church and Gilbert (18) for 'Genomic Sequencing'. These authors report the detection of 3 fg of DNA in 10 day exposures, which probably represents the highest sensitivity of detection yet achieved. Detailed protocols are given in reference (18). In outline, the procedure uses DNA cross-linked, by u.v. irradiation, to nylon membranes and hybridized with very high specific activity ^{32}P-labelled RNA in a solution of 1% (w/v) BSA, 1 mM EDTA, 0.5 M $NaHPO_4$ pH 7.2 and 7% (w/v) sodium dodecyl sulphate. It is not known which of these features results in the sensitivity.

4.2 Northern hybridization

The method for Northern analysis is virtually identical to that for Southern analysis and is detailed in *Table 5*.

RNA probes have proved much more sensitive than DNA probes for Northern analysis. Melton *et al.* (5) report a 10-fold increase in sensitivity and this has been found to be generally true. RNA/RNA hybrids are more stable in formamide solutions than equivalent DNA/DNA hybrids and this causes problems of non-specificity of hybridization. In particular, detection of ribosomal RNA by cross-hybridizing probes has been a significant problem with some probes, and it is important to vary stringency of washing to identify the specific hybridization. In general it is best to be suspicious of bands that are the same size as ribosomal 28 or 18S RNAs until further evidence substantiates the belief that it is the result of specific and not non-specific hybrid formation. Some workers suggest a wash in a low concentration of RNase to eliminate the non-specific hybrids. The filters cannot then be re-used.

4.3 RNase protection

RNase protection (13) is probably the most sensitive and technically simple method

Table 6. RNase protection assay.

A.	*Materials*
	Recrystallized, deionized formamide[a]
	Hybridization buffer[b]
	80% formamide
	40 mM Pipes pH 6.7
	400 mM NaCl
	1 mM EDTA
	RNase solution[c]
	40 μg/ml RNase A
	2 μg/ml RNase T1
	10 mM Tris pH 7.5
	5 mM EDTA
	300 mM NaCl
B.	*Method*
1.	Precipitate RNA samples to be assayed as described in *Table 1*. 40 μg of total RNA is a suitable amount.
2.	Dissolve the RNA pellet in 30 μl hybridization buffer.
3.	Dissolve the radioactive probe in hybridization buffer and add 1 μl to each reaction. (Use $10^5 - 10^6$ c.p.m. per reaction.)
4.	Incubate at 45°C overnight[d].
5.	Add 300 μl RNase solution. Incubate at 30°C for 1 h.
6.	Add 30 μl 10% SDS and 50 μg proteinase K. Incubate at 37°C for 10 min.
7.	Extract with phenol/chloroform as described in *Table 1*, but then add 5 μg yeast tRNA carrier to the aqueous phase before carrying out the ethanol precipitation.

[a]Formamide is recrystallized by freezing and is deionized by stirring with Biorad mixed bed resin for 30 min.
[b]The formamide is kept frozen separately, and is added to the buffer just before use.
[c]Make up just before use, and remove any double-strand nuclease activity by heating in a boiling water bath for 5 min.
[d]It might be found useful at this stage to heat the reaction to 80°C for 10 min before the overnight incubation. If this is done, it is important to have removed the template from the probe by DNase digestion.

for detection and analysis of specific RNA. As little as 0.1 pg of a specific RNA can be detected by the protocol (13). Its advantages over nuclease S1 analysis (10) are in ease of probe preparation, sensitivity of assay and in greater robustness in its final enzymatic steps (RNase digestion compared to nuclease S1 digestion). There seems to be much less sensitivity to overdigestion with RNase compared to nuclease S1.

4.3.1 *Method*

Table 6 gives a method for RNase protection.
  The following points should be noted.

(i)   A control hybridization with probe alone or with yeast tRNA should be included to identify background fragments and check that the digestion is complete.

(ii)   Hybridization at 45°C in 80% formamide has been shown to work for many different probes. Hybridization with some probes might require a different temperature, if the A+U or G+C composition is very different from normal or if the region of homology between probe and test RNA is particularly short.

(iii)   It is more critical to control the temperature of RNase digestion. Although the digestion is fairly insensitive to excess enzyme, the signal-to-noise ratio varies considerably according to digestion conditions. Increased temperature will

Table 7. Polyacrylamide/urea gel electrophoresis.

A.	*Materials*
1.	1 × Tris-borate electrophoresis buffer (TBE) is made up as a 20× stock. For 1 litre add:

      216 g Tris base
      110 g´boric acid
       20.4 g disodium EDTA

2.   Gel mix contains 57 g acrylamide (ultrapure for electrophoresis), 3 g bisacrylamide, and 460 g urea. This is dissolved in about 900 ml of water. It helps to warm the solution. Once dissolved, add about 20 g Biorad mixed bed resin and stir for about 30 min to deionize. Do not stir with resin for much longer than this. Filter through a 0.45 μm nitrocellulose filter. Add 50 ml 20 × TBE and make up to 1 litre.

3.   Loading buffer is 7 M urea, 1 × TBE, 0.1% xylene cyanol, 0.1% bromophenol blue.

B.   *Methods*

1.   Assemble the gel plates. It is best to use very thin (0.3 mm) spacers, and to siliconize one plate to facilitate separation after electrophoresis.

2.   De-gas the gel mix by evacuating in a dessicator for a few minutes. About 75 ml will provide an excess for the large (30 cm wide) 'sequencing' gel. The gel mix should be at room temperature as colder mix may not polymerize rapidly enough to form the wells.

3.   Add 650 μl freshly made 10% ammonium persulphate and 100 μl TEMED (*N,N,N′,N′*-tetramethyl-ethylene-diamine). Pour the gel, insert well former (or flat side of shark's tooth comb). Leave to set for at least 1 h.

4.   Place the gel in the running apparatus. Pre-electrophorese for 30 min or longer under the run conditions (see step 6).

5.   Add 5 μl of loading buffer to each sample. Vortex briefly to dissolve. Place in a boiling water bath for 5 min.

6.   Load the samples. Run the gel limiting on power at 40 Watts for a 30 cm wide gel or 25−30 Watts for a 20 cm gel. The voltage will increase during pre-electrophoresis and run from around 950 volts to 1200 volts.

7.   The length of run depends on the expected size of protected fragments. As a rough guide, on these 6% polyacrylamide gels the bromophenol blue dye runs at about 40 bases, and the xylene cyanol runs at about 120 bases.

8.   Following electrophoresis, separate the plates carefully. Fix the gel on the plate by soaking it in 10% methanol, 10% acetic acid for 15 min, then drain dry for 15 min. The gel and plate can then be wrapped in Clingfilm and autoradiographed, or the gel can be transferred to filter paper by firmly pressing a dry sheet of Whatman 3MM onto the gel and peeling it away from the plate. After covering with Clingfilm, the gel can be dried onto the paper on a heated vacuum drier and autoradiographed in a standard cassette. Dried gels provide a much sharper and more sensitive signal.

generally reduce the background, but it has been suggested that poly(U:A) stretches are sensitive to RNase digestion, resulting in artefactual fragments after gel electrophoresis (Robb Krumlauf, personal communication).

(iv)   After RNase digestion the protected fragments are separated by electrophoresis on polyacrylamide/urea gels and visualized by autoradiography. These gels are identical to those used in DNA sequencing and a method for their use is given in *Table 7*. Dilutions of the unhybridized undigested probe should be run alongside. Appropriate dilutions are usually 1 in 1000 or 1 in 10 000 of the input to the hybridizations, but choice should be governed by the expected abundance of the protecting RNA.

     Size markers for electrophoresis can be made from a series of templates directing synthesis of transcripts of known length. The templates can usually be transcribed together to provide a mixture of known fragments for electrophoresis.

Table 8. Model calculation of estimation of the abundance of mRNA by RNase protection.

1.	Probe synthesis conditions: 25 μm CTP. 1 μl of the reaction has 5×10^6 c.p.m. on Cherenkov counting, before TCA precipitation. Thus 25 pmol CTP has 5×10^6 c.p.m.
2.	Probe is 600 nucleotides long, and contains 150 C-residues. Therefore 5×10^6 c.p.m. is in 25/150 pmol of probe. Probe input to the hybridization reaction is 10^6 c.p.m. of TCA precipitable counts, which is $25/150 \times 10^6/5 \times 10^6$ pmol, or 0.033 pmol.
3.	On scanning the autoradiograph, the protected fragment (200 nucleotides long) is 20% the intensity of a 1/1000 dilution of the input probe. As the protected fragment is shorter than the probe, equal numbers of protected molecules would have a signal of 200/600 the probe. Therefore the protected fragment is $0.033 \times 600/200 \times 0.2 \times 1/100$ pmol per reaction; or 1.98×10^{-17} mol.
4.	Avogadro's number is 6.02×10^{23} molecules per mol. Therefore the reaction protects $1.98 \times 6.02 \times 10^6$ molecules of assayed mRNA, or 12×10^6 molecules.
5.	Each hybridization contained 40 μg total RNA, which came from 8×10^6 cells. Therefore the cells contain 12/8 molecules or 1.5 molecules per cell.

4.3.2 *Quantitation of RNA by RNase protection*

Solution hybridization of RNA probes and RNase protection will allow an accurate measurement of the abundance of the protecting RNA species. A model calculation is shown in *Table 8*.

The specific activity of the labelled nucleotide triphosphate in the probe synthesis reaction is known, and thus the specific activity of the probe itself can be calculated. (It is the molar specific activity of the nucleotide divided by the number of residues of that particular base in the probe sequence.) If the sequence of the probe is not known, an estimate of the labelled base composition must be used (25% is probably good enough). The number of radioactive counts of probe added to each hybridization gives the number of moles of probe added.

Following gel electrophoresis and autoradiography, the band intensity of the protected fragment(s) is compared to the input probe dilutions (preferably by densitometer scanning of an autoradiograph exposed in the linear response range). After taking into account the differences in size between probe and protected fragment, and the dilution factor used, the proportion of the input probe protected from digestion can be calculated. Thus the number of moles of protected probe is determined. As the probe is in vast excess over any individual mRNA species, it can be assumed that all the particular mRNA will have hybridized. Hence the number of moles of the assayed mRNA in the hybridization reaction is known and, using Avogadro's number, the number of molecules can be calculated.

If the source of the test RNA is homogeneous, the yield of RNA per cell can be determined. Otherwise an approximation should be used (an average mammalian cell contains 5 pg total RNA). In this way the number of molecules of the assayed mRNA per cell is calculated.

If an estimate of the relative abundance of the mRNA is required the size of the message must be known, so that from the molarity of the protected species in the hybridization reaction, the mass of the mRNA in the reaction can be calculated. If the reaction contains total RNA, an estimate of the fraction of polyA+ RNA gives the mass of mRNA in the reaction, of which the mass of protected mRNA will be a fraction.

15

5. SPECIALIST PROCEDURES

This section is not intended as a source of detailed protocols and draws attention to specific techniques that may be useful. Detailed methods are generally available and are referenced.

5.1 *In situ* hybridization

Radioactive RNA molecules are finding a major role as probes for *in situ* hybridization to detect and localize mRNA in tissue sections. The methods were first described by Angerer's lab and readers are referred to the references (19,20) for detailed experimental protocols.

The radioactively labelled nucleotides used in the transcription reaction can be ^{32}P, ^{35}S or ^{3}H. ^{32}P gives a signal which cannot be localized to the single-cell level, but one that can be easily detected by only a few days' autoradiography. Note that ^{32}P is not detected efficiently by standard dipping emulsion, but the signal must rather be visualized by exposing the labelled slide to X-ray film (D.Davidson, personal communication; P.Koopman, personal communication). ^{35}S has a much shorter path-length than ^{32}P, and therefore gives better resolution, and is available at higher specific activity than tritiated nucleotides. Ribonucleotide thiophosphates are incorporated reasonably efficiently by SP6 or T7 polymerases.

Tritium-labelled probes give the best resolution after the tissue section has been dipped in emulsion. ^{3}H-labelled nucleotide triphosphates are available at only $40-60$ Ci/mmol, and thus they should be added to the reaction to a concentration of 100 μM or more without the addition of cold triphosphate.

An important control required for *in situ* hybridization is the hybridization of a probe which will not be expected to react with any RNA on the section. This eliminates the possibility that a positive signal is due to non-specific binding of radioactive probe to certain cell types, as is sometimes seen (R.Haffner, personal communication). A suitable control is usually the 'opposite strand' to the probe; that is, a molecule transcribed in the opposite direction. Use of vectors with bidirectional promoters such as the pGEM series facilitates synthesis of both strands.

5.2 Biological activity of *in vitro* transcribed RNA

5.2.1 *Capping and translation*

mRNA isolated from eukaryotic cells normally contains a cap structure at its 5' end which is required for optimum stability and translation of an mRNA. Such a structure can be enzymatically introduced onto the 5' end of *in vitro* synthesized RNA, but this is expensive. Methods have been published (6,21) which show that a cap analogue can be introduced into the transcription reaction and will be incorporated at the 5' end of the synthesized RNA. The method is as described in Section 3.3 but the cap analogue, G(5')ppp(5')G, mG(5')ppp(5')Gm or mG(5')ppp(5')G, is included at 500 μM and GTP at 50 μM. Further details can be found in ref. 6.

RNA, either with or without cap structures, have been translated *in vitro* in reticulocyte lysates and *in vivo* by microinjection into *Xenopus* oocytes (22,23).

5.2.2 *Other activities*

In vitro synthesized RNAs have been successfully used for *in vivo* and *in vitro* splicing, since they allow for synthesis of large quantities of pseudo-primary transcripts and can be labelled to high specific activity to enable detection of low level enzymatic activities (4). No particular protocols need be followed for generation of such substrates.

Transcripts of the opposite strand to mRNA, 'anti-sense' transcripts, have also been used in a variety of experiments, to block translation of injected mRNAs in *Xenopus* oocytes (24) or in *Drosophila* embryos (25) to block specific translation of the product of the Krüppel gene.

5.3 **Walking protocols**

Specialist cloning vectors have been made that contain SP6, T7 or T3 promoters immediately adjacent to cloning sites of phage and cosmid cloning vectors. These promoters allow rapid generation of radiolabelled probes that are specific for the 'ends' of the cloned DNA fragment and such probes are ideal for using in 'walking' protocols. This is a general method for isolating DNA that must be adjacent in the genome to cloned DNA molecules in the 'walking vector'. Application of such a system to cosmids is described in (26) and Chapter 2 of this volume.

5.4 **Sequencing RNA transcripts**

RNA can be sequenced by a method that is identical in concept to the dideoxy chain termination method of Sanger.

Detail protocols have been published for T7 and SP6 (27) and T3 (9). In outline the method uses 3' deoxy analogues of ribonucleoside triphosphates at low concentrations to produce RNA molecules that terminate at the modified base. Conventional sequencing gels are then used to establish the RNA sequence by reasoning and methodology that is identical to the Sanger protocols.

The full power of these methods has not yet been developed. In particular the use of radiolabelled 3' deoxy-nucleotides dramatically improves sequence clarity, and these are not all yet commercially available. The ability to sequence the RNA from the bidirectional promoter systems (pGEM, phagescript and bluescript vectors, for example) reduces cloning manipulations required to establish the sequence of both strands.

6. CONCLUSION

RNA probes have proved to be increasingly useful for generating specific hybridization probes and also for substrates and reagents for the analysis of a variety of biological processes. The extreme specificity of the phage encoded polymerases and the small size of their cognate promoters (15 base pairs in many cases) open up a number of new technical possibilities that should not be ignored. The ready commercial availability of components and kits for SP6, T7 and T3 generated RNAs makes them serious candidates when experimental protocols require labelled probes to be made and the many unique functions and specific properties of RNA in some cases make these enzyme systems irreplaceable.

7. ACKNOWLEDGEMENTS

PFRL was supported by a grant jointly from the Medical Research Council and Cancer Research Campaign, and IJJ is a fellow of the Lister Institute of Preventive Medicine and was funded by the Medical Research Council during the course of some of this work.

8. REFERENCES

1. Chamberlin,M., Kingston,R., Gilman,M., Wiggs,J. and de Vera,A. (1983) In *Methods in Enzymology*. Wu,R., Grosman,L. and Moldave,K. (eds), Academic Press, New York, Vol. 101, p. 540.
2. Butler,E.T. and Chamberlin,M.J. (1982) *J. Biol. Chem.*, **257**, 5772.
3. Losich,R. and Chamberlin,M. (eds) (1976) *RNA Polymerase*. Cold Spring Harbor Laboratory, Cold Spring Harbor, NY.
4. Green,M.R., Maniatis,T. and Melton,D.A. (1983) *Cell*, **32**, 681.
5. Melton,D.A., Krieg,P.A., Rebagliati,M.R., Maniatis,T., Zinn,K. and Green,M.R. (1984) *Nucleic Acids Res.*, **12**, 7035.
6. Krieg,P.A. and Melton,D.A. (1987) *Methods in Enzymology*, in press.
7. Nam,H.G., Loechel,S. and Fried,H.M. (1986) *Gene*, **46**, 57.
8. Schenborn,E.T. and Mierendorf,R.C. (1985) *Nucleic Acids Res.*, **13**, 6223.
9. Klement,J.F., Ling,M.-L. and McAllister,W.F. (1987) *Gene Analysis Techniques*, in press.
10. Berk,A.J. and Sharp,P.A. (1977) *Cell*, **12**, 721.
11. Jackson,I.J., Schofield,P. and Hogan,B. (1985) *Nature*, **317**, 745.
12. Lovell-Badge,R.H., Bygrave,A.E., Bradley,A., Robertson,E., Evans,M.J. and Cheah,K.S.E. (1985) *Cold Spring Harbor Symp. Quant. Biol.*, **50**, 707.
13. Zinn,K., di Maio,D. and Maniatis,T. (1984) *Cell*, **34**, 865.
14. O'Hare,K., Levis,R. and Rubin,G.M. (1983) *Proc. Natl. Acad. Sci. USA*, **80**, 6917.
15. Birnboim,H.C. and Doly,J. (1979) *Nucleic Acids Res.*, **7**, 1513.
16. Lis,J.T. (1980) In *Methods in Enzymology*. Grossman,L. and Moldave,K. (eds), Academic Press, New York, Vol. 65, p. 347.
17. Gosule,L.C. and Schellman,J.A. (1978) *J. Mol. Biol.*, **121**, 311.
18. Church,G.M. and Gilbert,W. (1984) *Proc. Natl. Acad. Sci. USA*, **81**, 1991.
19. Lynn,D.A., Angerer,L.M., Bruskin,A.M., Klein,W.H. and Angerer,R.C. (1983) *Proc. Natl. Acad. Sci. USA*, **80**, 2656.
20. Cox,K.H., DeLeon,D.V., Angerer,L.M. and Angerer,R.C. (1984) *Dev. Biol.*, **101**, 485.
21. Konarska,M.M., Padgett,R.A. and Sharp,P.A. (1984) *Cell*, **38**, 731.
22. Kreig,P.A. and Melton,D.A. (1984) *Nucleic Acids Res.*, **12**, 7057.
23. Drummond,D.R., Armstrong,J. and Colman,A. (1985) *Nucleic Acids Res.*, **13**, 7375.
24. Melton,D.A. (1985) *Proc. Natl. Acad. Sci. USA*, **82**, 144.
25. Rosenberg,U.B., Preiss,A., Seifert,E., Jackle,H. and Knipple,D.C. (1985) *Nature*, **313**, 703.
26. Cross,S.H. and Little,P.F.R. (1986) *Gene*, **49**, 9.
27. Axelrod,U.O. and Kramer,F.R. (1985) *Biochemistry*, **24**, 5716.
28. Maniatis,T., Fritsch,E.F. and Sambrook,J. (1982) *Molecular Cloning − A Laboratory Manual*. Cold Spring Harbor Laboratory, NY.

CHAPTER 2

Choice and use of cosmid vectors

PETER F.R.LITTLE

1. INTRODUCTION
1.1 Scope of the chapter
The ideal vector for cloning DNA from higher eukaryotes would have a cloning capacity that was as large as possible to reduce the number of rounds of library probing that was required to isolate overlapping cloned segments of a large gene. Cosmid vectors have the highest capacity of our current generation of cloning vehicles but are still relatively rarely used when compared to λ phage vectors. The reasons for this are in part that cosmid vectors have been unpredictable in behaviour and also that construction of cosmid libraries is intrinsically more difficult than equivalent phage libraries. The purpose of this chapter is to record a series of protocols for constructing cosmid libraries that have worked in our laboratory and also to document, in an anecdotal fashion, some of the distressingly common causes of failures to make representative libraries. We would stress that the technical difficulty of carrying out carefully controlled experiments has made difficult the detailed analysis of cosmid cloning. The protocols we have generated should be treated as guidelines and variation from them is possible. We would, however, advise that inexperienced users do not deviate until enough experience has built up to allow a basis for improvization.

1.2 Cosmid vectors
Cosmid vectors were first developed by Collins and Hohn (1) to overcome the technical problems of introducing large pieces of DNA into *Escherichia coli*. Most protocols for the preparation of competent *E. coli* allow efficient transfer of DNA molecules up to about 10−15 kb and attempts to use DNA larger than this results in dramatic reduction of transformation efficiencies. The major barrier to successful incorporation of large plasmids into bacterial cells appears to be in the transfer of DNA across the cell membrane or perhaps, in the events immediately following entry of the DNA into the periphery of the cytoplasm.

To overcome these problems, Collins and Hohn (1) introduced the bacteriophage λ *cos* sequence into a conventional 4 or 5 kb plasmid cloning vector. This allowed the use of λ phage *in vitro* packaging protocols (2) which completely overcomes the size effects seen in transfection. *cos*, and about 200 bp of DNA either side, is a DNA sequence that is required for packaging DNA into preformed λ phage particles. There are no other specific λ DNA segments that are necessary for this and for successful packaging of DNA, there must be two *cos* sequences contained on the same DNA molecule, separated by 38−52 kb, which are the packaging limits of lambda. Generation of recombinant cosmid molecules was possible by joining 30−45 kb of, say, human DNA and cut cosmid vector DNA in ligation reactions that favoured the formation of long concatermers of cosmid/human/cosmid DNA. This created the necessary distribution of *cos* sites to be used in *in vitro* packaging reactions that have nearly identical biological properties to the *in vivo* processes. *In vitro* packaging is remarkably efficient with up to 10^9 plaques formed per microgram of λ DNA. This corresponds to 5% efficiency with respect to the DNA molecules, but efficiency of cosmid transduction is much lower − rarely greater than 10^6 colony forming units (c.f.u.) per microgram and generally considerably less.

1.3 Choice of vectors

The first criterion for choosing a cosmid vector must be to establish whether a cosmid-size clone is actually required. If this is not the case, then construction of phage libraries is always easier and quicker.

There are many different cosmid vectors available [see Maniatis *et al.* (3) and Pouwels *et al.* (4) for listings]. Features that are important are drug resistance, replicon and convenient restriction sites. These are discussed in turn.

1.3.1 *Drug resistance*

Cosmids often cause cells to grow slowly for reasons that are complex and not well understood. Slow growth is often associated with partial resistance to commonly used antibiotics such as ampicillin, which may reduce selection pressure on the cosmid. Satellite colony formation may also be a problem in the initial, slow, phase of cosmid growth. The majority of cosmid vectors contain this drug resistance marker, but if other features allow, this is not the optimal drug resistance determinant. Tetracyclin resistance does not suffer from these disadvantages, but the drug is significantly unstable. Kanamycin (or neomycin) resistance is used in several vectors and this is a stable drug for which there are two different genes encoding drug resistance. Its major disadvantage is that long pre-expression times are required to allow full expression (see Section 3.5.3).

Several cosmids carry, in addition to the prokaryotic drug resistance marker, genes that allow selection with eukaryotic cells. Thymidine kinase and G418 resistance (4) are the most convenient, but several others could, in principle, be constructed. The use of the selectable marker to facilitate re-introduction of DNA into cells may be a defining criterion for the choice of the vector. Schemes have been published that allow rescue of cosmid DNA from such experiments and these often require particular combinations of drug resistance (5).

1.3.2 *Replicon*

Most cosmids that are suitable for use in *E. coli* are derived from pBR322 and based upon the pMB1 replicon. The control of this replicon is not ideal for use in a vector cosmid [discussed in Little and Cross (6)] and can lead to overgrowth of libraries by small cosmids, derived by recA independent deletion events. There are in addition problems with interference of the replicon by adventitious promoters in the insert DNA (discussed in 6−8). The use of the phage λ origin of replication has overcome some, but not all of these problems (7). The R6K origin is used in two cosmids. It is not known how this compares to the pMB1 or λ replicons. The choice of replicon is undergoing serious scrutiny in several large cloning experiments and preliminary data has been published by Coulson *et al.* (9).

1.3.3 *Restriction sites*

Primary consideration should be the presence of the appropriate cloning site (discussed in Section 1.4.1). Additional points worth considering are location of sites in the correct position to allow construction of vector 'arms' using the procedure of Ish-Horowicz and Burke (10), the presence of sites flanking cloning site(s) that allows cleavage of the insert DNA away from the vector and the presence of sites between pairs of *cos* sequences that allows even more simple generation of cosmid arms (11).

1.4 **Cloning strategies**

1.4.1 *Choice of cloning enzyme*

Generally, cloning strategies follow the conventional path of using *Sau*3AI partial digests inserted into a *Bam*HI site. This is satisfactory and many *Bam*HI vectors are available. However, the analysis of such clones for identification of cosmid overlaps, for example, is difficult since the ends of the insert DNA are lost to the analysis − the fusion of a *Sau*3AI and *Bam*HI site destroys the *Bam*HI site in most cases. It is therefore difficult to analyse the DNA that most critically defines the overlap (i.e. the extreme ends). The cloning of partial digests with 6-cutting restriction enzymes into the same 6-cutting site allows analysis of all fragments. The representation of libraries made in this fashion is theoretically very good (12) and in practice the distribution of clones in partial *Eco*RI and partial *Sau*3AI libraries is very similar or identical (9). The advantage of facile analysis is significant in walking or mapping protocols.

1.4.2 *Cloning procedure*

There are two basic protocols available for preparing eukaryotic DNA of a suitable size range − either physical separation of partially digested fragments of the correct size (Section 2.1.3) or dephosphorylation of a partial digest and making use of the natural size selectivity of *in vitro* packaging to isolate 35−45 kb fragments (Section 2.1.4). The former is expensive on starting material − 300 μg of DNA will be required to yield sufficient DNA to construct a library with high efficiency ($\sim 10^6$ colonies per microgram of eukaryotic DNA). The phosphatase method is more economic in its use of starting DNA but significantly less efficient (never greater than 5×10^4 per microgram and in our hands usually less).

2. METHODS

2.1 **Preparation of insert DNA**

2.1.1 *Isolation of DNA from cells or tissues*

The quality of the DNA that is used to make the cosmid library is probably the most

Table 1. Preparation of high molecular weight eukaryotic DNA.

Solutions

1. Resuspend or homogenize approximately 10^8-10^9 cells (or between 0.5–1 g tissue) in 5 ml of 1 × SSC[a]. Make sure resuspension is complete.

2. Add 5 ml of 100 mM Tris-HCl pH 7.5, 100 mM NaCl, 10 mM EDTA, 1% Sarkosyl. Mix carefully for about 2–3 min to lyse the cells. Add Proteinase K to 100 μg/ml. Incubate at 55°C for 2 h.

3. Extract once with phenol, by adding an equal volume of phenol saturated with TE. Mix by gently inverting the covered tube and separate the phases by centrifugation (Table 1, Chapter 1). Remove the aqueous phase into a clean tube and carry out a further extraction with an equal volume of phenol:chloroform (1:1). Finally extract once with an equal volume of chloroform alone. If too many cells have been used, the first phenol extraction will be virtually solid. If this has happened dilute the DNA with the lysis solution used in step 2. The first phenol extraction is often messy but the interface should be as far as possible left with the phenol phase. The subsequent phenol-chloroform and chloroform extractions will be much cleaner.

4. Dialyse the final aqueous phase against 4 l of TE[b] containing 100 mM NaCl at 4°C for 17 h (overnight) or longer.

5. Repeat the dialysis for 24 h against 4 l of TE at 4°C.

6. The DNA is now ready for use. The concentration must be estimated by running on a gel against known concentrations of λ DNA, since the preparation still contains RNA and so a reading of u.v. absorption at 260 nm will give an inaccurate measure of DNA concentration. If this procedure is followed, the DNA will be at a concentration of between 100–300 μg/ml.

---

[a]1 × SCC is 0.15 M NaCl, 0.015 M trisodium citrate.
[b]TE is 10 mM Tris-HCl pH 7.5, 1 mM EDTA.

critical component of the success or failure of library construction. 40–50 kb partial DNA isolated from molecules of starting size 100 kb has only about a third of its molecules with restriction sites at both ends. The broken molecules compete in the ligation reaction and make a successful library impossible to construct. The most important advice is to check DNA at every stage of the isolation (partials, gradients, etc.) on 0.2% agarose gels. Instructions for using these gels are included in Section 3.4.

We use the method detailed in *Table 1* to make high molecular weight DNA. It may be used for fresh or frozen, cell lines or tissue samples.

2.1.2 *Partial digestion*

We carry out test partial digestions by 2-fold dilution and use the method of Seed *et al.* (13) to identify correct partials. We tend to use 2–3 different partial conditions to allow for inhomogeneity of site cleavage rates. The method described here is very similar to that described in Maniatis *et al.* (3).

(i) Use the DNA, purified as described in Section 2.1.1, and not further diluted unless necessary for ease of use. Take 180 μl and add 20 μl of the appropriate 10 × concentrated restriction endonuclease digestion buffer and mix carefully.

(ii) Remove a 40 μl aliquot into a tube and pipette 20 μl aliquots of the rest of the sample into 8 further tubes. Label these tubes 1–9.

(iii) Add an excess of restriction enzyme to tube 1 containing the 40 μl aliquot. We generally use 2 μl of restriction endonuclease at 10–20 units/μl (where 1 unit is that amount of enzyme that will cleave 1 μg λ DNA to completion in 1 h). Mix very carefully and *with a fresh tip* take out 20 μl and add to tube 2. Mix and repeat. Do not add anything to tube 9.

(iv) Incubate at 37°C for 30 min, then place the tubes on ice.

(v) Check the molecular length of the DNA by running 5 μl on a 1% agarose gel. You should see complete or virtually complete digestion in tube 1 and increasingly partial digestion towards tube 8. If this is observed, run 10 μl of the digest on a 0.2% agarose gel (see Section 3.4). Select the correct partial conditions by masking off the DNA in a photograph of the 0.2% agarose gel that is greater than 50 kb and less than 40 kb. The correct partial is *not* the one with most DNA in this range; it is the next more partial. The rationale for this is contained in (13). Use the correct partial conditions and the conditions of the adjacent digest (± 50% of the enzyme) and scale up for the preparative digests.

(vi) It is important to scale up the reaction to reproduce the above conditions *exactly*. You will need to pre-warm the DNA solution since it is a larger volume. Calculate the volume of enzyme required for the appropriate partials. Do not attempt to change buffer, enzyme or DNA concentration. Make as much partial DNA as possible. You will need 200−300 μg per gradient (see Section 2.3).

(vii) Check the DNA by electrophoresis on a 1% gel − you can just see a smear, with care, below the exclusion limit of the gel. If this is seen, keep a small sample from each partial digest for analysis on a 0.2% agarose gel.

(viii) Pool the partial digests and extract once with phenol, once with chloroform and ethanol precipitate as described in Table 1 of Chapter 1. Resuspend in TE so that you have about 300 μg DNA per ml.

2.1.3 *Gradient purification of partial 30−50 kb fraction*

(i) We use sucrose gradients for this purpose. Make 40% and 10% sucrose (w/v) solutions, in 1 M NaCl, 20 mM Tris-HCl, pH 7.1, 20 mM EDTA, 0.3% (v/v) Sarkosyl.

We use the Beckman SW 28/27.1 rotor and 38 ml gradients. Pour the gradients using a gradient maker about 1−1.5 h before the run and make sure there is sufficient room for the DNA sample − take off one or 2 ml if necessary. Alternatively equal volumes of 40%, 35%, 30%, 25%, 20%, 15% and 10% sucrose can be successively layered into the tubes and left to diffuse overnight before use. Carefully layer 1 ml of DNA solution, not more than 300 μg per gradient, onto each tube. We generally use three gradients and one balance. Centrifuge at 26 000 r.p.m. for 16 h at 10°C.

(ii) Fractionate the gradients by piercing the bottom of the tube with a needle attached to tubing through a pump. Collect 0.7−1 ml fractions. The DNA of appropriate size should be around fraction 15−25. Check 15 μl of each sample by electrophoresis on a 0.2% gel. Do not forget to add into the marker tracks sucrose solution in the high salt buffer used for the gradient to about 30%. This is important since the high salt strongly affects DNA mobility.

(iii) Precipitate DNA from fractions that seem to be the correct size by adding two volumes of ethanol. To avoid precipitation of sucrose it is a good idea to add a further 2 ml of 70% ethanol. Mix thoroughly and leave at −20°C for at least overnight or longer if possible. Pellet the DNA by centrifugation as described in Table 1 of Chapter 1. Carefully wash the pellets twice with 70% ethanol and resuspend in about 50 μl of TE. Run 1 μl or so of this on a 0.2% gel to identify

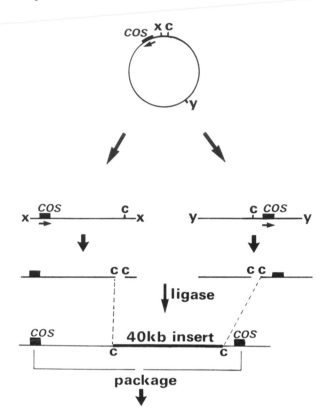

Figure 1. Constructing recombinants using the Ish-Horowicz and Burke protocol (10). c is the cloning site, x and y are other unique cleavage sites. The cosmid is cut separately with x and with y and phosphatased. Each sample is cut with c. The correct 'arms' are those which contain the *cos* site (cos) in the correct orientation (indicated by small arrow). It is not necessary, but advantageous, if the appropriate fragment is isolated prior to ligation. The protocol is designed to avoid generating polymers of the cosmid which would package efficiently.

the useful fractions (50−40 kb). Pool these fractions and adjust to 0.3 M NaCl. Precipitate the DNA with two volumes of ethanol. Pellet by centrifugation and resuspend the DNA in TE to give a concentration of about 1−2 μg/μl.

2.1.4 *Phosphatase procedure*

(i)   Carry out the preparation of the partial digests as described in Section 2.1.2 but resuspend the DNA at about 200 μg/ml in 10 mM Tris-HCl pH 7.5, 10 mM EDTA after the ethanol precipitation.

(ii) Add excess calf intestinal phosphatase (CIP). Use about 0.5 units per μg of DNA, but this may be varied according to experience. Incubate at 37°C for 20 min, then adjust the NaCl to 200 mM.

(iii) Phenol extract, ethanol precipitate and wash with 70% ethanol as described in Table 1 of Chapter 1.

(iv) Finally resuspend the DNA in TE at about 1 μg/μl.

Table 2. Preparation of cosmid vector 'arms'.

1.	Cut two samples of LoristB to completion one with *Sst*I and one with *Bst*EII. Use the manufacturer's conditions for cleavage. Keep back a small aliquot for the test in step 3.
2.	Treat each restriction digest with CIP (Boehringer Molecular Biology Grade). Add excess CIP directly to the restriction digest and continue incubation for 30 min at 37°C. (In our experiments we have dephosphorylated 150 µg with 56 units of CIP in about 500 µl). Extract with phenol and then with chloroform as described in Table 1, Chapter 1. Precipitate the DNA with isopropanol, wash with 70% ethanol and resuspend in TE (150 µg is resuspended in 300 µl TE).
3.	Remove aliquots of phosphatased arms and check that they will not religate in an overnight ligation using standard ligation buffers and conditions (Section 2.3). You can use the aliquot from step 1 as control.
4.	If no ligation is seen, cut both samples with *Hin*dIII. Make sure you use good enzyme and the minimum to allow complete digestion. Check for completion of the reaction by the electrophoresis of an aliquot on a 1% agarose gel.
5.	If the digestion in step 4 is complete, set up a ligation reaction with an aliquot from each digest separately. Check that ligation is complete by electrophoresis of the reaction mix on a 1% agarose gel. You will see a fragment of about 10 kb which is the large fragment of each digest ligating to itself. There should be nothing higher. We find that ligation buffer and enzyme can cause aberrant mobility of fragments, so run appropriate controls for this.
6.	If all samples ligate correctly, phenol extract the entire reaction mixture from step 4. Precipitate DNA from the aqueous phase with isopropanol as described in Table 1, Chapter 1, wash with 70% ethanol and take up in a small volume of TE. You will need each arm at about 1 µg/µl.

It is important to include high EDTA in the CIP reaction to avoid activation of DNase by divalent cations.

2.2 Vector preparation

The enzymes that are used to doubly cleave the cosmid vector for making 'arms' via the Ish-Horrowitz and Burke protocol (10) will depend on the actual cosmid used. In *Figure 1* we show the general procedure for any cosmid vector. The procedure detailed in *Table 2* applies to the Lorist family of cosmids (7,8) where enzyme X is *Sst*I, enzyme Y is *Bst*EII and the cloning site is *Hin*dIII.

An alternative procedure is to phosphatase the vector, cleaved at the cloning site. This is dependent upon a good batch of CIP being available and using the minimum amount (in the buffer used in Section 2.1.4) to produce the desired non-ligatable DNA arms.

Our experience has always been that CIP not only removes terminal phosphates but can also produce damaged sticky ends. Cloning with phosphatased material has always been less efficient than similar experiments with 'arms' and this latter protocol, whilst being more laborious, is less prone to this problem.

2.3 Ligation reactions

Ligations should be set up using the manufacturer's recommended buffers. Take great care to use neutralized ATP, since the pH of the resultant buffer can be significantly non-optimal if non-neutralized ATP is used.

(i)   Set up the following reaction mixture:

Insert DNA	3 μg
Arm 1	1.5 μg
Arm 2	1.5 μg
10 × ligase buffer	2 μl
Water to 20 μl final volume	
5 units T4 DNA ligase	

(ii)   Incubate at 22°C for 2 h or 15°C for 17 h.

(iii) After this, check an aliquot by electrophoresis on a 0.2% agarose gel. Ligation of the vector should be obvious and, with care, ligation of the insert can also be seen. This should not be too apparent since a 10-fold molar excess of arms has been used.

(iv)   If ligation of the vector has occurred, proceed to the packaging reaction. If no ligation is seen, the normal problem is carry-over of the sucrose and/or sarkosyl from the gradient. To overcome this, re-precipitate the DNA with two volumes of ethanol. Pellet by centrifugation, re-wash the insert DNA with 70% ethanol. Allow the pellet to air-dry, redissolve in ligase reaction buffer and repeat.

2.4 Packaging

Commercially available packaging extracts have high efficiencies but are costly. Nevertheless, they are the most convenient, and we have successfully used Amersham and Stratagene extracts.

(i)   Package 4 μl of the ligation mixture precisely as recommended by the manufacturers. Do not be tempted to add more of the reaction.

(ii)   Dilute the extract at the end of the reaction with 1 ml of phage dilution buffer [10 mM Tris-HCl pH 7.4, 10 mM MgSO$_4$ 0.01% (w/v) gelatin].

(iii) Titre 1 and 10 μl of the reaction as described in Section 2.5.3.

2.5 Plating the library

2.5.1 Choice of plating cells

The major consideration is to use a cell that is recombination deficient. Generally, this will be a consequence of a *rec*A mutation which makes the cell both recombination deficient and u.v. sensitive. *rec*A mutations can readily revert and it is important to use a *rec*A that reverts at low frequency (a *rec*A deletion for example). We have had good success with ED8767 which is *rec*A56 *sup*E *sup*F *hsd*S⁻ *met*⁻ (ref. 14), and 1046 which is probably identical to ED8767. Cells should be tested for the *rec*A allele by sensitivity to u.v. − see ref. 3 for methods.

The use of other *rec* mutations should be approached with caution. The *rec*BC *sbc*B background, reported to stabilize λ phages containing head-to-head DNA repeats (15), does not support the growth of pMBl derived plasmids, and we have had severe problems in propagating pBR322 and λ derived cosmids on *rec*BC *sbc*B *rec*A backgrounds which have been reported to support normal pBR322 growth (16).

Table 3. Adsorption and plating of packaged cosmids.

1.	For every ml of packaging reaction, add 10 ml of a fresh saturated culture of *E. coli* ED8767. Leave at 37°C for 30 min.
2.	Dilute with 25 ml of pre-warmed L Broth (not containing the selective antibiotics) and incubate at 37°C for 1 h.
3.	Spin the cells at low speed (5 min at 2000 r.p.m.) in a preparative centrifuge such as a Sorvall RC5 or its equivalent and resuspend in 1.2 ml of L Broth.
4.	Plate not more than 500 μl of this mix onto the appropriate plates.

2.5.2 *Preparation of plating cells*

We grow ED8767 to saturation (overnight) at 37°C with vigorous aeration in L Broth supplemented with 10 mM $MgSO_4$ and 0.1% (w/v) Maltose. This latter supplement is probably not critical. There are several protocols for preparing cells in more laborious fashions and these may be marginally more efficient, but we have not found it necessary to use them.

2.5.3 *Adsorption of packaged cosmids to E. coli*

Packaging extracts can kill cosmid containing bacteria. If the ratio of diluted packaging extract to saturated cell culture exceeds between 1:4 and 1:2, titers of cosmids will be dramatically reduced. We also find that some component of the packaging reaction can inhibit growth of bacteria spread on plates, even when present at ratios of less than 1:4. We have developed the protocol in *Table 3* that appears to overcome this problem and also allows sufficient time for even the slow-expressing neomycin phosphotransferase (Km^r) gene to be fully expressed.

   This protocol should be scaled up or down as required for analytic or preparative scale platings, but care should be taken not to plate greater than 500 μl of the final solution.

2.5.4 *Efficiencies*

The efficiency of cosmid construction can be very variable and final yield of $10^4 - 10^6$ colonies per microgram of eukaryotic DNA can be expected. We generally achieve between 5×10^4 and 5×10^5 and the lower figure is reasonably routine. A complete human library defined by the statistics of Clarke and Carbon (17) requires 345 000 cosmids for a 99% representative library (assuming a vector capacity of 40 kb and a genome size of 3×10^9).

2.6 **Plating out**

2.6.1 *Plating on agar for library amplification*

Generally, it is possible to spread $400 - 500$ μl of the cells prepared as in Section 2.5.3 per 14 cm diameter plate. This should give from an average experiment (50 000 cosmids per packaging reaction) about 17 000 colonies per plate, which is fine. Use L agar plates supplemented with the appropriate drug and make them thick (use 100 ml/plate).

If possible, use plates that are 1−2 days old so they are not too wet. After spreading, dry the plates, if necessary, in a sterile tissue culture hood and then incubate upside down for 24 h.

The plates can then be scraped. Add 2 ml of L Broth plus 15% glycerol (just add sterile glycérol to the L Broth), scrape each plate and pool. Mix carefully and store at −70°C or in liquid N_2. Titres of bacteria should be about 1−2 × 10^9/ml, so you will have many libraries' worth.

We have had some success with screening amplified libraries. We have, however, seen differential growth of colonies − both large ones and very small ones. The λ origin cosmids can be used in this fashion, but abherent representation of specific clones is observed and cannot be predicted in advance.

2.6.2 *Plating directly onto filters*

All the filters we have used, both nylon and cellulose nitrate, are mildly toxic to bacteria. Washing the filter in water and sterilization helps but does not eliminate the problem. Our best success is with cosmids that are adsorbed to *E. coli* exactly as described in Section 2.5.3 and then plated. A reduction in titre of 20% can be expected and may be as much as 100%. Some *E. coli* strains do not grow at all well on nylon membranes and it is important to check plating efficiencies on these membranes, compared to agar. ED8767 is quite reliable.

If the library is plated directly, then it is important to follow the protocol in Section 2.6.3 for the optimal preparation of replicas. The time allowed for the growth of colonies is particularly critical, since we find bacteria on filters tend to grow slower than on agar.

2.6.3 *Replica plating for library screening*

We work from preference with nylon Pall/Biodyne 1.2 micron filters and use the methods of Hanahan and Meselson (18) to make master and replica filters. We have found it very difficult to mix filter types in making replicas (e.g. Biodyne does not replicate well onto nitrocellulose) and therefore use only a single filter type for all operations.

The instructions in *Table 4* refer to use of an amplified library stock but need only appropriate and obvious modification for primary libraries.

2.7 **Screening cosmid filters**

Filters can be screened by a variety of methods. We favour one which allows use of either RNA or DNA probes without significant changes in technique (*Table 5*).

Probes must be high specific activity, $\geq 10^8$ c.p.m. per μg, and can be labelled by any conventional method.

We have had our best screening results with RNA probes made with either SP6 or T7 RNA polymerase (see Chapter 1 and Section 3.3, *Table 11*). Care must be taken against degradation of the probe. Our normal procedure is to use an SP6 or T7 reaction with enough [^{32}P]UTP and DNA template to give 30−80% incorporation into RNA. The reaction is terminated by a single chloroform extraction, isopropanol precipitated and the pellet resuspended in a small volume of TE containing 10 mM vanadyl nucleotide complex (VNC). There is no need to remove unincorporated nucleotides. Do not denature the RNA before use.

Table 4. Preparation of replica filters for hybridization.

1. Make dilutions of the amplified stock. You will need about 50 ml of a solution of about 2×10^4 cells/ml. Titre this by spreading onto L-agar plates containing 30 μg/ml kanamycin with filters. (Assume that the titre will be reduced by about 20% when plated onto filters due to reduced bacterial viability).

2. Place a filter, with a number written in pencil at one side, onto a fresh F agar plate containing antibiotic and allow the filter to become wet. Do not use plates that are very wet − dry them first to remove obvious excess moisture. Spread 0.5 ml of the appropriate dilution of cells onto the filter. Make sure you leave about 1−0.5 cm gap between the spread bacteria and the edge of the filter and take care to maintain sterility. Leave the plates upright and check that the liquid is being adsorbed into the filter. When dry, incubate the plates upside down at 37°C for about 12 h. Spread sufficient bacteria to give 20 000 colonies per plate and 3×10^5 in total (or more as necessary).

3. After 12 h, the colonies should be small (~0.5 mm). This size is critical and so the incubation time should be adjusted as necessary. Make a replica from this as follows:

    (a) Place the required number of filters, labelled in pencil, onto L-agar plates containing antibotic to pre-wet.

    (b) Put some filter paper (Whatman 3MM) onto a flat surface and place the master filter, colonies up, onto this.

    (c) Very carefully put a second filter on top of the master − do not adjust the position if they are not perfectly superimposed.

    (d) Put a second sheet of 3MM paper on top of the filters and a strong glass plate on top of this. Press down hard and uniformly over the plate.

    (e) Remove the plate and the 3MM filter above the bacterial filters and with a needle carefully stab the two filters to make key markers. Make two stabs close together and three others asymmetrically over the filters.

    (f) Then peel apart the two filters with a single reasonably firm motion and place the filters, colonies up, onto the two plates.

    The master can now be frozen away for further use [use the Hanahan and Meselson methods (18)] or held at 4°C for up to 1 month. The replica should be grown for about 3−5 h at 37°C. The colonies will again be about 1 mm diameter or less. These can then be worked up for screening.

4. Colonies are lysed and processed exactly as described in the Pall/Biodyne literature. Lysis is by placing the filter onto 0.5 M NaOH, 1.5 M NaCl for 5 min and then onto 3 M sodium acetate pH 5.5 for 5 min. Air dry and bake at 80°C for 1 h. Store at 4°C.

5. Rinse the filters in an excess of 5 × SSC^c before pre-hybridization. Take care to note the orientation of the filters, since the replica is a mirror image of the master.

^{a}L-agar is 10 g Difco bacto-tryptone, 5 g Difco yeast extract, 5 g NaCl and 15 g agar made up to 1 litre with water.
^{b}F-agar is L-agar plus 5% glycerol.
^{c}SSC is defined in the footnotes to *Table 1*.

After hybridization, the filters should be dried in air (do not allow the filters to dry completely if you wish to re-hybridize them with another probe − see the Pall/Biodyne literature) and exposed at −70°C using Kodak XAR-5 film. An overnight exposure normally gives very intense positives with RNA, less intense with DNA, but this can depend on the specific cosmid.

Colonies will then need to be picked and rescreened anything up to three times more before a single colony can be clearly identified. Do not attempt to be too specific in the first round pick. The filters shrink at −70°C and make it very hard to be absolutely accurate in picking colonies. Pick an area, streak and rescreen. It is surprisingly easy to get the picking wrong, so be prepared to repeat the pick as required. It may be possible

Table 5. Hybridization of filters.

1.	Wash the filters in an excess of 5 × SSC for 5 min at room temperature.
2.	Pre-hybridize the following solution:

> 5 × Denharts [0.1% (w/v) Ficoll 400, 0.1% (w/v) bovine serum albumin, 0.1% (w/v) Polyvinylpyrolidine]
> 5 × SSC[a]
> 50 mM sodium phosphate buffer pH 6.5
> 0.1% SDS
> 250 µg/ml salmon sperm DNA, denatured and sonicated
> 10 µg/ml poly(C)
> 10 µg/ml poly(A)
> 50% Formamide (deionized)

For DNA hybridizations, pre-hybridize at 42°C for between 4 h and overnight. For RNA hybridizations, pre-hybridize for 1 h. In both cases use 3−5 ml per filter.

3. Hybridization is carried out in 2.5−3.0 ml of fresh buffer per filter. The buffer has the same composition as that in step 2 and contains in addition 10⁶ c.p.m. per ml of the appropriate ³²P-labelled RNA or DNA probe. For RNA probes, supplement the reaction with 10 mM VNC and hybridize for 17 h at 50°C. For DNA, simply hybridize at 42°C for 2 days. We generally include the denatured cosmid vector as competitor in the pre-hybridization at 0.5−1 µg/ml.

4. After hybridization, filters are washed identically whether DNA or RNA probes are used. The first three washes are with 1 l of 2 × SSC, 0.1% SDS at room temperature for 20 min each wash. The final wash is for 30 min at 65°C with 0.1 × SSC, 0.1% SDS. This stringent wash can be modified as required and is for an homologous probe.

[a]SSC is defined in the footnotes to *Table 1*.

with the high copy number λ origin vectors to expose at room temperature to avoid the shrinkage problem.

An alternative procedure to streaking is to pick the positive area and resuspend the cells in 1 ml of L Broth plus drug. Aliquots of this (between 1 and 100 µl generally) can be spread directly onto fresh filters and screened directly (as in Section 2.6).

2.8 Storing cosmid libraries

2.8.1 *Storing bacteria*

Amplified libraries are stable virtually indefinitely when frozen at −70°C or in liquid nitrogen in L Broth plus 15% glycerol. Aliquot the amplified library (Section 2.6.1) into 1 ml vials and store. Thaw out as required. We have seen no obvious reduction in titre with two or three rounds of thawing, but have usually discarded the vials after this.

2.8.2 *Storing packaged cosmids*

Cosmids can be stored as packaged phage particles for at least 6 months at 4°C. It is not advised that the packaging reaction is stored, since we have observed gradual reduction in titres after storage for even 1 week. Lorist cosmids can be packaged out of the *E. coli* by either packaging by superinfection or by plating onto specialized *in vivo* packaging strains.

2.8.3 *Packaging cosmid libraries by superinfection*

This is a useful method for recovering a library that may have become contaminated

Table 6. Packaging of cosmids by liquid culture superinfection.

1.	Grow up 100 ml of the cosmid library in L broth supplemented with antibiotic and 10 mM $MgSO_4$. Inoculate sufficient bacteria to give an initial A_{600} of about 0.08. Grow with vigorous aeration until A_{600} is 0.4. This may be fast (2 h) or much slower (>4 h).
2.	Infect *E. coli* with an m.o.i. of 1 or greater with any λ phage that is incapable of lysogeny, i.e. CI^- (do not use λ *vir*). We have used several vector phages − L47.1 (19) and SepB (3) most conveniently.
3.	Monitor cell growth at A_{600}. It should increase to about 1.0 then collapse to about 0.5 as lysis occurs within a period of not greater than 4 h. When lysis is visible, add 1 ml of chloroform, shake for 1−2 min. Pellet the debris by centrifugation at 4000 r.p.m. in a standard bench centrifuge or a Sorvall RC5 or its equivalent. Keep the supernatant.
4.	Titre the supernatant as though it was a freshly packaged cosmid library.

Table 7. Packaging of cosmids by superinfection of plate cultures.

1.	Plate 200 μl of a saturated (overnight) culture of the cosmid-containing bacteria plus 2.5 ml of molten top agar at 55°C onto a single 9 cm diameter L-agar plate containing the selective antibiotic.
2.	Allow the top agar to solidify and then spot 5−10 μl of an appropriate superinfecting phage (see Section 2.8.3) containing $10^4−10^5$ p.f.u. in phage dilution buffer[a] onto the centre of the plate. Leave to dry and then incubate at 37°C overnight.
3.	The next morning, a clear area can be seen where the phage has lysed the cells. Pick this area with the end of a Pasteur pipette and put into 1 ml of phage dilution buffer (See Section 2.4). Add three drops of chloroform and shake gently. Leave at 4°C for 2−5 h and then titre the supernatant − be careful not to remove chloroform droplets when doing this. Use whatever cell is required as recipient. Titres will be variable − generally it is easiest to plate 1, 10 and 100 μl with 200 μl of saturated cells directly into top agar.

[a]Phage dilution buffer is 10 mM Tris-HCl pH 7.4, 10 mM $MgSO_4$, 0.01% (w/v) gelatin.

or is full of small deletion derivatives. It does, however, mean a further amplification of the library has occurred and it will almost certainly be non-representative. The protocol is detailed in *Table 6*.

The lysate will contain packaged cosmids and also the superinfecting phage, e.g. SepB or L47-1, and titres will depend very much on the efficiency of the growth and infection cycle. It often is about $10^6−10^7$ cosmids or phage per ml. The superinfecting phage can cause problems by lysing the cosmid-containing cells when attempting to plate onto the packaged cosmids. To overcome this, it is easiest to use ED8767 which has been lysogenized by a phage with the same immunity as L47-1 (imm^{434}) or SepB (imm^{21}). These cells are, by definition, immune to superinfection. Note that λ origin cosmids confer immunity to $λimm^λ$ and it is only possible in this case to use imm^{21} or imm^{434} CI^- superinfecting phages. The use of λvir superinfecting phages is not recommended since they are capable of growing on all lysogens.

Libraries packaged in this way are stable at 4°C for extensive periods of time and can be handled using identical procedures to packaged cosmid or phage libraries.

2.8.4 *Packaging individual cosmids by superinfection*

This is useful for storage purposes, for transforming cosmids to specialist cell lines, and for rescuing cosmids that have started to become unstable (see Section 4.7.1). The protocol is detailed in *Table 7*. To store the packaged cosmid, simply centrifuge the plug of top agar and phage dilution buffer picked as in step 3 of *Table 7*. The centrifugation speed should be just sufficient to clarify the suspended agar. Remove and store the supernatant over a drop of chloroform.

2.8.5 *Packaging in helper cell lines*

The background to the use of specialist packaging cells is in ref. 20.

Cell lines have been constructed that contain defective λimm^{434} lysogens that have the following genotype and biological properties. They are CI^{ts} and hence stable only at 32°C and induce to produce virus at 42°C; they are *Sam7*, a defect in lysis to allow high yield of phage particles; they also contain the *b2* deletion which dramatically reduces the efficiency of excision from the chromosome, and finally, they are *red3*, which eliminates the phage recombination system. If a cosmid is put into these cells (via *in vitro* packaging) then the cell may be successfully propagated in the presence of the appropriate antibiotic at 32°C. However, if the cell is shifted to 42°C, the repressor (*CI* gene product) is inactivated, the prophage attempts to excise from the *E. coli* genome, fails to do so but synthesizes large amounts of head and tail components which can package the resident cosmid. The cells are then lysed with chloroform and will give high yields of cosmid and low yields of helper phage (10^9 cosmids per ml compared to 10^4 phage). This process is an example of *in vivo* packaging.

It is in principle possible to construct libraries directly in such cell lines, but in practice plating efficiency is always lower in these temperature-sensitive strains. Two strains have been used for *in vivo* packaging — BHB3175 and DK22. Both cells are lysogenized with the same phage λ3169 (λimm^{434} CI^{ts} *b2 red3 Sam7*). BHB3175 is HL202 lysogenized with λ3169 (20) and DK22 is DK1 lysogenized with λ3169 (D.Kurnit, personal communication). Both strains are *recA*.

The protocol for *in vivo* packaging is in *Table 8*.

The procedure is useful for preparation of large amounts of packaged cosmids

Table 8. Preparation of phosmids by *in vivo* packaging cell lines.

1.	Infect the appropriate packaged cosmid into *E. coli* BHB3175 or *E. coli* DK22. Do not allow the cells to warm up to more than 32°C at any stage. Plate out onto L-agar plates containing the selective antibiotic and grow at 32°C overnight.
2.	Pick drug resistant colonies and streak onto two plates and incubate one plate at 32°C and the other at 42°C. Streak onto the 42°C plate before the 32°C plate. Grow overnight.
3.	Select a colony that shows no growth at all at 42°C. Do *not* attempt to use a colony that shows any sign of growth at the non-permissive temperature. If the colony is large enough, inoculate it into L broth containing antibiotic at 32°C and grow to A_{600} of 0.3.
4.	Rapidly warm the culture to 45°C and hold it at this temperature for 14 min. Measure the A_{600}, which should have increased from step 3.
5.	Transfer to a 37°C shaking incubator and grow for at least 3 h and not more than 17 h. Check the A_{600} in the early stages — it should increase to about 0.6–0.7. An increase of more than this means there are non-lysogen cells growing in the culture.
6.	After the appropriate time, lyse the cells by the addition of chloroform (2 ml/l). Heavy debris should be visible upon lysis. Spin out the debris at 4000 r.p.m. in a preparative centrifuge and titre the cleared lysate. In this case the helper phage is not very viable and there is no need to use a λ lysogen to titre the cosmids. Use the protocol detailed in Section 2.5.3 to titre.

(phosmids). The λ DNA within a phage particle is linear with single strand cohesive ends (*cos*). This is also true for packaged cosmids and we therefore define a phosmid as a cosmid that is linear around *cos*. *In vivo* packaging by this procedure works best with cosmids that are at high yield in the cell and we have had good success with λ origin cosmids and several pBR322 derivatives, but in the latter case only if they are high yielding cosmid clones. Phosmids can also be used in the rapid restriction mapping protocols briefly detailed in Section 3.2, using the so-called *cos*-mapping procedure (6,21).

Phosmids may also prove useful in cellular microinjection and transfection experiments.

2.8.6 *Storing DNA*

Cosmid DNA can be packaged *in vitro* identically to λ DNA. However, the efficiency with which cosmids are packaged is very much lower than λ phage DNA, since it is predominantly monomeric circles with only a single *cos* and so not a substrate for the packaging reaction. Generally efficiencies will be between 10^3 and 10^6 per microgram of DNA. It is a convenient fail-safe if bacterial or phosmid storage is not successful.

2.9 **Cosmid DNA preparations**

There are numerous protocols for preparing plasmid DNA from bacterial cells. The one we describe here is simple and reasonably reproducible but is almost certainly replaceable by other techniques. We describe conditions for growth of the Lorist λ origin cosmids. Modification for other cosmid vectors is minor and obvious.

2.9.1 *Growth of bacteria*

Grow cells in L Broth plus 30 μg/ml kanamycin sulphate. Never grow cosmid-containing cells in the absence of antibiotic and always aerate vigorously. For mini preps we grow 5 ml in 50 ml tubes, for maxi preps we use 500 – 1000 mls in a 2 l flask shaken vigorously. Start the growth by inoculation of a single colony or small volume of saturated culture. Grow overnight (17 h) at 37°C. Some cosmids grow badly and may not be saturated by then. Simply grow longer. For non λ origin cosmids we do not recommend chloramphenicol amplification. This may increase yields but also may allow over-replication of deletion derivatives of the parent recombinant.

2.9.2 *Mini preps*

The method in *Table 9* is derived from ref. 10 and is a slight further modification.

For restriction enzyme analysis of mini-prep DNA, digest 5 μl of the DNA in a 10 μl final reaction mix. Add 1 μg RNase (boiled) to the digest at the start — do not remove RNA before this, since it stabilizes the crude preparation. With care, this protocol will yield DNA that is cleavable every time. If you find this is not the case, phenol extract the preparation, ethanol precipitate the nucleic acids, wash the pellet with 70% ethanol (Table 1, Chapter 1), re-dissolve it and try again. This is definitely not routinely necessary. The commonest cause of failure is incomplete removal of the precipitate and bad washing out of the salt solutions.

Table 9. Cosmid DNA 'mini' preps.

1.	Spin down 1.5 ml of saturated culture in a microcentrifuge for 1 min at room temperature.
2.	Pour off the culture medium and swab out any excess with a cotton bud. Add 200 μl of cold solution I[a] to the pellet. Resuspend the cells very carefully. Add a few flakes of lysozyme (store lysozyme in freezer over dessicant − it goes off rather fast). Mix and leave for 5 min at room temperature.
3.	Add 400 μl of freshly made solution II[b] at room temperature. Mix by inverting 2/3 times. Do *not* vortex or shake too vigorously but make sure the solution is uniform. Place on ice for 5−10 min.
4.	Add 200 μl of cold solution III[c], mix by fairly vigorous shaking but do not use vortex and leave on ice for 10 min.
5.	Spin in a microcentrifuge at room temperature for 10 min.
6.	Pick out the rather sticky and gelatinous pellet with a toothpick. The pellet is often smeared over the side of the tube and looks horrible − don't worry, this is normal.
7.	Add 480 μl of propan-2-ol at room temperature and mix well. Freeze on dry ice and then transfer whilst still frozen to a microcentrifuge. Spin for 10 min at room temperature. There is no need to leave tubes in dry ice for long − just until they are frozen.
8.	Pour off the supernatant − there should be an easily visible pellet at the bottom of the tube. Add 1 ml of 70% ethanol at room temperature. Shake the tube hard to dislodge the pellet, spin for 5 min in a microcentrifuge, and pour off the supernatant. Leave the tubes upside down to drain for 10 min. Swab off the excess ethanol with a cotton bud. Resuspend the pellet in 50 μl of TE and put at 55°C for at least 10 min to dissolve.

[a]Solution I is 25% (w/v) glucose, 50 mM Tris-HCl, pH 8.0, 10 mM EDTA pH 8.0. Store and use cold.
[b]Solution II is 0.2 M NaOH, 1% (w/v) SDS. Make this fresh and use NaOH solutions that have been stored in plastic bottles not glass.
[c]Solution III is 3 M potassium acetate pH 4.8 with acetic acid. Store and use cold.

2.9.3 *Large scale preparations of 500−1000 ml cultures*

The method is detailed in *Table 10.*

Yields from this process are always disappointing − much less than the mini preps would lead you to believe. However, 500 ml of culture will yield at least 2−300 μg of cosmid.

Yields of non-recombinant λ origin cosmid vectors are also low − we rarely get more than 200 μg/litre. This is due to the nature of replication control of these λ derivatives.

3. SPECIALIST TECHNIQUES

This section covers in broad outline techniques that may prove useful to some workers in the field. It is not intended to be a detailed protocol for all aspects of the techniques.

3.1 **Cloning by recombination**

This procedure was first developed by Lehrach *et al.* (20) and by Linderman *et al.* (22). Detailed protocols are found in both these references and Chapter 3 of this volume.

Cloning by recombination is a method that allows very large numbers of cosmids to be screened with a minimum of labour. It takes advantage of the observation that λ is not a generalized transducing phage − that is it will only package DNA that is contained between two *cos* sequences the appropriate distance apart.

In outline, the method uses two vectors, one cosmid and one plasmid that have no DNA sequence homology and different drug resistances, say *Km*[r] and *Ap*[r]. Both are

Table 10. Large scale cosmid DNA preparations.

1.	Pellet the cells from a 500 ml culture by centrifugation and add 20 ml of cold solution I[a] to the pellet. Add crystals of lysozyme (the tip of a spatula worth) and resuspend carefully. Mix and leave for 10 min at room temperature.
2.	Add 60 ml of solution II[b], and mix with a pipette or similar instrument. Do not shake vigorously. Leave on ice for 10 min.
3.	Add 45 ml of cold solution III[c]. Mix as in step 2. Leave for 30 min on ice.
4.	Centrifuge for 15 min at 5000 r.p.m. in the GSA rotor of the Sorvall RC5 (or equivalent). Pour off the supernatant through gauze to remove large floating clumps of debris. Keep the supernatant and add 0.6 volumes of propan-2-ol. Leave on ice for 30 min then centrifuge to pellet the precipitate which is heavy and does not have to be spun hard. Drain off the supernatant and resuspend in TE. The volume will depend on the size of the ultracentrifuge tube that will be used. We use the VTi65 vertical rotor that takes 5 ml and so resuspend the sample in 5 ml of TE and divide the sample between two tubes.
5.	Suppose the volume of the DNA solution measures y ml, then add 0.1y ml of 10 mg/ml ethidium bromide, and 1.1y g of CsCl. We have found any grade or make works. Leave in the dark for 30 min at room temperature. A heavy precipitate of protein and other debris will form. Spin the sample at moderate speeds for 5 min and this will cause any debris to either float (if it is protein) or sink. Carefully remove the clear solution taking care to miss the debris. Centrifuge this for the appropriate time in the ultracentrifuge at 20°C − we use 17 h at 50 000 r.p.m. in a Beckman VTi 75 rotor.
6.	Harvest the (lower) supercoiled plasmid band in the smallest volume possible (x ml) and put in a 50 ml disposable polypropylene tube (a Falcon 2070 tube or one of similar type).
7.	Fill the tube with water saturated *N*-butanol, cap and shake. Allow the phases to separate and pour off the top, organic layer. Generally this will be about 45 ml.
8.	Repeat step 2. The CsCl/DNA solution will increase in volume as it becomes diluted with the water from the saturated *N*-butanol solution. Remove all traces of the organic phase.
9.	Add x ml of distilled water to give y ml of DNA/CsCl solution.
10.	Add y ml of propan-2-ol, freeze on dry ice, thaw and centrifuge in a middle speed centrifuge. Wash the pellet carefully with room temperature 70% ethanol, dry in air and resuspend the DNA in 10 mM Tris pH 7.4, 1 mM EDTA (see Table 1, Chapter 1). Incubate at 55°C for 10 min to dissolve, and use as required.

[a]Solution I is described in footnote a of *Table 9.*
[b]Solution II is described in footnote b of *Table 9.*
[c]Solution III is described in footnote c of *Table 9.*

grown transiently in *rec*[+] versions of the *in vivo* packaging strains (Section 2.8.5) and cells contain both episomes.

Induction of the prophage results in packaging of the *Km*[r] cosmid but not the *Ap*[r] plasmid. However, if there is homology between DNA cloned into both the cosmid and the plasmid, then recombination between the homologous sequences can occur, with a frequency of about 10^{-3}, which will result in the two vectors becoming linked together as one large circular cosmid. Packaging then will result, only in this case, in both *Km*[r] and *Ap*[r] transduction. Thus to clone a gene, it is only necessary to insert a small DNA fragment into the 'probe' plasmid contained in the helper cell line, superinfect with a cosmid library (packaged as in Section 2.8.5), induce the prophage of the helper cell and plate out on Km and Ap plates. Colonies that are doubly drug resistant will in principle contain the gene, cloned into the cosmid, with the probe plasmid integrated through the region of homology.

The method is powerful, technically exacting and requires careful strain testing to

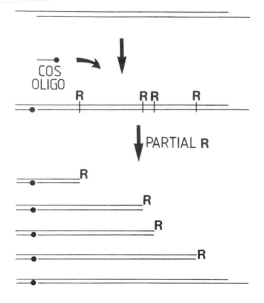

Figure. 2. *Cos* mapping. Radiolabelled oligonucleotides complementary to the left or right cohesive end are annealed to the appropriate end. Partial digestion with restriction enzyme R, separation of fragments by agarose gel electrophoresis followed by autoradiography, will only detect the partial fragments containing the radiolabel. Simple subtraction allows the molecular weight of each fragment to be calculated.

work efficiently. It should be a serious consideration where much repetitive isolation of the same gene is required from different libraries or where detailed and specific joining of DNA sequences is needed. It significantly reduces the amount of work required to isolate a gene but inevitably results in disruption of the DNA at the point of recombination. Techniques exist to isolate the reverse recombination event that excises the integrated probe plasmid.

3.2 *Cos* mapping

Cos mapping was developed by Rachwitz *et al.* (21) to map phage λ clones. It has been extended to cosmid clones (6). The major problem with restriction mapping analysis of cosmid clones is that of size − there are too many sites for most commonly used enzymes to allow rapid mapping. *Cos* mapping overcomes this by using partial digestion to identify map order and sites. The process is shown schematically in *Figure 2*. The left or right cohesive end is labelled by annealing to it a ^{32}P-labelled 12 base DNA fragment that is complementary to the left or right sticky end of phage λ. The DNA is then partially digested and radioactive fragments, by definition starting at labelled end, are detected by autoradiography after size fractionation on agarose gels.

The method can be extended to cosmids by analysis of cosmids packaged *in vivo* in helper cells − the phosmids detailed in Section 2.8.5. Detailed protocols can be found in ref. 6. Attention is drawn to the discussion in Section 2.8.5 of phosmid isolation from non-λ origin cosmids.

The procedure is initially a little complex but, once established as a routine system, it has proved to be versatile and extremely rapid. The major problem has been transferring the individual cosmids from *E. coli* ED8767 cells into *E. coli* BHB3175. This can be done by the process detailed in Section 2.8.4, but *E. coli* BHB3175 is somewhat unpredictable in its behaviour − it frequently reverts to non-temperature sensitive or spontaneously induces. DK22 has proved somewhat more stable in our hands.

3.3 **Walking**

Vectors that contain SP6, T7 or T3 promoters immediately adjacent to the cloning sites have recently been constructed (8 and unpublished results). These allow rapid and facile preparation of ^{32}P-labelled RNA probes that are specific for the extreme ends of the cloned DNA and therefore well suited to use as probes for the identification of new cosmids that overlap the starting cosmid. This process of isolating overlapping clones is known as 'walking' and the use of SP6/T7/T3 promoter systems can significantly reduce the time and labour involved in carrying out a walk, by reducing the requirement to identify ends of clones by restriction mapping and physical isolation for probe preparation.

The transcription reactions are most efficiently carried out using a CsCl purified template (see Section 2.9.3). It is important to purify the DNA carefully using the follow-

---

Table 11. *In vitro* transcription of cosmids.

1.	We use 20 μg of recombinant cosmid per transcription (this is equivalent to about 2 μg of a small pUC-derived vector). If cleavage of the template to give a specific run-off site is required, cut with the appropriate enzyme and then clean up the DNA by extracting once with phenol and once with chloroform. Precipitate the DNA with propan-2-ol, wash with 70% ethanol, dry and resuspend in TE for use. If required uncleaved the DNA can be used directly.
2.	Transcription reactions should be set up at room temperature to avoid spermidine precipitation. Set up 100 μl reactions with the following reactants at final concentrations or amounts.

> 20 μg DNA
> 40 mM Tris-HCl pH 7.5[a]
> 6 mM $MgCl_2$[a]
> 2 mM spermidine HCl (Sigma)[a]
> 100 μg/ml bovine serum albumin[a] (Pentex fraction V or other high quality)
> 10 mM dithiothreitol
> 100 units RNasın
> 400 μM ATP
> 400 μM CTP
> 400 μM GTP
> 50 μCi ^{32}P-UTP (800 Ci/mmol Amersham SP6 grade) (cold UTP as required)
> 40 units SP6 or T7 polymerase (Biolabs, Boehringer or others)

3.	Incubate at 40°C for 60 min. Take an aliquot for assay before the addition of enzyme and at 60 min.
4.	Terminate the reaction by adding an equal volume of chloroform. Shake and separate the phases by centrifugation. Precipitate nucleic acids from the aqueous phase using isopropanol. Pellet by centrifugation and resuspend in TE containing 10 mM Vanadyl Nucleotides. Use at once if possible and do not denature or attempt to remove the template − it is not necessary.

---

[a]These reagents can be kept as the following 5× concentrated buffer, which can be sterilized by filtration and stored at 4°C: 200 mM Tris-HCl pH 7.5, 30 mM $MgCl_2$, 10 mM spermidine-HCl, 500 μg/ml bovine serum albumin.

ing procedure, which has both the advantages of working and not requiring much effort.

(i)   Take the plasmid off the gradient in x mls (probably $0.5-1$ ml).
(ii)   Extract twice with 50 ml of water saturated *N*-butanol; the ethidium will partition with the butanol and the DNA solution will expand in volume.
(iii)   Add x ml of water to give final volume of y.
(iv)   Add y ml of propan-2-ol, mix well, freeze on dry ice and centrifuge to pellet the DNA.
(v)   Wash the pellet with 70% ethanol at room temperature.
(vi)   Collect the pellet by centrifugation, allow it to air dry and resuspend in the appropriate volume of TE (*Table 1*, Chapter 1).
(vii)   Transcription reactions are carried out as detailed in *Table 11*.

It is important to assay the transcription reactions since we see low efficiency of incorporation in some cases and this normally yields degraded probes that are not suitable for hybridization. Assay by TCA precipitation, DE81 filters or Whatman 540 filters (see Chapter 1, for the method). Incorporation in the absence of cold UTP will be up to 90% with T7 or $30-60\%$ with SP6 polymerase (SP6 is always less efficient than T7 polymerase in our hands).

RNA transcripts can be made that are specific for the ends of the cloned DNA either by cleavage with a restriction enzyme or by the use of limiting UTP concentrations. At $0.5~\mu M$, the transcripts average about $800-1000$ bp without a run-off cleavage site (see ref. 8 for discussion).

RNA probes are very efficient for screening libraries — they tend to give higher signal than double stranded radiolabelled DNA probes but are, of course, more sensitive to degradation. Hybridization conditions are detailed in Section 2.7.

3.4 **0.2% agarose gels**

These can be made using any standard agarose gel box. Gels should be cast on glass plates since they are quite difficult to move onto the u.v. transilluminator.

(i)   Use the lid of a polycarbonate box, for example, that fits into the normal gel area, leaving a 2 cm gap all round.
(ii)   Place a weight on this and pour 1% agarose to 0.5 cm depth round the lid. This will act as a more rigid mould to contain the 0.2% gel. There is no need to cover the bottom of the well with 1% agarose.
(iii)   When this has solidified, carefully remove the lid.
(iv)   Place the slot former in position about 2 cm away from the supporting agarose, pushing the teeth through the edges of the 1% agarose — do not worry about this breaking up the agarose slightly. Then fill the central well with 0.2% agarose and leave to solidify.
(v)   Remove the slot former very gently — the slots will look collapsed but will open up under buffer.
(vi)   Very gently flood the gel — do not pour buffer on top of the 0.2% since it goes straight through the gel.

The gel can be made up with ethidium bromide ($0.5~\mu g/ml$) in the gel and in the running buffer which is easier than trying to stain the gel after the run. It will reduce, very slightly, the resolution of the gel.

The gels are very sensitive to overloading and a few practice runs will establish the correct volume and amount of DNA to be loaded. We use slots that are 0.75 × 0.15 cm embedded in a gel of 0.5 cm depth. These will hold about 20−25 μl comfortably and will fractionate about 100 ng of DNA without overloading too badly.

The gels can be run fast to give approximate sizes but need to be run at low voltage gradients (1 V/cm at most) for optimum resolution. The gel running buffer is as with standard agarose gels.

Markers are most conveniently λ DNA either run as multimers or digested to give a 25−30 kb fragment. The λ multimers do not resolve particularly well on the gels run as described here but clear resolution of 48 and 96 kb should be possible.

The DNA that is used to make the library must be of lower mobility than the 95 kb λ dimer with no material running faster. Be careful, however, since an overloaded gel can have DNA running with both greater and lesser mobility than expected.

Analysis of sucrose gradients is possible by running samples directly off the gradient. It is imperative that the markers contain the sucrose/salt/EDTA mixture, or very abherent mobility occurs compared to the gradient samples.

It should be possible to obtain very high resolution gels using OFAGE or field inversion gel electrophoresis (23,24). We have found that the high salt in the gradients makes this hard for field inversion. We have not tried OFAGE.

4. PROBLEMS

The purpose of this section is to detail some of the commonest problems we have experienced in our attempts to construct libraries and suggest solutions.

4.1 **Starting DNA**

The starting DNA must be of very high quality. On a 0.2% gel there should be no DNA smaller than 100 kb. If there is, we have never had high enough efficiency to construct a library. RNase digestion and ethanol precipitation/resuspension seem to reduce the molecular weight of the DNA and we never use them. The protocol given in Section 2.1.1 works well and is very simple. Do not use old cells in culture or tissue that has been allowed to sit at room temperature since these are often slightly degraded.

4.2 **Sucrose gradients**

The DNA off sucrose gradients sometimes seems degraded. It can be seen if the high molecular weight fractions show appreciable streaking below 25 kb. We have seen similar problems with salt gradients. Make sure all solutions have been autoclaved − in the case of sucrose, 110°C is fine. We have never been successful in constructing a library if degradation has occurred. We have even seen DNA degrade on 0.2% gels run overnight. This is very hard to control − make sure the gel apparatus is clean and solutions fresh or autoclaved.

4.3 **Failure of ligation or packaging**

This is generally due to carry-over of salt, detergent or sucrose and can be seen if the vector fails to ligate to itself. Failure of packaging is difficult to identify — check extracts carefully against λ phage DNA and be careful to ensure there is no contamination of dilution buffers etc. with detergent from washing up or other glassware cleaning fluids. If the extracts are working, if ligation of the vector is seen and no colonies are seen after plating out, provided the plating cells are good, the insert DNA must be suspect. Re-precipitate it and repeat the ligation. If this does not work, then the sticky ends of the DNA are damaged and the DNA will have to be prepared fresh.

4.4 **Plating cells**

Always check that the plating cells are capable of supporting λ phage growth — do this routinely by plating a phage sample onto the cells. It is not uncommon that cells become λ resistant and these will not plate cosmids or any other packaged molecule. Always check plating cells for contamination by plating onto L-agar containing the selective antibiotic without added extracts. Check all solutions (SM, MgSO$_4$ etc.) in a similar fashion. In particular, be careful of slow growing contaminants (yeast and pseudomonads in particular) which behave very like slow growing cosmid-containing *E. coli*. Leaving plates out after analysis for a few days at room temperature can be very instructive in identifying contaminants. The easiest way of introducing such contaminants is by serial passage of plating cells — using one culture to start the next. *Always* go back to the stock. *E. coli* ED8767 is strong *recA* and rarely reverts, but it is worth checking u.v. sensitivity on a regular basis.

4.5 **Plating out**

Be very careful to follow the protocols detailed in Section 2.6. Plating onto filters can be impossible with some cell lines and it is strongly advised that cells be tested for their ability to grow on filters compared to directly plating them on L-agar containing antibiotic — make sure you use a recombinant cosmid in the bacteria.

Scale up of packaging/ligation reactions often is not a matter of simple multiplication — 10-fold more extract does not always make 10-fold more cosmids. Be very careful to control scale up — the best is to scale up *exactly*, as conditions of the small scale reaction dictate.

Most membranes will reduce viability of bacteria grown on their surface. This can be reduced to a minimum by pre-washing the filter, autoclaving and following the protocols in Section 2.6.2. However, always titre the library on filters and do not extrapolate directly from L-agar containing antibiotic — this can be wishful thinking.

4.6 **Differential growth of cosmids**

Amplified libraries do not show random representation of clones; under- and over-representation of clones will occur but this may not matter in particular circumstances. There are other reasons for this besides differential growth (Section 4.7) and some cosmids will always grow to give small colonies and slow growing cells.

4.7 **Vector problems**

4.7.1 *Unstable sequences*

Cosmids are seen quite often which are unstable and spontaneously re-arrange or become smaller (expect this to occur $1-5\%$ of the time). The cause of this is difficult to identify and can be any one of several reasons; inverted duplications, strong prokaryotic promoter homologies in the eukaryotic DNA, operator homologies and repressor binding sites are all candidate sequences for these [see (7) for discussion of these phenomena]. We have identified cosmids that cause their host cells to grow slowly and in bulk culture we would anticipate enriching cosmid deletion derivatives that do not cause growth interference. In practical terms, there is little that can be done about seriously unstable cosmids except to attempt to recover and store full length molecules from the deletion culture. This can be done by using *in vivo* packaging by superinfection on plates (Sections $2.8.3-2.8.6$). Cosmids recovered from the phage lysates will be enriched for full length cosmids since they will fall within the correct packaging limits. However, multimers of deletion derivatives can also be packaged and this process may not be effective.

To avoid deletion, it is important to store cosmids as early as possible after isolation (e.g. store some of the same bacterial suspension as was used to make initial minipreps) and grow cosmid stocks as little as possible. Storing packaged cosmids is also useful.

4.7.2 *Non-random clone representation*

Even in non-amplified libraries, under-representation and over-representation of individual clones has been seen. The basis of this is not entirely clear (7) but it can effectively render a sequence 'unclonable'. Under-representation by even a factor of two increases the probability of a clone not being contained within an otherwise statistically significant sized library.

One source of variability, transcriptional interference of the origin by promoter homologies in the inserted DNA, can be partially reduced by using cloning sites protected by RNA polymerase terminators. One such family of cosmids, based upon the λ origin, has been constructed (7).

5 CONCLUSION

Cosmid cloning is technically more difficult than λ phage cloning and should be avoided unless experience or biological problem requires its use. The protocols detailed in this chapter work under most circumstances but are not definitive. Other procedures have been detailed and almost certainly some degree of substitution is possible.

6. ACKNOWLEDGEMENTS

I am indebted to Sally Cross for her help in carrying out the experiments detailed in this Chapter and to Toby Gibson, Alan Coulson, John Sulston, Hans Lehrach, Noreen Murray amongst many others for much encouragement and discussion. The work was supported by a grant from the Medical Research Council and the Cancer Research Campaign.

7. REFERENCES

1. Collins,J. and Hohn,B. (1978) *Proc. Natl. Acad. Sci. USA,* **75**, 4242.
2. Becker,A. and Gold,M. (1975) *Proc. Natl. Acad. Sci. USA,* **72**, 581.
3. Maniatis,T., Fritsch,E.F. and Sambrook,J. (1982) *Molecular Cloning. A Laboratory Manual.* Cold Spring Harbor Laboratory Press, Cold Spring Harbor, NY.
4. Pouwels,P.H., Enger-Valk,B.E. and Brammar,W.J. (1986) *Cloning Vectors. A Laboratory Manual.* Elsevier, Amsterdam.
5. Brady,G., Funk,A., Mattern,J., Schutz,G. and Brown,R. (1985) *EMBO J.,* **41**, 2583.
6. Little,P.F.R. and Cross,S.H. (1985) *Proc. Natl. Acad. Sci. USA,* **82**, 3159.
7. Gibson,T.J., Coulson,A.R., Sulston,J.E. and Little,P.F.R. (1987) *Gene,* in press.
8. Cross,S.H. and Little,P.F.R. (1986) *Gene,* **49**, 9.
9. Coulson,A., Sulston,J., Brenner,S. and Karn,J. (1986) *Proc. Natl. Acad. Sci. USA,* **83**, 7821.
10. Ish-Horowicz,D. and Burke,J.F. (1981) *Nucleic Acids Res.,* **9**, 2989.
11. Bates,P.F. and Swift,R.A. (1983) *Gene,* **26**, 137.
12. Seed,B. (1982) *Biopolymers,* **21**, 1793.
13. Seed,B., Parker,R.C. and Davidson,N. (1982) *Gene,* **19**, 201.
14. Murray,N.E., Brammar,W.J. and Murray,K. (1977) *Mol. Gen. Genet.,* **150**, 53.
15. Leach,D.R.F. and Stahl,F.W. (1983) *Nature,* **305**, 448.
16. Vapnek,D., Alton,N.K., Bassell,C.L. and Kushner,S.R. (1976) *Proc. Natl. Acad. Sci. USA,* **73**, 3492.
17. Clarke,L. and Carbon,J. (1976) *Cell,* **9**, 91.
18. Hanahan,D. and Meselson,M. (1983) In *Methods in Enzymology.* Wu,R., Grossman,L. and Moldave,K. (eds), Academic Press, NY, Vol. 100, p. 333.
19. Loenen,W.A.M. and Brammar,W.J. (1980) *Gene,* **10**, 249.
20. Poustka,A., Rackwitz,H.R., Frischauf,A.-M., Hohn,B. and Lehrach,H. (1984) *Proc. Natl. Acad. Sci. USA,* **81**, 4129.
21. Rackwitz,H.R., Zehetner,G., Murialdo,H., Delius,H., Chai,J.H., Frischauf,A. and Lehrach,H. (1985) *Gene,* **40**, 259.
22. Lindenmaier,W., Dittmar,K.E.J., Hauser,H., Necker,A. and Sebald,W. (1985) *Gene,* **39**, 33.
23. Carle,G.F., Frank,M. and Olson,M.V. (1986) *Science,* **232**, 65.
24. Schwartz,D.C. and Cantor,C.R. (1984) *Cell,* **37**, 67.

CHAPTER 3

Genetic approaches to the cloning, modification and characterization of cosmid clones and clone libraries

ANNEMARIE POUSTKA and HANS LEHRACH

1. INTRODUCTION

The following chapter describes a genetic approach to the isolation, manipulation and analysis of cosmid clones or libraries. The techniques described include protocols to package cosmid clones or libraries as lambda particles, to genetically select cosmids (or plasmids) from complex libraries by homologous recombination and to modify isolated clones or groups of clones by the insertion or substitution of sequence elements.

Cosmid vectors, plasmids carrying the cos sequence recognized by the λ packaging system (1), represent a powerful tool in the cloning and analysis of large regions of genomes, in chromosome walking and in the cloning of genes larger than 20 kb in intact form. Though techniques have been developed to allow the construction and manipulation of cosmid clones or libraries, the inherent difficulties in handling or analysing the large libraries required to represent mammalian genomes, to analyse the inserts, and especially to introduce specific modifications independent of particular features of the restriction map can be quite formidable. In many cases the application of techniques developed in bacterial genetics can be used to advantage to simplify, or make possible, some of these manipulations.

2. MANIPULATION OF COSMID CLONES BY IN VIVO PACKAGING

Definition and usefulness of cosmid vectors rely on the use of an *in vitro* system to package DNA sequences containing *cos* sites into λ phage particles, creating infectious phage, which will then inject its DNA with high efficiency into a bacterial host. An analogous reaction can however be carried out *in vivo*, allowing the efficient and selective packaging of cosmids into λ phage particles (2–5). In this case the required packaging machinery is provided inside the bacterial cell either by a prophage, activated by heatinactivation of the temperature sensitive repressor protein, or by a helper phage newly introduced into the bacterial cell by infection. This pathway dramatically increases the flexibility for transferring the genetic information between different cells, and in converting the different physical forms (circles, linears with protruding end sequences) of the DNA (*Figure 1*).

In our experience both superinfection and induction of prophages will give high titre cosmid lysates. The superinfection approach has the obvious advantage, that the requirement for special *in vivo* packaging strains is avoided. It will, however, often yield

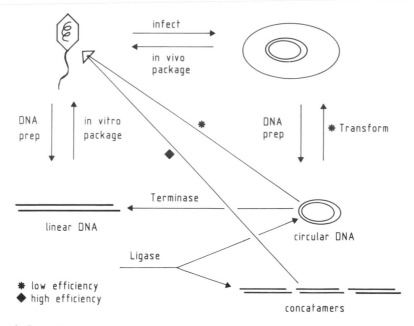

Figure 1. Conversion of cosmid forms.

more variable titres, and, due to the contamination of the resulting lysate with packaging phage, this approach can not be used to prepare clean linearized cosmid DNA. In addition, the higher packaging phage concentration in the lysate can necessitate the use of recipient strains carrying the same immunity, (e.g. BHB3169 or BHB3175), (5) to avoid lysis of the recipient bacteria. In general the induction of a resident prophage gives more reproducible titres of packaged cosmids. In addition, by the use of appropriate mutations in the phage attachment site of the helper prophage contamination of the DNA with helper (or defective particles) can be drastically reduced or, in the case of *cos* minus helper phages, be completely eliminated.

In vivo packaging of cosmid clones or clone libraries has application in the handling, manipulating and screening of cosmid libraries. A major advantage of the use of *in vivo* packaging during the amplification of cosmid libraries is that cosmids packaged into phage particles are easily handled. Just like λ libraries, cosmids packaged as phage particles can be stored at 4°C as phage suspensions, can be easily titrated before plating, and, due to their stability at room temperature, can be easily distributed.

Amplification followed by *in vivo* packaging, like any other library amplification, does however carry the risk of reducing the library complexity and can lead to repeated isolation of identical clones. As in other amplified libraries, this risk can be reduced by separate amplification and packaging of independent fractions of the cosmid library.

Another type of application taking advantage of the *in vivo* packaging reaction relies on the action of the λ encoded enzyme terminase, which either during packaging, or in a separate *in vitro* reaction, will linearize the originally circular cosmid molecule. DNA isolated from the phage particles formed during the *in vivo* packaging reaction is linearized selectively at the *cos* sequence, creating 12 base pair single-stranded ends.

Such linear DNA will for example be required for restriction analysis of cosmid clones by partial mapping techniques (6,7), for the analysis of clones by EM heteroduplex techniques (3) and for linearization and/or concatamerization of cosmids before introduction into eukaryotic cells (4). Similarly the protruding single-stranded ends offer a handle for the selective labelling of one or the other end by radiolabelled complementary oligonucleotides, for example. Alternatively the single strand ends could be used to isolate fragments extending from one or the other end by hybridization.

A third type of application is the use of *in vivo* packaging as a way to transfer cosmids selectively and with high efficiency between different host strains. Using cycles of packaging and re-infection, cosmids or cosmid libraries can be transferred readily (and selectively) between hosts with different genetic backgrounds, and can be exposed either transiently or permanently to other genetic elements (plasmids, transposons). Therefore *in vivo* packaging is an essential step in many approaches to manipulate cosmid clones genetically. This is especially true of the cosmid recombination protocol described here. In this application *in vivo* packaging provides two different essential functions: the transfer of cosmids between the different host strains; and an essential part of the genetic selection for cosmid clones which have recombined with the probe plasmid.

3. SELECTION OF COSMIDS BY HOMOLOGOUS RECOMBINATION

3.1 **Homologous recombination in *E. coli* can be used as alternative to colony hybridization**

Identification of specific cosmid clones can either, in rare cases, be carried out using selection systems specific for the sequence to be cloned, or, much more commonly, by the identification of clones carrying sequences homologous to a specific DNA probe. This identification will usually be carried out by high density colony hybridization techniques (8).

Since genetic selection systems, where applicable, involve considerably less work than screening protocols, it was a challenge to develop approaches allowing the selection of clones containing sequences homologous to arbitrary probe sequences, thereby extending the applicability of the selection to an area usually reserved for the more work intensive (and often less specific) screening techniques. In general terms, this approach relies on the fact, that, while most specific eukaryotic sequences will not be selectable in *E. coli*, pairs of vectors can be engineered to allow selection for the products of homologous recombination mediated by a sequence homology between the clones. Such selections are based on the fact, that processes like DNA replication, transcription, plasmid mobilization or packaging of DNA into phage particles will only take place in *cis* to the required recognition elements (replication origins, promoter, mobilization or packaging signals). To rule out recombination between vector sequences, pairs of vectors without sequence homology, (or, in the case of phage-phage recombination, with no vector homology within the interval defined by the markers used in the selection) have to be used. Implementations of this basic concept have been developed for the screening of phage clones by phage-phage (9) and phage-plasmid recombination (10) and the screening of cosmid (or plasmid libraries) by cosmid-plasmid recombination (4,11). In the following we will concentrate on this last approach, designed to allow the selection of specific clones from libraries representing the complexity of the mammalian genome.

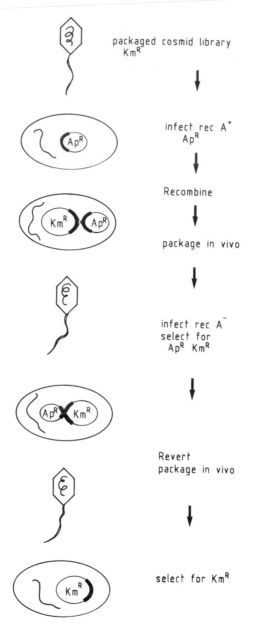

packaged cosmid library
Km^R

infect rec A$^+$
Ap^R

Recombine

package in vivo

infect rec A$^-$
select for
Ap^R Km^R

Revert
package in vivo

select for Km^R

Figure 2. Principle of cosmid recombination.

3.2 **Principle of cosmid-plasmid recombination**

The basic requirements in such a cosmid-plasmid recombination experiment are first of all two vectors without sequence homology, which are therefore unable to recombine by homologous recombination. Secondly, it is necessary to introduce the cosmid library, originally constructed and amplified in a *recA⁻* host, into a recombination proficient host containing the selection plasmid(s). Finally, one needs a selection for recombinant cosmids after re-transfer into a *recA⁻* host, a step that is necessary to ensure the stability of the clones during further propagation.

The basic protocol used is outlined in *Figure 2*. Cosmid libraries constructed in a *recA⁻* host are packaged into λ particles to give a high titre lysate of transducing particles. Aliquots of the packaged library are then used to infect a *rec⁺* host, containing the probe sequence (or sequences) cloned into a plasmid without sequence homology to the cosmid vector. After a period of between 30 min and 2 h to allow recombination to occur, the cosmids are again packaged into phage particles. The packaged cosmids are used to infect a *recA⁻* host, selecting for the antibiotic resistances of both plasmid and cosmid. Since the plasmid does not carry a *cos* sequence, it will only be transferred to the recipient cell, if it has recombined with the sequences in the cosmid clone. To regenerate the original cosmid, the two clones can be separated again by a second recombination event and, after transfer to a new host, revertants can be identified on indicator plates. As outlined later, exact restoration will however not always be possible (or intended).

3.3 Selection of recombinants

The easy and selective transfer of cosmid clones made possible by *in vivo* packaging can be used as component of the selection for recombinants, since only sequences *cis* to the *cos* sequence will be packaged into the phage particle. A recombinant, formed by one recombination step (or an odd number of recombination events) contains the selection plasmid integrated into the cosmid, and will therefore, after packaging, be able to transmit the antibiotic resistances of both cosmid and plasmid to recipient cells. Such cells, and therefore clones of the recombinant molecules, can be easily selected by plating cells infected with a mixture of packaged cosmids containing a few recombinants on plates and selecting for both antibiotic resistance markers.

This selection system combines a highly *cis* selective step provided by the selective packaging of sequences containing a *cos* sequence with the very strong, but in itself not *cis* selective selection for antibiotic resistance genes. This combines to give a very low background. (As outlined later, a slight background of unknown origin can however occasionally be observed).

Alternative selection approaches can be considered, and might become useful to complement or substitute for the selection using packaging. Such alternatives might be required under special circumstances, for example if one needs to select recombinants too large to be packaged in λ particles, or for the selection of high frequency recombination events. Such selections could, for example, take advantage of conditional replication of one of the two replication origins (e.g. using cosmid derivatives with a temperature sensitive R6K origin); or of specific mobilization of either plasmid or cosmid sequences.

3.4 Vectors

Since, partly for historic reasons, many plasmid (or cosmid) vectors have been constructed using a small number of very similar replication origins (ColE1, PMB1 and pA15) (12), special vectors using other origins have to be used. Only recently, and partly motivated by their potential use in cosmid recombination systems, have such vectors become available. For this purpose we have constructed and used a family of cosmids (pcos2EMBL, pcos3EMBL, pcos5EMBL, pcos6EMBL) and plasmid (ps1EMBL) vectors, using the β and γ origins of the naturally occurring multicopy plasmid R6K (13) as origin of replication and a kanamycin resistance gene from transposon Tn903 as selection marker (4, Ehrich *et al.*, in preparation; Craig, unpublished results).

All the cosmid vectors mentioned above have no sequence homology to pUC8 (14) or similar plasmids. Recombination between clones in cosmid libraries constructed in these vectors and clones of sequences in pUC or similar plasmids will therefore depend on sequence homology within the inserted sequences. In addition, libraries constructed in pcos3, pcos4, pcos5 and pcos6 can also be screened with sequences cloned into pBR322 (15) and similar plasmids, which carry the same tetracycline resistance gene. This tetracycline resistance gene is, however, also present in pcos2EMBL and so libraries constructed in this cosmid cannot be screened with pBR322 recombinant plasmids. Conversely the selection plasmid ps1EMBL (5) has no sequence homology to many commonly used pMB1 derived cosmid vectors [e.g. pcos4EMBL (Poustka, Brady, Schuetz and Lehrach, unpublished)], and can therefore be used in recombination experiments with cosmid libraries constructed in these vectors. PS1EMBL is a 4.2 kb construct, carrying a Kanamycin resistance gene, the R6K origin sequences and the *lacZ* α complementation sequence plus a polylinker derived from M13mp9 (16).

More recently additional plasmid or cosmid vectors with non-ColE1 family origin sequences have become available. These could also be used in combination with available vectors in recombination experiments. Examples are selection plasmids based on the R1 origin (11) plasmids and cosmids based on pSC101 (17) and cosmid vectors using the λ replication origin (18).

3.5 Strains

The key strains in the selection of specific clones by homologous recombination are the *recA*⁻ and *rec*⁺ *in vivo* packaging strains used in the amplification and recombination steps. The strains originally constructed and used by us (5), and which later were also used in a similar system (11), are: BHB3175, derived from HL202, a *supO* derivative of DH1 [*endA1*, *hsdR17*(rk⁻, *mk*⁺),*supE44*, *thi-1*,*recA1*, *gyrA96*, *relA1*] (19) by lysogenization with λ 3169 (λ *imm434, cIts, b2, red3, Sam7*); and BHB3169 which was analogously derived from W3110*rk*⁻*mK*⁺ (10). λ 3169, the phage used in lysogenization, carries a temperature sensitive (*imm 434*) CI repressor gene, allowing induction by temperature shift. Additional genetic features of the prophage responsible for the *in vivo* packaging reaction are the *Sam7* mutation, which blocks bacterial lysis, thereby increasing the packaging yields, the *b2* deletion used to reduce the frequency of excision of the prophage, and a mutation in the *red* gene, to block *red* mediated recombination.

One complication in the use of BHB3175 has been the extremely low plating efficiency of primary libraries constructed from mammalian DNA, which we expect to be due to the induction of the prophage by *recA* mediated repressor cleavage (20), triggered by some feature of the mammalian DNA. In contrast, the plating efficiencies of packaged cosmid clones already amplified in *E. coli* is identical to that found with DH1. In agreement with this model, an analogous packaging strain carrying an *ind⁻ cI857* prophage (Craig, unpublished results) has been found to plate primary libraries as efficiently as libraries previously amplified in *E. coli*. This strain has however been found to have lower packaging efficiency. Other strains have also been described (4,21 and Chapter 2).

3.6 Genetic selection of clones

As described before, the protocols described here can be used to select unique cosmid clones (or plasmids) from complex libraries, using the genetic selection as an alternative to the screening of libraries by colony hybridization protocols. This approach has been tested extensively, and has been used successfully to isolate a number of both mouse and human cosmid clones, using sequences cloned into pUC8 or pUC9 as selection (e.g. 5,6,22).

To demonstrate the generality of the genetic approach, amplified libraries were screened both by the genetic protocol, and by hybridization, with essentially all clones being recovered by both procedures. As mentioned before, a complication inherent in the genetic protocol is the necessity for library amplification, which can lead to reduction in library complexity and the repeated recovery of identical clones. This complication is avoided in the hybridization screen of primary libraries. This difficulty can however be reduced considerably by the amplification (and *in vivo* packaging) of independent fractions of the primary library.

A number of other potential difficulties have to be considered. One of these is the necessary exposure of the cosmid clones to the recombination system of the host, which could lead to rearrangements of the cosmid sequences. In our experience such rearrangements are quite rare, possibly due to the short time of exposure to *rec⁺* conditions, as well as the selection for at least close to full length clones, inherent in the selection system. Stability of cosmids during the recombination and reversion steps have for example been tested by multiple cycles of recombination and reversion and no evidence of rearrangements was observed (5).

A theoretical limitation inherent in the mechanism of selection is the size limit imposed on the recombinant by the λ packaging system (23). Using fairly small (2.9−5 kb) selection plasmids, we have not observed serious difficulties with this limitation. The average size of cosmid clones in our libraries is approximately 45 kb, usually leaving sufficient room for the size increase predicted for the recombination product. In addition, the size limitation imposed by a single packaging step might be expected to be less stringent than that imposed by the repeated packaging necessary for plaque formation (24).

A difficulty in the use of the genetic recombination protocol can also arise, if the sequences carried by the selection plasmid and the cosmid clone differ e.g. by base pair differences in the case of polymorphisms or gene families, or the presence of intron sequences in the cosmid DNA, absent in cDNA sequences used for selection. Since the crossovers leading to integration and separation of the two clones will in general take place at different positions within the region of homology, and additional unpredictable sequence changes can occur during repair of transiently arising mismatches, the sequence recovered in the reverted cosmid (or selection plasmid) can differ from the original sequence. Since potential sequence changes are restricted to the region of sequence homology, this problem can be solved quite easily by the re-isolation of the same cosmid, using a different sequence homology. This problem will not arise in the case of chromosome walking, in which each sequence to be used in the next step is already available in unmodified form on the previous clone. In addition to homologous recombination, other recombination mechanisms are active in the cell, and will generate occasional background clones, identifiable due to the powerful selection system. These low frequency background events are obviously especially noticeable (and misleading), if no clones with homologous sequences are contained in the library. Often such background clones formed by non-homologous recombination mechanisms can be identified at the reversion step, since usually a very low frequency of revertants will be observed in this case. As a general precaution, characterization of revertants should include a check for remaining selection plasmid vector sequences.

The major advantage of the genetic approach is speed and efficiency of this procedure. A fairly large number of experiments can be carried out in parallel, and essentially no re-screening is required, making this approach especially useful in applications requiring the repeated isolation of many cosmids (e.g. in chromosome walking experiments). A second advantage of the genetic approach is the fact, that homologous recombination is quite sensitive to sequence mismatches (25,26). This feature can be especially useful, for example in attempts to isolate cosmids containing members of gene families, or in chromosome walking experiments. Such chromosome walking experiments are simplified in some of our newer vectors (Ehrich *et al.*, in preparation), which contain *Not*I sites flanking the insertion site, allowing the rapid and selective cloning of insert end fragments in derivatives of pUC18 or pEMBL18 containing *Not*I sites in the polylinker.

It is not only possible to select specific cosmid clones from complex libraries, but it should also be feasible to use specific cosmids to isolate clones from complex plasmid libraries. A potential use of this approach would be to isolate cDNA clones containing sequences encoded in the cosmid clones.

3.7 Modification of clones

A second, powerful application of homologous recombination aims to take advantage of the sequence changes taking place during recombination and/or reversion to introduce specific or even random changes into the cosmid structure. These changes can be targeted to any position within the insert or vector, irrespective of the availability of unique restriction sites, and can be combined with the isolation of the clones by homologous recombination.

Two basic possibilities can be distinguished: constructs can be generated in one step, for example, using recombination targeted by a short region of homology to introduce sequence elements carried on the selection plasmid into a specific position of the cosmid (*Figure 3*). Examples are the positioning of enhancer or promoter sequences upstream of a gene; or the positioning of selectable or indicator genes (neomycin resistance,

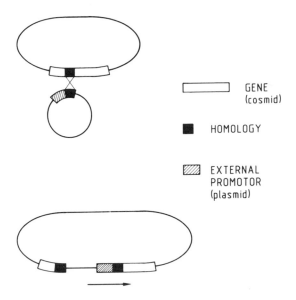

Figure 3. Integration of sequences by homologous recombination.

chloramphenicol transferase, β-galactosidase) as fusions under the control of a cosmid carried promoter; or the construction of random fusions between homologous genes carried on cosmid and plasmid. If necessary, transfer into hosts not permissive to replication of one of the components can be used to select against independently replicating plasmids arising by secondary recombination events. Similarly selection plasmids with sequence homology to the cosmid vector can be used to introduce specific sequences (e.g. markers selectable in eukaryotic cells, or elements allowing transposon mediated deletions) into either all clones of a library, or into isolated cosmid clones.

Alternatively a two step process leading to a sequence exchange between cosmid and plasmid can be used. Using the appropriate selection or transfer systems, either the cosmid, or the plasmid, can be isolated separately. Such a series of steps can, for example, serve to introduce mutations generated in a short region of a gene cloned in a single strand packagable plasmid back into the cosmid. Conversely one could transfer a sequence carried by the cosmid clone into a plasmid for further analysis. As illustrated in *Figure 4*, such a process can be especially well controlled in a two step protocol, in which initially a biological marker sequence (e.g. a *lac* operator) is introduced by double recombination into the position of the cosmid to be mutagenized. Exchange of this sequence for sequences carrying the desired mutations can then be easily scored, using the *lac* operator test outlined in the reversion protocol.

Modification of cosmid clones by homologous recombination is a highly selective, and extremely efficient process. In most cases, in which intact cosmids have to be manipulated, appropriate restriction sites will either not be available, or too difficult to identify. Usually therefore genetic manipulation will be the only realistic possibility, or will involve considerably less work.

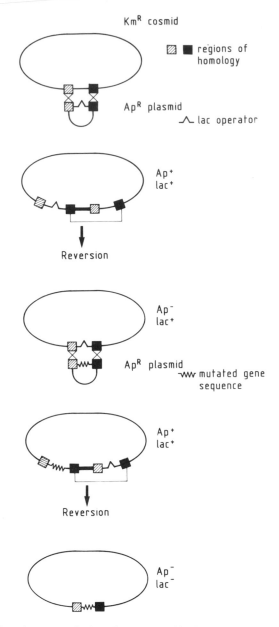

Figure 4. Substitution of sequences by homologous recombination.

4. PROTOCOLS

4.1 Construction of cosmid libraries

Construction of cosmid libraries can be carried out by any of the standard protocols (see Chapter 2). We use a protocol developed by ourselves (5) and also in similar form by Bates and Swift (27). This is based on the availability of two *cos* sites separated

Table 1. Media and protocols for plating cosmid libraries.

A. *Materials*

1. *L Broth*
   10 g Bacto Tryptone (Difco), 5 g Yeast Extract (Difco), 10 g NaCl water to 1 litre, adjust to pH 7.2 and autoclave.

2. *L agar*
   L Broth containing 15 g Agar/litre.

3. *Ampicillin stock*
   30 mg/ml ampicillin in 50% ethanol stored at $-20°C$.

4. *Kanamycin stock*
   30 mg/ml kanamycin in water stored at $-20°C$.

5. *L agar with antibiotic*
   Melt L agar and allow it to cool to below 50°C. Add 1 ml of stock antibiotic solution per litre of L-agar.

6. *Xgal (5-bromo-4-chloro-3-indolyl-beta-D-galactoside)*
   Dissolve 20 mg/ml Xgal in N-N-dimethyl formamide. Use 40 μl per plate.

7. *λ Diluent*
   10 mM Tris-HCl pH 7.6, 10 mM MgSO$_4$, 1 mM EDTA.

8. *10 × HMFM*
   Dissolve 6.3 g K$_2$HPO$_4$, 0.45 g sodium citrate, 0.09 g MgSO$_4$.7H$_2$O, 0.9 g (NH$_4$)$_2$SO$_4$, 11.8 g KH$_2$PO$_4$, 44 g of glycerol in a final volume of 100 ml of water.

B. *Plating of cosmid libraries*
   Preparation of DH1 plating cells

1. Pick a single colony into L Broth medium.

2. Culture at 37°C overnight shaking vigorously.

3. Pellet the cells by centrifugation for 10 min at 4000 r.p.m. in a Sorvall HB4 or GSA rotor.

4. Resuspend the pellet in 0.5 × the culture volume of 10 mM MgSO$_4$. Plating cells prepared in this way are usable for 2−4 weeks.

   Preparation of BHB3175 plating cells

1. Pick a few independent colonies, by toothpicking onto duplicate L-agar plates. Culture one plate at 30°C and the other at 42°C to verify temperature sensitivity.

2. Streak out a checked (temperature sensitive) colony on an L-agar plate and grow overnight at 30°C.

3. Scape off the cells from one half of the plate into 500 ml L broth and culture at 30°C until the OD$_{600}$ is 0.3[a].

4. Pellet the cells by centrifugation for 10 min at 4000 r.p.m. in a Sorvall HB4 or GSA rotor.

5. Resuspend the pellet in 25 ml of 10 mM MgSO$_4$.

   Plating

1. For a standard (10 cm diameter) plate take 0.1 ml of plating cells, up to 10^4 packaged cosmids, mix, and pre-incubate at the appropriate temperature (30°C for temperature sensitive lysogens, 37°C for other strains) for 15 min.

2. Dilute 10-fold with L broth, culture for one hour at the appropriate temperature, and concentrate the cells again by centrifugation as described above.

3. Plate onto selective media or onto nitrocellulose or nylon membrane filters on L Broth plates for one hour, before transferring to selection plates[b]. Scale up 10-fold for Nunc (22 × 22 cm) plates.

[a]Plating cells containing a prophage seem to be more stable on storage after preparation from exponentially growing cells.
[b]If ampicillin selection is being used, there is no need to allow the 1 h pre-expression period.

by a blunt end cloning site in our vectors. This protocol, a modification of the cosmid cloning procedure described by Ish-Horovitz and Burke (28), uses partial cleavage with *Sau*3A or *Mbo*I for random DNA fragmentation, and relies on dephosphorylation of the partially-digested DNA (rather than size separation) to avoid the recovery of clones containing religated insert sequences. Cosmid vector arms are generated by *Pvu*II cleavage, dephosphorylation of the cleaved *Pvu*II sites to further rule out formation of vector oligomers, and cleavage at the *Bam*HI site. Control of the ligatability of ends by phosphatase treatment together with the size selection inherent in the λ packaging system ensures, that only constructs of the correct structure will be generated. Using an analogous series of selections, both cosmid and λ replacement vector libraries can be generated in parallel. Cloning yields of approximately 10^5 cosmid clones and approximately 10^6 λ clones per ug of DNA are routinely achieved. Cosmid libraries are amplified by plating for single colonies at high density (up to 10^5 clones per 22 × 22 cm plate). After overnight growth the colonies are scraped off into LB+HMFM (*Table 1*), divided into aliquots, and stored at $-70°C$. Media and materials used, protocols for the preparation of plating cells, and the titration and plating of cosmid libraries are described in *Table 1*. Titration of packaging phage requires a *sup*F host (e.g. NM538, 29).

4.2 In vivo packaging

The protocol in *Table 2* describes the *in vivo* packaging of an amplified cosmid library by superinfection. Aliquots of the amplified library are transferred to liquid culture grown to early log phase (approximately 0.3 OD_{600}), and infected with λ3169 at a high multiplicity of infection to allow *in vivo* packaging to proceed. Good aeration is re-

Table 2. *In vivo* packaging using superinfection.

1.	Dilute an aliquot of the library in *E. coli* DH1 to 0.05 OD_{600} in L Broth containing antibiotics.
2.	Grow the cells with good aeration to 0.3 OD_{600} and superinfect with *red-S7* phage[a] using a m.o.i. of approximately 50.
3.	Incubate for 30 min at 42°C, then transfer to 37°C and shake for 3−4 h[b].
4.	Collect the cells by centrifugation in the Sorvall GSA rotor for 10 min at 5000 r.p.m. Resuspend in 1/20 × culture volume of λ diluent[c], and add $CHCl_3$ to 5−10%. Shake well at room temperature, remove the debris by centrifugation.
5.	Titrate the cosmids in the supernatant by plating on BHB3175 as described in *Table 1*. The expected titre of cosmids is $10^8−10^9$ c.f.u./ml, and the expected titre of the helper phage is 10^{11} p.f.u./ml.

[a]We usually use a phage recovered by heat induction from BHB3169.
[b]Titres increase at least up to 4 h, but drop on overnight incubation.
[c]See *Table 1*.

Table 3. Amplification and *in vivo* packaging by induction of a lysogen.

1.	Scrape off cells from BHB3175 plates into L Broth or (for storage at $-70°C$ into L Broth+Hogness freezing medium[a]). Inoculate the cells into 400 ml L Broth containing antibiotics in a 2 l Erlenmeyer flask to give an OD_{600} of 0.05.
2.	Culture at 30°C to an OD_{600} of 0.30.
3.	Transfer the flask to a 45°C water bath for 25 min. Check that the temperature of the culture reaches 45°C. Transfer to a shaking incubator and shake for 4 h at 37°C.[b]
4.	Collect the cells by centrifugation as described in *Table 1* and resuspend the pellet in 1/20 × culture volume of λ diluent.
5.	Lyse the cells and titrate the cosmids as described in *Table 2*. The expected titre of the cosmids is $10^8−10^9$/ml[c].

[a]Hogness freezing medium is 3 g NaCl, 12.6 g K_2HPO_4, 0.9 g sodium citrate, 0.09 g $MgSO_4$, 1.8 g $(NH_4)_2SO_4$, 3.6 g KH_2PO_4, 88 g (70 ml) glycerol per litre.
[b]Titres increase at least up to 4 h, but drop on overnight incubation.
[c]Titres can be quite variable, though much more so in packagings with superinfection. It is often preferable in this case to repeat a packaging reaction, rather than to attempt experiments with lysates of too low titre. In a *recA*⁻ host, the concentration of infectious packaging phage is quite low, while the contamination with DNA due to abortive packaging products can be quite high. The background of helper is higher with *rec*⁺ hosts.
Libraries can be stored at 4°C for extended periods (in λ diluent or L Broth+10 mM $MgSO_4$). For very long term storage it might be advisable to concentrate the cosmids further by CsCl step gradient centrifugation (use titration to detect cosmids) and store aliquots in CsCl. Dialyse against a small volume of λ diluent before use.

quired. Packaging yields increase for at least 3−5 h. After the packaging, the bacteria are concentrated by centrifugation, resuspended at a ten-fold higher concentration, and the cosmids are released by lysing the bacteria with chloroform. Titrations should be carried out on hosts carrying immunity to the helper phage used (*inm 434* in the case of λ3169) to avoid killing of recipient cells by helper phage. Alternatively helper phage titres can be determined, and titrations can be carried out at sufficiently low multiplicity of infection and cell numbers to reduce the interference by packaging phage.

Table 3 shows the protocol for an analogous *in vivo* packaging reaction on libraries contained in an *in vivo* packaging host (e.g. BHB3175). This step can be used to amplify a cosmid library a second time, following an amplification by superinfection of a primary library. Alternatively this protocol can be applied to amplify and package libraries constructed directly in appropriate *in vivo* packaging hosts.

A protocol analogous to the protocol described in *Table 3* can also be used in packaging reactions carried out to prepare larger amounts of linearized cosmid DNA for example for analysis by electron microscopy. In this case inoculation from a liquid culture prepared from a tested, temperature sensitive colony will be sufficient. After preparation of the lysate, a standard protocol for the preparation of λ DNA can be followed.

Small scale packaging reactions used to transfer cosmid clones between different host cells for example, can be carried out in an analogous manner, using either superinfection or the induction of a prophage.

4.3 Cosmid recombination

For the selection of unique clones from complex (mammalian) libraries, the protocol in *Table 4* is used. The packaged cosmids can either be derived from a library packaged by superinfection (*Table 2*) or by induction of a lysogen (*Table 3*).

If the selection plasmid carries an ampicillin resistance, we find it necessary to plate

Table 4. Recombination.

1.	Distribute bacteria from two single colonies of the BHB3169 cells containing the probe plasmid each over half of an ampicillin L-Plate. Incubate overnight at 30°C. Incubate a duplicate plate at 42°C overnight. Prewarm 100 ml of L Broth containing 30 μg/ml ampicillin at 30°C overnight.
2.	Inoculate the 200 ml of prewarmed L Broth containing 30 μg/ml ampicillin temperature sensitive BHB3169 cells carrying the probe plasmid − scraped from a plate prepared in step 1.
3.	Shake the culture at 30°C until the OD_{600} is 0.3.
4.	Add $MgSO_4$ to 5 mM and then add lysate containing approximately 10^9 cosmids. Leave the flask to stand at 30°C for 15 min. Transfer the flask to a shaking incubator at 30°C for 90 min before adding 15 μg/ml kanamycin.
5.	Induce at 42°C in a shaking waterbath for 25 min.
6.	Transfer to 37°C and shake vigorously for 3 h.
7.	Pellet the cells by centrifugation in the Sorvall GSA rotor at 6000 r.p.m. for 10 min.
8.	Carefully pour off the supernatant as completely as possible. Keep an aliquot for titration.
9.	Resuspend the cell pellet in 10 ml of λ Diluent (*Table 1*).
10.	Add 1 ml $CHCl_3$ and shake vigorously from time to time over a period of 30 min or longer at room temperature.
11.	Clarify by centrifugation for 10 min in a table top centrifuge. Pour off the supernatant.
12.	Titrate the lysate with DH1 plating cells (*Table 1*) on Kanamycin plates. The expected titre is $10^8 - 10^9$.[a]

[a]As controls plate the plating cells alone, as well as the product of a mock recombination using the selection plasmid vector (e.g. pUC8). As positive control a plasmid with cosmid vector homology can be used (expected recombination frequency $10^{-2} - 10^{-3}$).

Table 5. Selective plating of recombinant cosmids.

1.	One day before wishing to carry out the large scale selective plating set up two overnight cultures of BHB3175 cells at 30°C. This is to ensure at least one culture of temperature sensitive cells is available for the following day. Check the temperature sensitivity by plating some of the innoculum for culture at 30°C and 42°C.
2.	Take a volume of lysate of no more than 2 ml containing $10^8 - 10^9$ cosmids, and evaporate the $CHCl_3$ from within it by leaving it at 37°C for 10 min in an open vial. Allow to cool and add 2 ml of BHB3175 plating cells.
3.	Leave at 30°C for 15 min. Add 15 ml L Broth and shake at 30°C for 60 min.
4.	Centrifuge for 5 min in a HB4 rotor at 4000 r.p.m. Remove the supernatant very thoroughly and resuspend in 1.5 μl L Broth.
5.	Plate on a 24 × 24 cm L-agar plate containing 15 μg/ml kanamycin and 30 μg/ml ampicillin which has been covered by a Schleicher and Schuell nitrocellulose filter. Incubate for 24 – 36 h at 30°C.

[a]The expected frequency of recovering recombinants for a unique sequence in a cosmid library of the mammalian genome is 2×10^{-6} to 10^{-8}, varying with the type of sequence, its length, and the homology. Colonies growing in groups, at the edges or at folds of the filter are often background. After 24 – 36 h the good colonies are almost transparent, not thick, round and brownish.

Table 6. Repackaging of potential recombinants[a].

1.	Pick up to 24 colonies, resuspend each in 200 μl L Broth containing 15 μl/ml kanamycin, 30 μg/ml ampicillin.
2.	Grow with aeration at 30°C for 2 – 3 h, place at 42°C for 15 min. Replace at 37°C and shake for 2 h.
3.	Add a drop of $CHCl_3$, shake, and leave at room temperature for 15 min. Clarify by centrifugation and keep the supernatants.
4.	Take an L-agar plate covered with Schleicher and Schuell filter, and distribute 150 μl of DH1 plating cells (*Table 1*) on filter. Spot 5 μl of each supernatant on to the plated cells.
5.	Incubate for 2 h at 37°C.
6.	Transfer the filter to an L agar-plate containing ampicillin and kanamycin.
7.	Incubate overnight at 37°C.

[a]This step gets rid of false positives caused by cells that have survived the $CHCl_3$ treatment or that have been transformed with probe plasmid. It also works as a colony purification step and eliminates mixed colonies originating from a cell infected by more than one cosmid. Alternatively a scaled down version of *in vivo* packaging by superinfection (*Table 2*) can be carried out.

Table 7. Selection of reverted cosmids.

1.	Pick the small colonies that have grown after repackaging into 200 μl L Broth containing 15 μg/ml kanamycin, 5 mM $MgSO_4$.
2.	Grow for 2 h at 37°C. Add 20 μl red^+ phage 3171 of a titre of approximately 10^{11} p.f.u./ml.
3.	Shake for 2 h at 37°C and add a drop of $CHCl_3$.
4.	Clarify by centrifugation and take the supernatants.
5.	Add 5 μl of the supernatant to 150 μl DH1 plating cells (*Table 1*). Plate on L-agar plates containing 30 μg/ml kanamycin onto which 40 μl of 2% Xgal in dimethyl formamide (*Table 1*) has been distributed.
6.	Incubate overnight at 37°C. White colonies containing reverted cosmid clones should appear at a frequency of 0.1 to 90% among a background of blue colonies containing recombinant cosmids.

the cells infected with the recombinant cosmids on nitrocellulose filters covering the ampicillin selection plates (*Table 5*). Plating on filters reduces the degradation of the ampicillin in the plates by ampicillinase carried over in the lysate. Analogous precautions might be required for some other antibiotic selection markers.

Small scale recombination experiments, used to integrate or substitute sequences in single cosmids (see section 4) for example, can be carried out in an analogous manner, using reduced volumes (see *Tables 6* or *7*). *In vivo* packaging can be carried out by prophage induction or superinfection. We routinely test and purify recombinants by small scale repackaging reactions (*Table 6*), to overcome a variable and still unexplained background of double resistant colonies containing unrecombined cosmid and plasmid sequences.

To remove the selection plasmid again, use the protocol described in *Table 7*. Reversion can also be carried out in a rec^+ *in vivo* packaging strain, analogous to the protocol described in *Table 6*. Revertants are identified using the effect of the *lac* operator sequence carried by the pUC selection plasmid, which in a lac^+ host will bind the *lac* repressor and therefore induce the chromosomal *lac* gene. Cells still containing the pUC plasmid component are therefore blue, while the products of the reversion event have lost the selection plasmid, and can therefore be recognized as white colonies.

5. ACKNOWLEDGEMENTS

We thank Anna-Maria Frischauf for contributing to the protocols used.

6. REFERENCES

1. Hohn,B. and Collins,J. (1980) *Gene*, **11**, 291.
2. Fukamaki,Y., Shimada,K. and Takagi,Y. (1976) *Proc. Natl. Acad. Sci. USA*, **73**, 3238.
3. Vollenweider,H.J., Fiandt,M., Rosenvold,E.C. and Szybalski,W. (1980) *Gene*, **9**, 171.
4. Lindenmaier,W., Hauser,H., Greiser de Wilke,I. and Schuetz,G. (1982) *Nucleic Acids Res.*, **10**, 1243.
5. Poustka,A., Rackwitz,H.-R., Frischauf,A.-M., Hohn,B. and Lehrach,H. (1984) *Proc. Natl. Acad. Sci. USA*, **81**, 4129.
6. Rackwitz,H.R., Zehetner,G., Murialdo,H., Delius,H., Poustka,A., Frischauf,A.-M. and Lehrach,H. (1985) *Gene*, **40**, 259.
7. Zehetner,G., Frischauf,A.-M. and Lehrach,H. (1987) In *Nucleic Acid and Protein Sequence Analysis — A Practical Approach*, Bishop,M.J. and Rawlings,C.J. (eds), IRL Press, Oxford, UK, p. 147.
8. Hanahan,D. and Meselson,M. (1980) *Gene*, **10**, 63.
9. Carroll,D. and Aijoka,R.S. (1980) *Gene*, **10**, 273.
10. Seed,B. (1983) *Nucleic Acids Res.*, **11**, 2427.
11. Lindenmaier,W., Dittmar,K.E.J., Hauser,H., Necker,A. and Sebald,W. (1985) *Gene*, **39**, 33.
12. Pouwels,P.H., Enger-Valk,B.E. and Brammar,W.J. (1986) *Cloning Vectors, A Laboratory Manual*, Elsevier, Amsterdam.
13. Kolter,R. and Helinski,D.R. (1978) *Plasmid*, **1**, 571.
14 Messing,J. and Vieira,J. (1982) *Gene*, **19**, 259.
15. Bolivar,F., Rodriguez,R.L., Greene,P.J., Betlach,M C., Heynecker,H.L. and Boyer,H.W. (1977) *Gene*, **2**, 95.
16. Yanisch-Perron,C., Vieira,J. and Messing,J. (1985) *Gene*, **33**, 103.
17. Brady,G., Jantzen,H.M., Bernard,H.U., Brown,R. and Hashimoto-Goto,H. (1984) *Gene*, **27**, 223.
18. Little,P.F.R. and Cross,S.H. (1985) *Proc Natl. Acad. Sci. USA*, **82**, 3159.
19. Hanahan,D. (1983) *J. Mol. Biol.*, **166**, 577.
20. Ossanna,N., Peterson,K R. and Mount,D.W. (1986) *Trends Genet.*, **2**, 55.
21. Cami,B. and Kourilsky,P. (1978) *Nucleic Acids Res.*, **5**, 2381.
22. Hofker,M.H., vanOmmen,G.J.B., Bakker,E., Burmeister,M. and Pearson,P.L. (1986) *Hum. Genet.*, **74**, 270.
23. Feiss,M., Fisher,R.A., Crayton,M.A. and Egner,C. (1977) *Virology*, **77**, 281.
24. Struck,D.K., Durica,D.S. and Young,R. (1986) *Gene*, **47**, 221.
25. Shen,P. and Huang,H.V. (1986) *Genetics*, **112**, 441.
26. Watt,V.M., Ingles,C.J., Urdea,M.S. and Rutter,W.J. (1985) *Proc. Natl. Acad. Sci. USA*, **82**, 4768.
27. Bates,P.F. and Swift,R.A. (1983) *Gene*, **26**, 137.
28. Ish-Horovitz,D. and Burke,J.F. (1981) *Nucleic Acids Res.*, **9**, 2989.
29. Frischauf,A.-M., Lehrach,H., Poustka,A. and Murray,N. (1983) *J. Mol. Biol.*, **170**, 827.

CHAPTER 4

The purification of eukaryotic polypeptides expressed in *Escherichia coli*

FIONA A.O.MARSTON

1. INTRODUCTION

With the advent of techniques for *in vitro* manipulation of DNA in the 1970's, two potential developments of this technology were envisaged. One was the production of proteins of limited natural availability and the second, the engineering of novel proteins using *in vitro* mutagenesis techniques. The expression of cloned genes is now possible in a variety of prokaryotic and eukaryotic host organisms. With *E. coli* in particular, both efficient and controlled production of recombinant polypeptides can be achieved.

Genes can be constructed so that the foreign proteins specified by them may either be located in the *E. coli* cytoplasm or, by incorporating a leader sequence before the coding sequence, the proteins may be secreted through the cell membrane. In general recombinant polypeptides accumulate to higher levels when expressed intracellularly (up to 25% of total cell protein) than when they are secreted (<1% of total cell protein). However, many of the polypeptide products located in the cytoplasm are insoluble and aggregated (1) and specific solubilization techniques are required.

This chapter concentrates primarily on the techniques which have been developed for recovering active soluble products from the insoluble proteins in the *E. coli* cytoplasm. Because of the empirical nature of the solubilization and refolding protocols developed for each protein, selected examples are described. The methods used for the purification of eukaryotic polypeptides expressed as soluble products in the cytoplasm, or by secretion, will also be considered. The chapter cannot describe all the methods published, but a more extensive review of the literature has been published (1).

1.1 Expression vectors

High level accumulation of a 'foreign product' in the host organism, is often dependent on initiation of transcription by a strong promoter (2) and the presence of multiple copies of the heterologous gene in each cell (3). It is of central importance, however, to have controlled expression from plasmids, which are retained by the organisms through successive generations (4). This is because the synthesis of recombinant products is a metabolic burden to the cells (5); cells which lose their plasmids soon outgrow plasmid-containing cells during a fermentation. Tight control of expression allows cells to be grown first to high biomass in the absence of heterologous gene expression, followed

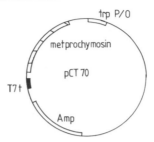

Figure 1. pCT70, an *E. coli* plasmid capable of expressing met-prochymosin under the control of the tryptophan promoter. Reproduced with permission from (4).

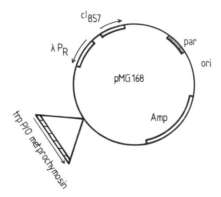

Figure 2. pMG168, an *E. coli* dual-origin vector capable of expressing met-prochymosin at high levels at temperatures above 37°C. Reproduced with permission from (4).

by growth for a limited number of generations with heterologous gene expression switched on.

The earliest expression plasmids used the strong metabolic promoters *trp* or *lac* to direct transcription (*Figure 1*), with the recombinant gene inserted downstream of the promoter/operator region. However, using the systems of metabolic regulation known to control these operons, it was found that expression from the plasmids was constitutive rather than controlled (6) and as a result, plasmids were lost from the cells during fermentation. Better control is achieved by using temperature regulated expression plasmids (4) incorporating promoters such as P_R and P_L, obtained from the bacteriophage λ. These promoters can be controlled by the temperature sensitive λ repressor gene product cI_{857} which itself is denatured at temperatures greater than 37°C. A plasmid incorporating the λ promoter P_R is illustrated in *Figure 2*. Another feature of this vector is that it has two origins of replication which improve the efficiency of product accumulation by allowing control of plasmid copy number (7). One is a low copy number origin, and the other a high copy number origin controlled by the λP_R promoter. At 34°C or below, plasmids replicate from the low copy number origin. Replication from the other origin is controlled by the cI_{857} repressor. During this phase, growth to high biomass can be achieved before the fermentation temperature is increased to 38−42°C at which point the cI_{857} repressor is denatured, plasmid copy number is amplified and heterologous gene expression is switched on (8). Using such expression vectors high level expression of recombinant proteins is achieved, commonly 20−25% of total cell protein (4). Successful fermentations have been performed at scales from laboratory shake flasks up to 100−200 litres fermentation volume. In the future, there is scope for development, particularly in aspects of the microbial physiology and process engineering of the temperature inducible systems (4).

1.2 Modes of expression

There are two general strategies for the synthesis of proteins which are located intracellularly. The gene can be cloned in frame with synthetic or bacterial coding sequences and expressed as a fusion protein; alternatively the foreign gene is expressed directly. The need to express eukaryotic polypeptides as fusion proteins resulted from the discovery that levels of expression in *E. coli* were limited because the polypeptides were recognised as foreign and degraded (9). This was particularly apparent with small polypeptides. By linking the eukaryotic gene with a bacterial gene, fused products were synthesized, which accumulated to significantly greater levels (10,11). However, if the eukaryotic polypeptide alone is required then a strategy is needed for correct cleavage of the fusion protein. In contrast, direct expression of eukaryotic genes can yield the correct protein product. However, the primary products of translation do possess an N-terminal methionine residue. *E. coli* possesses enzymes which catalyse the efficient removal of methionine from natural proteins, when required; but these enzymes do not work with the same efficiency on recombinant polypeptides (1). Therefore, directly expressed proteins may possess an unnatural N-terminal methionine residue.

Proteins possessing a signal sequence may be secreted through the *E. coli* cytoplasmic membrane into the periplasmic space or to the outer cell membrane and into the extracellular medium. Expressing foreign proteins via secretion offers several advantages over intracellular expression. If the signal sequence is correctly processed, the amino terminal of the recombinant protein will be identical to the authentic product. Secretion into the periplasm can also prevent degradation of the polypeptide. The greatest advantage of this type of expression system is that disulphide bond formation occurs with secretion and correctly folded, active products are produced.

2. CELL LYSIS TECHNIQUES

The *E. coli* cell wall is complex in structure, consisting of three distinct layers; a lipopolysaccharide (LPS) outer layer, lined by a membrane bilayer (the outer cell membrane), and a peptidoglycan layer, which is tightly associated with the outer cell membrane. The *E. coli* cytoplasmic membrane is separated from the peptidoglycan layer by the periplasmic space.

Both the *E. coli* cell wall and the cytoplasmic membrane must be disrupted to release insoluble or soluble recombinant proteins located in the cytoplasm. More care is required in releasing proteins secreted into the periplasm; techniques are used which remove part or all of the cell wall, but do not rupture the cytoplasmic membrane.

2.1 Total cell lysis

E. coli may be lysed using enzymes such as lysozyme in conjunction with detergents (12). Alternatively mechanical techniques, reliant on liquid shear to break the cells,

Table 1. Lysis of 10 g wet weight of *E. coli* using lysozyme and deoxycholate (adapted from ref. 13).

1.	Suspend 10 g (wet weight) of *E. coli* in 30 ml of lysis buffer[a] using a blender or overhead homogenizer, and maintaining the temperature below 10°C.
2.	Add 80 μl of 50 mM PMSF[b], followed by 0.8 ml of lysozyme[c].
3.	Incubate the suspension on ice for 20 min, stirring occasionally.
4.	Add 40 mg deoxycholic acid, with stirring.
5.	Transfer the suspension to a water bath heated at 37°C and stir with a glass rod.
6.	Once the suspension becomes viscous, and difficult to stir, add 200 μl of deoxyribonuclease[d], with stirring.
7.	Incubate the suspension at room temperature for 30 min or until the suspension is no longer viscous.

[a]Lysis buffer is 50 mM Tris-HCl pH 8.0 1 mM EDTA, 100 mM NaCl.
[b]Stock solution of PMSF (phenylmethylsulphonylfluoride) is at 50 mM in 100% methanol. Prepared fresh.
[c]Stock solution of lysozyme is 10 mg/ml in lysis buffer. Stored at −20°C.
[d]Stock solution of deoxyribonuclease is 1 mg/ml in lysis buffer. Prepared fresh.

Table 2. Preparation of *E. coli* spheroplasts.

1.	Suspend 1 g wet weight of cells in 25 ml of 200 mM Tris-HCl pH 8.0.
2.	Dilute the suspension with an equal volume of 200 mM Tris-HCl pH 8.0, 1 M sucrose.
3.	Add 0.5% volume (v/v) of 100 mM EDTA pH 7.6.
4.	Add lysozyme to a final concentration of 60 μg/ml.
5.	Dilute the suspension two-fold in water and incubate at 23°C.
6.	Take a small portion of the suspension, dilute it 50-fold in water and monitor the absorbance at 450 nm. Spheroplast formation is complete when the optical density falls 80−85% within 10 sec; this usually occurs in less than 30 min.
7.	Add Mg^{2+} to a final concentration of 20 mM to stabilize the spheroplasts.

can be employed; for example, using a French press or a Manton-Gaulin homogenizer. A third alternative is the use of sonication, but this technique can only be used with limited volumes.

A method for effecting cell lysis with lysozyme and deoxycholic acid (DOC) is given in *Table 1*. *E. coli* producing recombinant proteins in an insoluble form can become resistant to lysis. This was observed for *E. coli* cells producing tissue-type plasminogen activator (13). It was necessary to increase the ratio of lysis buffer to cells from 3:1 to 9:1 to obtain efficient lysis.

The use of sonication to lyse *E. coli* producing recombinant proteins has been described in a number of reports. Using a microprobe, a typical procedure (14) is as follows.
(i)   Suspend 1 g wet weight of cells in 6 ml of lysis buffer (see footnote to *Table 1*.)
(ii)   Add lysozyme to a final concentration of 1 mg/ml.
(iii)   Incubate the suspension at 25°C for 15 min.
(iv)   Place the suspension on ice and cool to <4°C.
(v)   Sonicate (for example with a Model W225R sonicator, Heat System, Ultrasonics Inc.) with two 15 sec bursts.
        Alternatively steps (i) and (iii) above may be omitted, and sonication increased to three 20 sec bursts.

In order to estimate the efficiency of cell lysis, intact cells are counted under the light microscope before and after the lysis procedure. Alternatively the release of soluble protein is measured.

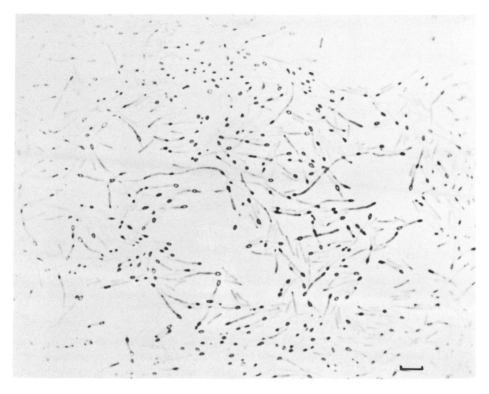

Figure 3. Phase contrast micrograph of *E. coli* HB101 cells producing prochymosin.

2.2 Preparation of spheroplasts

In order to release the contents of the periplasm, *E. coli* cells are treated with lysozyme, then subjected to a mild osmotic shock (15; *Table 2*). In the method described, a high concentration of Tris HCl is used to destabilize the outer cell membrane and allow the lysozyme to penetrate the peptidoglycan layer. EDTA facilitates this procedure, while Mg^{2+} prevents it.

3. INSOLUBLE PROTEINS

Insoluble recombinant proteins generally accumulate in *E. coli* in the discrete form of inclusion bodies. It is possible to visualize these inclusion bodies using phase-contrast light microscopy (*Figure 3*). They are seen as large, refractile aggregates, often located at the poles of the cells. Accumulation of product during a fermentation can be monitored by the appearance of inclusion bodies as well as by SDS-polyacrylamide gel electrophoresis (SDS-PAGE).

3.1 Isolation of inclusion bodies

3.1.1 *Centrifugation procedures*

Using the cell lysis procedures described for *E. coli* inclusion bodies are released, usually with no accompanying solubilization of expressed protein. Because the recombinant

Figure 4. Electron micrograph of prochymosin inclusion bodies isolated from *E. coli*. Contaminating material can be seen associated with the inclusion bodies. (Provided by and reproduced with the permission of R.Sugrue, R.Newsam and the University of Kent Electron Microscopy Unit, Canterbury, UK).

protein is in a discrete form, isolation from the cell lysate can be used as a purification step. Inclusion bodies are dense, and isolation is therefore effected by centrifugation. The mean size and density of the inclusion bodies can vary with the protein expressed (16). This is supported by data from the published literature where inclusion body isolation is reported using centrifugation speeds varying between 500 *g* and 12 000 *g* (1). It is generally possible to define empirically a centrifugation speed and time which pellets the inclusion bodies, leaving a proportion of other particulate matter in suspension with the soluble proteins. A typical procedure to define the optimum separation is as follows.

(i)   Centrifuge the cell lysate at speeds varying between 500 *g* and 12 000 *g* for 10 min.
(ii)   Decant the supernatants.
(iii)   Dilute the supernatants and pellets in SDS-PAGE sample buffer a to protein concentrations of 5 mg/ml.
(iv)   Analyse the supernatants and pellets by SDS-PAGE (17), using loadings of 50−150 μg protein.

The relative purity and yield of the expressed protein in the pellets may define the optimum separation parameters or can be used to design an experiment in which steps (i)−(iv) are repeated with different centrifugation parameters.

3.1.2 *Procedures for washing inclusion bodies*

Contaminating material does co-purify with the inclusion bodies as illustrated in *Figure 4*. Further purification can be achieved by washing the inclusion bodies with solutions which solubilize the contaminants but not the recombinant protein. Two major contaminants of prochymosin inclusion bodies were tentatively identified as *E. coli* outer membrane proteins (18) based on the fact that they were substantially solubilized by

Table 3. Triton X-100 and EDTA washing procedure.

1.	Lyse the cells with lysozyme and deoxycholate (*Table 1*).
2.	Centrifuge the cell lysate at 12 000 g for 5 min at 4°C.
3.	Resuspend the pellet in nine volumes (v/v) of lysis buffer[a] containing 0.5% (v/v) Triton X-100 and 10 mM EDTA.
4.	Incubate the suspension for 5 min at room temperature.
5.	Centrifuge the suspension at 12 000 g for 5 min at 4°C.
6.	Analyse the pellet and supernatant using SDS-PAGE (17).

[a]See footnote a of *Table 1* for lysis buffer composition.

Table 4. Urea washing procedure.

1.	Suspend 1 g wet weight of frozen cell pellet in 5 ml of 0.1 M Tris-HCl pH 7.3.
2.	Lyse the cells by treatment with lysozyme followed by sonication (see Section 2.1).
3.	Centrifuge the lysate at 1000 g for 5 min at 4°C.
4.	Centrifuge the supernatant at 27 000 g for 15 min at 4°C.
5.	Suspend the pellet in 1 ml of water and divide the suspension into 100 μl aliquots in conical microfuge tubes.
6.	Centrifuge the suspensions at 27 000 g for 15 min at 4°C.
7.	Resuspend each pellet in 100 μl of 0.1 M Tris-HCl pH 8.5 containing urea at the desired concentration (e.g. 0.5 M, 1.0 M, 2.0 M, 5.0 M).
8.	Centrifuge the suspensions at 27 000 g for 15 min at 4°C.
9.	Resuspend each pellet in 100 μl of water.
10.	Analyse 10 μl samples of the supernatants and resuspended pellets using SDS-PAGE (17).

Triton X-100 and EDTA (in the absence of Mg^{2+}). The method used for washing the prochymosin inclusion bodies with these components (18) is described in *Table 3*.

Urea has been used to wash bovine growth hormone (bGH) inclusion bodies, as reported by Schoner *et al.* (14). Since denaturants are commonly used to solubilize proteins from inclusion bodies, it is important to use a concentration of urea which gives minimum levels of solubilization. In the method used for bGH (*Table 4*) successive washing with 0.5 M, 1.0 M and 2.0 M urea solubilizes most of the contaminating proteins but not the bGH. 5.0 M urea solubilizes approximately 10% of the bGH, while 5.0 M urea containing 1% Triton X-100 partially solubilizes the bGH but not the contaminating proteins.

Contaminating proteins can affect the efficiency with which recombinant proteins are solubilized, cleaved or refolded. Therefore isolated washed inclusion bodies are often the preferred starting material for these processes.

3.2 Cleavage strategies for fusion proteins

As described in Section 1, fusion proteins consist of a bacterial or synthetic polypeptide linked to the eukaryotic polypeptide. In general, it is the eukaryotic polypeptide alone which is required. The strategy used to allow this is to construct the fusion with a cleavage site placed between the bacterial or synthetic sequence and the coding sequence of the eukaryotic gene. A number of cleavage strategies have been reported, which can broadly be divided into two types; chemical or enzymatic (*Table 5*). The choice of strategy is determined by the foreign protein itself, as the ideal situation is to use a cleavage site which is not present in the sequence of the foreign protein.

Table 5. Strategies for cleaving fusion proteins.

Sequence recognized	Cleavage effector	Reference
-asp↓pro-	Acid pH	19
-met↓	Cyanogen bromide	11
-arg↓ ⎫ or ⎬ -lys↓ ⎭	Trypsin	10
-arg↓	Clostripain	20
-lys↓	Endoproteinase lys C	21
-(asp)$_4$-lys↓	Enterokinase	22
-ile-glu-gly-arg↓x-	Factor Xa	23
-pro-x↓gly-pro-y↓	Collagenase	24

↓ indicates peptide bond cleaved.

Table 6. Acid cleavage of *trpLE*-bGH fusion proteins.

1.	Prepare a cell lysate using sonication.
2.	Centrifuge the cell lysate at 12 100 *g* for 10 min at 4°C.
3.	Resuspend the pellet in 70% formic acid and 6 M guanidine hydrochloride at a protein concentration of 0.85−1.0 mg/ml.
4.	Incubate for up to 72 h at 37°C.
5.	Dialyse cleaved samples against a 1000-fold excess volume of 50 mM Tris-HCl pH 7.6, 0.1 mM EDTA and 1 mM PMSF, at 4°C.
6.	Analyse the dialysed samples using SDS-PAGE (17).

3.2.1 *Chemical cleavage*

One example of a sequence susceptible to chemical cleavage is the aspartyl-proline bond, which is acid labile. This dipeptide was used to bridge each of two bGH fusion proteins; *trpE*-bGH and *trp LE*-bGH (19). The *trip LE*-asp-pro-bGH fusion was expressed to 5% of total cell protein in *E. coli* and aggregated in the form of inclusion bodies. The protocol used to isolate and cleave this fusion protein (19) is given in *Table 6*. The incubation conditions used for cleavage, 70% (v/v) formic acid and 6 M guanidine hydrochloride, are severe, and likely to unfold the aggregated fusion proteins, making the asp-pro bond accessible to the solvent. Dialysis is used to remove the denaturant, adjust the buffer conditions and allow the bGH to refold. One problem associated with this cleavage strategy is that the recombinant protein is left with a proline residue at the N-terminus, which may be unnatural. In the example given, the receptor binding activity of the bGH released from the fusion protein was compared with that of untreated authentic bGH and found to be significantly lower. There were a number of possible reasons for this; the extra proline residue, modification of amino acid residues at low pH, or incorrect refolding of the bGH after denaturation and acid cleavage (19).

A common approach for polypeptides which do not contain methionine is to use a methionine residue to bridge the fusion protein and then cleave with cyanogen bromide. One example of this is the fusion of β-galactosidase to insulin A chain and to insulin B chain (11), for which the cleavage protocol is described (*Table 7*). The A chain and B chain fusion proteins are cloned and expressed separately. Before cleavage with cyanogen bromide, the aggregated proteins are incubated in 6 M guanidine hydrochloride

Table 7. Cyanogen bromide cleavage of β-galactosidase-insulin A or -insulin B chain fusion proteins.

1.	Resuspend inclusion bodies isolated from 24 g wet weight of cells in 40 ml of 6 M guanidine hydrochloride, 1% (v/v) 2-mercaptoethanol (2-ME).
2.	Centrifuge the suspension at 21 000 *g* for 1 h.
3.	Dialyse the supernatant overnight against 20 l of water.
4.	Dissolve the precipitate which forms, in 25 ml of 70% (v/v) formic acid.
5.	Add 1.3 g of cyanogen bromide.
6.	Incubate the mixture overnight at room temperature.
7.	Remove the formic acid and excess cyanogen bromide by rotary evaporation.

```
... cys-asn-arg-arg-asn-ser-met-phe ...
    TCG AAC AGG CAC AAT TCT ATG TTT
```

Figure 5. Structure at the proinsulin domain junctions of β-galactosidase-multidomain proinsulin fusion proteins (25).

and 1% (v/v) 2-mercaptoethanol. Such treatment would unfold the fusion proteins and reduce any existing intermolecular or intramolecular disulphide bonds. Again, this pre-treatment may be necessary to make the met-X bond accessible, for cleavage.

In many fusion proteins the recombinant polypeptide constitutes only a small pro-portion of the hybrid molecule. In an effort to improve yields, fusion proteins have been constructed which consist of multiple copies of the eukaryotic gene linked to a single bacterial gene sequence. An example of this is the fusion of tandem-linked pro-insulin genes to an amino-terminal fragment of β-galactosidase (25). The sequence of the residues between proinsulin units is shown in *Figure 5*. Cyanogen bromide was used to effect cleavage. Using this strategy however, only one authentic proinsulin molecule is released from each fusion protein, at the C-terminus. All the other monomeric proinsulin molecules released have an extra pentapeptide sequence (arg-arg-asn-ser-homoserine) at their C-termini. Therefore further digestion with trypsin and carboxypeptidase B is required to yield authentic proinsulin. Using this expression system, similar levels of recombinant protein were obtained using an 'unfused' system consisting of tandem-linked proinsulin genes alone.

3.2.2 *Enzymatic cleavage*

From the procedures described in *Tables 6−8*, it is clear that stringent solvent condi-tions, such as 6 M guanidine hydrochloride, or 8 M urea, are required to solubilize fusion proteins before cleavage. When the sequence linking the bacterial and eukaryotic polypeptides is to be cleaved enzymatically, then conditions are required in which the fusion protein is soluble and the enzyme is still active. A chloramphenicol acetyltrans-ferase (CAT)-lys-arg-calcitonin fusion protein was constructed and expressed in *E. coli*; the aim being to cleave the fusion protein with clostripain, which cleaves on the C-terminal side of arg residues. The fusion protein is insoluble when synthesized in *E. coli*, but is still cleavable because clostripain is stable in up to 6 M urea. Isolated inclu-sion bodies are first incubated in 8 M urea and 2-mercaptoethanol to unfold the fusion protein (*Table 8*). The urea concentration is then reduced two-fold by dilution before addition of clostripain. After acid precipitation to remove some *E. coli* proteins and

Table 8. Clostripain cleavage of CAT-calcitonin fusion proteins.

1.	Suspend 10 g wet weight of cells in 30 ml of lysis buffer[a] and lyse the cells using the protocol outlined in *Table 1*.
2.	Centrifuge the cell lysate at 12 000 g for 30 min at 4°C.
3.	Resuspend the pellet in nine volumes (v/v/) of lysis buffer containing 0.5% (v/v) Triton X-100 and 10 mM EDTA.
4.	Incubate the suspension for 5 min at room temperature.
5.	Centrifuge the suspension at 12 000 g for 30 min at 4°C.
6.	Resuspend the pellet to a final protein concentration of 40 mg/ml in 100 mM Tris-HCl pH 7.8 containing 8 M urea and 0.14 M 2-mercaptoethanol.
7.	Incubate for 10 min at 37°C.
8.	Dilute the suspension with an equal volume of water.
9.	Add one part by weight of clostripain to 40 parts by weight fusion protein.
10.	Incubate for 15 min at 37°C.
11.	Add trifluoroacetic acid to a final concentration of 5% (v/v).
12.	Incubate for 20 min at 4°C.
13.	Remove acid-precipitated *E. coli* proteins by centrifugation at 15 000 g for 10 min at 4°C.

[a]Lysis buffer is described in the footnote to *Table 1*.

```
     1                          5                             10
  Tyr - Gly - Gly - Phe - Met - Thr - Ser - Glu - Lys - Ser -

                             15                            20
  Gln - Thr - Pro - Leu - Val - Thr - Leu - Phe - Lys - Asn -

                             25                            30
  Ala - Ile - Ile - Lys - Asn - Ala - His - Lys - Lys - Gly
```

Figure 6. Nucleotide and amino acid sequence of β-endorphin (10).

the clostripain, calcitonin is purified by reverse-phase h.p.l.c. (20). At this stage the calcitonin exists as a mixture of reduced and oxidized forms. Resuspension of the calcitonin in buffer at pH 8.5, in the presence of EDTA, promotes thiol-disulphide interchange and the formation of the 1,7 disulphide bond. The oxidized calcitonin is finally purified using a second reverse-phase h.p.l.c. step.

In general, unique cleavage sites are engineered into fusion proteins. Thus, for example, calcitonin contains no arginine residues and clostripain catalysed cleavage can be performed without the risk of cleaving the eukaryotic polypeptide. In contrast the β-galactosidase-β-endorphin fusion protein expressed in *E. coli* contains internal cleavage sites in the β-endorphin sequence (10; *Figure 6*). The fusion protein was designed for cleavage with trypsin, which cleaves peptide bonds specifically on the C-terminal side of lysine and arginine residues. In this fusion protein an arginine residue was placed immediately before the N-terminus of the eukaryotic polypeptide, and while there are no internal arginine residues in β-endorphin (*Figure 6*), there are five lysine residues. To prevent internal cleavage, these lysine residues are reversibly blocked, *in vitro*. The insoluble fusion protein is isolated from cell lysates by centrifugation (*Table 9*; reproduced from 10) and treated with citraconyl anhydride at pH 9. Under these conditions, lysine residues are modified with citraconyl groups. After digestion with trypsin, PMSF is added to inhibit the protease followed by acidification to pH 3.0 to remove the

Table 9. Trypsin cleavage of a β-galactosidase-β-endorphin fusion protein.

1.	Prepare cell lysates by sonication (Section 2.1) and isolate inclusion bodies by centrifugation at 21 000 *g* for 30 min.
2.	Suspend the pellet obtained from 6 g wet weight of cells in 10 ml of 6 M guanidine hydrochloride, 1% 2-mercaptoethanol.
3.	Centrifuge at 36 000 *g* for 60 min.
4.	Add 30 μl of citraconic anhydride (Fisher) in three 10 μl aliquots over a 15 min period. During this time, maintain the pH between 9 and 11 by the addition of 2 M NaOH.
5.	Dialyse the solution overnight against 50 mM ammonium bicarbonate.
6.	Add trypsin (Worthington) to a final concentration of 0.5 mg/ml and incubate for 12 h at 37°C.
7.	Add PMSF to a final concentration of 1 mM and continue the incubation for a further 60 min.
8.	Add formic acid to a final concentration of 1% (v/v), then lyophilise the solution completely.
9.	Dissolve the dried β-endorphin in Tris-HCl pH 7.6 to yield a protein concentration of 0.5 – 1.0 μg/μl.
10.	In a 15 ml plastic centrifuge tube add 0.5 ml of horse serum (Grand Island Biological) to 0.5 ml β-endorphin and then add 50 mg glass powder[a] (140 mesh; Corning Glass Works).
11.	Vortex the suspension for 30 sec, then centrifuge for 5 min at 2000 *g*.
12.	Discard the supernatant and add 3 ml of water to the pellet.
13.	Vortex and centrifuge the suspension as in step 11.
14.	Discard the supernatant and resuspend the pellet in 1 ml 50% (v/v) acetone in 0.25 – 5.0 M HCl.
15.	Vortex for 30 sec, then centrifuge as in step 11.
16.	Transfer the supernatant to a clean tube and evaporate the acetone completely with a fine stream of nitrogen; incubating the tube at 45°C in a water bath.
17.	Dried samples are reconstituted in Tris-HCl pH 7.6.

[a]Before use, the glass powder is washed once with water, heated for 24 h at 120°C and stored in a dessicator until required.

citraconyl groups. The recombinant polypeptides released from the fusion proteins are lyophilized, resuspended and purified by glass extraction. The opiate activity of β-endorphin prepared by this method was demonstrated in an *in vitro* cell culture system; additionally the polypeptides were shown to specifically bind to β-endorphin receptors. This was the first published report of a biologically active eukaryotic polypeptide synthesized in and isolated from *E. coli* (10).

The examples of enzymatic cleavage discussed in the text employ the use of proteases which recognize single amino acid residues. There are proteases which recognize sequences of amino acids (*Table 5*) and clearly, the longer the cleavage site recognized, the less chance there is of that sequence existing in the recombinant polypeptide. One example is the tetrapeptide sequence recognized by the blood coagulation factor Xa; Nagai and co-workers (23) inserted this sequence at the junction between λcII and β-globin sequences. The expressed fusion protein is insoluble and therefore inclusion bodies are isolated and washed before solubilization with urea (*Table 10*). Protein contaminants, which might later interfere with refolding of the β globin, are removed by ion-exchange chromatography and gel filtration. Both of these purification steps are performed in the presence of denaturants. The purified fusion protein is dialysed against buffer, to remove denaturant before cleavage with factor Xa (23).

There are also examples of eukaryotic polypeptides expressed in multiple forms, containing enzymatically cleavable sites at the junctions between repeated sequences. The pentapeptide enkephalin was expressed as the product of a concatenated gene containing eleven enkephalin sequences; each being separated from the previous sequence by

Table 10. Cleavage of a λcII - β-globin fusion protein with blood coagulation factor Xa.

1.	Suspend 100 g wet weight of *E. coli* in 8 ml of 50 mM Tris-HCl pH 8.0, 25% (w/v) sucrose, 1 mM EDTA.
2.	Add 200 mg of lysozyme, followed by $MgCl_2$, $MnCl_2$ and deoxyribonuclease I to final concentrations of 10 mM, 1 mM and 10 μg/ml respectively.
3.	Incubate for 30 min, then add 200 ml of 0.2 M NaCl, 1% (w/v) deoxycholic acid, 1.6% (v/v) Nonidet P-40, 20 mM Tris-HCl pH 7.5, 2.0 mM EDTA.
4.	Centrifuge the lysate at 5000 *g* for 10 min, to isolate inclusion bodies.
5.	Suspend the pellet in Triton X-100 and EDTA as described in step 3 of *Table 3*, but using 1 mM EDTA.
6.	Wash and centrifuge the inclusion bodies as described in steps 4 and 5 of *Table 3*.
7.	Repeat steps 5 and 6 in this Table until a tight pellet is obtained.
8.	Dissolve the pellet in urea buffer[a].
9.	Equilibrate a 4 × 10 cm CM-Sepharose (Pharmacia) column with urea buffer and apply the urea-solubilized fusion protein.
10.	Wash the column with urea buffer until the absorbance at 280 nm of the column eluate returns to zero.
11.	Elute the fusion protein with a 1 1 linear gradient of 0−0.2 M NaCl in urea buffer.
12.	Equilibrate a 5 × 600 cm Sephacryl S-200 (Pharmacia) column with 5 M guanidine HCl. 50 mM Tris-HCl pH 8.0, 1 mM EDTA, 1 mM DTT.
13.	Apply the fusion protein eluted from CM-Sepharose to the Sephacryl S-200 column and elute with the equilibration buffer described in step 12.
14.	Analyse the fractions from the gel filtration column by SDS-PAGE (17) and pool those fractions containing fusion protein (approximately 160 mg).
15.	Dialyse the purified fusion protein extensively against 50 mM Tris-HCl pH 8.0, 100 mM NaCl.
16.	Add 5 mg activated[b] blood coagulation factor Xa to the dialysed fusion protein.
17.	Dialyse the cleaved fusion protein extensively against water and lyophilize to dryness.

[a]Composition of urea buffer; 8 M urea, 25 mM Tris-acetate pH 5.0, 1 mM EDTA, 1 mM DTT.
[b]Blood coagulation factor Xa was activated with Russell's viper venom immobilized on Sepharose 6B.

two arginine residues (26). These genes were linked to a portion of the small-t antigen of SV40 and were expressed as fusion proteins. Release of monomers involves incubation with trypsin to effect cleavage and then removal of the arg residues with carboxypeptidase B. The isolation and cleavage protocol is as follows.

(i)   Boil intact cells for 5 min in 60 mM Tris-HCl pH 6.8, 2% (w/v) SDS, 5% 2-mercaptoethanol, 3 M urea.

(ii) Separate the proteins by SDS-PAGE on a 12.5% gel (17).

(iii) Elute the protein from the polyacrylamide gel; the appropriate gel slice being crushed and shaken for 16 h at 37°C in 50 mM Tris-HCl pH 8.0, 1 mM $CaCl_2$ and 0.1% (w/v) SDS.

(iv) Clarify the eluate by filtration and incubate it in trypsin (Worthington; TPCK-treated) at a final concentration of 10 μg/ml for 16 h at 37°C.

(v)   Boil the digest for 15 min, cool and then incubate with carboxypeptidase B (Serva) at a final concentration of 0.1 μg/ml for 60 min at 37°C.

(vi) Boil the digests once more for 15 min.

The peptide hormones produced and isolated by this procedure had opioid activity as measured by inhibition, *in vitro* of the contraction of guinea pig ileum.

3.3 Fusion proteins that facilitate purification

Fusion proteins can be constructed to facilitate purification. The bacterial or synthetic nucleic acid sequences fused to the eukaryotic gene, code for polypeptides which bind

Table 11. Some examples of fusion proteins that facilitate purification.

Fusion protein	Purification ligand or matrix	Reference
β- Galactosidase-X	p-Aminophenyl-β-D-thiogalactoside	27
CAT-X	Chloramphenicol	20
Protein-A-x	IgG	28
X-polyarginine	Cation-exchanger	29

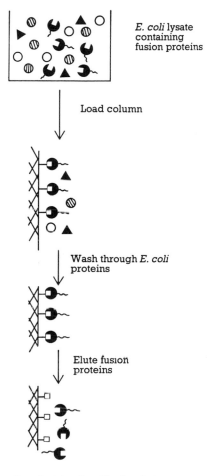

Figure 7. Diagram illustrating the principle of purification fusions.

selectively to certain chromatographic matrices. In three of the examples listed (*Table 11*) the fusion proteins are designed for isolation by affinity purification. As shown schematically in *Figure 7*, the process then followed is as given below.

(i)   Lyse the cells and isolate inclusion bodies.

(ii)   Solubilize the inclusion bodies in denaturant.

(iii)   Load the solubilized proteins onto the affinity column and wash off *E. coli* proteins with equilibration buffer, containing denaturant.

71

Table 12. Purification and cleavage of a urogastrone polyarginine fusion protein.

1.	Culture *E. coli* cells in a 7 l fermenter to an A_{600} of 2.2.
2.	Harvest the cells from an 800 ml portion of this fermentation by centrifugation at 4000 *g* for 20 min at 20°C.
3.	Resuspend the cells in 20 ml Tris/urea buffer pH 9.5[a] and lyse by sonication (see Section 2.1).
4.	Centrifuge the cell lysates at 16 000 *g* for 60 min at 20°C.
5.	Decant the supernatant and adjust the pH to 5.5 with HCl.
6.	Equilibrate a 1 × 2 cm SP-Sephadex (Pharmacia) column with Tris/urea buffer pH 5.5[b].
7.	Apply the supernatant to the SP-Sephadex column, then wash the column with 10 ml of Tris/urea buffer pH 5.5.
8.	Elute the fusion protein with a 45 ml linear gradient of 0−300 mM NaCl in Tris/urea buffer pH 5.5. Collect 1.5 ml fractions.
9.	Pool the fractions containing fusion proteins and adjust the pH of the solution to 8.1 with 1 M NaOH.
10.	Add 100 µl of carboxypeptidase B-Sepharose[c] and incubate for 2 h at 22°C with gentle end-over-end rotation.
11.	Remove the carboxypeptidase B-Sepharose on a sintered glass funnel.
12.	Dialyse the digested fusion protein overnight at 4°C against 8 l of 40 mM Tris-acetate pH 5.5.
13.	Add urea to a final concentration of 5 M and apply the sample to an SP-Sephadex column (1 × 1 cm), previously equilibrated with Tris/urea buffer pH 5.5.
14.	Wash the column with 5 ml equilibration buffer and elute the urogastrone with a 30 ml linear gradient of 0−125 mM NaCl in buffer pH 5.5.
15.	Collect 1 ml fractions and analyse for urogastrone activity (31).

[a]Tris/urea buffer pH 9.5 is 5 M urea, 40 mM Tris-acetate NaOH pH 9.5.
[b]Tris/urea buffer pH 5.5 is 5 M urea, 40 mM Tris-acetate pH 5.5.
[c]20 mg carboxypeptidase B-DFP Type 1 (Sigma, UK) suspended in 10 ml of 0.1 M Na_2HCO_3 pH 8.3 is added to 10 ml CNBr-Sepharose and reacted for 16 h at 4°C.

(iv)   Specifically elute the fusion protein.

The CAT-calcitonin fusion protein (20; *Table 11*) was constructed with the objective of purification by substrate-affinity chromatography. When the fusion protein was found to be in an insoluble form, this strategy was no longer feasible. The other examples of purification fusions listed in *Table 11* are also designed for isolation by affinity chromatography. *p*-Amino-β-D-thiogalactoside is a substrate analogue of β-galactosidase (27), and Protein A specifically binds to the F_c region IgG (28). These fusion proteins expressed in *E. coli* are soluble and their purification is described in Section 4.

The approach taken by Sassenfeld and Brewer (29) differed in that the fusion protein was designed for purification by cation-exchange chromatography. Human urogastrone (epidermal growth factor) was produced with a C-terminal polyarginine fusion. Arginine is a basic amino acid, therefore at acid pH the polyarginine is positively charged and binds strongly to a cation-exchanger. In contrast, most *E. coli* proteins are acidic and therefore do not bind. The urogastrone-polyarginine fusion protein is insoluble, but the strategy described (from ref. 29) does not include a step for isolating inclusion bodies (*Table 12*). Instead, cells are disrupted by sonication in a pH 9.5 buffer containing 5 M urea, and the fusion protein is located in the soluble fraction. Two cation-exchange chromatography steps are performed, one before enzymatic cleavage of the fusion protein (steps 6−8, *Table 12*) and one after cleavage (steps 13−15, *Table 12*). In the first cation-exchange step, the fusion protein binds, acidic *E. coli* proteins wash through the column and the fusion protein is eluted with salt. The polyarginine residues are

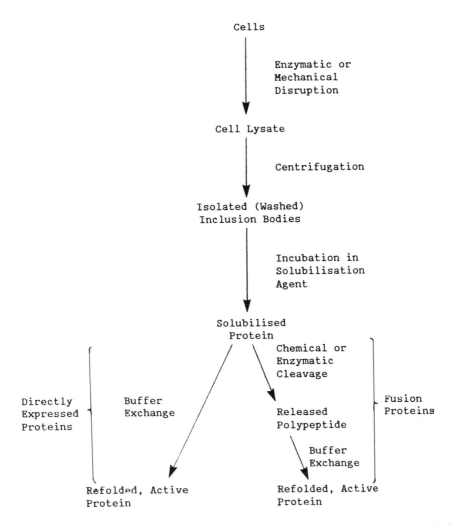

Figure 8. Diagram of the stages in the recovery of active, soluble eukaryotic proteins from inclusion bodies in *E. coli.*

digested with carboxypeptidase B, and in the second cation-exchange step the urogastrone (pI = 5.8 ± 0.3; ref. 31) washes straight through the column while any positively-charged proteins or peptides are retarded. This procedure yields 39% of the urogastrone, greater than 95% pure. Two critical features of this approach are the accessibility of the polyarginine and the efficiency with which carboxypeptidase digests the arginine tail to yield the correct C-terminus.

3.4 Solubilization of directly expressed proteins and fusion proteins

The recovery of soluble, active products from the insoluble starting material isolated from *E. coli* requires at least a two stage process (*Figure 8*). Inclusion bodies, if isolated, are first solubilized and then refolded. If necessary, fusion proteins are cleaved before refolding (Section 3.2). There are a number of agents which will release polypeptides

Table 13. Reagents which release eukaryotic polypeptides from inclusion bodies into solution.

Reagent	Eukaryotic polypeptide solubilized[a]
Guanidine HCl (5−8 M)	Insulin A & B chains
	Bovine growth hormone
	Urokinase
Urea (6−8 M)	Prochymosin
	Interferon-γ
	Salmon growth hormone
SDS	Interferon-β
	Interleukin-2
Alkaline pH (>9.0)	Prochymosin
	Chicken growth hormone
Acetonitrile/propanol	T_4 *reg A* protein

[a]For references, see ref. 1.

Table 14. Strategy for examining the efficiency with which eukaryotic polypeptides are solubilized from inclusion bodies.

1.	Isolate inclusion bodies and if appropriate, wash to remove contaminating proteins (see Section 3.1).
2.	Suspend inclusion bodies in the solubilization reagents to a final protein concentration of 5 mg/ml or less. For small volumes, inclusion bodies are suspended by vortex mixing; large volumes are suspended with an overhead homogenizer, taking care to minimize foaming.
3.	Incubate the suspensions for varying amounts of time at room temperature; 1−16 h being a suggested initial range. Large volumes may be gently stirred.
4.	Centrifuge the suspensions to pellet any insoluble material. 12 000 *g* for between 10 min and 30 min is usually adequate.
5.	Resuspend the pellets and dilute the supernatants in sample buffer[a]. Analyse the protein profiles by SDS-PAGE (17).

[a]Sample buffer (2-fold concentrated): 20% (v/v) glycerol, 10% (v/v) 2-mercaptoethanol, 6% (w/v) SDS, 0.125 M Tris-HCl, pH 6.8.

from inclusion bodies into solution (*Table 13*). Denaturants such as urea and guanidine hydrochloride will disrupt ionic interactions; native proteins exposed to high concentrations of these solvents completely unfold, but covalent interactions such as disulphide bonds, remain intact. Using extremes of pH ionic interactions between polypeptide chains are disrupted, while detergents and organic solvents disrupt hydrophobic interactions between polypeptide side-chains. The efficiency with which each of these agents solubilizes a protein can vary. This is because the interactions between proteins in inclusion bodies differ; being dependent on the protein itself (1).

A strategy which can be used as a starting point for studying solubilization is described in *Table 14*. It is possible to examine the effect of a large number of solubilization agents if incubation volumes of 1−2 ml are used. As the aim is to recover active, soluble protein, having identified the effectiveness of a particular solubilization reagent, further optimization of solubilization is examined in conjunction with refolding.

The polypeptides in solution may still be aggregated because covalent intermolecular bonds exist, such as disulphide bonds. If it is necessary to disrupt these interactions completely, then thiol reagents such as dithiothreitol (DTT) or 2-mercaptoethanol (2-ME) are included with the solubilization reagent. Another method which can be used to disrupt

Table 15. Preparation of S-sulphonated derivatives of insulin A chain or insulin B chain.

1.	Insulin A chains or B chains are isolated from β-galactosidase fusion proteins (see *Table 7*), starting with 24 g wet weight of cells.
2.	After CNBr cleavage and rotary evaporation, suspend the residue in 50 ml of 8 M guanidine hydrochloride.
3.	To prepare S-sulphonated derivatives, add 1 g of sodium tetrathionate and 2 g of sodium sulphite.
4.	Adjust the pH to 9 with NH_4OH.
5.	Incubate the mixture for 24 h at room temperature, with stirring.
6.	Adjust the pH to 5 with acetic acid.
7.	Dialyse the mixture twice against 3 l of water.

intermolecular disulphides is derivatization to form S-sulphonates. This was the approach taken for insulin A chain and insulin B chain (11; *Table 15*). The need to disrupt these interactions completely can only be ascertained by examining refolding and recovery of activity. It is not always necessary to disrupt intermolecular disulphide bonds completely; conditions which promote thiol-disulphide interchange can be used during refolding (Section 3.5) to produce monomeric molecules containing intermolecular disulphide bonds.

Once effective solubilization agents are identified, conditions in the solubilization reaction mixture are examined. A number of variables at the solubilization stage can influence the yield of active protein recovered after refolding.
(i)   pH.
(ii)   Incubation temperature.
(iii)   Time of exposure to solvent.
(iv)   Ionic components of the solvent.
(v)   Concentration of solubilization agent.
(vi)   Concentration of total protein.
(vii)   Ratio of solubilization agent to protein.
(viii) Presence or absence of thiol reagents.
(ix)   Derivatization of thiol groups, e.g. by S-sulphonation.

The conditions used to solubilize polypeptides from inclusion bodies are stringent (*Table 13*) and could result in derivatization of amino acid residues. Cyanate ions in urea solutions can derivatize lys residues and cross-link the polypeptide chains. To avoid this, urea solutions are prepared immediately before use and as a further precaution may be deionized using a mixed bed resin. Because of the nature of the solubilization agents, the aim should be to minimize the time the polypeptides are exposed. This is particularly pertinent when pH values of 9 or greater are being used. Under these conditions asparagine and glutamine residues may be deamidated. There are also a number of sequence-specific derivatizations which can occur at alkaline pH.

3.5 Refolding

After solubilizing the eukaryotic polypeptides, refolding is effected by changing the buffer condition, out of the denaturant or other solubilization agent. This can be achieved by dialysis or by dilution. The rate at which the concentrations of the solubilization agent and the recombinant polypeptide are changed can be controlled simultaneously, using dilution. As for solubilization there are a number of variables which influence the yield of active protein obtained.

(i)   Rate of change from solubilization to refolding environment.
(ii)   Purity of the recombinant polypeptide.
(iii) Concentration of the recombinant polypeptide.
(iv)   pH.
(v)   Ionic components of the solvent.
(vi)   Presence or absence of thio reagents.

There are protocols which use two stages to effect refolding; it is thought that in the first stage the proteins fold into forms approximating their native state and in the second stage, folding is completed. Examples include dilution of prochymosin from 8 M urea into buffer at pH 10.7; after incubation the pH is adjusted to 8.0 (18). Another approach is to transfer the solubilized proteins into low concentrations of urea to allow partial refolding (30).

The purity of the recombinant polypeptide may be important as contaminants can interfere with refolding. In this respect, isolation of inclusion bodies is useful and furthermore, it is possible to purify the polypeptides in the presence of certain solubilization reagents before refolding. Ion-exchange chromatography can be performed in the presence of urea, even at concentrations of 8 M. Guanidine hydrochloride is charged, and precludes the use of ion-exchange chromatography, but not the use of gel filtration. H.p.l.c. and f.p.l.c. can be used to purify the polypeptides in the presence of a number of the solubilization conditions listed (*Table 13*); h.p.l.c. in particular can be used in conjunction with organic solvents. Other methods which have been used to purify recombinant polypeptides before refolding are high speed centrifugation (30) and organic extraction (31).

The concentration of the recombinant protein during refolding is critical, in order to ensure that intramolecular interactions occur in preference to intermolecular interactions. This is particularly important if the native, active protein contains intramolecular disulphide bonds. When the disulphide bonds in the inclusion bodies are disrupted by the use of thiol reagents or derivatization to S-sulphonates, then the formation of correct disulphide bonds is promoted by mixtures of reduced and oxidized thiol reagent such as glutathione. Both the concentration and ratio of reduced: oxidized reagent must be optimized, and with the pH of the refolding buffer at 8 or above, thiol-disulphide interchange occurs rapidly.

It is possible to promote thiol-disulphide interchange at high pH in the absence of exogenous thiol reagents; the protein itself can act as a source of free thiol (18).

During the development of a refolding protocol, the efficiency of refolding must be assessed to allow optimum conditions to be established. There are a number of ways in which refolded polypeptides can be analysed and some methods are listed (*Table 16*). SDS-PAGE and analytical h.p.l.c. or f.p.l.c. can be used to examine the state of aggregation of the final product. SDS-PAGE analysis in the presence and absence of 2-ME may reveal incorrect, intermolecular disulphide bonds. If there are contaminating proteins still remaining, interpretation of a stained gel may be difficult. This problem can be overcome by Western blotting onto nitrocellulose and using a specific antiserum to probe the blot. The best measure of the efficiency of refolding to yield active protein is to assay biological activity and this is feasible for many enzymes. However, the biological activity of peptide hormones and metabolic modulators may

Table 16. Methods for analysing refolding of eukaryotic polypeptides isolated from *E. coli.*

1.	SDS-PAGE, in the presence and absence of 2-mercaptoethanol followed by staining.
2.	SDS-PAGE, in the presence and absence of 2-mercaptoethanol followed by Western blotting and immunological analysis.
3.	Analytical h.p.l.c. or f.p.l.c.
4.	Biological activity assay.
5.	Immunoassay e.g. RIA, ELISA.
6.	Receptor assay — for peptide hormones.

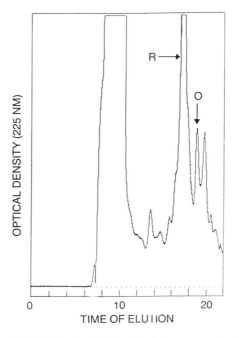

Figure 9. Purification of a clostripain digest of CAT-calcitonin by reverse-phase h.p.l.c. R and O indicate elution positions of reduced and oxidized calcitonin respectively (20).

require *in vivo* assays and cost or resource may be a limitation. Under these circumstances immunoassays or receptor assays are used to give some indication that a biologically active conformation has been regained.

3.6 **Examples of eukaryotic polypeptides solubilized and refolded from *E. coli***

Small polypeptides synthesized as insoluble fusion proteins in *E. coli* require solubilization but may not require extensive empirical definition of refolding conditions. β-endorphin is a typical example (10); this polypeptide apparently folds spontaneously either when it is released from the fusion protein (see *Table 9*) or during purification by glass extraction. Human calcitonin is a 32 amino acid polypeptide and contains two cysteine residues which form a disulphide bond in the biologically active molecule. When the *E. coli* product is released by cleavage of the fusion protein (see *Table 8*), the calcitonin exists in two forms, reduced and oxidized, which can be detected by

Table 17. Analysis of human calcitonin released by clostripain digestion of a CAT-calcitonin fusion protein.

1. Isolate CAT-calcitonin fusion protein from *E. coli*, solubilize and cleave it (see *Table 8*).
2. Equilibrate a 1.0 × 25 cm Synchropak RP-P h.p.l.c. column with 30% (v/v) acetonitrile, 0.1% (v/v) TFA.
3. Load the supernatant from step 13 of *Table 8* onto the reverse-phase column at a flow rate of 2 ml/min. Monitor the absorbance at 225 nm.
4. Elute the calcitonin with a linear gradient of 30% (v/v) — 45% (v/v) acetonitrile in 0.1% (v/v) TFA, over a 20 min period (*Figure 8*).
5. Pool peaks R and O, and lyophilize to dryness.
6. Redissolve the polypeptide to a final concentration of 0.5 mg/ml in 50 mM Tris-HCl pH 8.5, 2 mM EDTA.
7. Monitor the oxidation of the calcitonin by analytical reverse-phase h.p.l.c. as described in steps 2 and 3 above.
8. When oxidation is complete re-purify the oxidized calcitonin by reverse-phase h.p.l.c., as described in steps 2 and 3 above.

Table 18. Solubilization and refolding of calf prochymosin from *E. coli*.

1. Suspend 100 g wet weight of *E. coli* in 300 ml of lysis buffer[a] and break the cells using lysozyme and deoxycholate (see *Table 1*).
2. Isolate inclusion bodies and wash with Triton X-100 and EDTA (see *Table 3*).
3. Suspend the pellets in 900 ml 8 M urea (de-ionized), 50 mM Tris-HCl pH 8.0, 1.0 mM EDTA, and 50 mM NaCl.
4. Incubate the suspension for 1 h at room temperature.
5. Add the suspension slowly, with stirring, to nine volumes (v/v) of 50 mM KH_2PO_4 pH 10.7, 1 mM EDTA, 50 mM NaCl and maintain the pH at 10.7 throughout the dilution with KOH.
6. Incubate the solution for 15−30 min at room temperature.
7. Adjust the pH of the solution to 8.0 with HCl.
8. Incubate the solution for 30 min at room temperature.
9. Dilute the solution with an equal volume of 20 mM Tris-HCl pH 8.0, 1 mM EDTA and concentrate the solution 4-fold (Amicon hollow fibre concentrator; H1P10-8 cartridges).
10. Add 300 ml (settled bed volume) of DE-52, previously equilibrated with ion-exchange buffer[b], stir and incubate for 1 h at 4°C.
11. Collect the DE-52 on a sintered funnel using a low vacuum.
12. Resuspend the DE-52 in 3 volumes (v/v) of ion-exchange buffer containing 350 mM NaCl and incubate for 30−60 min at 4°C.
13. Collect the DE-52 on a sintered glass funnel under low vacuum, taking care to minimize foaming. The prochymosin is in the filtrate.

[a]See *Table 1* for the composition of lysis buffer.
[b]Ion exchange buffer: 20 mM Tris-HCl pH 8.0, 1 mM EDTA, 50 mM NaCl.

analytical h.p.l.c. (*Figure 9*). Conditions were therefore established to convert all the calcitonin to the oxidized form (20; *Table 17*).

Recovery of β-globin from fusion proteins synthesized in *E. coli* is an example of a process incorporating the purification of the polypeptide in a denatured state (23). The intact fusion protein was first purified by ion-exchange chromatography in the presence of 8 M urea and subsequently by gel filtration in the presence of 5 M guanidine hydrochloride (see *Table 10*). Several other examples of this approach are given in ref. 30.

The solubilization and two-stage refolding of calf prochymosin (18) is described in *Table 18*. The time of incubation in urea is important and influences the overall yield.

Table 19. Summary of the purification of prochymosin from *E. coli* (18).

Purification stage	Volume (ml)	Chymosin (mg/ml)	Protein (mg/ml)	Purity	Yield %
Cell lysate	400	*1.4 (3.37)	17.5	0.08	100
Urea/alkali extract	5000	0.06	0.15	0.40	53.5
DE-52 (Batch)	515	0.32	0.53	0.60	29.4
DE-52 (Column) Pooled prochymosin peak	67	1.85	1.86	0.995	22.2

It is thought that this reflects the time required for the urea to penetrate and disrupt the interactions in the inclusion bodies. The yield of active enzyme is also dependent on the protein concentration in urea and alkali. In urea, this may reflect the efficiency with which the inclusion bodies are disrupted, as the ratio of denaturant: protein is increased. At alkaline pH, it is thought that thiol-disulphide interchange is occurring between prochymosin molecules and therefore the optimum protein concentration is that at which monomers form in preference to aggregates. While the correct disulphide bonds may start to form at pH 10.7, the period of incubation at pH 8.0 probably allows complete refolding into a stable, native conformation. Purification of the refolded prochymosin by batch ion-exchange (*Table 18*) and column ion-exchange (18) gave a yield of 22% prochymosin, greater than 90% pure (*Table 19*).

Apolipoprotein E is an example of a eukaryotic polypeptide synthesized directly in *E. coli* which is insoluble, but is purified by affinity chromatography in the presence of denaturant (32; *Table 20*). The method used is heparin-Sepharose chromatography in the presence of 2 M urea. The eukaryotic protein must attain partial native conformation under these conditions, in order to recognize the ligand. Two further purification steps are used, one being gel filtration on Sephacryl S-300 in the presence of 6 M guanidine HCl. Then after dialysis to refold the protein, final purification involves preparative isoelectric focusing on an Immobiline gel.

The polypeptides for which solubilization and refolding protocols have been described so far are either small polypeptides, or proteins which contain six or less cysteine residues, forming three or less disulphide bonds. Proteins with predicted complex structures have been expressed directly in *E. coli*; namely urokinase (33) and tissue-type plasminogen activator (tPA. 13). The solubilization protocols for these proteins are given in *Tables 21* and *22*, respectively. Both proteins were solubilized in the absence of exogenous thiol reagents, but refolded in the presence of reduced and oxidized glutathione. In both examples, a defined protein concentration, ratio and concentration of thiol reagents are required during refolding. The overall yields of urokinase are not given, but with tPA they were low, being <0.1% of total cell protein. This can be attributed to the fact that tPA has a complex, multidomain structure containing 10 or more disulphide bonds and is therefore difficult to refold efficiently. Another contributory factor could be the lack of glycosylation of the *E. coli* derived protein.

Multi-subunit proteins have also been produced in *E. coli* and recovered from an

Table 20. Solubilization and refolding of human apolipoprotein E from *E. coli*.

1.	Mix 33 g wet weight of cells and 22 g of alumina (Buehler, Evanston, IL) and grind to a fine powder in a chilled (4°C) mortar and pestle.
2.	Extract the ground cells with 300 ml of 6 M urea in 0.1 M ammonium bicarbonate buffer[a].
3.	Centrifuge the extract at 25 000 r.p.m. for 50 min at 4°C (Beckman SW28 rotor).
4.	Re-extract the pellet with 200 ml of 6 M urea in 0.1 M bicarbonate buffer and centrifuge as in step 3.
5.	Pool the supernatants from steps 3 and 4 and dialyse against three changes of 2 M urea in 25 mM ammonium bicarbonate buffer[b].
6.	Equilibrate 200 ml (settled bed volume) of heparin-Sepharose with 2 M urea in 25 mM ammonium bicarbonate buffer.
7.	Add the dialysed supernatant to the heparin-Sepharose and incubate on a rotating platform, overnight at 4°C.
8.	Pack the heparin-Sepharose into a glass column (4 × 3.5 cm).
9.	Wash the column by pumping 300 ml of 2 M urea buffer in 25 mM ammonium bicarbonate through the column at a flow rate of 25 ml/h.
10.	Elute the bound material with 50 ml of 1.0 M ammonium bicarbonate in 2 M urea.
11.	Dialyse the eluate against 5 mM ammonium bicarbonate and lyophilize to dryness.
12.	Dissolve the dried protein in 6 M guanidine-HCl in gel filtration buffer[c].
13.	Equilibrate a Sephacryl S-300 column (2.5 × 300 cm) with 4 M guanidine-HCl in gel filtration buffer.
14.	Apply the solubilized protein to the Sephacryl S-300 column and elute with 4 M guanidine-HCl in gel filtration buffer.
15.	Dialyse the eluted Apolipoprotein E exhaustively against 5 mM ammonium bicarbonate and lyophilize to dryness.

[a]0.1 M ammonium bicarbonate buffer is 0.1 M NH_4HCO_3 pH 7.8, 2 mM PMSF, 0.1% (v/v) Trasylol (Mobay, New York, NY).
[b]25 mM ammonium bicarbonate buffer is 25 mM NH_4HCO_3 pH 7.4, 2 mM PMSF, 2 mM EDTA, 0.1% (v/v) Trasylol, 0.1% (v/v) 2-mercaptoethanol.
[c]Gel filtration buffer is 0.1 M Tris-HCl pH 7.4, 1 mM EDTA, 1% (v/v) 2-mercaptoethanol.

Table 21. Solubilization and refolding of urokinase from *E. coli*.

1.	Suspend 100 g wet weight of cells in 900 ml of 0.05 M Tris-HCl pH 8.0, 0.005% (v/v) Tween 80.
2.	Break the cells by one pass through a Manton-Gaulin homogenizer at 5000 p.s.i.
3.	Centrifuge the lysate at 4700 g for 45 min at 4°C.
4.	Resuspend the pellet in 5 M guanidine hydrochloride, 0.005 M Tris-HCl pH 8.0, 0.05% (v/v) Tween 80 and incubate overnight, with stirring, at 4°C.
5.	Centrifuge the suspension at 4700 g for 45 min at 4°C.
6.	Decant the supernatant and dilute it to a final absorbance at 280 nm of 1.0 and a final buffer concentration of 1.0 M guanidine hydrochloride, 0.05 M Tris-HCl pH 8.0, 0.005% (v/v) Tween 80, 2.0 mM reduced glutathione and 0.02 mM oxidized glutathione.
7.	Incubate the solution for 18−36 h at 4°C.
8.	Dialyse the solution into 0.05 M Tris-HCl pH 8.0, 0.005% (v/v) Tween 80, 0.05 M NaCl and clarify by centrifugation.
9.	Equilibrate a 5 × 5 cm DE-52 (Whatman) column with 0.05 M Tris-HCl pH 8.0, 0.005% (v/v) Tween 80, 0.05 M NaCl.
10.	Load the supernatant from step 8 onto the DE-52 column and collect the solution which flows straight through.
11.	Equilibrate a 2.5 × 10 cm benzamidine-Sepharose column with 0.05 M Tris-HCl pH 8.0.
12.	Load the sample from step 10 and wash the column with 0.05 M Tris-HCl pH 8.0, 1 M NaCl until the absorbance at 280 nm is constant.
13.	Elute the urokinase from the benzamidine-Sepharose column with 0.05 M Tris-HCl pH 8.0 containing 1 M arginine.

Table 22. Solubilization and refolding of tPA from *E. coli.*

1.	Suspend 1 g wet weight of cells in 9 ml of lysis buffer[a] and break the cells using lysozyme and deoxycholate (see *Table 1*).
2.	Isolate inclusion bodies by centrifugation at 12 000 g for 5 min at 4°C.
3.	Resuspend the inclusion bodies in nine volumes (v/v) of urea buffer[b] using an overhead homogenizer.
4.	Incubate the suspension for 1 h at 30°C.
5.	Add the suspension slowly, to nine volumes (v/v) of 20 mM Tris-HCl pH 8.5, 0.01% (v/v) Tween 80, 0.25 M NaCl, 1 mM reduced glutathione, 0.1 mM oxidized glutathione, at 30°C.
6.	Incubate for a further 2 h at 30°C.
7.	Adjust the pH of the solution to 7.4.
8.	Dialyse the solution extensively against 20 mM Tris-HCl pH 8.5, 0.01% (v/v) Tween 80, 0.25 M NaCl, 1 mM reduced glutathione 0.1 mM oxidized glutathione at 4°C, to remove residual denaturant.

[a]Lysis buffer is 50 mM Tris-HCl pH 7.5, 50 mM NaCl, 1 mM EDTA.
[b]Urea buffer is 8 M urea (deionised) in 20 mM Tris-HCl pH 8.5, 0.01% (v/v) Tween 80, 0.25 M NaCl.

Table 23. Reconstitution of anti-CEA IgG from γ-heavy chain and $\varkappa$-light chain synthesized separately in *E. coli.*

The following protocol is either for cells containing γ-heavy chain or for cells containing $\varkappa$-light chain.

1.	Suspend 1 g of frozen cell paste in 9 ml lysis buffer[a].
2.	Add 2-mercaptoethanol to a final concentration of 0.1 M.
3.	Incubate the suspension for 1 h at 37°C.
4.	Centrifuge the suspension at 15 000 r.p.m. (Sorvall SS-34 rotor) for 30 min

To reconstitute the IgG:

5.	Mix and dilute the γ-heavy chain and $\varkappa$-light chain supernatants from stage 5 to give a potential IgG content of 25 μg/ml in 8 M guanidine hydrochloride, 50 mM Tris-HCl pH 8.0, 1 mM EDTA.
6.	Dialyse the solution for 1−2 h at 4°C against 20 volumes of 8 M urea (de-ionized) in dialysis buffer[b].
7.	Transfer the dialysis bag(s) to 20 volumes of the same buffer and add N$_2$ saturated dialysis buffer over a period of 15 h to give a final urea concentration of 1 M.
8.	Add serum albumin to each dialysis bag to a final concentration of 0.5 mg/ml.
9.	Transfer the dialysis bags to phosphate buffered saline containing 0.1 mM PMSF (which is not degassed).
10.	Dialyse for 2 h at 4°C.

[a]Lysis buffer is 7.6 M guanidine hydrochloride, 50 mM Tris-HCl pH 8.0, 1 mM EDTA.
[b]Dialysis buffer is 50 mM sodium glycinate pH 10.8, 10 mM glycine ethyl ester, 1 mM EDTA, 1 mM reduced glutathione, 0.1 mM oxidized glutathione.

insoluble state. In order to produce mutant haemoglobins, β-globin was expressed in *E. coli* as a β-galactosidase-β-globin fusion protein and processed as described in Section 3.2.2. (23; *Table 10*). After cleavage of the fusion protein, dialysis and lyophilization, the haemoglobin is reconstituted as follows (23).

(i) Dissolve the β-globin to a final concentration of 5 mg/ml in 8 M urea, 50 mM Tris-HCl pH 8.0, 1 mM DTT.

(ii) Dilute the β-globin to 0.3 mg/ml protein.

(iii) Mix the β-globin with a 1.2 molar excess of cyanohaem and α-globin.

(iv) Reduce the reconstituted haemoglobin with sodium dithionite under an atmosphere of CO in the presence of 1 μg/ml catalase.

Two examples of multi-subunit eukaryotic proteins synthesized entirely in *E. coli* are insulin (11) and IgG (anti-carcinoembryonic antigen; CEA; ref. 34). In both cases the subunits were cloned and expressed in separate organisms. The insulin A chains and B chains were expressed as fusion proteins and were isolated, cleaved and S-sulphonated as described in *Tables 7* and *15*. The S-sulphonated derivatives were purified by ion-exchange chromatography and reverse-phase h.p.l.c. before reconstitution. Insulin A (SSO_3^-) and insulin B (SSO_3^-) were reconstituted at pH $9.6-10.6$ and yielded $10-15\%$ radioimmune active insulin (11).

The reconsitution of anti-CEA IgG is described in *Table 23*. The approach taken (34) is to completely reduce and solubilize the heavy and light chains in crude extracts; then dialysis is used to achieve a gradual return to native conditions in the continual presence of a mild redox buffer that promotes thiol-disulphide interchange. The best yield of anti-CEA activity, from *E. coli* extracts, as measured in an ELISA was $3-5\%$ of the expected maximum.

4. SOLUBLE PROTEINS

4.1 Intracellular expression

There are examples of eukaryotic polypeptides synthesized in *E. coli* as fusion proteins or by direct expression which are soluble (1). In some cases only a proportion of the polypeptide is soluble; the remainder being located in inclusion bodies. Many of the purification procedures published for these soluble proteins include an affinity chromatography step; either immunopurification, or substrate affinity chromatography (1).

As mentioned earlier in the text (Section 3.3) the pre-S2 protein of hepatitis B virus was produced as a fusion to β-galactosidase (pre S2-β-gal), to facilitate purification as well as to optimize expression (27). The fusion protein was expressed to 30% of total cell protein. Purification from the supernatant after cell lysis is effected by affinity chromatography on an immobilized substrate analogue column (see *Table 11*). The fusion protein is eluted from this column with 0.1 M sodium borate, pH 10.0. Using this one-step procedure, the fusion protein is purified 75-fold to >90% homogeneity, with almost no loss.

Human lymphotoxin (35) and the AIDS retrovirus p24 *gag* protein (36) were each synthesized directly in *E. coli* in a soluble form. In both examples, immunopurification was used as a single step; purifying the recombinant protein from total soluble *E. coli* protein. The lymphotoxin purification procedure was as follows.

(i)   Equilibrate a 20 ml monoclonal antibody—Sepharose column with 0.05 M Tris-HCl pH 7.0, 0.15 M NaCl, 2 mM EDTA (TBS).

(ii) Equilibrate the column with 0.1 M acetic acid pH 4.5, 150 mM NaCl.

(iii) Re-equilibrate the column with TBS.

(iv) Add ammonium sulphate to a final concentration of 40% (w/v) to an *E. coli* lysate, and collect the pellet by centrifugation.

(v)   Dissolve the pellet in a small volume of 0.1 M Tris-HCl pH 7.4, 5 mM EDTA and load it onto the column at a flow rate of one column volume per h.

(vi) Wash the column with TBS containing 0.05% (v/v) Tween 20 until the absorbance at 280 nm is constant.

(vii) Elute the lymphotoxin with 0.1 M acetic acid pH 4.5, 150 mM NaCl.

(viii)   Adjust the pH of the eluate to 7.8 immediately with 0.1 volume 1 M Tris-HCl pH 8.5.

The AIDS p24 *gag* protein is eluted from the immunoadsorbent with 2 M potassium thiocyanate (KSCN) (36) and the chaotropic agent removed by dialysis against phosphate-buffered saline.

In a recent publication (37) the direct expression of human Cu/Zn superoxide dismutase (SOD) in *E. coli* was reported. The protein was soluble, enzymically active and expressed at a level of ~13% of total cell protein. Purification from soluble *E. coli* proteins involved several steps.

(i)   Addition of SDS to a final concentration of 2% (w/v) (to specifically precipitate bacterial SOD).

(ii)   Addition of KCl to the supernatant to a final concentration of 0.3 M to remove traces of SDS.

(iii)   60% (w/v) ammonium sulphate precipitation of contaminating proteins.

(iv)   Dialysis against 20% potassium phosphate.

(v)   Ultrafiltration (concentration) and gel filtration on Fractogel 55.

(vi)   Ion-exchange chromatography on DE-52 (isocratic elution with KCl).

The SOD was purified to >90% homogeneity, but the yield was only 10%. However, this was equivalent to a yield of 2 g of SOD from 50 l *E. coli* harvested at an absorbance at 600 nm of 20. This is an excellent example of the amount of recombinant protein which can be purified from *E. coli* when expression levels are high and the protein is soluble; even if the yield after purification is moderate.

Table 24. Systems used for the secretion of heterologous proteins from *E. coli*.

Derivation of signal sequence	Proteins secreted from *E. coli*	Reference
β Lactamase	Proinsulin	38
	IgG light chain	39
	A-α fibrinogen	40
omp A	FMDV VP1	41
	Human growth hormone	42
omp F	β-endorphin	43
pho A	Epidermal growth factor	44
Human growth hormone	Human growth hormone	45
Urokinase	Urokinase	46

Table 25. Purification of β-endorphin secreted into the culture medium from *E. coli*.

1.   Lyophilize 1 l of culutre medium to dryness.
2.   Dissolve the pellet in 50 ml of water and desalt by passage through a 2.6 × 95 cm column of Sephadex G-10 equilibrated with 0.1 M acetic acid.
3.   Lyophilize the excluded fraction from the G-10 column to dryness.
4.   Dissolve the pellet in 4 ml of water and apply the solution to a 1.2 × 140 cm Sephadex G-25 (fine) column equilibrated with 0.1 M acetic acid.
5.   Develop the column at a flow rate of 20 ml/h and collect 2 ml fractions.
6.   Equilibrate a reverse phase column (RP-300, 4.6 × 250 mm, Brown Lee) with 0.1% (v/v) TFA.
7.   Analyse aliquots of the G-25 eluate by RP-h.p.l.c., eluting with a linear gradient of 0.1% (v/v) TFA — 50% (v/v) acetonitrile/0.075% (v/v) TFA over 50 min at a flow rate of 1 ml/min.

Table 26. Assay for β-lactamase.

1.	Prepare a 19 mM nitrocefin solution in dimethyl sulphoxide.
2.	Dilute the nitrocefin 100-fold in 0.1 M phosphate buffer pH 7.0.
3.	Equilibrate 1 ml of the nitrocefin solution in a cuvette placed in a spectrophotometer at a temperature of 30°C.
4.	Add 0.1 ml of appropriate diluted sample.
5.	Measure the change in absorbance at 495 nm.
6.	Calculate the β-lactamase activity using $\epsilon_{mM}^{495nm} = 1.406$ (1 cm light path).

Table 27. Assay for alkaline phosphatase.

1.	Warm 2-amino-2-methyl-1-propanol (2A2M1P) at 35°C until it completely liquifies.
2.	Weigh 86 g 2A2M1P in a 1 l beaker, add 500 ml of water and mix.
3.	Add approximately 120 ml of 1 M HCl and mix.
4.	In a separate beaker, weight 264 mg of $MgSO_4.7H_2O$ and dissolve with 200 ml of water.
5.	Pour the magnesium solution into the 2A2M1P solution and mix.
6.	Warm the solution to 30°C, and maintaining this temperature, adjust the pH to 10.5 with 1 M HCl.
7.	Make the volume of the solution up to 1 litre with water.
8.	Mix 1.4 ml of the $2A2M1P/Mg^{2+}$ solution and 50 μl of appropriately diluted sample in a cuvette.
9.	Equilibrate the solution in a spectrophotometer at a temperature of 30°C.
10.	Add 50 μl of 0.48 M 4-nitrophenyl phosphate and mix.
11.	Measure the charge in absorbance at 405 nm.
12.	Calculate the alkaline phosphatase activity using $\epsilon_{mM}^{495nm} = 1.881$ (1 cm light path).

Table 28. Assay for alcohol dehydrogenase.

1.	Place 950 μl of 0.1 M glycine pH 10.0, 2.5 mM NAD^+ in a cuvette.
2.	Add 50 μl of 1 M ethanol, mix and equilibrate the solution in a spectrophotometer at a temperature of 25°C.
3.	Add 0.5 ml of appropriately diluted sample.
4.	Measure the change in absorbance at 340 nm.
5.	Calculate the alcohol dehydrogenase activity using $\epsilon_{mM}^{495nm} NAD^+ = 6.22$.

4.2 Secretion

E. coli does not naturally secrete high levels of protein. However, several eukaryotic polypeptides have been successfully secreted into the periplasm, and a few into the medium, by *E. coli* (*Table 24*). Expression levels are low (<1% of total *E. coli* protein) compared with the levels achieved by intracellular expression; but the extent of purification necessary is less than that required for cytoplasmic products.

A method for the purification of β-endorphin secreted into the medium by *E. coli* (43) is given in *Table 25*. To confirm that the β-endorphin was truly secreted into the medium and had not leaked from the periplasm the activities of the periplasmic marker enzymes β-lactamase (47; *Table 26*) and alkaline phosphatase (48; *Table 27*) were assayed. After purification of the recombinant polypeptides in the medium by gel filtration and reverse-phase h.p.l.c., amino acid composition and N-terminal sequence were analysed. The latter results indicated heterogeneity at the N-termini, but the signal sequence had been removed from all the peptides. The heterogeneity was probably indicative of proteolysis (42).

Secretion of a fusion protein, Protein A-insulin-like growth factor-1 (IGF-1), from

E. coli has been achieved (28). This fusion protein was designed both for secretion and to allow affinity purification (*Table 11*). The *Staphylococcus aureus* Protein A signal sequence is recognized and cleaved by *E. coli*, and the protein A-IGF is secreted into the medium. Purification is achieved using IgG-Sepharose and the eluted fusion protein is cleaved with hydroxylamine, pH 9.0 to release the IGF.

When secretion into the periplasm is being estimated, assays of the periplasmic marker enzymes are used to assess the efficiency of spheroplast formation. In addition, the activity of a cytoplasmic enzyme, such as alcohol dehydrogenase (49), (*Table 28*) is assayed to check for cell lysis.

The maximum expression level achieved in the examples listed in *Table 23* is about 0.02% (42) which is equivalent to 2 mg/l of culture medium. Thus, while secretion from *E. coli* overcomes insolubility and facilitates purification, further development is required to improve yields. It is of interest to note that a secretion level of 1% total cell protein is considered to be adequate for the commercial production of proinsulin (51).

5. CONCLUDING REMARKS

A large variety of protocols are described in this chapter on the methods required to recover active soluble proteins from insoluble aggregates in *E. coli*. The unique structure of each protein appears to necessitate a specific solubilization and refolding protocol, which must be determined empirically.

With one or two exceptions, the purification protocols outlined have been performed on an analytical scale, using 50 g wet weight of cells or less. If scale-up of solubilization and refolding is required for production purposes, certain problems are apparent.

Processes requiring high concentrations of urea or guanidine are not only expensive, but generate large amounts of waste denaturant for disposal. A major problem however, is the fact that many of the processes are complex and therefore can prove difficult to scale-up, e.g. reversible citraconylation of lysine residues and refolding of multisubunit proteins such as IgG.

The removal of non-protein contaminants from recombinant polypeptides has not been considered. If the polypeptides are to be administered to animals or ultimately to be used in human therapy then removal of LPS is essential. There have been two recent reviews of this subject (51,52).

If a eukaryotic protein is synthesized in *E. coli*, are the structure and conformation of that protein identical to those of the authentically produced molecule? In certain instances, the answer to this question is no. Direct expression can produce molecules with unnatural N-terminal methionine residues. Also *E. coli* does not perform certain post-translational modifications characteristic of eukaryotic cells, such as acetylation, amidation and glycosylation. However, acetylation and amidation have been successfully performed *in vitro* on purified recombinant proteins (1).

Analytical techniques such as circular dichroism and X-ray crystallography can be used to probe the conformation of refolded and soluble recombinant proteins. The limited results available to date are encouraging. For example, the circular dichroism spectra of refolded prochymosin (53) and secreted human growth hormone (42) are not significantly different from their authentic counterparts. Also, refolded *E. coli* β-globin incorporated into haemoglobin, has been crystallized. X-ray diffraction analysis to 2.8 Å resolution reveals slight differences between authentic and mutant recombinant products; these differences being attributable to the engineering changes (23). Although there are problems associated with the purification of eukaryotic polypeptides from *E. coli*, it is being used as a production system for several therapeutic proteins (1).

6. ACKNOWLEDGEMENTS

I would like to thank Tim Harris and Peter Lowe for helpful discussions and for their criticisms of the manuscript. I am particularly grateful to Margaret Turner for preparing the typescript. The author would also like to thank all those who have granted permission for their data to be reproduced in this chapter.

7. REFERENCES

1. Marston,F.A.O. (1986) *Biochem. J.*, **240**, 1.
2. Harris,T.J.R. (1983) In *Genetic Engineering*. Williamson,R. (ed.), Academic Press, London, UK, Vol. 4, p. 127.
3. O'Farrell,P.H., Polisky,B. and Gelfand,D.H. (1978) *J. Bacteriol.*, **134**, 645.
4. Caulcott,C.A. and Rhodes,P.M. (1986) *Trends Biotechnol.*, **4**, 142.
5. Carrier,M.J., Nugent,M.E., Tacon,W.C. and Primrose,S.B. (1983) *Trends Biotechnol.*, **1**, 109.
6. Caulcott,C.A., Lilley,G., Wright,E.M., Robinson,M.K. and Yarranton,G.T. (1985) *J. Gen. Microbiol.*, **131**, 3355.
7. Yarranton,G.T., Wright,E., Robinson,M.K. and Humphreys,G.O. (1984) *Gene*, **28**, 1293.
8. Wright,E., Humphreys,G.O. and Yarranton,G.T. (1986) *Gene*, in press.
9. Wetzel,R. and Goeddel,D.V. (1983) In *The Peptides*. Gross,E. and Meienhofer,J. (eds), Academic Press Inc., New York, Vol. 5, p.1
10. Shine,J., Fettes,I., Lan,N.C.Y., Roberts,J.L. and Baxter,J.D. (1980) *Nature*, **285**, 456.
11. Goeddel,D.V., Kleid,D.G., Bolivar,F., Heyneker,H.L., Yansura,D.G., Crea,R., Hirose,T., Kraszewski,A., Itakura,K. and Riggs,A.D. (1979) *Proc. Natl. Acad. Sci. USA*, **76**, 106.
12. Burgess,R.R. and Jendrisak,J.J. (1975) *Biochemistry*, **14**, 4634.
13. Harris,T.J.R., Patel,T., Marston,F.A.O., Little,S., Emtage,J.S., Opdenakker,G., Volckaert,G., Rombauts,W., Billiau,A. and De Somer,P. (1986) *Mol. Biol. Med.*, **3**, 279.
14. Schoner,R.G., Ellis,L.F. and Schoner,B.E. (1985) *BIO/TECHNOL.*, **3**, 151.
15. Witholt,B., Boukhout,M., Brock,M., Kingma,J., van Heerikhuizen,H. and de Leij,L. (1976) *Analyt. Biochem.*, **74**, 160.
16. Taylor,G., Hoare,M., Gray,D.R. and Marston,F.A.O. (1986) *BIO/TECHNOL.*, **4**, 553.
17. Laemmli,U.K. (1970) *Nature*, **227**, 680.
18. Marston,F.A.O., Lowe,P.A., Doel,M.T., Schoemaker,J.M., White,S. and Angal,S. (1984) *BIO/TECHNOL.*, **2**, 800.
19. Szoka,P.R., Schreiber,A.B., Chan,H. and Murthy,J. (1986) *DNA*, **5**, 11.
20. Bennett,A., Rhind,S.K., Lowe,P.A. and Hentschel,C.C.G. (1984) *U.K. Patent* GB2140810A.
21. Allen,G., Paynter,C.A. and Winther,M.D. (1985) *J. Cell Sci. Suppl.*, **3**, 29.
22. Belagaje,R.M., Mayne,N.G., Van Frank,R.M. and Rutter,W.J. (1984) *DNA*, **3**, 120.
23. Nagai,K., Perutz,M.F. and Poyart,C. (1985) *Proc. Natl. Acad. Sci. USA*, **82**, 7252.
24. Lee,J.M. and Ullrich,A. (1984) *European Patent Application No.* 0128733.
25. Shen,S.-H. (1984) *Proc. Natl. Acad. Sci. USA*, **81**, 4627.
26. Hostomsky,Z., Smrt,J. and Paces,V. (1985) *Gene*, **39**, 269.
27. Offensperger,W., Wahl,S., Neurath,A.R., Price,P., Strick,N., Kent,S.B.H., Christman,J.K. and Acs,G. (1985) *Proc. Natl. Acad. Sci. USA*, **82**, 7540.
28. Uhlen,M. and Nilsson,B. (1986) Abstracts of the Engineering Foundation 3rd Conference on Recovery of Bioproducts, Uppsala, Sweden, p 20.
29. Sassenfeld,H.M. and Brewer,S.J. (1984) *BIO/TECHNOL.*, **2**, 76.
30. Builder,S.E. and Ogez,J.R. (1985) *US Patent No.* 4511502.
31. Konrad,M.W. and Lin,L.S. (1984) *US Patent No.* 4450103.
32. Vogel,T., Weisgraer,K.H., Zeevi,M.I., Ben-Artzi,H., Levanon,A.Z., Rall,S.C.,Jr, Innerarity,T.L., Hui,D.Y., Taylor,J.M., Kanner,D., Yavin,Z., Amit,B., Aviv,H., Gorecki,M. and Mahley,R.W. (1985) *Proc. Natl. Acad. Sci. USA*, **82**, 8696.
33. Winkler,M.E., Blaber,M., Bennett,G.L., Holmes,W. and Vehar,G.A. (1985) *BIO/TECHNOL.*, **3**, 990.
34. Cabilly,S., Riggs,A.D., Pande,H., Shirely,J.E., Holmes,W.E., Rey,M., Perry,L.J., Wetzel,R. and Heyneker,H.L. (1984) *Proc. Natl. Acad. Sci. USA*, **81**, 3273.

35. Gray,P.W., Aggarwal,B.B., Benton,C.V., Bringman,T.S., Henzel,W.S., Jarnett,J.A., Leung,D.W., Moffat,B., Ng,P., Svederesky,L.P., Palladino,M.A. and Medwin,G.E. (1984) *Nature*, **312**, 721.
36. Dowbenko,D.J., Bell,J.R., Benton,C.V., Groopman,J.E., Nguyon,H., Vetterlein,D., Capen,D.J. and Laskey,L.A. (1985) *Proc. Natl. Acad. Sci. USA*, **82**, 7748.
37. Hartman,J.R., Gelles,T., Yavin,Z., Bartfield,D., Kanner,D., Aviv,H. and Gorecki,M. (1986) *Proc. Natl. Acad. Sci. USA*, **83**, 7142.
38. Talmadge,K. and Gilbert,W. (1982) *Proc. Natl. Acad. Sci. USA*, **79**, 1830.
39. Zemel-Dreasen,O. and Zamir,A. (1984) *Gene*, **27**, 315.
40. Lord,S.T. (1985) *DNA*, **4**, 33.
41. Henning,U., Cole,S.T., Bremer,E., Hindernach,I. and Schaller,H. (1983) *Eur. J. biochem.*, **136**, 233.
42. Hsiung,H.M., Mayne,N.A. and Becker,G.W. (1986) *BIO/TECHNOL.*, **4**, 991.
43. Nagahari,K., Kanaya,S., Monakata,K., Aoyagi,Y. and Mizushima,S. (1985) *EMBO J.*, **4**, 3589.
44. Oka,T., Sakamoto,S., Miyoshi,K.-I., Fuwa,T., Yoda,K., Yamasaki,M., Tamura,G., Miyake,T. (1985) *Proc. Natl. Acad. Sci. USA*, **82**, 7212.
45. Gray,G.L., Baldridge,J.S., McKeown,K.S., Heyneker,H.L. and Chang,C.N. (1985) *Gene*, **39**, 247.
46. Jacobs,P., Cravador,A., Loriau,R., Brockly,F., Colau,B., Churchana,P., Van Elsen,A., Herzog,A. and Bollen,A. (1985) *DNA*, **4**, 139.
47. Bush,K. and Sykes,R.B. (1984) In *Methods in Enzymatic Analysis IV*. Bergmeyer,H.U. (ed.), Verlag Chemie, GmBH, p. 280.
48. Bretaudiere,J.-P. and Spillman,T. (1984) In *Methods in Enzymatic Analysis IV*. Bergmeyer,H.U. (ed.), Verlag Chemie, GmbH, p. 75.
49. Wagner,F.W., Burger,A.R. and Vallee,B.L. (1983) *Biochemistry*, **22**, 1857.
50. Emerick,A.W., Bertolani,B.L., Ben-Bassat,A., White,T.J. and Konrad,M.W. (1984) *BIO/TECHNOL.*, **2**, 165.
51. Sofer,G. (1984) *BIO/TECHNOL.*, **2**, 1035.
52. Sharma,S.K. (1986) *Biotechnol. Appl. Biochem.*, **8**, 5.
53. Sugrue,R., Lowe,P.A., Marston,F.A.O., Pain,R. and Freedman,R.B. (1987) in preparation.

8. APPENDIX

Host-vector combinations used for expression

Polypeptide expressed	Mode of expression	E. coli strain	Plasmid	Reference
AIDS p. 24 *gag*	Direct	294	p24 DE p24 De Δ *Hin*D III	36
Apolipoprotein E	Direct	c600	pTV 170 pTV 194	32
Human Calcitonin-gly	Fusion	E103S	pMG	20
β-endorphin	Fusion	RR1	pβ-gal pβ-gal-end	10
β-endorphin	Secretion	RR1 N99	pNM101	43
Enkephalin	Fusion	CSR603	pRE31	26
Epidermal growth factor (Urogastrone)	Secretion	C600 YK537	pTA1529	44
Fibrinogen A α-chain	Secretion	JM105	p116.9	40
β-globin	Fusion	Q413	pLc IIFx- β-globin (*nic⁻*)	23
Bovine growth hormone	Direct	RV308	pCZ101	14

Bovine growth hormone	Fusion	HB101	pTEBGH pSBBGH	19
Human growth hormone	Secretion	RV308	pOmpA-hGH2	42
Human growth hormone	Secretion	294	pPreHGH 207-2 p APH 1	45
Hepatitis B virus pre S2	Fusion	JM83	pWS3	27
IgG heavy chain	Direct	W3110	pγCEA trp 207-7	34
IgG light chain	Direct	W3110	pKCEA trp 207-1	34
IgG light chain	Secretion	HB101	pRI 12	39
Insulin A-chain	Fusion	294	pIA1	11
Insulin B-chain	Fusion	D1210	pIB1	11
Preprourokinase	Direct	MM294	pULB1135	46
Prochymosin	Direct	HB101	pCT 70	18
Proinsulin	Fusion	JM103	pTac/PI plac 239/PI	25
Proinsulin	Secretion	HB101 PR13	p287.47 p241.1947 p241.CB15 p234.CB16	38
Tissue plasminogen Activator	Direct	E103S	pMG178	13

CHAPTER 5

Production and purification of polyclonal antibodies to the foreign segment of β-galactosidase fusion proteins

SEAN B.CARROLL and ALLEN LAUGHON

1. INTRODUCTION — EXPRESSION VECTORS FOR β-GALACTOSIDASE FUSION PROTEINS

The expression of cloned eukaryotic genes in *Escherichia coli* has greatly facilitated the study of a large number of proteins of basic research and therapeutic interest. When the expression of a native, unfused protein is unsatisfactory, the expression of proteins or parts of proteins as hybrid proteins fused to *E. coli* polypeptides such as β-galactosidase has often been more successful. Furthermore, fusion proteins may be more easily purified by chromatographic procedures established for β-galactosidase. Eukaryotic proteins expressed as hybrid products have been useful for studying the immunodominant regions of surface antigens (1), the function of recombinant polypeptides (2), and for the development of immunological probes to study previously undetected antigens (3–6) and the expression of variant protein subunit forms (7), and for the isolation and verification of DNA clones recovered from expression libraries (8–10). The expression vector technology has developed to the point where virtually any coding region may be expressed at a significant level in *E. coli* as a hybrid product and a variety of biochemical procedures can be employed to isolate the hybrid product for use in functional studies or as an immunogen. The fusion of a foreign polypeptide to β-galactosidase appears to significantly enhance the stability of that polypeptide in *E. coli*. Protein stability, rather than promoter strength, appears to be the most important factor in recombinant protein expression in bacteria.

   This chapter describes the use of two proven vector systems for the expression of cloned genes as proteins fused to *E. coli* β-galactosidase and techniques for the isolation of the fusion polypeptides and production and purification of polyclonal antibodies specific for the foreign segment of the β-galactosidase fusion. The vectors described are the λgt11 system developed by Young and Davis (8) and the pUR plasmid-based system developed by Rüther and Müller-Hill (11). The phage vector has become the system of choice for isolating genes by using antibody probes to screen cDNA libraries and the plasmid system has proven to be a simpler and more efficient system for the expression of characterized cloned DNA. The procedures described in this chapter will be most useful to investigators who have isolated λgt11 clones using antibodies and want to purify and manipulate the expressed fusion protein and by investigators who want to express DNA cloned by other methods.

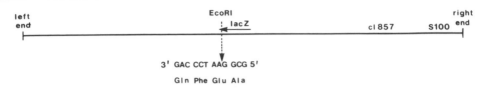

Figure 1. Structure of λgt11. *Eco*RI cleaves within a glutamine codon that is seventeen codons from the 3' end of the *lac*Z coding region (8).

1.1 λgt11

The λgt11 expression vector has been described in detail in a previous chapter in this series (12). The basic features of the system are outlined in *Figure 1*. The phage contains the *lac*Z gene with a unique *Eco*RI cloning site. Insertion of foreign DNA sequences at the *Eco*RI site results in the loss of β-galactosidase activity. The chromogenic substrate 5-bromo-4-chloro-3-indolyl β-D-galactoside (X-gal) is used to detect the presence (blue plaques) or absence (colourless plaques) of enzyme activity. When a foreign protein coding region is fused in register with the *lac*Z open reading frame, the synthesis of a foreign protein β-galactosidase hybrid protein results. In addition, the phage encodes a temperature-sensitive repressor (cI857) and is defective in lysis due to an amber mutation (S100) such that large quantities of phage encoded products, including β-galactosidase fusion proteins, accumulate in cells after induction by a shift from 32°C to 42°C. The phage can be propagated lytically in the amber suppressor-containing host, RY1090, or maintained as a lysogen in the strain RY1089.

It is not the authors' intention to describe protocols for generating fusion protein constructions in λgt11, since a detailed chapter covering these methods has already appeared in this series (12). We will describe methods for screening and purifying λgt11 fusion proteins applicable to both clone verification and the generation of antisera to fusion proteins.

1.2 pUR plasmid vectors

In many cases, smaller sizes and simpler restriction maps make it easier to assemble the desired recombinant constructions in plasmids rather than in phage. Rüther and Müller-Hill (11) have built a useful series of plasmids, pUR290, 291 and 292, for the purpose of expressing foreign proteins as β-galactosidase hybrids in *E. coli* (*Figure 2*). Four unique restriction sites have been introduced to the 3' end of the *lac*Z coding region (*Figure 2B*) (a second *Cla*I site is contained within the vectors in addition to the *Cla*I site at the 3' end of the *lac*Z gene). The positions of the inserted restriction sites have been shifted with respect to the *lac*Z coding region in each of these vectors such that any foreign coding region can be inserted into one of the vectors in the same frame as *lac*Z.

Unlike λgt11, pUR-encoded β-galactosidase fusion proteins usually retain enzymatic activity. Apparently the 18 carboxy-terminal β-galactosidase amino acid residues absent in λgt11 fusions are critical for enzyme activity. In our experience, the foreign segments of β-galactosidase fusion proteins are also more stable in *E. coli* when expressed in pUR than in λgt11, perhaps indicating that the conformation of β-galactosidase influences the folding of the foreign protein segment.

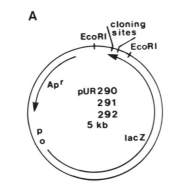

B

```
EcoRI
▼
Glu Phe Gln Leu Ser Ala Gly Arg Tyr His Tyr Gln Leu Val Trp Cys Gln Lys
GAA TTC CAG CTG AGC GCC GGT CGC TAC CAT TAC CAG TTG GTC TGG TGT CAA AAA TAA LacZ
```

```
                   BamHI   SalI          PstI   HindIII ClaI
                      ▼      ▼             ▼      ▼      ▼
TGG TGT CAA AAA GGG GAT CCG TCC ACC TGC AGC CAA GCT TAT CGA TGA         pUR290

TGG TGT C       GG GGA TCC GTC GAC CTG CAG CCA AGC TTA TCG ATG         pUR291

TGG TGT CA      G GGG ATC CGT CGA CCT GCA GCC AAG CTT ATC GAT         pUR292
```

Figure 2. Structure of pUR290, 291 and 292 plasmids. **A.** Location of cloning sites at the 3' end of the *lacZ* coding region. **B.** Sequence of the pUR cloning sites in all three frames at the 3' end of *lacZ*. The sequence of wild-type *lacZ* from the *Eco*RI site to the end of the coding region is shown above (11).

The pUR plasmids also contain the portion of pBR322 containing an origin of replication and the β-lactamase gene that confers ampicillin resistance. Expression of *lacZ* is repressed by maintaining these plasmids in a host, 71-18 (Δ*(lac pro)F' lacI^q lacZ* Δ*M15 pro$^+$ supE*), that overproduces lac repressor due to the *lacI^q* allele. β-galactosidase synthesis is induced with isopropyl β-D-thiogalactopyranoside (IPTG).

2. CONSTRUCTION AND SCREENING OF β-GALACTOSIDASE FUSIONS

There are three different starting points from which one approaches the use of β-galactosidase fusions depending upon the project objectives. These starting points are as follows.

(i) One has cloned a DNA sequence without any molecular characterization of the encoded product. One wants to obtain an antibody in order to study the gene product.

(ii) One has an antibody to a protein(s) and has isolated a putative DNA clone by expression library screening (e.g. λgt11). One then wants to verify the clone by showing that antibodies purified using the clone identify a specific antigen.

(iii) One has a characterized cDNA but wants antibodies because the protein is of low abundance or hard to purify or because one wants to produce region-specific or subunit-specific antisera. This latter approach is far more direct than screening a group of monoclonal antibodies and is much easier than isolation of peptide fragments by enzymatic or chemical cleavage.

Regardless of how one obtains a DNA clone, sequencing the clone first will reveal the location of any open reading frames and convenient restriction sites. DNA sequence analysis allows the prediction of the molecular weight of the fusion protein and aids in assessing the degree to which the protein is degraded. Then, one may proceed with the construction of gene fusions (if applicable), the isolation of fusion proteins and production of specific antibodies.

Gene fusions may be constructed without knowing the sequence of the foreign DNA segment. The foreign DNA is fused to *lacZ* in each of the possible three reading frames and the synthesis of a fusion protein larger than β-galactosidase is detected by SDS polyacrylamide gel electrophoresis (PAGE). There are potential problems with this approach. Usually, without a complete DNA sequence the boundaries of the coding region of a gene are not known, making it necessary to guess in choosing a restriction site for the fusion junction. To circumvent this problem, build fusions at several restriction sites, so that one construction should include most of the coding region. A second problem that we have encountered is the presence of two overlapping open reading frames in a single gene. In the case of the *Antennapedia* gene of *Drosophila*, DNA sequence analysis was crucial in determining which of two open reading frames encoded a protein *in vivo* (13). Finally, proteolysis of fusion proteins occurs *in vivo* in *E. coli* and in many cases the major fusion protein product is not full length, confusing the interpretation of fusion constructs made without the knowledge of the cloned DNA sequence.

2.1 Construction of λgt11 fusions

A complete protocol for cloning cDNAs in λgt11 has been described in an earlier chapter in this series by Huynh, Young and Davis (12). The bacterial strains RY1088, RY1089 and RY1090 that are required for constructions in the λgt11 system are available through the American Type Culture Collection, 12301 Parklawn Drive, Rockville, MD 20852, USA. 8mer, 10mer or 12mer *Eco*RI linkers are available commercially (New England Biolabs), and are used to ligate the ends of a given restriction fragment such that the coding region is ligated in-frame into the *Eco*RI site of λgt11. We have found it useful to insert linkered DNA fragments into the *Eco*RI site of a convenient plasmid such as pUC18 or pEMBL18 as an intermediate step in constructing λgt11 fusions.

2.2 Construction of pUR fusions

Insert foreign DNA into *Bam*HI, *Sal*I, *Pst*I, *Hin*dIII or *Cla*I sites in pUR290, 291 or 292 using naturally occurring restriction sites or by adding the appropriate restriction site in the form of a synthetic DNA linker. If possible, direct the orientation of the foreign DNA insert by generating two different cohesive ends (e.g. *Bam*HI and *Hin*dIII ends).

2.2.1 *Preparation of vector DNA*

The percentage of clones containing foreign insert DNA is increased dramatically by treating the ends of vector DNA with calf intestinal phosphatase (CIP) prior to ligation. Removal of 5' phosphates from the ends of vector DNA prevents intramolecular ligation. Because RNA competes effectively as a substrate for alkaline phosphatase, it is important that the pUR plasmid DNA be RNA-free.

(i) Prepare DNA by standard methods (14) and purify twice by equilibrium density centrifugations in 50% w/w CsCl (14).

(ii) Cleave 1−5 μg of the DNA with the chosen restriction endonuclease at a concentration of 100 μg DNA/ml.

(iii) Upon completion of the digest, add 10 units of CIP (Boehringer) and incubate for 15 min at 37°C.

(iv) Purify the linear pUR DNA by electrophoresis in a 0.8% low melting temperature agarose gel (14).

2.2.2 *Preparation of foreign DNA insert*

Cleave 1−5 μg of foreign DNA with the appropriate restriction enzyme and purify the desired restriction fragment by agarose gel electrophoresis. If the addition of DNA linkers is necessary, first make the DNA blunt-ended after restriction endonuclease cleavage. Generate blunt ends by repairing recessed 3′ ends with DNA polymerase I Klenow fragment or by removing extended 3′ ends with the 3′ to 5′ exonuclease activity of T_4 DNA polymerase (14). After ligation of linkers to the blunt-ended fragment (14), generate cohesive ends by cleaving the linker DNA with the appropriate restriction endonuclease. Recover the desired DNA fragment after fractionation by agarose gel electrophoresis.

2.2.3 *Ligation and transformation of pUR fusions*

Ligate approximately 0.1 μg of purified, phosphatased pUR DNA to an equal molar amount of purified foreign insert DNA in a 10 μl ligation reaction. Use the ligation mixture to transform competent *E. coli* strain 71-18 (15), plating cells on 1XYT plates (8 g tryptone, 5 g yeast extract, 5 g NaCl, 15 g agar per litre) containing 50 μg/ml ampicillin.

2.3 **Screening of λgt11 fusions**

2.3.1 *Screening phage DNA for foreign inserts*

After ligation and *in vitro* packaging plate the phage on RY1090 in top agar containing X-gal and IPTG (12). Plaque purify phage from colourless plaques (indicating the presence of a foreign insert). Prepare phage DNA (12) and digest with *Eco*RI to detect

Table 1. Screening λgt11 lysogens for fusion proteins.

1.	Grow overnight cultures of lysogens in NZCYM[a] at 30°C.
2.	Dilute the overnight cultures 1:100 into 2 ml of NZCYM and grow to a density of 4×10^8 cells/ml at 30°C.
3.	Add IPTG to 1 mM and shift the cultures to a 45°C waterbath for 15 min.
4.	Incubate the induced cultures for 2 h at 37°C and harvest the cells by centrifugation in 1.5 ml microcentrifuge tubes for 1 min.
5.	Lyse the pelleted cells in 200 μl of SDS PAGE sample buffer[b] and heat to 100°C for 5 min.
6.	Vortex briefly and clear the lysates by centrifugation for 5 min in a microcentrifuge.
7.	Fractionate 25 μl of each of the supernatants by electrophoresis on a 7.5% SDS polyacrylamide gel.

[a]NZCYM contains 10 g of NZ-amine, 5 g of NaCl, 5 g of yeast extract, 1 g of casamino acids, 1 g of $MgSO_4$ per litre, adjusted to pH 7.5 with 2 M NaOH.
[b]SDS PAGE buffer is 80 mM Tris-HCl pH 6.9, 2% SDS, 0.1 M dithiothreitol, 0.004% bromophenol blue.

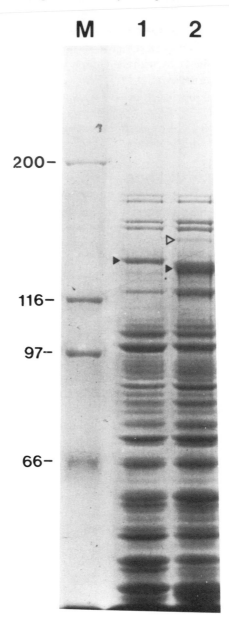

Figure 3. Two examples of anomalous fusion protein behaviour. A fragment from an *Antennapedia* cDNA clone was inserted into the λgt11 vector in two different reading frames. The larger major product (**lane 1**) is actually the incorrect reading frame, but because of an exceptionally high GC content and abundant proline residues, a product was made that migrated with the predicted molecular weight of the *bona fide* reading frame (solid arrow, **lane 1**). The second reading frame (**lane 2**) is the correct frame, the major product (**lane 2**, solid arrow) is also of the predicted size. However, this protein is not the full-length fusion. A larger product of much lower abundance is detectable by the gel stain (**lane 2**, open arrow), by anti-β-galacto-sidase blotting (data not shown), and by blotting with an antibody probe for the C-terminal region of the protein (data not shown). The high proline content of the fusion protein caused a 10−15 kd increase in the apparent molecular weight, leading to a tentative conclusion that the low-mobility degradation product was full-length.

the insert fragment and with a restriction endonuclease that cleaves within the insert to determine insert orientation.

2.3.2 *Screening for λgt11 fusion proteins*

Package candidate fusion phage and infect RY1089 at 32°C to generate lysogens (12). Lysogens will grow at 32°C but not at 42°C due to the temperature-sensitive repressor. Lysogens can be cultured and prepared for analysis by SDS-polyacrylamide gel electrophoresis as described in *Table I*. An example of two λgt11 fusion protein profiles on an SDS-polyacrylamide gel is shown in *Figure 3*.

2.4 Screening of pUR fusions

2.4.1 *Screening plasmid DNA for foreign inserts*

Pick ampicillin-resistant transformants with sterile toothpicks into 1 ml cultures of 2XYT containing 50 μg/ml ampicillin and grow overnight at 37°C. Prepare plasmid DNA from the cultures using the rapid boiling method described in Maniatis *et al.* (14). Digest plasmid DNAs with a restriction endonuclease that cleaves at sites within the insert DNA and in the flanking pUR DNA to detect the presence and orientation of foreign DNA cloned in the vector.

2.4.2 *Screening for pUR fusion proteins*

Dilute overnight cultures of candidate clones 1:100 into 2XYT containing 50 μg/ml ampicillin and grow at 37°C for 2 h. Harvest and lyse cells and fractionate lysate by electrophoresis as described in Section 2.3.2 and *Table 1*. An example of a pUR fusion protein profile on an SDS-polyacrylamide gel is shown in *Figure 4*.

2.5 Insert size versus yield

Size of the foreign protein segment is an important consideration in constructing β-galactosidase fusions. Stability (and therefore yield) of fusion proteins generally decreases as the length of the foreign protein segment increases. In many cases it may be desirable to use short protein segments in fusion proteins. This approach has been demonstrated to be effective for raising specific antibodies with as little as 200 bp of foreign DNA encoding antigen (16). One potential problem with using short segments is that the small ratio of foreign protein mass to β-galactosidase mass may result in proportionally low titres of foreign protein-specific antibodies in immunized animals. Affinity purification of antibodies is also made less efficient by the low capacity of affinity columns built with short fusion proteins. One way around these problems is to increase the molar ratio of foreign segment to β-galactosidase. This is accomplished by ligating multiple tandem copies of a DNA fragment in-frame to *lac*Z. *Figure 5* shows the result of ligating one versus five copies of a coding segment from the *ftz* gene of *Drosophila* into pUR291. The yield of 1-mer fusion protein is about ten times that of the 5-mer fusion.

2.6 Verifying fusion protein integrity

There are several problems that can arise in interpreting the expression of a fusion protein in *E. coli*. First, if a DNA fragment has been inserted into a vector without

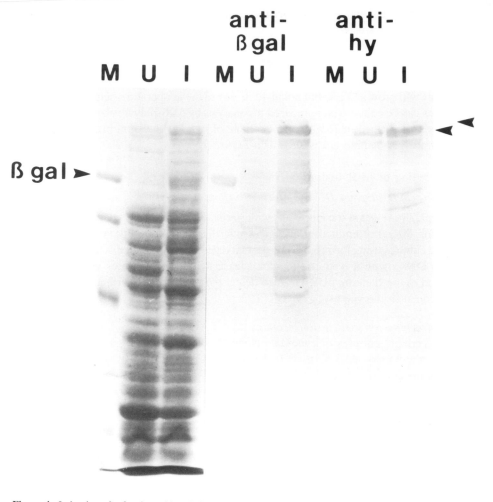

Figure 4. Induction of a β-galactosidase-hairy fusion protein. Triplicate panels show identical lanes of 7.5% SDS polyacrylamide gels loaded with protein markers (**M**) or extracts from uninduced (**U**) or IPTG-induced (**I**) 71-18 cells harboring a fusion plasmid between β-galactosidase and the *hairy* gene of *Drosophila*. The left-hand set of three lanes shows the pattern of Coomassie-stained protein, the centre set shows a Western blot stained with affinity-purified rabbit anti-β-galactosidase antibody (anti-β-gal) and the right-hand set shows a Western blot stained with affinity-purified rabbit anti-*hairy* antibody (**anti-hy**). For both Western blots, alkaline phosphatase-conjugated goat anti-rabbit IgG was used as a secondary antibody (*Table 1*). The fusion plasmid is pUR290 ligated to the 1011 bp open reading frame of a cDNA derived from transcripts of the *hairy* gene. The left-hand arrow points to β-galactosidase (116 000 mol. wt) that is stained by anti-β-galacto-sidase antibodies but not by anti-*hairy* antibodies. The lower arrow on the right points to the 160 kd β-galacto-sidase-hairy fusion protein in the induced extracts that stains with anti-β-galactosidase and anti-*hairy* antibodies. The fusion protein is still detectable at lower levels in uninduced cells indicating that repression of fusion protein synthesis by *lacI*^{q} is not complete. The upper arrow on the right points to a faint band in the induc-ed lanes stained with anti-β-galactosidase and anti-*hairy* antibodies. The band is 5000 daltons larger than the 160 000 mol. wt band indicating that the major product is at least 5000 daltons smaller than the full length fusion protein. Extracts were prepared as described in Section 2.4.2. Affinity purification of antibodies was according to Section 4.2. The *hairy* cDNA clone used for the fusion construction was kindly provided by C.Rushlow.

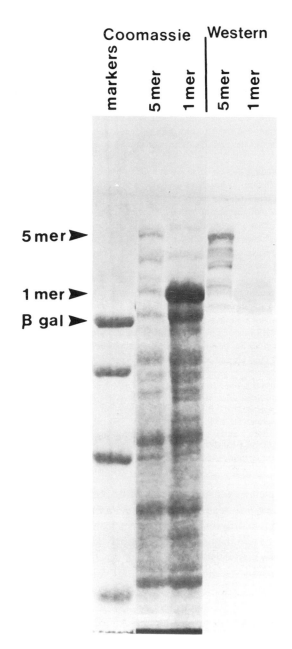

Figure 5. Fusion protein size and stability. Duplicate 7.5% SDS polyacrylamide gels were stained with Coomassie brilliant blue or transferred to nitrocellulose by Western blotting and stained with affinity-purified antibody to the fusion insert. The lanes were loaded with IPTG-induced extracts from 71−18 cells harboring pUR291-*ftz* homeobox fusion plasmids. 1mer lanes were from plasmids containing a single copy of a 268 bp *ftz* homeobox sequence fused to *lacZ*. 5mer lanes were from a plasmid containing 5 tandem, in-frame copies of the 268 bp *ftz* homeobox sequence fused to *lacZ*. Arrows point to the positions of the corresponding 1mer and 5mer *ftz* fusion proteins. Extracts were prepared according to Section 2.4.2, and Western blots performed as described in *Table 2*. The yield of fusion proteins from SDS extracts of cells was approximately 50 μg/ml for the *ftz* 1mer and 5 μg/ml for the *ftz* 5mer.

Table 2. Western blotting to detect antibodies to individual antigens.

1.	Prepare fusion protein lysates as described in Section 2 and *Table 1* for loading onto an analytical 7.5% SDS-polyacrylamide gel. Apply high molecular weight protein standards including β-galactosidase as size markers in adjoining lanes.
2.	After electrophoresis, transfer the proteins to nitrocellulose using an electro-blotting apparatus (e.g. Hoefer Transphor TE 41) following manufacturers instructions.
3.	After transfer, temporarily stain the nitrocellulose blots with Ponceau S stain diluted 1:10 in distilled water for 3 min, and rinse the blot with distilled water to destain. The stained blot will indicate the efficiency of transfer and the location of sample lanes, mark the blot with a pencil to indicate lane borders.
4.	Block protein binding sites on the nitrocellulose by immersing the blot in PBS[a] containing 3% (w/v) bovine serum albumin overnight at 4°C or 2 h at 37°C.
5.	After blocking, blot strips are incubated for $2-3$ h with specific antibodies diluted in PBS containing 5% (v/v) normal goat serum. Affinity purified antibodies should be effective at $0.5-5.0$ μg/ml and whole antisera at a minimum dilution of 1:50. After incubation, wash the blots with two changes each of large volumes of PBS, BBS-Tween[b] and PBS successively involving at least 60 min (10 min/wash). Extensive washing is important to minimize background staining; shorter washing times may suffice for some applications.
6.	Apply the secondary antibody, goat anti-rabbit IgG alkaline phosphatase conjugates, diluted to 1 μg/ml (1:1000 usually) in PBS containing 5% normal goat serum for $2-3$ h at room temperature. After incubation, wash the blots with PBS, BBS-Tween, and TBS[c] successively over 60 min including at least two washes with each buffer.
7.	After the final TBS wash, immerse the blots in freshly prepared alkaline phosphatase substrate buffer[d]. Once the colour has developed, rinse three times in distilled water. Let the blot stand in water for 10 min and then air dry on a paper towel.

[a]PBS is phosphate-buffered saline; 10 mM KPO_4, 150 mM NaCl pH 7.2.
[b]BBS-Tween is borate-buffered saline with Tween 20; 0.1 M boric acid, 0.025 M sodium borate, 1 M NaCl, 0.1% (v/v) Tween 20, pH 8.3.
[c]TBS is Tris-buffered saline; 50 mM Tris-HCl pH 7.5, 150 mM NaCl.
[d]Alkaline phosphatase substrate buffer contains 2 ml of Nitro Blue Tetrazolium (Sigma) at 1 mg/ml in 50 mM Na_2CO_3 pH 9.5, 2 ml of 0.5 M Na_2CO_3 pH 9.5, 15.5 ml dH_2O, 0.1 ml of 1 M $MgCl_2$ and 0.2 ml of bromo-chloro-indolylphosphate (Sigma) dissolved at 5 mg/ml in dimethyl sulphoxide.

knowledge of its sequence, a fusion protein may be observed that is of significant length, but is not in the *bona fide* reading frame. An example is shown in *Figure 3*, where fusion of a cDNA in two different reading frames from the same restriction site resulted in the accumulation of two major products of nearly identical size. One fusion migrated with an apparent molecular weight of 135 kd, but was in the wrong reading frame (*Figure 3*, lane 1). This underscores the desirability of obtaining sequence information prior to fusion constructions.

Second, degradation of a fusion protein can occur *in vivo*, leading to the accumulation of a major product that is not full-length. An example is shown in *Figure 3* (lane 2) of a fusion where the major product is approximately 10 kd·shorter than the full-length product. Sequence analysis of this unusual cDNA revealed that a third type of anomalous behaviour was being exhibited by this particular clone. The major fusion product, though incomplete, migrated with the predicted mobility of the full length protein. This was probably due to an unusually high proline content that increased the apparent molecular weight of the protein.

To reduce the chances of misleading results, we recommend that one employ a Western blot analysis of the fusion protein lysate with anti-β-galactosidase antibody to detect any minor products present (see *Figure 3*, middle panel) and confirm all results with complete sequencing of the insert DNA. A second antibody specific for epitopes expected to be present on the fusion protein will also aid clone verification. Because of the high-level expression of the fusion proteins, we recommend immunoenzymatic detection of antigens by Western blotting (*Table 2*) due to its safety and speed.

3. FUSION PROTEIN EXPRESSION AND PURIFICATION

Depending upon the vector employed, the level of fusion protein expression, and its solubility, a variety of methods may be applied in order to isolate pure intact protein for immunological purposes. On some occasions, enough native fusion protein may be readily purified for biochemical studies on the activity of the foreign segment. In this section, we detail procedures for purifying fusion proteins with a variety of expression characteristics. The schemes are designed to obtain 1 − 10 mg of fusion protein per purification run. These quantities should suffice for the hyper-immunization of medium-sized animals (e.g. rabbits) with fusion proteins with any sized insert. While, in general, it would be best to use a full-length cDNA clone for producing an antiserum with the highest activity for the native protein, we have had success in raising antisera to fusion proteins with small inserts (< 10 kd). Antisera to small inserts may be especially useful as functional or topological probes (see Section 2.5).

3.1 Induction of fusion proteins

The maximum level of fusion protein expression is partly a function of the induction conditions employed. For the two vector systems described here, induction is straightforward and we have observed little variation between proteins in their induction characteristics.

3.1.1 *Induction of λgt11 lysogens*

For large-scale purification of λgt11-derived fusion proteins, cure the lysogen of the pMC9 (*lacI*q) ampicillin resistance plasmid. Normally, removal of *lac* repression may lead to selective pressure for mutations of the fusion protein; however, for a 3- to 4-fold increase in yield, a cured lysogen may be passaged for a limited period of time. Keep permanent stocks of the pMC9-containing lysogen to avoid clone loss through negative selection. Pass the lysogen through several cycles of growth at 32°C without drug selection in NZCYM (see footnote a of *Table 1* for composition of NZCYM). Test for loss of drug resistance by replica plating lysogens on NZCYM plates ± ampicillin. The cured lysogen will produce more protein when devoid of the *lacI*q product than the uncured lysogen will when under full induction with IPTG.

Grow a culture of the lysogen overnight at 32°C. Dilute the stationary culture 1:100 and grow for 2 h at 32°C with good aeration. One litre of culture typically yields 2 − 20 mg of fusion protein. Induce the culture by rapidly bringing the temperature to 42°C by immersion in a pre-heated 44°C water bath. Monitor the temperature of the culture with a thermometer over the induction period, about 15 min. Return the culture to 37°C and continue growth for 2 − 3 h.

3.1.2 *Induction of pUR fusion clones*

Grow an overnight culture in 2XYT containing 50 μg/ml ampicillin. Dilute the overnight culture 1:100 in 2XYT + 50 μg/ml amp and grow at 37°C for 2 h. A 0.5 litre culture typically yields 5–50 mg of fusion protein. Add IPTG to 0.5 mM and continue growth at 37°C for 2 h.

3.2 **Cell harvest and extraction of fusion proteins**

Chill the induced cells in an ice-bath and add phenylmethylsulphonylfluoride (PMSF) to 1 mM to reduce proteolysis. Centrifuge the cells at 5000 g for 5 min. Resuspend the cell pellets in one of the following extraction buffers.

(i)   For preparative gel electrophoresis (Section 3.3.1), resuspend in 1/12 volume of SDS-PAGE sample buffer containing 1.5% SDS with vigorous vortexing. Heat the extract at 100°C for 5 min.

(ii)   For purification by either immunoaffinity chromatography (Section 3.3.2) or gel filtration chromatography (Section 3.3.3), resuspend the cells in 1/50 volume of a buffer containing 50 mM $NaPO_4$ pH 7, 10 mM 2-mercaptoethanol, 10 mM EDTA, and 1 mM PMSF at 4°C. Add lysozyme to 0.2 mg/ml and incubate on ice for 30 min. Freeze the extract at −70°C for 30 min. Thaw the extract rapidly in a 37°C water bath, not allowing the temperature to rise above 4°C and sonicate it thoroughly using five 20-sec bursts of a microprobe with intermittent cooling to maintain the temperature at 4°C. Add NaCl (5 M) to 0.5 M, mixing thoroughly, then centrifuge the extract at 13 000 g for 10 min to clarify. Keep the extract chilled at 4°C for all subsequent procedures.

(iii)   For APTG-agarose chromatography (Section 3.3.4), resuspend the cells in 1/50 volume of 0.2 M Tris-HCl pH 7.6, 10 mM MgOAc, 5% glycerol, 10 mM 2-mercaptoethanol, 0.25 M NaCl, and 1 mM PMSF on ice. Add lysozyme to 0.2 mg/ml for 30 min on ice and quick freeze at −70°C for 30 min. Sonicate and clarify the extract as in (ii) above, omitting the NaCl addition.

(iv)   Some proteins are not extracted well by the procedures given in (ii) and (iii) above. Fusion proteins may remain in the cell debris pelleted by centrifugation after sonication. We have solubilized some of the more difficult fusion proteins by urea extraction of the cell debris. Extract the cell debris by suspension in about 20 ml of urea buffer (8 M urea, 0.5 M Tris-HCl pH 7.9, 0.5 M NaCl, 1 mM EDTA, 30 mM 2-mercaptoethanol, and 1 mM PMSF) per litre of original cell culture. Vortex the suspension vigorously and centrifuge at 13 000 g for 10 min. Dialyse the soluble extract against 50 mM Tris-HCl pH 7.9, 0.5 M NaCl, 10% glycerol twice (25-50 volumes), first at room temperature for 2–3 h, then overnight at 4°C. Cenrifuge the extract at 13 000 g for 10 min. This urea extract may be enriched for fusion protein which can then be purified by any of the methods given in Section 3.3. An example of the enrichment provided by the urea extraction procedure is shown in *Figure 6*.

3.3 **Fusion protein purification—choosing a method**

For the widest array of immunological studies, we have found that it is best to obtain as large a quantity of native protein as possible. This is best achieved by using the

UREA SDS SALT APTG

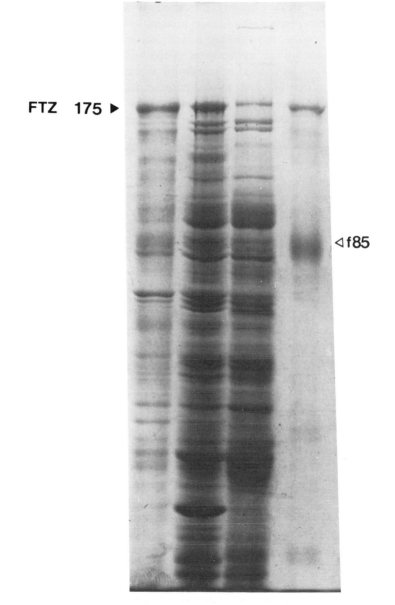

FTZ 175 ▶

◁f85

Figure 6. Extraction and purification of a β-galactosidase fusion protein. A comparison of the yield and purity of a λgt11-*ftz* fusion lysogen that was extracted with either 8 M urea, 1.5% SDS, or 50 mM NaPO₄, pH 7. The equivalent of 200 μl of original culture volume of each extract was applied to a 7.5% SDS-polyacrylamide gel and was stained with Coomassie blue. The urea extract is enriched for the 175 kd full-length fusion protein (FTZ, solid arrow). Protein from the NaPO₄ extract was further purified by APTG-agarose chromatography (for right lane). APTG-agarose purified material consisted mainly of full-length protein and one major β-galactosidase 85 kd degradation product (f85, open arrow). Figure is from ref. 6, copyright MIT press.

classical chromatography techniques detailed in Section 3.3.3 and has been most successful with fusion proteins produced using the pUR system. The other methods have been utilized when the yield, solubility, or stability of a fusion protein has been problematic. For example, preparation of fusion proteins by an SDS-PAGE method should be considered a last resort, not a first approach simply due to its ease, because SDS denatured proteins are not the immunogens of choice for raising anti-native protein antisera. If antisera are to be used primarily for Western blots, SDS denatured immunogens may be sufficient for this limited purpose. Immunoaffinity purification can be performed efficiently on a moderate scale, unfortunately, the eluted protein is usually irreversibly denatured by the reagents required to disrupt antibody-antigen complexes. APTG chromatography can yield pure, soluble protein, but it is not very efficient and is very poor for use with proteins of low abundance or stability. The choice of method can be readily identified after pilot extractions and purifications are analysed.

3.3.1 *Preparative SDS-PAGE of fusion proteins*

Preparative acrylamide gels may be utilized at any stage of the fusion protein purification scheme to obtain intact, but denatured immunogen. SDS lysates of whole cells prepared as in Section 3.2 above may be loaded after clarification by centrifugation directly onto slab gels. The protein from about 15 ml of cells that is solubilized in 1.25 ml of 1.5% SDS samples buffer can be accommodated by one slab gel having a cross-sectional area of 2.0 cm^2. Enriched extracts obtained by partial purification may afford the purification of 1 mg or more of intact fusion protein per slab gel.

To identify the region of the gel containing the fusion protein, soak the gel after electrophoresis in chilled 0.1 M KCl. The cold K$^+$ precipitates with the SDS in gel bands, giving a white precipitin line. The fusion protein precipitin line can be cut out of the gel with a razor blade, obviating the need for fixing and Coomassie staining of the gel band or parallel gel lanes.

3.3.2 *Immunoaffinity purification of fusion proteins*

Extracts prepared as in Section 3.2 (ii), (iii) or (iv) may be applied directly to affinity columns containing anti-β-galactosidase antibody without any previous fractionation (e.g. removal of nucleic acids). Thus, for proteins of low abundance or stability, the fusion protein may be rapidly purified from dilute extracts without the degradation that may occur over longer purification schemes.

(i)   Anti-β-galactosidase columns may be prepared as described in Section 4 or purchased commercially. The repetitive yield of a column is a function of the properties of the antibody (monoclonal or polyclonal) and the strength of the eluents employed. Polyclonal antibody columns constructed as described here may be eluted more than 20 times without a significant decrease in binding capacity. A column containing 5 mg of affinity-purified polyclonal anti-β-galactosidase usually binds at least 1 mg of fusion protein.

(ii)   Load the fusion protein extract at 4°C to minimize proteolysis. Wash the columns with one column volume of PBS (see footnotes to *Table 2*) at 4°C, perform all subsequent steps at room temperature. Wash the column with BBS-Tween

Table 3. Gel filtration chromatography of fusion proteins.

1.	To the extract prepared as described in Section 3.2 (ii), add 0.1 vol of a 30% (w/v) streptomycin sulfate solution equilibrated in extraction buffer.
2.	Stir for 15 min at 4°C and centrifuge at 13 000 g for 10 min.
3.	To the supernatant, add saturated $(NH_4)_2SO_4$ pH 8.0 to between 25% and 40%, depending upon the fusion protein. Gently stir the protein extract while adding the $(NH_4)_2SO_4$ dropwise. Continue stirring for 30 min at 4°C.
4.	Centrifuge at 13 000 g for 30 min. Aspirate and discard the supernatant, extrude the residual ammonium sulphate by spinning the pellet for 1 min at 4000 g. Carefully remove the remaining solution. Dissolve the pellet using 5 ml of column buffer[a] per litre of original culture.
5.	Centrifuge this solution at 13 000 g before applying it to a 2.5 cm × 50 cm Sephacryl S-300 column equilibrated in column buffer[a].
6.	Adjust the flow rate to 1 ml/min. The elution profile of the fusion protein may be followed by using a colorimetric assay for β-galactosidase activity; however we have found that the first major elution peak at 280 nm contains the fusion protein.
7.	The fusion protein elution peak is collected in about 20 ml and may be concentrated by precipitation with $(NH_4)_2SO_4$.

[a]Column buffer is 20 mM Tris-HCl pH 7.5, 150 mM NaCl, 20 mM 2-mercaptoethanol, 1 mM PMSF. Triton X-100 may be added to 0.1% (v/v) to facilitate solubility of some proteins.

(see footnotes to *Table 2*) until the effluent is free of protein. Equilibrate with PBS. Elute the column with 4 M guanidine-HCl, 10 mM Tris-HCl pH 8.0 and collect the peak and dialyse it against PBS with several changes. Most of the protein will precipitate and can be collected by centrifugation. For immunization, resuspend the precipitate in a small volume of PBS and follow the instructions in Section 4. Re-equilibrate the column with PBS immediately after each use. Other eluents may be used, but weaker elution agents will fail to disrupt high affinity antigen−antibody complexes and the capacity of the column will be diminished as high affinity sites become occupied.

3.3.3 *Gel filtration chromatography of fusion proteins*

For most forms of chromatography, it is desirable to remove nucleic acids from protein extracts. After these steps, fusion proteins may be purified by a number of chromatographic procedures (17). The simplest procedure involves gel filtration to separate the larger fusion proteins from smaller *E. coli* polypeptides. The nucleic acid is removed and the protein within an extract is concentrated by streptomycin sulphate and ammonium sulphate precipitation (*Table 3*). Some fusion proteins can be efficiently precipitated and substantially purified by precipitation with low concentrations (25%) of ammonium sulphate. Others require higher concentrations. This may be determined on a pilot scale by testing a range of $(NH_4)_2SO_4$ concentrations. Sephacryl (registered trademark, Pharmacia) S-300 is a good separation medium for β-galactosidase fusion proteins. β-galactosidase is a tetrameric protein (monomer mol. wt 116 kd) such that fusion proteins will elute at >460 kd. A 2.5 cm × 50 cm column equilibrated in column buffer is suitable for chromatography of a 5 ml extract from one litre of cell culture. A profile of a typical fusion protein purification run on S-300 and SDS-PAGE analysis of peak fractions is presented in *Figure 7*.

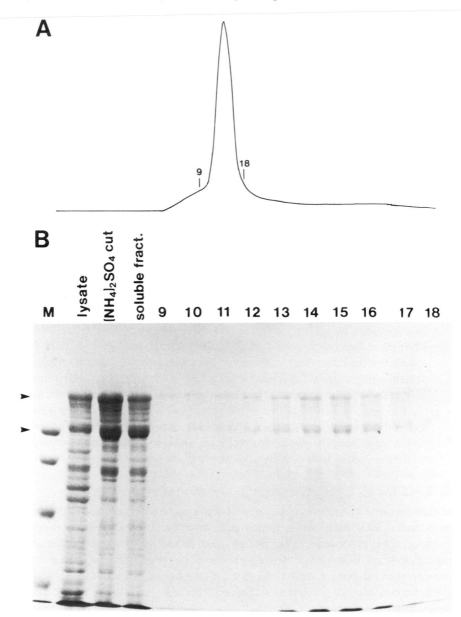

Figure 7. β-galactosidase fusion protein purification. **A**. Elution profile of the β-galactosidase-*hairy* fusion protein chromatographed on Sephacryl S300 as described in Section 3.3.3. Tracing is of absorbance at 280 nm. A 5 ml extract from a 500 ml culture of IPTG-induced cells was loaded on a 2.5 × 50 cm S300 column. After approximately 40 ml of void volume, 2 ml fractions were collected. The fusion protein peak is contained within fractions 9 to 18. **B**. Coomassie-stained 7.5% SDS polyacrylamide gel of cell extracts and S300 peak profile. Arrows at the left indicate the positions of the β-galactosidase-*hairy* fusion protein (upper) and β-galactosidase (lower). Lanes were loaded as follows: **M**, marker proteins; **lysate**, 20 μl out of 10 ml crude lysate [3.2 step (ii)]; **(NH₄)₂SO₄ cut**, 20 μl out of 5 ml resuspended 25% (NH₄)₂SO₄ pellet (3.3.3 and *Table 3*); **solution fraction**, 20 μl out of 5 ml from soluble fraction of resuspended 25% (NH₄)₂SO₄ pellet (3.3.3 and *Table 3*); **9** to **18**, 20 μl samples from 2 ml fractions collected from S300 elution peak.

Table 4. APTG affinity chromatography.

1.	Streptomycin sulphate and ammonium sulphate precipitate the extract prepared as in Section 3.2 (iii) according to Section 3.3.3 and *Table 3* steps 1−4.
2.	Resuspend the ammonium sulphate precipitate in 5 ml/l original culture volume of 10 mM Tris-HCl pH 7.6, 0.25 M NaCl, 10 mM MgCl$_2$, 1 mM EDTA, 10 mM 2-mercaptoethanol, 1 mM PMSF, and 0.1% (v/v) Triton X-100.
3.	Dialyse the extract against 100 volumes of this same buffer with one change over 3 h.
4.	Centrifuge the extract to remove precipitates and apply to a 10 ml APTG-agarose (Sigma) column.
5.	Wash the column with 3−5 volumes of the above buffer with Triton X-100, then with 2−3 volumes of the same buffer without Triton X-100, until the effluent is essentially free of protein.
6.	Elute the column with 0.1 M sodium borate pH 10.0.
7.	Precipitate the eluted protein with ammonium sulphate added to 50% saturation. Resuspend the precipitate in a convenient buffer, PBS is best for immunization.

3.3.4 *Amino phenyl thiogalactopyranoside (APTG) affinity chromatography*

As first developed by Steers (18) and utilized for fusion protein chromatography by Germino *et al.* (2), β-galactosidase derived polypeptides can be isolated on the basis of their affinity for the lactose analogue APTG. In practice, this method yields material of excellent purity, but is not very efficient and is ineffective for purification of proteins of low abundance (19). An example of an APTG-agarose purified protein preparation is shown in *Figure 6*.

3.3.5 *Summary of fusion protein purification methods*

The features of the different fusion protein purification schemes described in this section are summarized in *Table 5*. Depending upon the initial concentration and stability of the fusion protein and the experimental objective, these four different approaches may be employed. All of the chromatographic procedures may be scaled up to accommodate the purification of larger quantities of protein.

4. POLYCLONAL ANTIBODY PRODUCTION AND PURIFICATION

Using the methods described in Section 3, fusion proteins may be obtained in a variety of forms and in differing amounts. In our experience, for the widest variety of applications, it is best that an antiserum be raised against a more native form of the antigen injected in moderate amounts. The choice between polyclonal and monoclonal antibodies is not clear cut. Each can have superior performance for some applications. We recommend that polyclonal antibodies be produced initially or in conjunction with a monoclonal production effort mainly because one is virtually assured of getting a reagent that is functionally antigen-specific in some immunoassays. Any fusion protein that can elicit a strong specific polyclonal response is a good candidate for immunization in hybridoma protocols. The immunization schedules for different antigen forms to be injected into rabbits are given below.

4.1 **Immunization schedules**

(i)   For SDS denatured antigens obtained from gel slices, the gel should contain as much protein as can be accommodated in one ml of gel volume. This will range between 0.1 mg and 1.0 mg depending upon the stability of the fusion protein

Table 5. Comparison of fusion protein purification methods.

Procedure	Purity of antigen	Yield	Degree of native structure	Comments
Preparative SDS-PAGE	Highest intact fusion protein to β-galactosidase ratio, degradation products not isolated, little E. coli protein contamination	0.1–1.0 mg per gel	Poor, antigen is SDS denatured	Easy, rapid procedure
Immunoaffinity purification	All β-galactosidase derived products isolated, no E. coli contaminants	1–2 mg per column run	Poor, but better than SDS treatment, antigen is mostly insoluble precipitate	Easy, rapid procedure
Gel filtration	Some contamination with E. coli polypeptides	1–10 mg per column run	Soluble, native protein	Longer procedure, proteolysis sometimes a problem
APTG-agarose chromatography	Mostly large β-galactosidase derived products, little E. coli protein contamination	1–5 mg per column run	Mostly soluble protein (pH denaturation variable)	Longer procedure, inefficient yield of low abundance proteins, proteolysis sometimes a problem

and whether it has been enriched before electrophoresis. Acrylamide is not well tolerated by the animal and a minimal volume should be injected. Macerate the gel slice by passing it several times through a syringe. Mix five parts complete Freund's adjuvant (Gibco) with four parts gel (v/v) using two Luer-lock tip syringes with a stainless steel connector. (This connector can be made by brazing two 18 gauge steel needles together near their base.) Emulsify the antigen completely so that the suspension is of a firm consistency and stable and inject the restrained or anaesthetized rabbit (5–6 lb) at several sites intramuscularly. 14 and 21 days later, repeat the injections using antigen emulsified in incomplete adjuvant. On day 28, bleed the animal (~20 ml is a safe volume) from the ear vein. Blood may be collected weekly so long as the animal is healthy and additional boosts of antigen may be given about every 6–8 weeks.

(ii)   For antigens derived from chromatography procedures so that they are at least partially soluble, mix from 0.2–2.0 mg of intact fusion protein in 1 ml of saline or PBS with 1.25 ml of complete Freund's adjuvant and emulsify completely as above. Inject the restrained rabbit at several sites subcutaneously. Repeat the injections with 0.2–1.0 mg of antigen on days 14 and 21 in incomplete adjuvant and begin bleeding on day 28. Monitor bleeds weekly for specific antibody titre and boost rabbits with 0.2–1.0 mg of antigen when the antibody titre begins to taper off. When satisfactory amounts of antisera have been obtained and while the titre is still high, exsanguinate the rabbit under anaesthesia by heart puncture.

4.2 Antiserum purification and assay

For many applications, it is necessary or desirable to utilize affinity purified antibodies specific to an antigen. The procedures below detail methods for fractionating the whole antiserum against the fusion protein to obtain antibodies specific for the foreign portion of the hybrid. The general scheme that we describe is outlined in *Figure 8*.

4.2.1 *Antiserum preparation from whole rabbit blood*

Collect the blood into a 50 ml centrifuge tube. Apply a wooden applicator stick around the wall of the tube to free any clots that have formed and place the stick in the clot forming in the centre of the tube. Place the blood in a refrigerator (4°C) overnight. The next day, remove the clot attached to the applicator stick and centrifuge the remaining liquid at 13 000 *g* for 10 min. The serum obtained should be yellow with little or no trace of hemolysis. To the serum add 20% NaN_3 (w/v) (highly toxic!) to a final concentration of 0.02% and freeze until needed at −20°C.

4.2.2 *Absorption of the anti-β-galactosidase fraction of antisera*

In order to measure the amount of hybrid specific antibody initially present in the serum, and to purify hybrid specific antibody that is free of anti-β-galactosidase reactivity, the anti-fusion protein antiserum is first applied to a β-galactosidase affinity column. The column is prepared using 5–7 mg of purified *E. coli* β-galactosidase (Sigma) dialysed against PBS following the procedure detailed in *Table 6*.

The antiserum is purified following the procedure in *Table 7*. Since the anti-hybrid

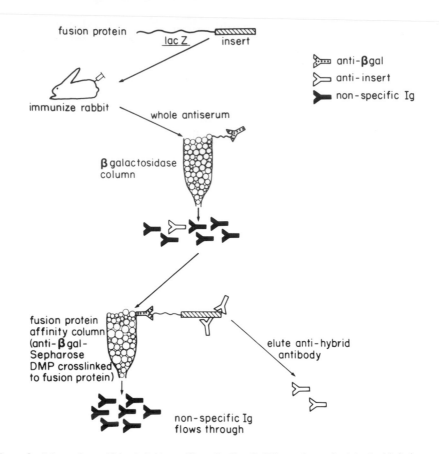

Figure 8. Scheme for purifying hybrid-specific antibodies. Rabbits are immunized (top) with fusion protein isolated by any of several methods. The whole antiserum is first passed over a β-galactosidase-Sepharose column to remove most of the anti-β-galactosidase antibodies. The flow-through of this column is applied to a column containing fusion protein that has been covalently bound to the resin by dimethylpimelimidate-2 HCl coupling of immobilized anti-β-galactosidase to the β-galactosidase portion of the fusion protein. Bound antibodies are eluted and assayed for their specificity for the fused portion of the hybrid, after a final absorption on β-galactosidase (not shown).

fraction of the antiserum is in the effluent of the column, this fraction is collected through the initial PBS wash without significant losses. The eluted anti-β-galactosidase fraction is a good specificity control for experiments utilizing the anti-hybrid antibodies and can be used to construct fusion protein affinity columns (see below).

4.2.3 *Purification of the antibodies specific for the foreign segment of the hybrid*

The procedure described in this section is the most reliable method we have devised for purification of anti-hybrid antibodies. We have found it to be applicable to even the most problematic fusion proteins. As described, it is aimed at the purification of 1−2 mg of hybrid specific antibody per run. The method circumvents solubility and yield problems by immobilizing the fusion protein immediately from a crude extract

Table 6. Coupling of proteins to CNBr-activated Sepharose 4B.

1.	All procedures must be performed in a safe chemical hood, cyanogen bromide can be lethal. All vessels and instruments that contact CNBr should be decontaminated by wiping or soaking in dilute NaOH and left overnight in the hood to allow the volatile gas to dissipate.
2.	Wash the Sepharose 4B (Pharmacia) with five volumes of chilled, distilled water on a coarse grained scintered glass funnel. Prepare at least $1-2$ ml of Sepharose 4B for every 10 mg protein to be coupled or every $1-2$ ml of protein solution.
3.	Suspend the washed Sepharose in an equal volume of 2.5 M potassium phosphate buffer pH 12.2[a] in a beaker with gentle stirring and immersed in an ice bath.
4.	In a separate vessel and with the hood closed as much as possible, dissolve 1 g CNBr in 1 ml of acetonitrile per 10 ml of gel to be activated.
5.	Add the CNBr solution dropwise to the gently stirring gel over a period of 2 min. Continue stirring for 8 min more.
6.	Pour the activated Sepharose onto the scintered glass funnel and wash the cake carefully with 10 volumes of cold distilled water followed by 10 volumes of cold PBS[b].
7.	Remove filter from hood and add activated Sepharose cake to protein solution, agitate slowly overnight. The protein solution must not contain Tris or free amino groups and should be dialysed to equilibrium in PBS.
8.	The next day, collect the uncoupled filtrate on the scintered glass funnel and save it to measure the uncoupled protein concentration. Suspend the Sepharose 4B in an equal volume of 1 M ethanolamine-10 mM Tris-HCl, pH 8.5 for 2 h at 4°C to block the remaining protein-reactive sites. Finally, wash and equilibrate the coupled Sepharose in $PBS-0.02\%$ NaN_3 and store at 4°C. The resin is stable for more than one year and will retain most of its activity after many elution cycles.

[a]2.5 M potassium phosphate buffer pH 12.2 is composed of 353.4 g K_3PO_4 and 145.4 g K_2HPO_4 per litre.
[b]PBS is described in the footnotes to *Table 2*.

Table 7. Affinity chromatography for purification of antibodies.

1.	Pour the antigen affinity resin into a column such that the bed height is sufficient to slow the flow rate to 1 ml/min or less.
2.	Equilibrate and pack the column in PBS, then pre-elute the column to remove non-covalently bound antigen. Elute with full-strength elution buffer (e.g. 4 M guanidine-HCl or 0.5 M acetic acid or 1 M glycine-HCl pH 2.8) to prevent contamination of antibody eluate with free antigen. Monitor the column effluent at 280 nm using absorbance monitor/recorder. When the peak has completely eluted, wash the column with $3-5$ volumes of PBS to re-equilibrate it.
3.	Apply $10-20$ ml of antiserum to the 5 mg β-galactosidase column or to a 5 ml cross-linked fusion protein column (*Table 6*). Collect the flow through in PBS[a], then wash the column with BBS-Tween[a] until the effluent is free of protein. Equilibrate the column with PBS. Elute the bound antibody using 4 M guanidine-HCl to achieve most complete elution. Dialyse the collected peak against 100 volumes of PBS[a] with at least three changes allowing at least 3 h of dialysis per change. Re-equilibrate the column with $3-5$ volumes of PBS.
4.	To calculate the antibody yield, measure protein from dialysate by a Biuret assay, or measure A_{280}. An A_{280} of 1.4 = 1 mg/ml IgG. Store IgG in 0.02% azide and freeze at -20°C in aliquots. Avoid refreezing.

[a]The composition of these buffers is given in the footnotes to *Table 2*.

using an antigen-specific resin that can be activated to covalently cross-link the fusion protein (6,20) (*Table 8*).

(i)   Prepare the anti-β-galactosidase column by coupling $5-10$ mg of affinity purified anti-β-galactosidase (purified as described in *Table 7*) to 5 ml of Sepharose 4B that has been activated with CNBr as described in *Table 6*.

Table 8. Preparation of a cross-linked fusion protein affinity column.

1.	Prepare a 5 ml Sepharose 4B column containing 5−10 mg of affinity purified anti-β-galactosidase antibody as in *Table 6*.
2.	Equilibrate the column in PBS[a] at 4°C. Apply an enriched extract of induced lysogen or pUR-bearing clone containing at least 3−5 mg of intact fusion protein to the column at 4°C. Wash the column with 1 volume of PBS at 4°C then transfer to room temperature and apply 3 volumes of BBS-Tween[a], 2 volumes of 0.1 M sodium borate pH 8.2, and 2 volumes of 0.2 M triethanolamine pH 8.2 to remove unbound protein and prepare for cross-linking of the bound fusion protein to the immobilized anti-β-galactosidase.
3.	To cross-link the protein, remove the resin from the column by flushing with 10 volumes of 0.2 M triethanolamine that is also 50 mM dimethylpimelimidate-2 HCl (Pierce) adjusted to pH 8.2. Gently rock the cross-linking mixture for 45 min at room temperature.
4.	After cross-linking, gently centrifuge the resin for a few seconds in a table-top clinical centrifuge to settle the beads. Aspirate the cross-linking solution, and wash the beads once in 10 volumes of 20 mM triethanolamine pH 8.2. Resuspend the beads in 2 volumes of PBS and repour the column in PBS.
5.	Before attempting affinity purification of anti-fusion protein antibodies, pre-elute the column as described in *Table 7*.
6.	The column should be stored at 4°C in PBS[a] + 0.02% NaN$_3$. The resin is stable for more than one year and retains most of its antibody-binding activity after many repeated cycles.

[a]The composition of these buffers is described in the footnotes to *Table 2*.

(ii)   Apply the fusion protein-containing extract as described in *Table 8*. The fusion protein extract (see Section 3) can be in any buffer and need not be depleted of nucleic acids or contaminating proteins. If a particular fusion protein is soluble in a non-denaturing extraction buffer (e.g. 0.1 M KPO$_4$ pH 7) it may be applied directly to the column.

(iii)   Wash and cross-link the column (*Table 8*).

(iv)   Pre-elute the column with elution buffer and re-equilibrate in PBS as described in *Table 7*. Apply the flow-through from the β-galactosidase column, wash, and elute the hybrid antibody fraction using the same procedure as in *Table 7*. Dialyse the antibody against several changes of PBS and assay its protein content.

(v)   Using a higher sensitivity on the column absorbance monitor, apply the dialysed antibody fraction from (iv) once more to the β-galactosidase affinity column equilibrated in PBS to remove any residual anti-β-galactosidase antibody. The flow-through of this column should be entirely specific for the foreign segment of the fusion protein.

4.2.4 *Western blot assay of antibody specificity*

In order to determine the specificity of the anti-hybrid antibody at any stage in its purification, it is important to discriminate between antibody to the β-galactosidase portion of the fusion protein and antibody to the foreign segment of the hybrid. The easiest way to do so is to assay the activity of the antibody fraction on a Western blot (21) where fusion protein and β-galactosidase are presented in adjacent lanes and the relative binding to the antigens may be observed.

(i)   Prepare lysates of induced and uninduced cells carrying the expression vector as described in Section 2.

(ii)   Blot the samples after SDS-PAGE as described in *Table 2*.

(iii)   Apply the antibody fractions and assay as described in *Table 2*.

(iv)   A typical purified antibody preparation prepared as described in this section will exhibit no binding to β-galactosidase or to *E. coli* antigens, and will react with all forms of the fusion protein containing the antigenic determinants of the foreign segment (*Figure 4*, far right panel).

5. ACKNOWLEDGEMENTS

The experiments with fusion proteins were conducted in the laboratory of Dr Matthew Scott. We are grateful for his support. Some of the general immunological methods are derived from protocols established in the laboratory of Dr B.David Stollar (Tufts University, Boston, MA) and were learned by S.B.C. during his graduate training there. We thank Dr John Tamkun for a critical reading of the chapter and for insightful discussions on several different aspects of fusion protein technology. We thank Cathy Inouye for preparation of the manuscript. This work was supported by grant # HD 18163 from the NIH and grant # NP502 from the ACS to Matthew P.Scott. A.L. was supported by an American Cancer Society Postdoctoral Fellowship; S.B.C. was supported by Damon Runyon-Walter Winchell Cancer Fund Fellowship DRG-659 and NIH Postdoctoral Fellowship GM-09756.

6. REFERENCES

1. Collins,W.E. *et al.* (1986) *Nature*, **323**, 259.
2. Germino,J., Gray,J.G., Charboneau,H., Vanaman,T. and Bastia,D. (1983) *Proc. Natl. Acad. Sci. USA*, **80**, 6848.
3. White,R.A.H. and Wilcox,M. (1984) *Cell*, **39**, 163.
4. Beachy,P.A., Helfand,S.L. and Hogness,D.S.(1985) *Nature*, **313**, 545.
5. DiNardo,S., Kuner,J.M., Theis,J. and O'Farrell,P.H. (1985) *Cell*, **43**, 59.
6. Carroll,S.B. and Scott,M.P. (1985) *Cell*, **43**, 47.
7. Paul,J.I., Schwarzbauer,J.E., Tamkun,J.W. and Hynes,R.O. (1986) *J. Biol. Chem.*, **261**, 12258.
8. Young,R.A. and Davis,R.W. (1983) *Proc. Natl. Acad. Sci. USA*, **80**, 1194.
9. Young,R.A. and Davis,R.W. (1983) *Science*, **222**, 778.
10. Schwarzbauer,J.E., Tamkun,J.W., Lemischka,I.R. and Hynes,R.O. (1983) *Cell*, **35**, 421.
11. Rüther,U. and Muller-Hill,B. (1983) *EMBO J.*, **2**, 1791.
12. Huynh,T.V., Young,R.A. and Davis,R.W. (1984) In *DNA Cloning: A Practical Approach*, Glover,D. (ed.), IRL Press, Oxford, Vol. I, p. 49.
13. Laughon,A., Boulet,A.M., Bermingham,J.R., Laymon,R.A. and Scott,M.P. (1986) *Mol. Cell. Biol.*, **6**, 4676.
14. Maniatis,T., Fritsch,E.F. and Sambrook,J. (1982) In *Molecular Cloning, A Laboratory Manual*. Cold Spring Harbor Laboratory Press, Cold Spring Harbor, NY.
15. Morrison,D.A. (1979) In *Methods in Enzymology*. Wu,R. (ed.), Academic Press, NY, Vol. 68, p. 326.
16. Tamkun,J.W., DeSimone,D.W., Fonda,D., Patel,R.S., Buck,C., Horwitz,A.F. and Hynes,R.O. (1986) *Cell*, **46**, 271.
17. Fowler,A.V. and Zabin,I. (1983) *J. Biol. Chem.*, **258**, 14354.
18. Steers,E., Cuatrecasas,P. and Pollard,H.P. (1971) *J. Biol. Chem.*, **246**, 196.
19. Struck,D.K., Maratea,D. and Young,R. (1985) *J. Mol. Appl. Gen.*, **3**, 18.
20. Schneider,C., Newman,R.A., Sutherland,D.R., Asser,V. and Greaves,M.F. (1982) *J. Biol. Chem.*, **257**, 10766.
21. Towbin,H., Staehelin,T. and Gordon,J. (1979) *Proc. Natl. Acad. Sci. USA*, **76**, 4350.

CHAPTER 6

Production of monoclonal antibodies against fusion proteins produced in *Escherichia coli*

SARA E.MOLE and DAVID P.LANE

1. INTRODUCTION

The production of monoclonal antibodies against the product of a genetically identified open reading frame (ORF) opens up a wider perspective to the immunochemical and functional analysis of that product. The procedure is more complex than that described in the previous chapter for the production of polyclonal antibodies to an ORF and should clearly be seen as an additional and complementary technique rather than an alternative approach. The overall scheme is summarized in *Figure 1*. We would certainly advise any investigator to prepare polyclonal antibodies as well as monoclonals. The major benefits of monoclonal antibodies, namely their unlimited supply and defined specificity, really come into their own when the investigation of the product of the ORF has reached a more advanced stage than its simple detection. The preparation of monoclonal antibodies will facilitate the quantitative assay of the ORF product and often provides a fast route to its purification in biologically active form. The specificity of the monoclonal antibodies can also be exploited by the fine mapping of the location of their binding sites (epitopes) on the ORF product and by combining this information with the antibodies' ability to promote or inhibit the biological activity of the ORF product.

In order to raise monoclonal antibodies, sufficient quantities of the immunogen are required to elicit a strong immune response. It is not always possible to extract large amounts of the native protein. However, the cloning of the gene in a suitable bacterial vector which allows over-expression of the encoded protein, and purification of this product will allow its use as an immunogen. This system will also allow the cloning of smaller defined fragments of a gene encoding a known protein, or indeed of an unknown reading frame in order to produce monoclonal antibodies against defined regions of that product and to fine map the location of epitopes recognized by existing antibodies.

Bacterial expression vectors which are particularly suited to this technique include the pUR system (1) in which a number of discrete restriction enzyme sites are present at the 3' end of the *lac*Z gene (see Chapter 5, Figure 2). These sites exist in each of the three possible reading frames which allows any restriction fragment containing an open reading frame to be expressed as part of a fusion protein with β-galactosidase. This is advantageous since there are few bacterial proteins of greater size than β-galactosidase, and *lac*Z gene expression can be induced using isopropyl β-D-thiogalactosidase (IPTG) resulting in the abundant production of the fusion protein,

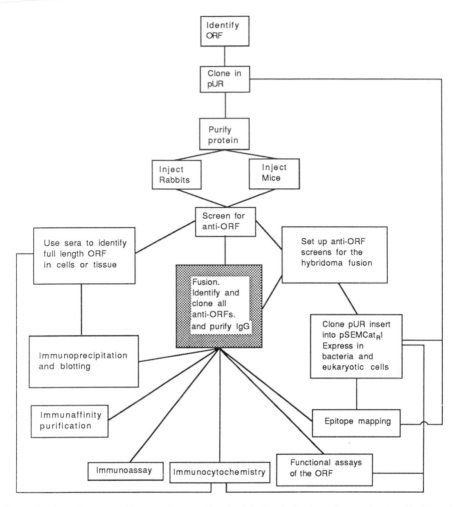

Figure 1. Flow diagram to illustrate the steps involved in the derivation of monoclonal antibodies using fusion proteins produced in *E. coli* and their potential uses.

thus facilitating the identification and isolation of the fusion protein using SDS−polyacrylamide gel electrophoresis.

Potential difficulties in the raising of monoclonal antibodies include the production of sufficient quantities of immunogen and the subsequent screening of sera for the desired immunological activity. The use of over-expressed fusion proteins can solve both these problems since purification of large amounts using either electrophoretic or chromatographic procedures is possible. Screening of the sera and of the subsequent hybridoma clones obtained can make use of radioimmunoassay (RIA) or enzyme-linked immunosorbent assay (ELISA) techniques.

A particular advantage in using the fusion protein approach in the production of monoclonal antibodies is that strong or weak immunogenic regions of the native protein may exhibit a changed immunogenicity when expressed as part of a larger fusion protein.

114

This is particularly desirable in the raising of antibodies to immunogenically silent regions of a protein. In the case of SV40 large T antigen, there are many monoclonals which recognize binding sites at the N and C termini of the native protein but few which recognize more centrally located regions. We have successfully used this approach to raise antibodies to this immunologically silent region of large T.

2. CLONING AND EXPRESSION OF GENE FRAGMENTS

Most of the methods used in this section are based on detailed protocols found elsewhere (2). New or significantly different methods required are given in *Tables 1–3*.

The choice of expression vectors such as the pUR series takes advantage of the different restriction enzyme sites available for the cloning of a gene fragment. The pUR vectors require a bacterial strain that does not express β-galactosidase in order to be able to identify *lac*Z expression resulting from the induction of expression of the vector

Table 1. Colony screening by blotting.

1.	Grid out colonies on a nitrocellulose filter laid on an L-agar plate containing 100 μg/ml of ampicillin (Sigma Chemical Company) and 500 μM of IPTG (Sigma Chemical Company) and onto a replica master plate. If possible, include negative and positive controls. Grow overnight at 37°C.
2.	Lyse the bacteria by incubating the nitrocellulose filter in chloroform-saturated vapour for 30 min.
3.	Incubate the filter in blocking buffer consisting of 25% dried milk proteins diluted 1 in 2 in phosphate-buffered saline (PBS[a]) for 30 min at room temperature.
4.	Rinse in PBS and incubate with the screening antibody[b] diluted, if necessary, in PBS containing 1% bovine serum albumin (BSA, Sigma Chemical Company), 5% fetal calf serum (FCS), for at least 1 h at room temperature.
5.	Rinse in PBS, followed by two 15 min washes in PBS containing 1% NP-40 (Sigma Chemical Company), and two 15 min washes in PBS.
6.	Incubate in pre-adsorbed second antibody[c] coupled to horse-radish peroxidase for at least 1 h at room temperature.
7.	Rinse in PBS, followed by two 15 min washes in PBS containing 1% NP-40, and two 15 min washes in PBS.
8.	Freshly dilute 50 mg of 4-chloro-1-naphthol (Aldrich), dissolved in 1 ml of ethanol, 1:100 in PBS and filter. Add hydrogen peroxide (30%) at a dilution of 1:5000 and use to stain the filter. Once colonies show up positive, rinse the filter in PBS and dry. Keep in the dark.

[a]PBS is 150 mM NaCl, 3 mM KCl, 8 mM Na$_2$HPO$_4$, 1.5 mM KH$_2$PO$_4$.
[b]The screening antibody could be monoclonal antibodies or polyclonal sera.
[c]It is advisable to pre-adsorb the second antibody with a lysed *E. coli* extract (see *Table 2*). The second antibody should be specific for the species used as host in the preparation of the screening antibody, e.g. rabbit anti-mouse immunoglobulin coupled to horse-radish peroxidase (DAKO) or goat anti-rabbit immunoglobulins, etc.

Table 2. Pre-adsorbtion of second antibody coupled to horse-radish peroxidase with lysed *E. coli* extract.

1.	Grow up a 2 ml overnight culture of the relevant *E. coli* strain (such as BMH 71-18 containing pUR290, induced for *lac*Z expression using IPTG).
2.	Transfer 1 ml to a 1.5 ml microcentrifuge tube and spin for 30 sec.
3.	Suspend in 50 μl of 5% SDS and boil for 5 min to lyse the cells.
4.	Allow to cool and dilute the suspension 1:50 in PBS containing 1% BSA, 5% FCS. Store at -20°C.
5.	Add the second antibody coupled to horse-radish peroxidase at a 1:100 dilution to the lysed cell extract. Incubate overnight at 4°C.
6.	This can be spun to pellet any immune complexes formed and the supernatant used directly.

Table 3. Preparation of samples for SDS−polyacrylamide gel electrophoresis.

1.	Grow up a 2 ml overnight culture of the positive clone in L broth containing 100 μg/ml ampicillin and 500 μM IPTG. Alternatively, if degradation of the fusion protein is a problem add the IPTG when the culture is in mid-log phase (OD_{600} of 0.5) and grow for 1−2 h.
2.	Cool on ice and transfer 1.5 ml to 1.5 ml microcentrifuge tubes.
3.	Spin for 30 sec and discard the supernatant.
4.	Wash the pellet in PBS and resuspend finally in 300 μl of 1× sample buffer.
5.	Boil for 5 min before loading 5−25 μl on the gel.

gene. Two strains have been used successfully, both of which are *lac*Z: BMH 71-18 (3); (*lac pro*)Δ *thi supE* F' *lac*I^{Q}Z$^-$ΔM15 *pro*$^+$ and F'11*rec*A (4); (*lac pro*)Δ *thi rif*A *str*A *rec*A F'*lac*I^{Q1}Z$^-$ *pro*$^+$. The main difference is the *rec*A phenotype of the second strain which should serve to minimize rearrangements occurring with construction. However, we find that fusion protein expression is greater with BMH 71-18 as the host. To avoid loss of a construct by possible rearrangements, it is therefore advisable to prepare a plasmid stock of a new construction as soon as possible.

2.1 Construction of the fusion protein expressing vector

To clone the ORF insert, carry out the following steps.

(i)   Ligate the gene fragment or ORF into the restriction site in the relevant framing (if known) of pUR.

(ii)   Transform into *Escherichia coli* which is *lac*Z and competent for DNA uptake.

(iii)   Screen the colonies obtained for successful insertion. This can be performed in two ways.

    (a) Screen for successful insertion of the DNA fragments by radiolabelling the same DNA fragment and using it as a probe. The presence of the insert, under suitable conditions, will allow hybridization of the radiolabelled probe and subsequent detection of positive colonies using autoradiography. This method detects the presence of one or more copies of the insert, in either orientation.

    (b) Screen for the presence of epitopes expressed by the cloned fragment. This method permits the identification of clones containing an insert in frame and in the correct orientation for fusion protein expression. The protocol, which makes use of existing monoclonal antibodies or polyclonal sera against the polypeptide encoded by the cloned gene fragment, is found in *Table 1*.

(iv)   Analyse bacterial extracts of positive clones by SDS−polyacrylamide gel electrophoresis (a 7.5−8.5% gel is preferable) for fusion protein production. Expression can be induced using IPTG (*Table 3*).

(v)   Check clones for the number of inserts present. This can be performed by digestion with *Eco*RI since the cutting of *Eco*RI sites flanking the polylinker containing the insert should produce a fragment (the '*Eco*RI cassette') larger by approximately 100 bases than the cloned insert if a single insert is present, and approximately twice the size if a double insert is present. If there are *Eco*RI sites within the cloned insert, then a partial *Eco*RI digest will be required to verify the number of inserts.

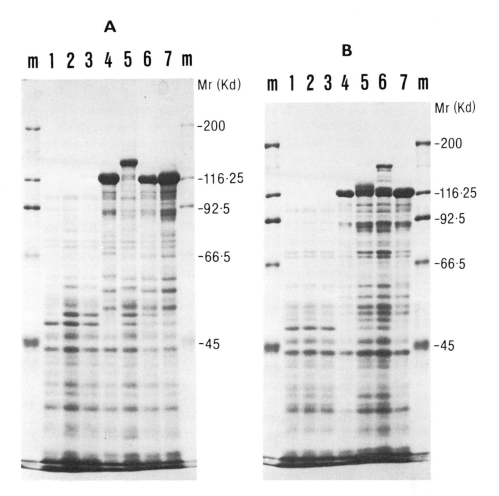

Figure 2. Coomassie blue stained SDS−polyacrylamide gels showing β-galactosidase fusion protein expression. (**A**) Bacterial host strain, BMH 71-18. **Lane M**, molecular weight (Mr) markers; **lane 1**, host, uninduced; **lane 2**, host, induced; **lane 3**, host containing pUR292, uninduced; **lane 4**, host containing pUR292, induced; **lane 5**, host containing pUR292 with SV40 *Hind*III D fragment insert (β-galactosidase-large T fusion protein, large T amino acids 271−448), induced; **lane 6**, host containing pUR290 with SV40 *Hind*III D fragment insert, induced; **lane 7**, host containing pUR291 with SV40 *Hind*III D fragment insert, induced. (**B**) Bacterial host strain, F'llrecA. **Lane M**, molecular weight (Mr) markers; **lane 1**, host, uninduced; **lane 2**, host, induced; **lane 3**, host containing pUR290, uninduced; **lane 4**, host containing pUR290, induced; **lane 5**, host containing pUR290 with SV40 *Hind*III A fragment insert (β-galactosidase-large T fusion protein, large T amino acids 448−708), induced; **lane 6**, host containing pUR291 with SV40 *Hind*III A fragment insert (β-galactosidase-VP1 fusion protein), induced; **lane 7**, host containing pUR292 with SV40 *Hind*III A fragment insert. This figure is taken from Figure 1, ref. 9, and reproduced with kind permission.

2.1.1 *Example*

A selection of the clones derived from the cloning of the *Hind*III D and *Hind*III A fragments of SV40 were analysed for *lacZ* expression using SDS−polyacrylamide gel electrophoresis. This is shown in *Figure 2*.

The high copy number of the expression vector, coupled with the induction of *lacZ* gene expression, resulted in the abundant production of the fusion proteins. This, in addition to their high molecular weight, makes them easily identifiable on the gel. It was estimated that a 1 ml IPTG-induced, overnight culture of the fusion protein expressing the SV40 *Hin*dIII D fragment contained approximately 40 μg of fusion protein.

The *Hin*dIII D fragment of SV40 encodes amino acids $271-447$ of large T antigen and is present in frame with *lacZ* in pUR292 (βgal.T.HD). The *Hin*dIII A fragment of SV40 encodes amino acids $447-708$ of large T antigen in one orientation, which is present in frame with *lacZ* in pUR290 (βgal.T.HA), and encodes amino acids $69-362$ of VP1 in the opposite orientation, present in frame with *lacZ* in pUR292 (βgal.VP1. HA).

It can be seen from the SDS$-$polyacrylamide gel analysis of the fusion protein constructions that the βgal.T.HA and βgal.VP1.HA fusion proteins appear to be partially degraded, whereas the βgal.T.HD fusion protein appears completely stable. There was no difference in the pattern of degradation observed in the case of βgal.T.HA when smaller lengths of induction time with IPTG were used, which suggests that certain cloned gene fragments, when expressed as a fusion protein construction in the bacterial host, are subjected to proteolysis very soon after they are first synthesized.

Western blotting of the βgal.T.HA fusion protein, probed with existing anti-large T monoclonal antibodies, demonstrated that the fusion protein was degraded throughout its whole length. For example, in *Figure 3*, PAb423, which recognizes an epitope located at the extreme C terminus of large T, only binds to the highest molecular weight band visible on SDS$-$polyacrylamide gel electrophoresis, the full length fusion protein. PAb204, which recognizes an epitope located between amino acids 453 and 469 (5), lights up in a pattern of bands ranging from the full length fusion protein product to polypeptides of lower molecular weight than β-galactosidase.

The solubility of the fusion proteins varies, as well as their stability. Of six fusion proteins constructed in the pUR vectors using different fragments of SV40 large T, two were found predominantly in the supernatant fraction of a lysed cell extract, three were found predominantly in the insoluble portion of the prepared cell extract and one was found in equal amounts in both portions.

3. DERIVATION OF MONOCLONAL ANTIBODIES TO FUSION PROTEINS

Monoclonal antibody producing cell lines are usually derived from rodents, such as mice or rats, showing a good immune response to an immunogen. A suspension of their spleen cells is prepared and the cells fused with a myeloma cell line. The fused cells produced thus exhibit characteristics derived from both parental cells, combining the property of unlimited cell division of the myeloma parent with the property of specific antibody production of the spleen B cell. Isolation of a clone of cells derived from the fusion of one antibody producing cell allows the production of a monoclonal antibody.

Cloning of ORFs in fusion protein expression vectors permits immunization with large amounts of pure protein, and this makes the production of monoclonal antibodies directed to sequences within that ORF a straightforward, if somewhat laborious, task. The primary practical requirements are for good tissue culture facilities and a sensitive screening assay that will distinguish antibodies directed against the ORF from those

Table 4. Purification of the fusion protein by SDS−polyacrylamide gel electrophoresis.

A. *Preparation of extract*

This procedure works for an insoluble fusion protein found in the cell pellet fraction of a lysed cell extract.

1. Grow a 150 ml overnight culture of the fusion protein in L broth containing 100 μg/ml ampicillin and 500 μM IPTG.
2. Pellet the cells by centrifugation at 2500 r.p.m. for 5 min at 4°C in a Sorvall GS-3 rotor and re-suspend the cell pellet in 10 ml of 10 mM Tris-HCl pH 8.0, 2 mM EDTA, 50 mM NaCl containing 0.25 mg/ml lysozyme.
3. Incubate at room temperature for 15 min then add Triton X-100 to 0.2% (v/v), MgCl$_2$ to 10 mM and DNase to 1 μg/ml. Incubate for 30 min at room temperature.
4. Centrifuge at 5000 r.p.m. for 5 min at 4°C in a Sorvall SS-34 rotor and suspend the cell debris fraction containing the fusion protein in 30 ml SDS−polyacrylamide gel sample buffer. Store at −20°C.

B. *Preparative gel electrophoresis*

1. Run on an SDS−polyacrylamide gel using one large preparative well.
2. Remove a small vertical strip and stain with Coomassie Blue.
3. Line up the remaining gel, and excise the region of the gel corresponding to the fusion protein.
4. Electroelute protein out of the gel slice into SDS−polyacrylamide gel electrophoresis running buffer.
5. Store in aliquots at −20°C.
6. The concentration can be estimated by comparison with known amounts of pure β-galactosidase on an SDS−polyacrylamide gel.

that recognize the vector derived sections of the fusion protein. It is the establishment of this assay that is the chief stumbling block in the procedure. Once insert specific monoclonal antibodies have been obtained they can be used to identify, quantitate and purify the product of the ORF.

3.1 Preparation of the antigen

The purification of β-galactosidase fusion proteins has been described in detail in the previous chapter. The amounts needed for immunization of mice are relatively small so all methods of preparation are suitable. Whilst material derived from preparative SDS−polyacrylamide gels may not be as immunogenic as a more native preparation, it does have the advantage of inducing a response to denaturation resistant epitopes. The protocol we follow for insoluble fusion proteins is detailed in *Table 4*. Monoclonal antibodies directed to such epitopes are often disproportionately useful in the subsequent detailed immunochemical analysis of protein antigens. Absolute purity of the immunogen is not required as only monoclonal antibodies directed to epitopes specific to the cloned insert will be selected. The previous chapter considers the purification of soluble fusion proteins in detail.

3.2 Immunization protocol

The aim of the initial immunizations is to obtain a detectable antibody response to the insert sequence and to use the resulting polyclonal sera to establish an insert-specific screening assay. For routine use, 3−6 month old female BALB/c mice are suitable. The initial two injections should be given in Freunds complete adjuvant, and subsequent

Table 5. Immunization protocol.

Day[a]	Injection	Adjuvant[b]	Test-bleed
1	–	–	Pre-bleed
3	50 μg	Complete Freunds adjuvant	–
24	50 μg	Complete Freunds adjuvant	–
34	–	–	Test-bleed
35	50 μg	Incomplete Freunds adjuvant	–
42	–	–	Test-bleed
43	50 μg	Incomplete Freunds adjuvant	–
50	50 μg	Incomplete Freunds adjuvant	–
57	–	–	Test-bleed

[a]This protocol may be continued as required.
[b]The volume of all injections is 100 μl of protein in PBS (500 μg/ml) and 100 μl adjuvant. Mix the adjuvant with the protein solution using two syringes connected by a double Luer fitting. Inject intraperitoneally.

injections in incomplete adjuvant, except for the final pre-fusion boost which should be given in the absence of adjuvant (see later). All injections can be given intraperitoneally. Mice should be immunized in groups of four to six animals to give a reserve of fusion donors should a fusion fail. A suitable protocol is given in *Table 5*. Whilst a response to β-galactosidase is usually detected after two injections, antibodies specific to the insert may not appear until much later. It is therefore worth persevering with an immunization schedule for at least seven injections before concluding that the immunogen is unsuitable.

3.3 Detection of insert-specific antibodies

It is vital to establish that antibodies specific to insert sequences are present in the sera of the immunized mice. There are a number of distinct approaches that can be taken, depending on the availability of the full length native product of the ORF. If it is known that the ORF is expressed by a tissue culture cell line or is present at reasonable levels in a particular tissue, then the reactivity of the sera with the cell line or tissue in immunocytochemical, immunoprecipitation or Western blotting procedures can be measured. In our experience of mammalian and viral ORFs, the crude polyclonal sera can be used in all three of these methods without serious background problems. Control sera should include the pre-bleed of the test mouse and hyperimmune sera directed to β-galactosidase. If nothing is known about the expression of the ORF, then an alternative strategy must be adopted that exploits the available ORF sequence. One approach, which is detailed in the previous chapter, is to remove selectively anti-β-galactosidase antibodies from the sera by immunoabsorption on a column of solid phase β-galactosidase and then to test the unbound fraction in a Western blot procedure for reaction with the fusion protein but not with β-galactosidase. An alternative approach, which is described in Section 5, is to subclone the ORF into an alternate fusion protein vector. The reactivity of the sera with the new construct either in colony blot or Western blot procedures will then confirm the presence of antibodies specific to the insert with the caveat that, following the procedure in Section 5, 16 amino acids of the C terminus of β-galactosidase are transferred to the CAT vector as part of the *Eco*RI cassette. Again, tests with the

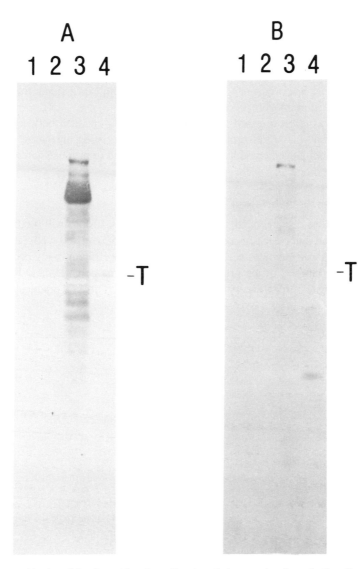

Figure 3. Western blotting of β-galactosidase large T antigen fusion proteins. **Lane 1,** *E. coli* strain BMH 71-18 containing pUR292. **Lane 2,** *E. coli* strain F'llrecA containing a β-galactosidase large T fusion protein (large T amino acids 271−448). **Lane 3,** *E. coli* strain F'llrecA containing a β-galactosidase large T fusion protein (large T amino acids 448−708). **Lane 4,** SVA31E7 cell extract containing large T antigen. **Panel A** was probed with PAb204 which binds to a site on large T between amino acids 453 and 469. **Panel B** was probed with PAb423 which binds to a site at the extreme C terminus of large T. An immunoperoxidase detection system (as described in *Table 8*) was used to visualize binding of the antibodies. This figure is taken from Figure 1, ref. 9, and reproduced with kind permission.

same control sera are required, and in addition, all sera should be checked for reactivity with the new vector alone (with and without the pUR polylinker). The convincing establishment of an anti-insert specific response by at least one of these methods is an absolute prerequisite before proceeding to the next stage.

3.3.1 *Example*

Figure 4 shows SV40-infected CV1 cells immunoprecipitated with an existing mono-clonal antibody, PAb204, in panel A and the mouse anti-fusion sera in panel B. Both specifically immunoprecipitate SV40 large T antigen demonstrating that a successful immune response had occurred against the fusion protein expressing a fragment of large T, used as the immunogen.

The fusion protein expressed a fragment of large T encoded between amino acids 271 − 448 which was not recognized by any of the existing anti-large T monoclonal antibodies tested. This method had therefore been used to produce antibodies to a pre-viously immunologically silent region of the protein.

3.4 **Setting up the hybridoma screen**

Successful fusions demand rapid, efficient screens. Most fusions will need to be screened three times, and since each fusion is plated out over 500 − 1000 wells, this means that up to 3000 separate samples need to be tested for specific antibody production. Fur-thermore, the kinetics of the growth of the hybridoma cells demand that the results of the screening test be known within 48 h of sampling. The only practical way to handle

Table 6. ELISA protocol for protein antigen.

Special equipment

1.	Plastic microtitre plates (Falcon 3912).
2.	Multichannel dispenser (Flow 8 channel 5−50 μl).
3.	ELISA plate reader (not absolutely essential).

Reagents

1.	Protein antigen solution: 0.1−1 μM in PBS.
2.	Blocking solution: 3% BSA in PBS.
3.	Wash solution: 0.1% NP-40 in PBS.
4.	Anti-globulin rabbit antibodies to mouse immunoglobulins coupled to horse-radish peroxidase (DAKO diluted 1/1000 in PBS containing 10% FCS).
5.	Substrate solution: dissolve 3'3'5'5' tetramethyl benzidine (Miles Chemicals) in dimethyl sulphoxide (Sigma Chemical Company) at a concentration of 1 mg/ml. Dilute 1/100 in PBS and filter through Whatman No. 1 paper. Finally add H_2O_2 to a concentration of 0.01%.
6.	Stop solution: 1 M H_2SO_4.

Method

1.	Prepare the microtitre plates by adding 50 μl of protein solution to each well and incubating over-night at 4°C. Remove the protein solution. Plates can be stored at −20°C almost indefinitely.
2.	Block the plates before use by incubating 50 μl of blocking solution per well for 1 h at room temperature. Remove this solution, rinse the plates in PBS and add hybridoma supernatant samples at 20−100 μl per well by direct transfer from the fusion master plates using the multichannel pipet-ter. (Rinse the tips between rows in 70% ethanol, and change the tips between plates.) Incubate for 3 h.
3.	Wash three times with the wash buffer and add the enzyme conjugated second antibody at 50 μl per well. Incubate for 1 h, then wash three times in wash buffer and once in PBS.
4.	Add 50 μl of freshly prepared substrate per well, and incubate for a suitable period. Stop the chromo-genic reaction by the addition of 50 μl of stop solution.
5.	Read the plates in the ELISA plate reader. The results are most conveniently analysed by a matrix plot in which the values for optical density are ranked on a scale of 1−10.

---

this kind of sample number is to use an assay based in microtitre plates that gives a direct visual readout. The screening assay need not be absolutely definitive and some false positives can be tolerated. The assay can then be backed up by a more definitive test which need only be carried out on the relatively small number of samples that scored positive in the initial screening assay. One of the most useful types of screening assay is an ELISA test, in which antigen is coated onto the bottom of plastic microtitre wells and bound antibody present in the hybridoma sample is detected with an enzyme conjugated anti-immunoglobulin. A basic protocol for this assay is presented in *Table 6*.

An alternative screening test which we have found to be surprisingly versatile is the direct immunocytochemical staining of fixed cells (*Table 7*). This method is quite prac-

Table 7. Cell staining.

1. For the screening of mouse sera, plate the cells out on 90 mm dishes marked on their backs with a 10×10 grid drawn with a marker pen. For the screening of hybridomas, plate the cells out in the microtitre wells at approximately 10^4 cells per well in a volume of 100 μl. Leave to settle overnight at 30°C.

2. Rinse in PBS and fix by incubating in 50% acetone:50% methanol for 2 min. Rinse in the same fixative and allow to dry.

3. Incubate with the crude monoclonal antibody supernatant or dilutions of mouse sera for 3 h in a humid environment (for the microtitre plate, use 50 μl of supernatant or diluted sera per well, for the 90 mm dish, spot 2 μl of each antibody onto the monolayer over a marked square on the grid).

4. Rinse five times with PBS. Incubate for 3 h in rabbit anti-mouse immunoglobulin coupled to horseradish peroxidase, diluted 1:100 in PBS containing 1% BSA, 10% FCS.

5. Rinse five times with PBS and stain as follows: take a saturated solution of *o*-dianisidine (Sigma Chemical Company) in ethanol and dilute it 1:100 in PBS. Filter this freshly diluted solution and add hydrogen peroxide (30%) at a dilution of 1:5000. Add the stain to the fixed cells and leave for 1 – 24 h in the dark. Wash in water and add sodium azide to a final concentration of 0.2% for storage.

Table 8. Western blotting.

1. Separate polypeptides in extracts by electrophoresis on an SDS−polyacrylamide gel. Include prestained protein molecular weight standards (BRL) if necessary.

2. Transfer proteins from the gel to a nitrocellulose sheet (Schleicher and Schuell) in an appropriate electroblot apparatus (15).

3. Incubate the nitrocellulose sheet in blocking buffer (3% BSA in PBS) for 1 h.

4. Rinse in PBS and divide into appropriate strips if required. Incubate each sheet in the screening antibody[a] for 3 – 18 h.

5. Rinse in PBS, followed by two 15 min washes in PBS containing 1% NP-40, and two 15 min washes in PBS.

6. Incubate in pre-adsorbed second antibody[b] coupled to horse-radish peroxidase for 3 – 18 h.

7. Rinse in PBS, followed by two 15 min washes in PBS containing 1% NP-40, and two 15 min washes in PBS.

8. Freshly dilute a 50 mg/ml ethanolic solution of 4-chloro-1-naphthol (Aldrich) 1:100 in PBS and filter. Add hydrogen peroxide (30%) at a dilution of 1:5000 and use to stain the filter. Once staining has occurred sufficiently, rinse the filter in PBS and dry. Keep in the dark.

[a]The screening antibody could be monoclonal antibodies or polyclonal sera.
[b]It is advisable to pre-adsorb the second antibody with a lysed *E. coli* extract (see *Table 2*). The second antibody should be specific for the species used as host in the preparation of the screening antibody, e.g. rabbit anti-mouse immunoglobulin coupled to horse-radish peroxidase (DAKO) or goat anti-rabbit immunoglobulins, etc.

Table 9. Immunoprecipitation[a].

A. *In vivo labelling of SV40 infected cells*

1.   Pre-incubate monolayers of 90% confluent CV-1 cells infected with SV40 in Dulbecco's modified Eagle's medium (DMEM, Flow) lacking methionine for 30 min at 37°C.

2.   Label by incubation with [^{35}S]methionine (50 μCi per 90 mm dish, Amersham) in DMEM lacking methionine for the desired time at 37°C.

B. *Preparation of cell extracts*

1.   Rinse the cells in Tris diluent[b]. Then add more Tris diluent containing 10 mM EDTA and incubate for 10−15 min at 37°C.

2.   Collect the cells by centrifugation at 1000 g for 5 min and lyse by incubating in NET$_{8.0}$[c] containing 1% NP-40 for 30 min at 4°C. Centrifuge at 15 000 g, 4°C, for 30 min or in a microcentrifuge for 5 min at 4°C to remove cell debris.

3.   Pre-clear the supernatant of non-specifically reacting material by incubating the preparation with normal rabbit serum (10 μl per 10^7 cells) for 1 h, then with *Staphylococcus aureus* Cowan 1[d] (50 μl per 10^7 cells) for 15 min on ice. Pellet the immune complexes by centrifugation for 1 min in a micro-centrifuge and incubate the supernatant with *S. aureus* Cowan 1 for a further 15 min on ice, and centrifuge as above. The supernatant is now ready for use in the immunoprecipitation assay.

C. *Immunoprecipitation*

1.   Perform each immunoprecipitation reaction with a volume of cell supernatant equivalent to approximately 3×10^6 cells. Incubate the cell extract with 100 μl of monoclonal antibody supernatant or 10 μl of mouse serum overnight at 4°C. In addition, incubate cell extracts that have been incubated with monoclonal antibody with 5 μg of rabbit anti-mouse immunoglobulins (DAKO) and 5 μl of normal rabbit serum for 2 h at room temperature.

2.   Incubate all cell extracts with 50 μl *S. aureus* Cowan 1 for 15 min at 4°C. Centrifuge for 1 min in a microcentrifuge.

3.   Wash the cell pellets sequentially by resuspending in the following buffers and repelleting by centri-fugation:
NET$_{8.0}$ containing 1% NP-40;
1% NP-40, 0.1% SDS, 500 mM LiCl, 50 mM Tris-HCl pH 8.0;
1% NP-40, 600 mM NaCl, 50 mM Tris-HCl pH 8.0;
1% NP-40, 0.1% SDS, 100 mM NaCl, 50 mM Tris-HCl pH 8.0;
0.05% NP-40, 1% BSA, 150 mM NaCl, 5 mM EDTA, 50 mM Tris-HCl pH 8.0;
NET$_{8.0}$.

4.   Suspend each pellet in NET$_{8.0}$, transfer to a fresh tube and centrifuge as above. Resuspend each pellet in 50 μl of SDS−polyacrylamide gel sample buffer[e], boil for 2 min and centrifuge. Transfer the supernatant to a fresh tube, boil for 5 min and electrophorese on an SDS−polyacrylamide gel.

5.   Stain and destain the gel, and incubate for 1 h in 3 gel volumes of EN^{3}HANCE (New England Nuclear). Wash in water for 1 h, dry and autoradiograph.

---

[a]This protocol describes the procedure we use in the analysis of sera raised against SV40 proteins. It would obviously have to be adapted if other virus or cellular proteins were being investigated.
[b]Tris diluent is 137 mM NaCl, 5 mM KCl, 0.7 mM Na$_2$HPO$_4$, 25 mM Tris-HCl pH 7.4.
[c]NET$_{8.0}$ is 150 mM NaCl, 5 mM EDTA pH 8.0, 50 mM Tris-HCl pH 8.0.
[d]Prepare *S. aureus* Cowan 1 cells by washing twice in 10 × volume of NET$_{8.0}$ containing 1% NP-40, then resuspend in original volume.
[e]SDS−polyacrylamide gel sample buffer is 62.5 mM Tris-HCl pH 6.8, 2% SDS, 100 mM DTT, 10% glycerol, 0.05% bromophenol blue.

tical as only wells that are visibly darkened on the addition of substrate need to be examined under the microscope, and the localization of the substrate deposition can give a great deal of information about the antibodies' specificity. As the plates can be stored, it is quite easy to screen a given fusion against a number of different cell lines. The range of the assay can be extended by using virus infected or stably transfected cell lines.

Once the initial screen has been established, it is worthwhile devising some supplementary screens that will definitively identify the antibody as being of the required specificity. These screens do not have the same restrictions placed on them as the preliminary screens and can utilize more laborious methods suitable only for small sample numbers. The Western blot and immunoprecipitation protocols described (*Tables 8* and *9*) are both suitable. If the ORF is not available in any other form than in the β-galactosidase expression vector, then the screens can include a preliminary ELISA on both β-galactosidase and fusion protein coated plates followed by Western blotting of the two proteins using the hybridomas that scored only against the fusion protein and not against the β-galactosidase control plates. However, we would recommend shuttling the insert into an alternate vector (as described in Section 5) if this is at all possible as this will permit detection of insert specific antibodies even in the presence of contaminating anti-β-galactosidase antibodies.

3.5 The fusion

The equipment and reagents needed for the fusion are listed in *Table 10*.

Once a clear-cut anti-insert specific response has been established in the immunized mice, preparation for the fusions can begin. Whilst a large number of empirical observations have been recorded about crucial factors that affect the success of fusions, there is still a background of variability in the technique that makes it worthwhile doing several fusions. It is the cloning and isolation of the antibodies and their characterization that requires most effort so working only with fusions that have a large number of healthy growing colonies (100+) is advisable.

3.5.1 *The final boost*

Prior to fusion the donor mouse should be given a final boost. The object of this booster injection is to stimulate selectively the proliferation of antigen reactive B cells and to localize them to the donor organ, in this case the spleen. The boost should not be given when there are still high concentrations of serum antibodies to the immunogen present. The immunized animal should therefore be rested for at least a month before the boost. If the fusion protein is soluble the final boost can be given by intravenous injection into a tail vein as this is particularly effective. Inject about 10 μg to 100 μg of protein in a volume of 0.5 ml of saline or PBS without adjuvant. Ensure the sterility of the antigen by filtering through a 0.22 μ filter before injection. If the fusion protein is poorly soluble, do not filter or attempt an intravenous injection, but instead inject the unfiltered material intraperitoneally six, five and four days prior to fusion. Fusion should then take place 72−96 h following the final boost.

3.5.2 *Preparation of the myeloma cells*

The hybridoma parent cells must be in very good condition for the fusion and should therefore be obtained from a cell culture reference centre (e.g. American National Type Culture Collection) or from a successful hybridoma laboratory. It is best not to keep

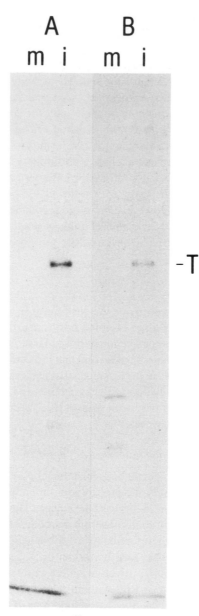

Figure 4. Immunoprecipitation of extracts of [^{35}S]methionine-labelled CV-1 cells infected and mock-infected wih SV40. **Lanes m**, mock-infected CV-1 cells, **lanes i**, infected CV-1 cells. **Panel A**, extract immunoprecipitated with an anti-large T monoclonal; **panel B**, extract immunoprecipitated with sera from a mouse immunized with a β-galactosidase large T fusion protein (large T amino acids 271−448) which did not show binding to any existing anti large T monoclonals. New monoclonals were derived from a fusion using spleen cells of this mouse. This figure is taken from Figure 4, ref. 9, and reproduced with kind permission.

them in culture for prolonged periods but to work from a frozen stock kept in liquid nitrogen. The cells should be thawed at least 10 days before the fusion so that they have been subcultured at least twice before use [in DMEM containing 10% fetal calf

Table 10. Equipment and reagents for cell fusions.

A.	*Equipment*
	Low speed centrifuge, laminar flow hood, CO_2 incubator, 37°C incubator, plastic tissue culture 96-well microtitre dishes, dissecting kit, multichannel dispenser and sterile tips, plastic round bottom centrifuge tubes, routine tissue culture plasticware and pipettes.
B.	*Reagents*
	Fetal calf serum. This should be purchased from a source that screens batches of serum to support hybridoma growth, e.g. Hybritech.
	Polyethylene glycol solution. This is available as a sterile pre-screened solution 50% w/v, in 75 mM Hepes (Cat. No. 783641 from Boehringer Mannheim GmbH, FRG).
	Selection medium. We prefer to use HA (hypoxanthine/azaserine) rather than the more conventional HAT (hypoxanthine/aminopterin/thymidine) medium as it allows more vigorous initial growth. HA is prepared as a 100 × stock by dissolving 136 mg of hypoxanthine and 10 mg of azaserine in 100 ml of sterile distilled water. The solution should then be sterilized by filtration and stored in small aliquots at −20°C.
	Tissue culture medium. Dulbecco's modified Eagle's medium (DMEM) containing 2 mM L-glutamine and 100 μg/ml gentamycin.
	Dimethylsulphoxide. DMSO.

serum (FCS)]. Split the cells 1 in 3 into fresh medium (DMEM containing 20% FCS) the evening before the fusion. Prepare the cells for fusion by washing twice in DMEM without serum and finally resuspend the cells in 5 ml DMEM. You will need 10^7 cells per fusion ($\sim 2 \times 90$ mm plates of subconfluent cells). Both SP20/AG14 and NS-1 myeloma lines work well.

3.5.3 *Preparation of the donor spleen cells*

(i)   Kill the mouse by cervical dislocation.

(ii) Soak the fur in ethanol and, using sterile instruments, remove the spleen to a sterile 90 mm Petri dish containing $3-4$ ml of DMEM with 10% FCS in the hood.

(iii) Using a pair of 19 gauge needles mounted on 1 ml syringes tease the spleen apart very thoroughly.

(iv) Add 15 ml of DMEM without serum and transfer the cells to a centrifuge tube. Let the cell suspension settle for about 5 min, then carefully decant the suspension free of any particulate matter to a fresh tube.

(v)   Wash the cells once in DMEM and resuspend in 5 ml DMEM.

3.5.4 *The fusion*

(i)   Mix the two cell types in a round bottom centrifuge tube and spin them down together.

(ii) Drain the cell pellet aggressively using an aspirator. Be sure that no medium remains, even to the extent of losing a few cells, then add 300 μl of the polyethylene glycol solution (33% in DMEM, held at 37°C).

(iii) Resuspend the pellet by vigorous flicking of the tube and centrifuge the tube at 1200 g for about 5 min.

(iv) Gently aspirate off the excess polyethylene glycol, add 5 ml of DMEM and resuspend the pellet very gently using a large bore pipette.

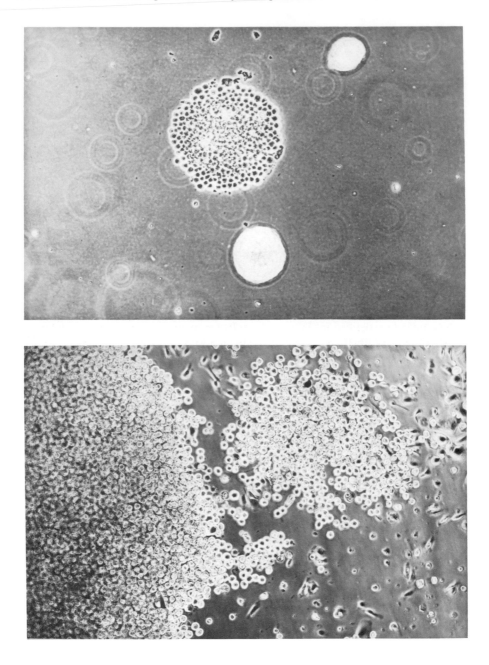

Figure 5. Appearance of growing hybridoma cell cultures. **(A)** A small colony of cells in a microtitre well. Such colonies are not visible macroscopically and should be present by 7−9 days post-fusion. **(B)** A large colony, taken at day 17. The colony is starting to fill the well, the media is turning yellow and the cells will need to be subcultured in the next day or two if the well contains antibodies of the desired specificity. (Photographs kindly provided by Dr E.B.Lane, ICRF, Clare Hall)

(v)   Transfer the cell suspension to 45 ml of DMEM containing 20% FCS and HA, and plate the cells out over five to ten 96-well plates using the multiwell pipette.

(vi)   Put the fusion plates in the CO_2 incubator and try to leave undisturbed for 10 days. Check once at day 3 for the absence of contamination and for the presence of massive cell death as the selection starts to take effect.

(vii) At day 10 examine the plates carefully by holding them up to the light and looking at the underside: positive growth of hybridoma cells is indicated by a yellowing of the media and by the presence of small white spots at the bottom of some wells. Under the microscope large spherical colonies of highly birefringent cells (*Figure 5*) should be visible in 10−30% of the wells.

(viii) At this stage, take 50 μl samples, either from all the wells or from all the wells containing macroscopic colonies, for testing in the screening assay.

(ix)   Repeat the screening test at day 13 and day 17.

All wells that scored positive may be subcultured by transferring the well contents to a 24-well plate and adding 0.5 ml of fresh medium. Cells from the 24-well plate can be used as a source for cloning of the hybridoma line and may also be expanded by subculturing into a 90 mm Petri dish and freezing. If the fusion has been very successful, it is easy to become swamped by trying to subculture and clone too many cells at once. Under these circumstances, it is best to choose just five or ten positives for immediate cloning and freeze the rest for later study. Once the positives have been expanded to the 24 well stage, they should be tested again in the screening assay and also in any alternative, more stringent screen that can be applied. If the fusion resulted in many wells with growth and anti-β-galactosidase activity but no insert specific antibodies, then the only option is to repeat the fusion under identical conditions. If, however, the fusion failed to produce many colonies at all, then certain alterations to the fusion protocol are worth trying. These include the use of media supplements and of feeder cells.

(i) *Feeder layers.* Successful fusions do not require feeders but if growth appears poor, then feeder layers may help. We use human diploid fibroblasts MRC5 plated 2 days before at 10^4 cells/well in the 96-well trays.

(ii) *Media supplements.* If the FCS batch is sub-optimal then the addition of a cocktail of soluble factors to the medium can be helpful. Make the DMEM medium up as usual with gentamycin and L-glutamine and then add bovine insulin (0.2 units/ml), pyruvate (0.45 mM) and oxalacetate (1 mM).

3.6 Freezing hybridoma cell lines

The myeloma parent cells and the hybridoma cells themselves can be safely and efficiently stored in liquid nitrogen freezers for an indefinite period (certainly for 10 years). The freezing procedure is straightforward but should be practised and checked using the parent cell before undertaking a fusion. The freezing mix is essential and mixes that work well for other cell types do not work for hybridomas, so stick to this method.

(i)   Cells for freezing should be growing well so feed them the night before by splitting them 1 in 3 in fresh medium.

Table 11. Cloning in soft agar.

A. *Reagents*

Solution A:, 3% low gelation temperature agarose (Sea prep 15145, FMC Corporation) in glass distilled water. Sterilize by autoclaving and hold at 37°C.
Solution B: double strength DMEM, sterilize by filtration and then add 20% FCS, 2 mM L-glutamine and 100 µg/ml gentamycin.

B. *Method*

1. Set up duplicate cloning tubes (Falcon 2054) containing 10^5, 10^4, 10^3 and 10^2 viable cells in 150 ml of normal strength DMEM. Pipette the cells to ensure that they are free of clumps, and hold all tubes at room temperature.
2. Mix equal volumes of solutions A and B together. Add 2 ml of the mix to each cloning tube and mix by pipetting. Hold the tubes at 4°C for 45 min then place them in a 37°C CO_2 gassed incubator.
3. Pick colonies from the lowest dilution tube possible when they become macroscopically visible (10 – 21 days) using a fresh sterile Pasteur pipette.
4. Place the agarose plug into 1 ml of fresh medium (DMEM containing 20% FCS, L-glutamine and gentamycin) in a 24-well tissue culture plate.
5. The wells can be screened for antibody 2 days later.
6. Cells grown in this way grow exceptionally vigorously so that freezing can take place only a few days after testing.
7. All colonies picked should be positive and the cloning procedure should be repeated until this is achieved.

(ii) Spin the cells down, drain off the supernatant, and gently resuspend in ice-cold freezing mix (94% FCS, 6% dimethylsulphoxide) at the ratio of 0.3 ml of mix to 5×10^6 cells.

(iii) Aliquot the cells into sterile freezing vials (0.2 – 0.3 ml per vial), pack the vials in a large polyurethane container filled with cotton wool and place at −70°C for 24 h. The vials should then be transferred to the liquid nitrogen container.

(iv) Ensure that the freezing has a good viability by thawing a test vial a few days later and always place vials from any given hybridoma in at least two different liquid nitrogen tanks.

3.7 Cloning hybridoma cells

Newly derived hybridomas must be single cell cloned to remove contaminating hybridomas and to select for a cell line which is genetically stable. There are a range of methods available for cloning but the procedure we have found most satisfactory is cloning in soft agarose. This is detailed in *Table 11*.

3.8 Contamination

Scrupulous technique and practice manipulating the microtitre plates will prevent contamination. It is vital not to overfill the wells so never have more than 100 µl of media in a well. If a well is contaminated in an important fusion plate then gently pipette into the well 100 µl of 70% ethanol, drain the well completely under gentle suction and leave dry. If an antibody secreting well is contaminated it may be saved by passage *in vivo*. Inject the entire contents of the well into a BALB/c mouse that has been injected with 200 µl of Freunds complete adjuvant intraperitoneally 2 – 10 days earlier.

With luck, an abdominal swelling will appear $10-14$ days later as a result of ascites tumour formation. Use a large gauge needle to tap some of the ascites fluid. Place 0.1 ml of fluid in 2 ml of tissue culture medium (DMEM plus supplements and 20% FCS) and examine under the microscope. The hybridoma cells are usually clearly visible and can be cloned immediately (see Section 3.7). The remainder of the ascites fluid sample can be tested for the presence of specific antibody and should be tested over a wide range of dilutions as it can be 1000 times more concentrated than tissue culture medium containing secreted antibody.

4. APPLICATIONS OF MONOCLONAL ANTIBODIES

Monoclonal antibodies are useful in a wide range of immunological techniques, some of which are considered in more detail later in this section. They are readily purified using Protein A Sepharose chromatography and can be efficiently labelled either directly by iodination or indirectly using anti-globulin reagents. Indirect labelling of biotin-coupled antibodies using streptavidin or avidin conjugates is particularly useful if more than one monoclonal antibody is being used in an experiment and we present an easy protocol for their biotinylation.

Because of their homogeneity and site specificity, monoclonal antibodies are especially useful for immunoaffinity chromatography. We present a powerful method for the preparation of immunoabsorbent columns (*Table 15*) and a set of elution conditions that have allowed us to purify very sensitive, low abundance macromolecules with high efficiency and retention of biochemical activity.

Monoclonal antibodies can be used effectively in immunoprecipitation and immuno-cytochemical procedures. In earlier studies, we experienced some background problems in both these methods which we had not seen with polyclonal antibodies. The procedures described in *Tables 7* and *9* have overcome these difficulties for us and we find that they work well in a range of systems.

We also describe an effective protocol for Western blotting with these reagents (*Table 8*). In our hands, monoclonals fall into two quite distinct groups: those that do Western blot and those that do not. There is not much variation in the efficiency of those that do blot, and no renaturation measure that we have tried has ever allowed us to recruit 'non-blotters' into the blotting groups. Interestingly, non-Western blotting antibodies will score in the colony blotting procedure (*Table 1*), allowing some mapping of their epitopes to be realized.

The derivation of multiple monoclonal antibodies against the same product allows the establishment of quantitative sandwich immunoassays for the protein using one antibody as a solid phase to 'capture' the antigen from solution, and the other antibody as a labelled 'probe' to detect the immobilized material. Whilst we have used both ^{125}I-labelled and enzyme-labelled (usually by biotin labelling the antibody and using an avidin enzyme conjugate) 'probes' we describe only the former protocol as this has proved more practical in our hands. This assay design can also be used to determine if two antibodies compete for binding to sterically associated sites and also to measure protein — protein interactions.

The full benefits of monoclonal antibodies are realized when the knowledge of their epitope site is combined with the results of their functional effects on the ORF product. This aspect is considered further in Section 5.

4.1 Purification of monoclonal antibodies

4.1.1 Subclasses IgG2a, IgG2b and IgG3

(i)   Grow the hybridomas in spinner vessels if possible, using 5% FCS for economy. Do not use adult serums as the immunoglobulins in these will contaminate your preparation.

(ii)   Allow the cells to grow to as high a density as possible by adding extra glucose to the medium (4.5 g/l) as the cells reach a density of 5×10^5 per/ml. Continue the culture until the medium becomes very acid and cell viability drops below 50%.

(iii)   Spin out the cells and debris (2000 g for 15 min) and pass the antibody containing supernatant through a Protein A Sepharose column (5 ml column bed per litre of supernatant) recirculating overnight at a flow-rate of 60 ml/h.

(iv)   Wash the column with 10 column volumes of PBS and then elute with citrate buffer pH 3.0.

(v)   Collect the eluted antibody into tubes containing 1 M Tris-HCl pH 8.5 so that it is immediately neutralized.

This method works very efficiently for all mouse IgG antibodies except those of the IgG1 subclass. These antibodies have a much lower affinity for Protein A and so the method must be modified to obtain a good yield. The purification of other immunoglobulin classes is not considered here as the vast majority of hybridomas isolated using the hyperimmunization and fusion protocols described will be of the IgG class. We do not recommend the production of ascites fluids (see Section 3.8) as quite adequate amounts of antibody of greater purity can be isolated using the protocols described above.

4.1.2 Subclass IgG1

(i)   Adjust the pH of the hybridoma supernatant to 8.5 by adding 0.1 volumes of 1 M Tris-HCl pH 8.5. Then slowly and with stirring, add solid ammonium sulphate to achieve a 50% saturation at 4°C and leave stirring overnight.

(ii)   Recover the precipitate by centrifugation at 10 000 g for 30 min and resuspend in 1/50 of the starting volume of high salt buffer (0.1 M Tris-HCl pH 8.5, 3 M NaCl) and then dialyse against this buffer overnight.

(iii)   Centrifuge again to clarify and apply to the Protein A column pre-equilibrated in the high salt buffer.

(iv)   Wash the column with 10 column volumes of high salt buffer and then elute as described for the other IgG subclasses in Section 4.1.1.

4.2 Solid phase radioimmunoassays

If two antibodies are isolated to sterically discrete sites on the ORF, they can readily be used to establish an ORF-specific radioimmunoassay. In these assays, one antibody (the capturing reagent) is immobilized by binding to the plastic wells of a microtitre plate. The other antibody is iodinated to a high specific activity (100 μCi/μg) using the iodogen method (*Table 12*). The procedure used for the establishment of this RIA is detailed in *Table 13*.

These assays do not require pure antigen, have very low backgrounds and are very

Table 12. Iodination of monoclonal antibody.

A. *Preparation of iodogen coated tubes*

1. Dissolve iodogen (Pierce Chemical Company, 28600) at 0.5 μg/ml in chloroform.
2. Dispense 100 μl aliquots into glass tubes (Gallenkamp TES 100 020G 2 × 6 mm soda glass). If this gives too fast a rate of iodination then prepare a further set of tubes containing 20 μl per tube.
3. Dry overnight in the fume hood to evaporate off the chloroform.
4. Store in a desiccator at room temperature. They last indefinitely.

B. *Iodination reaction*

1. Add 50 μl of antibody (at 1 mg/ml in 0.5 M sodium phosphate buffer, pH 7.5) to a coated tube.
2. Add 500 μCi ^{125}I-labelled sodium iodide (Amersham; ~5 μl of stock) and incubate for 2−10 min.
3. Transfer contents of the tube to 150 μl of PBS containing 1% BSA and 0.01% sodium azide.
4. Fractionate on a 5 ml G-50 column using the same buffer. Monitor fractions with a gamma counter and collect the first peak.
5. Store at 4°C or −20°C.

Table 13. Solid phase radioimmunoassay.

A. *Reagents*
Solid phase antibody 20 μg/ml in PBS;
iodinated antibody 10^6 c.p.m./ml in PBS containing 3% BSA and 0.1% NP-40;
blocking solution of 5% BSA in PBS;
wash solution of PBS containing 0.1% NP-40.

B. *Equipment*
Gamma counter, plastic microtitre plates, multichannel pipettes.

C. *Method*

1. Prepare antibody coated plates by adding 50 μl of the antibody solution to each well and incubating in a humidified box at room temperature overnight.
2. Shake out the antibody solution and add 50 μl of the block solution to each well.
3. After 1 h wash out the wells with two changes of the wash solution and add the antigen containing solution (the assay has a sensitivity range of 0.1 pM to 10 pM for most protein antigens). Incubate for 2 h at room temperature.
4. Wash out the antigen with four changes of the wash solution then one wash of PBS alone.
5. Add 50 μl of iodinated antibody (50 000 c.p.m.) per well and incubate for another 2 h at room temperature.
6. Finally remove the labelled antibody, wash the plate as before and dry off in a fume cupboard or with a hair dryer. Cut out the individual wells with scissors (or a hot wire machine) and count in the gamma counter.

reproducible (*Figure 6*). We have also found them exceptionally valuable for studying protein−protein interactions using pairs of monoclonal antibodies directed to different subunits of multisubunit protein complexes.

4.3 **Biotinylation**

Purified monoclonal antibodies are readily modified by the covalent coupling of biotin groups. This simple procedure acts as an alternative to direct labelling with iodine or a fluorochrome and allows detection of the modified antibody with commercially

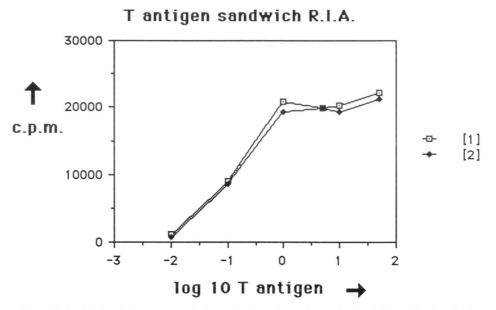

Figure 6. Sandwich radioimmunoassay for SV40 large T antigen using a pair of anti-T monoclonal antibodies binding to sterically distinct epitopes. The vertical axis is counts per minute of iodinated antibody bound to the plate over the range of antigen concentrations listed on the horizonal axis. The assay was carried out in duplicate and the data are plotted for both duplicates to show the consistency of the method.

available labelled streptavidin or avidin reagents. The protocol that we follow is detailed in *Table 14*.

4.4 Epitope mapping

To make full use of the specificity of large monoclonal antibody binding in functional assays, it is essential that the binding site is mapped as closely as possible. One simple and easy approach is by colony blotting on overlapping series of fusion proteins to specify an amino acid stretch of around 50 amino acids. The colony blotting protocol is outlined in *Table 1*. The next step would be to synthesize an overlapping series of peptides in order to define the site to a few amino acids. We have used this approach successfully in the mapping of PAb204, which inhibits the ATPase (6), helicase (7) and replicative functions of T antigen (8). Initially, we mapped the epitope to a region of 64 amino acids, between residues 448−509 of SV40 large T (9) using data obtained from the binding to a β-galactosidase large T fusion protein and from data on the reactivity of the antibody with deletion mutants.

PAb204 shows cross-reaction with a growth-regulated evolutionarily conserved host protein, p68 (10). A series of cDNA clones for p68 have recently been isolated (11) by screening a λgt11 library of human hepatoma cDNA (12) with PAb204.

One of the shortest clones that encoded the PAb204 epitope within p68 was sequenced. This sequence was then aligned with the sequence of 63 amino acids within large T that encompassed the epitope and a series of four synthetic peptides corresponding to this area were tested for their interaction with PAb204 in a solid phase ELISA assay.

Table 14. Biotin coupling of monoclonal antibody.

1.	Add a 10 mg/ml solution of biotin succinimide ester (Miles Ltd.) in DMSO to a 1−3 mg/ml solution of antibody in amino free buffer such as borate or sodium hydrogen carbonate at pH 8.8. Use a ratio of 1 mg protein to 25−250 μg ester. Mix well and incubate at room temperature for 4 h.
2.	Add 20 μl of 1 M NH$_4$Cl per mg of protein or per 250 μg of ester.
3.	Dialyse or fractionate on a G-50 column to remove the ester.
4.	Store at 4°C in PBS containing 1% FCS and azide.

Table 15. Coupling monoclonal antibody to Protein A.

A. *Reagents*
Protein A Sepharose (Pharmacia);
dimethyl-pimelimidate dihydrochloride (DPD, Sigma);
0.1 M borate buffer pH 9.0 (boric acid/sodium tetraborate);
0.1 M borate buffer pH 8.0;
0.02 M ethanolamine pH 8.0 (HCl);
0.1 M citrate pH 3.0 (citric acid/sodium citrate).

B. *Making the column*

1. Pump 100 ml of hybridoma supernatant (the antibody can be IgG2a, IgG2b or IgG3 but not IgG1) through 1 ml of Protein A Sepharose beads overnight at 4°C.
2. Wash the column thoroughly with 0.1 M borate buffer pH 9.0 and resuspend beads in the same buffer at room temperature. Keep an aliquot to check that the level of immunoglobulin bound is 0.5−2 mg per ml of beads.
3. Add 50 mg of DPD to crosslink. (This should be stored in a desiccator at −20°C and added to the beads immediately after weighing out.) Mix thoroughly and leave for 1 h at room temperature, with occasional mixing.
4. Harvest the beads by centrifugation, wash once in 0.1 M borate buffer pH 8.0 and incubate for 10 min in ethanolamine. Wash thoroughly and store the beads in 0.1 M borate buffer pH 8.0.

C. *Using the column*

1. Pre-elute the column with the chosen buffer for antigen elution (such as 0.1 M citrate pH 3.0). Check that no protein is released.
2. Equilibrate the column in a suitable buffer for the antigen sample (for SV40 T antigen we use 20 mM Tris-HCl pH 8.0, 120 mM NaCl, 1 mM EDTA, 0.1% NP-40).
3. Load the antigen by recirculating the extract through a very small 1 ml column and wash extensively with at least 100 ml of buffer.
4. Elute by pumping the elution buffer in a reverse direction of flow to the loading of the antigen. Collect 500 μl of fractions directly into neutralizing buffer (200 μl of 1 mM Tris-HCl pH 8.8).
5. After elution, re-equilibrate the column.

The results localized the epitope to a region of 17 amino acids extending from residue 453 to 469 of large T (5). The close proximity of this site to the consensus nucleotide binding site previously noted in the sequence of T antigen (13) is striking. This suggests that the region of the ATPase activity has been correctly identified.

5. FURTHER APPLICATIONS: SHUTTLING OF INSERT-CONTAINING *Eco*RI CASSETTES

A particular advantage in using the pUR series of expression vectors or λgt11 in the construction of fusion proteins is the presence of two *Eco*RI sites flanking the insertion

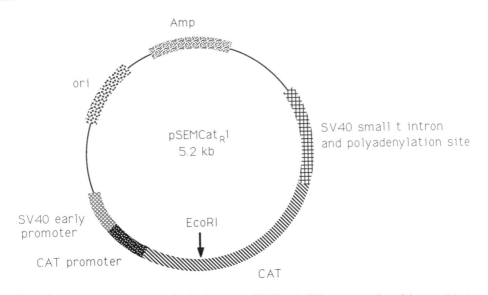

Figure 7. The prokaryotic−eukaryotic shuttle vector, pSEMCat$_R$1. This vector consists of, in an anticlockwise direction, the gene encoding ampicillin resistance and the origin of replication of pBR322; the SV40 early promoter region which includes a Goldberg−Hogness TATA box; the CAT core promoter region which includes a transcription start site; the gene encoding chloramphenicol acetyltransferase which confers resistance to the antibiotic chloramphenicol; the SV40 small t intron and the early region polyadenylation site.

site situated at the 3′ end of the *lac*Z gene. The power of these systems can be greatly extended by the transfer of the '*Eco*RI cassette' containing the insert from these constructions into another expression vector. One suitable vector is pSEMCat$_R$1 (*Figure 7*), which was constructed in our laboratory (5). This is a derivative of pSV2-cat^r (14) which has been considered in DNA Cloning Volume II. It is a prokaryotic−eukaryotic shuttle vector that can be propagated by ampicillin selection within a bacterial host. The vector also contains the gene encoding chloramphenicol acetyltransferase which can be expressed in a bacterial environment and also in a mammalian cell environment due to the presence of the SV40 early region promoter in tandem with the bacterial promoter region. The polyadenylation site and small t intron from SV40 is also contained 3′ to the CAT gene.

pSEMCat$_R$1 contains a single *Eco*RI site within the CAT gene which is in frame with that at the 3′ end of the *lac*Z gene. Transfer of the '*Eco*RI cassette' from a pUR fusion protein construction into this *Eco*RI site therefore allows the expression of a cloned gene fragment as a fusion protein with CAT in both bacterial and mammalian cell environments. This enables, for example, localization and functional experiments to be carried out within a mammalian cell environment on fragments of a gene expressed as a fusion protein with CAT. In addition, it allows the activity of the CAT fusion protein within bacterial and mammalian cells to be compared since the same construct can be used for each. Many of these experiments require the use of monoclonal antibodies specific to the fusion protein under investigation. Hence the construction of a fusion protein in pUR would allow the derivation of new monoclonals to an ORF. Transfer of this ORF to pSEMCat$_R$1 would then allow investigation of the *in vivo* ex-

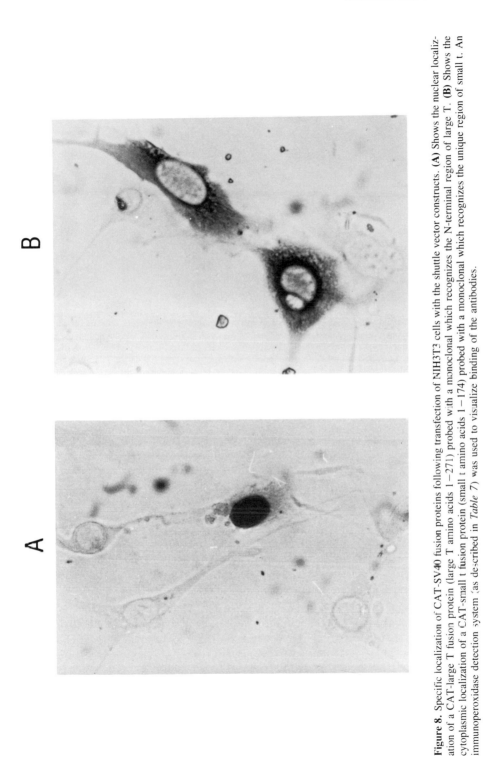

Figure 8. Specific localization of CAT-SV40 fusion proteins following transfection of NIH3T3 cells with the shuttle vector constructs. (**A**) Shows the nuclear localization of a CAT-large T fusion protein (large T amino acids 1–271) probed with a monoclonal which recognizes the N-terminal region of large T. (**B**) Shows the cytoplasmic localization of a CAT-small t fusion protein (small t amino acids 1–174) probed with a monoclonal which recognizes the unique region of small t. An immunoperoxidase detection system (as described in *Table 7*) was used to visualize binding of the antibodies.

137

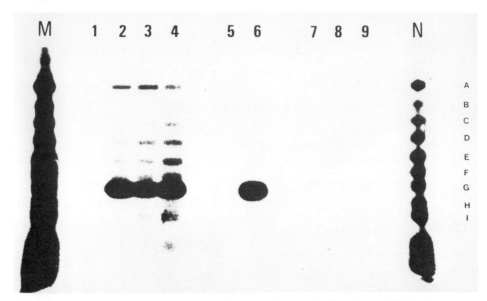

Figure 9. An immunoprecipitated CAT-large T fusion protein retains SV40 origin-specific binding activity. **Lanes M** and **N** contain end-labelled *Eco*RII-digested SV40 DNA (SV40 origin is contained within the *Eco*RII G fragment). **Lanes 1−4** show the immunoprecipitation of SV40 large T antigen bound specifically to the origin fragment. **Lane 1** contains a control antibody that does not recognize large T. **Lanes 2−4** contain monoclonals which recognize large T and so co-precipitate large T bound to the origin fragment. **Lanes 5** and **6** show the immunoprecipitation of a CAT-large T fusion protein (large T amino acids 1−271) bound to the origin fragment. **Lane 5** contains a control antibody that does not recognize the fusion protein. **Lane 6** contains a monoclonal which recognizes the fusion protein and co-precipitates it bound to the origin fragment. **Lanes 7−9** show the immunoprecipitation of a CAT-large T fusion protein (large T amino acids 271−708) which does not bind the origin fragment. **Lane 7** contains a control antibody that does not recognize the fusion protein. **Lanes 8** and **9** contain antibodies which recognize the fusion protein but no DNA is co-precipitated. This figure is taken from Figure 5, reference 5, and reproduced with kind permission.

pression and localization and functional analysis of the CAT fusion protein using the newly derived monoclonals.

5.1 Examples

We have transfected the N-terminal region of the SV40 large T (amino acids 1−271) as a CAT fusion protein construction in pSEMCat$_R$1 into CV-1 cells, where the expressed protein localizes to the nucleus of these cells (*Figure 8*). The CAT−SV40 large T fusion protein (amino acids 1−271) also shows specific binding to DNA containing the SV40 origin sequences *in vitro* (*Figure 9*), when various immunoprecipitating monoclonals are used which bind to epitopes localized to different regions of this functional domain. This region of large T is considered to have immortalizing activity which can be investigated *in vivo* using the CAT shuttle vector.

6. ACKNOWLEDGEMENTS

The early part of this work was supported by the Cancer Research Campaign and the latter part by the Imperial Cancer Research Fund.

7. REFERENCES

1. Rüther,U. and Müller-Hill,B. (1983) *EMBO J.*, **2**, 1791.
2. Maniatis,T., Fritsch,E.F. and Sambrook,J. (eds) (1982) *Molecular Cloning: A Laboratory Manual.* Cold Spring Harbor Laboratory Press, Cold Spring Harbor, N.Y.
3. Messing,J., Groneneborn,B., Müller-Hill,B. and Hofschneider,P.H. (1977) *Proc. Natl. Acad. Sci. USA*, **74**, 3642.
4. Rüther,U., Koenen,M., Otto,K. and Müller-Hill,B. (1981) *Nucleic Acids Res.*, **9**, 4087.
5. Mole,S.E., Gannon,J.V., Ford,M.J. and Lane,D.P. (1987) *Phil. Trans. R. Soc., Series B*, **317**, in press.
6. Clark,R., Lane,D.P. and Tjian,R. (1981) *J. Biol. Chem.*, **56**, 11854.
7. Stahl,H., Dröge,P. and Knippers,R. (1986) *EMBO J.*, **5**, 1939.
8. Smale,S.T. and Tjian,R. (1986) *Mol. Cell. Biol.*, **6**, 4077.
9. Mole,S.E. and Lane,D.P. (1985) *J. Virol.*, **54**, 703.
10. Lane,D.P. and Hoeffler,W.K. (1980) *Nature*, **288**, 167.
11. Ford,M.J. and Lane,D.P., in preparation.
12. de Wet,J.R., Fukushima,H., Dewji,N.N., Wilcox,E., O'Brien,J.S. and Helinski,D.R. (1984) *DNA*, **3**, 437.
13. Seif,I. (1984) *Virology*, **138**, 347.
14. Gorman,C.M., Moffat,L.F. and Howard,B.H. (1982) *Mol. Cell. Biol.*, **2**, 1044.
15. Burnette,W.N. (1982) *Anal. Biochem.*, **112**, 195.

CHAPTER 7

Expression and secretion of foreign genes in yeast

BRUCE L.A.CARTER, MEHER IRANI, VIVIAN L.MACKAY,
RON L.SEALE, ANDRZEJ V.SLEDZIEWSKI and ROBERT A.SMITH

1. INTRODUCTION

The yeast *Saccharomyces cerevisiae* is a useful host for the production of foreign proteins for either fundamental or applied studies. The first yeast-derived recombinant product, hepatitis B vaccine, is already on the market. The second is likely to be yeast-derived human insulin. This is a process developed for Novo Industri by ZymoGenetics in which a modified proinsulin is secreted into the medium by the yeast cells and is converted efficiently to insulin *in vitro*.

Expression of a foreign polypeptide can also be useful as a probe in studies of yeast physiology and biochemistry. The *Escherichia coli* β-galactosidase gene has been used in yeast to study such subjects as (i) nuclear targeting; (ii) promoter function; and (iii) secretion mechanisms.

Heterologous gene expression can also be used to gain information on the nature and activity of the foreign polypeptide. The expression of regions of p28[sis] from simian sarcoma virus in yeast led to the proof that biological activities associated with platelet-derived growth factor (PDGF) could be definitely ascribed to PDGF and not to cytokines that may contaminate PDGF when prepared from mammalian sources (4).

Yeast has long been a favourite organism of experimental biologists but with the discovery that yeast cells could be transformed with exogenous DNA (5,6), there has been an explosion of interest in yeast. This is largely because yeast is a eukaryotic cell that can be manipulated biochemically and genetically (both classical and molecular) with the same ease as *E. coli*. This permits a multi-disciplinary approach to fundamental problems of eukaryotic biology such as mitosis. In the last five years, there has also been considerable interest in the use of yeast as a host for the production of proteins of, for instance, therapeutic utility. This interest was fuelled by the realization that *E. coli* was not a suitable host for the production of many mammalian proteins. The problem in *E. coli* is often one of quality not quantity. It can be difficult to recover the protein of interest from *E. coli* without denaturation and renaturation cycles. These often result in the purification of a protein that only has a fraction of the proper biological activity.

It should not be thought that yeast is a panacea for cell expression problems but there are occasions such as with the hepatitis B vaccine mentioned earlier where yeast can solve a problem that was intractable in *E. coli*.

Yeast, in addition to cytoplasmic expression, offers the possibility of secretion of the heterologous protein into the medium. There are several reasons why the possibility of secretion may be an advantage. Many of the human proteins of therapeutic interest are those that are secreted by one cell type and exert their effect on another. Such proteins are often rich in cysteines; multiple disulphide bridges are one of the major difficulties in successfully renaturating *E. coli* produced proteins.

One advantage of secretion is that very few yeast proteins are secreted naturally into the medium and, given reasonable expression levels, this provides certain purification advantages. The secretion from yeast of proteins normally secreted from mammalian cells usually leads to proper disulphide bond formation and full biological activity. We have found that platelet derived growth factor which requires proper disulphide bond formation and dimerization can be assembled and secreted from yeast and appears to have the same biological activity as the material that can be recovered from human platelets (4).

Secretion also permits glycosylation of foreign proteins as the apparatus for glycosylation lies in the secretion pathway. The inner core carbohydrate is assembled after translocation to the endoplasmic reticulum and the outer core is added in the Golgi apparatus. It should be noted that outer core glycosylation in yeast is different from that observed in mammalian cells. Rapid secretion may also offset the toxic effects associated with cytoplasmic expression of some proteins in yeast.

Good expression of human proteins in yeast is protein dependent; there are successes, and there are the less publicized failures such as beta interferon which is produced at less than 0.1% of total cell protein. In addition, there are proteins such as many involved in blood coagulation that require the type of post-translational modification such as gamma-carboxylation of glutamic acid residues that is not possible in yeast (7).

1.1 Methods included in this chapter

In this chapter we will describe methods that are useful in the expression and secretion of foreign genes in yeast. Many of the DNA manipulations and plasmid constructions are done using *E. coli*. As such methods have been described adequately elsewhere (8,9), we will not describe them in detail here but will concentrate on those methodological aspects that are peculiar to yeast. Other useful sources of yeast methodology are Volumes 11 and 12 of Methods in Cell Biology (10) which are entirely devoted to research methods that have been developed with yeast cells. The Methods in Yeast Genetics Laboratory Manual (11) published by the Cold Spring Harbor Laboratory is a good source of chemical and molecular genetical methodologies. Various methods involved in the cloning of genes in yeast are covered in Wu *et al.* (12).

1.2 Expression vectors

There are many different types of plasmid that can be used to express foreign genes in yeast. The differences in them have been explained on numerous occasions (12). The expression plasmid shown in *Figure 1* is a YEp plasmid: it replicates episomally in yeast, hence the abbreviation for yeast episomal plasmid.

Most of the manipulations necessary for plasmid construction and propagation, are carried out in *E. coli*, and so such plasmids need an origin of replication which permits

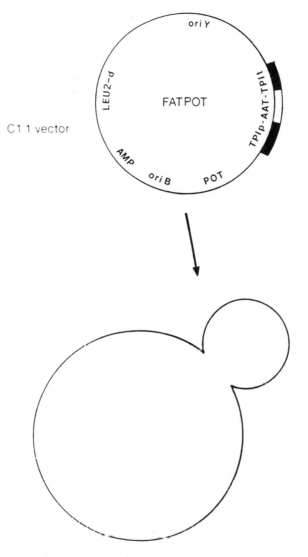

C1 1 vector

pep4 leu2 Δtpi yeast strain

Figure 1. A yeast expression vector. The vector has an origin of replication for yeast (ori Y) derived from the yeast 2-μm plasmid. It has a *leu2* gene for the selection of transformants in yeast. Sequences from pBR322 provide ori B, permitting replication in *E. coli* and AMP providing ampicillin resistance a selectable marker for transformants in *E. coli*. The plasmid utilizes the triose phosphate isomerase promoter and terminator. Ideally in an expression vector these are separated by a unique restriction site. In the plasmid illustrated, *alpha 1 anti-trypsin* has been inserted between promoter and terminator. The vector illustrated is a sophisticated vector allowing growth on complex media without apparent selection. Selection is provided by incorporating on the plasmid the *triose phosphate isomerase (tpi)* gene and promoter from *Schizosaccharomyces pombe* and transforming into a host in which the *tpi* gene has been deleted (Δtpi). Only the transformed cells can grow on glucose as untransformed cells lack an essential glycolytic enzyme. The host cell illustrated lacks a functioning *leucine 2* gene and therefore transformants can be selected on medium minus leucine. In addition the host cell lacks *pep4*; the advantages of this are discussed in the text.

143

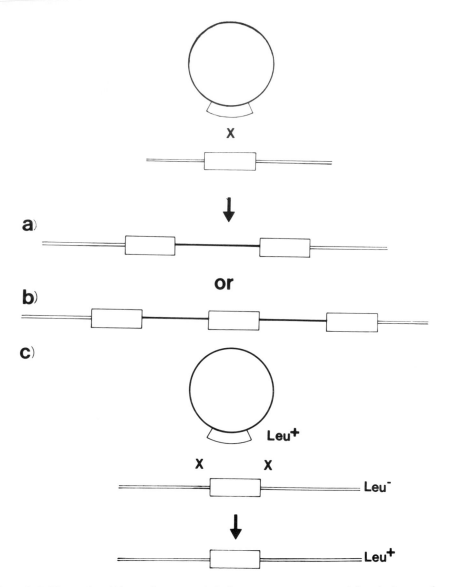

Figure 2. Different plasmid integration events. A single cross-over event can result in a single copy of vector sequence flanked by direct repeats of homologous DNA (**a**) or multiple tandem copies of vector sequences (**b**). A double crossover can result in replacement of chromosomal DNA with homologous plasmid derived sequences without the integration of plasmid vector sequences.

replication in *E. coli*. This is usually achieved by incorporating DNA sequences from plasmids such as pBR322 into the vector. In addition, a marker for the selection of transformants in *E. coli* is essential: in the plasmid in *Figure 1*, this is provided by the gene encoding ampicillin resistance.

Selection of transformants in yeast is vital and is often provided by the incorporation of a wild type copy of the *leucine 2* gene on the plasmid. If this is used to transform yeast host cells that have a defective *leucine 2* gene, only transformants can grow on medium that lacks leucine. Other auxotrophic combinations can be used. YEp plasmids can replicate in yeast because they contain the origin of replication of an endogenous yeast plasmid, the 2-μm circle. Propagation at high copy numbers of plasmids containing only the origin of replication function of the 2-μm plasmid requires transformation into a host cell containing the native 2-μm plasmid which provides two trans-acting functions. Hybrid plasmids containing the entire 2-μm plasmid genome are maintained at high copy number even in strains lacking the endogenous 2-μm plasmid; so called *cir*^{o} strains. The trans-acting proteins encoded by *rep1* and *rep2* can be provided by the native 2-μm plasmid or the hybrid plasmid that is used for expression. Broach (13) has discussed various aspects of the construction and use of 2-μm plasmid vectors for propagating cloned genes in yeast.

Although it might seem obvious that higher plasmid copy numbers are desirable for maximum expression level, this is not always the case. Some proteins are toxic to a yeast cell and result in selection for lowered expression levels: this is usually accomplished by reduction in, or complete loss of plasmids. In these cases, integration of the plasmid into one or another of the yeast chromosomes at low copy number gives stability and greater net expression levels (14).

Yeast integrating vectors (YIp) do not have DNA sequences capable of acting as origins of replication in yeast and consequently transformants can only be selected if recombination occurs and the plasmid becomes integrated into the yeast genome (6).

Integration occurs as a result of recombination between homologous sequences on the plasmid and a host cell chromosome. It results in an integrated copy of the plasmid vector sequences flanked by direct repeats of that region of the DNA that is homologous between plasmid and chromosome. *Figure 2* shows the results of a cross-over event within the *leucine 2* gene. Many transformants integrate plasmids in multiple copies in tandem array (*Figure 2*). A fraction of integrants result from a double cross-over (*Figure 2*). This can lead to replacement of DNA on the chromosome by a homologous region on the plasmid without integration of the plasmid vector DNA. Integration can occur at any place on the yeast genome for which there are homologous sequences on the plasmid. It does not only occur at the genomic site of the plasmid selectable marker.

YIp vectors transform at much lower magnitude (2−3 orders) then YEp vectors although their transformation frequency can be enhanced by the introduction of a double strand break in the region homologous to the yeast genome.

Whichever type of plasmid is used, a yeast promoter is necessary for efficient transcription initiation. The most commonly used are the glycolytic promoters. Since the glycolytic enzymes represent between 1% and 5% of total cell protein, although often encoded by single copy genes, it was assumed correctly that the promoters of the genes encoding these enzymes are strong. Effective transcription termination is another prerequisite for good expression. Yeast will often recognize the terminators of mammalian proteins but it is sensible to incorporate a yeast terminator as shown in *Figure 1*. The promoter and terminator are separated by a unique restriction endonuclease site which provides a convenient way to insert the structural genes of interest.

Plasmids such as that shown in *Figure 1* are suitable expression vectors for expression of foreign proteins within the cytoplasm of the cell. Such expression vectors have been developed in a number of industrial and academic laboratories and are available from at least some of these laboratories (15,16).

Increasingly attention is being paid to the development of conditional expression systems. This is because the glycolytic promoters are, for all practical purposes, constitutive. Constitutive expression of any gene on a multicopy plasmid must represent a significant metabolic strain to a transformed cell. With both yeast-derived and heterologous material, this strain may be accompanied by toxic effects which can vary in both mechanism and intensity in a protein-dependent manner. Slow transformation and poor growth rates are much more common than a perusal of the literature would indicate.

Conditional promoters may alleviate this situation by permitting biomass accumulation when gene expression is off. The aim is to turn gene expression on when the fermentor is full of cells in response to a simple change in the external environment. Conditional expression systems are discussed in some detail by Piggott *et al.* (17).

1.3 Secretion vectors

If secretion of a foreign polypeptide is desired, it is important to incorporate a yeast signal such as invertase or acid phosphatase, at the amino terminus of the mature protein. An alternative and superior method is to remove the signal or leader of the mammalian protein and substitute for it the alpha-factor leader from the yeast alpha-factor precursor molecule. Alpha-factor is a mating factor secreted by alpha mating type cells. Cells of the *a* mating type secrete *a* factor. The mating factors act by causing reciprocal G_1 arrest in cells of opposite mating type prior to conjugation (18). The MF α-1 gene has been cloned and sequenced (19). The secretion leader is complex, consisting of 20 amino acids whose composition is typical of a classic signal sequence, followed by a relatively hydrophobic stretch of 69 amino acids which contains glycosylation sites. Glycosylation and processing of prepro alpha factor has been extensively studied (20−22).

The sequence of the alpha-factor leader and immediate 5' promoter sequences is shown in *Figure 3*. The basic approaches to the utilization of the alpha-factor leader to drive the secretion of heterologous proteins have been outlined by Brake *et al.* (23). There is a *Hin*dIII restriction site in the MFα-1 structural gene which overlaps the glu ala repeats at the processing site for the first peptide repeat. This offers a natural means of appending mature foreign proteins to the secretion leader. Exploitation of the natural site, however, can lead to the extracellular secretion of product which has a large proportion of molecules with one or two N-terminal glu ala additions. The reason for this is that there is an insufficiency of the *ste13* gene product, the dipeptidyl amino-peptidase, that cleaves the glu ala repeats after initial endopeptidase cleavage by the *kex2* gene product after lys arg.

Brake *et al.* (23) addressed this problem in two ways. The first was to connect the mature foreign sequence to the natural *Hin*dIII site via a stretch of synthetic DNA which provides a second lys arg cleavage site immediately adjacent to the foreign protein. In the case of human epidermal growth factor, this arrangement lead to the secretion of material of which 80% had been processed in the desired manner at the downstream

```
 -70        -60        -50      C -40        -30       -20        -10
ACGATTCAAGAATAGTTCAAACAAGAAGATTACAAACTATCAATTTCATACACAATATAAACGACCAAA
                                     ▲

  1                 10               20    PstI      30         40                   50
AGA ATG AGA TTT CCT TCA ATT TTT ACT GCA GTT TTA TTC GCA GCA TCC TCC GCA
    met arg phe pro ser ile phe thr ala val leu phe ala ala ser ser ala


              60      Hinc II 70              80           90            100
TTA GCT GCT CCA GTC AAC ACT ACA ACA GAA GAT GAA ACG GCA CAA ATT CCG GCT
leu ala ala pro val ASN THR THR thr glu asp glu thr ala gln ile pro ala


   110            120            130            140           150
GAA GCT GTC ATC GGT TAC TCA GAT TTA GAA GGG GAT TTC GAT GTT GCT GTT TTG
glu ala val ile gly tyr ser asp leu glu gly asp phe asp val ala val leu


160            170            180            190          200           210
CCA TTT TCC AAC AGC ACA AAT AAC GGG TTA TTG TTT ATA AAT ACT ACT ATT GCC
pro phe ser ASN SER THR asn asn gly leu leu phe ile ASN THR THR ile ala


    220            230             AGC          250              Hind III
AGC ATT GCT GCT AAA GAA GAA GGG GTA TCT TTG GAT AAA AGA GAG GCT GAA GCT
ser ile ala ala lys glu glu gly val ser leu asp lys arg glu ala glu ala
                                      ▲▲▲
```

Figure 3. The alpha-factor leader sequence and immediate 5′ promoter sequence. Site directed mutagenesis at the site marked ▲ permits the creation of a *Hind*III site within the promoter such that completely heterologous signals can replace the alpha-factor leader sequences. Alternatively, the promoter can be used for cytoplasmic expression. Mutagenesis at the site ▲▲▲ permits the construction of fusion proteins in which the glu ala repeats do not occur. It is also possible to change sequences immediately upstream of the natural *Hind*III site in the leader.

lys arg pair, and 20% showed an N-terminal extension of glu ala glu ala ser leu asp lys arg, reflecting cleavage at the 'natural' primary processing site.

The second route to circumventing the glu ala addition problem is to generate, by site directed mutagenesis, a restriction site in the leader sequence which is sufficiently far upstream to eliminate the glu ala repeats from fusions, but sufficiently close to the primary cleavage site to allow it to be easily reconstituted by synthetic DNA linkers which do not interpose glu ala repeats in front of the foreign protein. This is illustrated in *Figure 3* (Piggott, unpublished data) where replacement of TCT by AGC using site directed mutagenesis permits the retention of the serine in the leader yet creates a *Hind*III cloning site. This type of approach has been successfully applied to human insulin (24), the interleukins (25), and platelet-derived growth factor (4).

A basic secretion vector utilizing the alpha-factor promoter (a strong promoter), the alpha-factor leader and the *adh1* terminator is shown in *Figure 4*. There is a unique *Hind*III site that permits the insertion of mature structural genes.

Construction of expression and secretion vectors containing foreign structural genes is performed by standard molecular genetical techniques (8,9). Ammerer (26) has written a useful methodological article on the expression of genes in yeast using the *adcI* promoter. The success of ligations can be checked by analysis of individual bacterial transformants. Bacterial transformation is done by standard procedures (8,9). The orientation

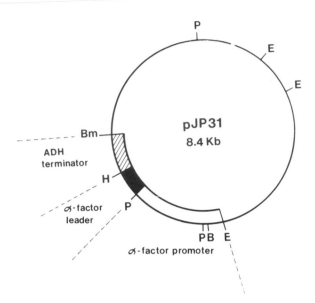

Figure 4. A basic secretion vector, p JP 31 (Piggott, unpublished results). The unmarked region represents the large *Eco*RI/*Bam*HI fragment of pJDB207 from which the *Hin*dIII site in the yeast 2-μm plasmid sequence has been removed by treatment with DNA polymerase 1 and DNA ligase. B = *Bgl*II; Bm = *Bam*HI; E = *Eco*RI; H = *Hin*dIII; P = *Pst*I.

of inserts can be monitored in plasmid preparations by restriction fragment length analyses. Plasmid DNA for yeast transformations can be purified by CsCl gradient centrifugation and is stored at 4°C.

2. YEAST STRAINS SUITABLE FOR EXPRESSION AND THEIR CONSTRUCTION

The yeast strains that produce the highest levels of foreign protein expression are often not available from the industrial companies that have developed them, for obvious reasons. Several useful strains, however, are available from both university and industrial laboratories and it is not difficult to construct suitable host strains oneself.

A perfectly adequte host for most purposes, strain X4003-5B is available from the Yeast Genetic Stock Center, Donner Laboratories, University of California, Berkeley, California, USA. This strain will permit studies of the expression and secretion of foreign proteins at the shake flask level. The genotype of X4003-5B is *mat a leu2 ade1 his4 met2 ura3 trp5 gal1*. Because this strain is *leu2⁻* it can be used in conjunction with plasmids carrying a wild type copy of the *leu2* gene. A danger in using a host cell with a single point mutation in the gene being used for selection of transformants is that genetic revertants may occur. This is only a problem in circumstances when only a few transformants are obtained. In these instances revertants can represent a high proportion of the cells growing on medium minus leucine and this is obviously a nuisance. To avoid this problem strains like LL20: *mat α can1 his3-11,15 leu2-3, 112* constructed by Leslie Lau at Cornell University and D 234-3B; *mat α his3-11,15 leu2-3,112 tcm1 trp1 ura3* constructed by P.Brown at the Dana-Farber Cancer Institute carry double mutations in two markers that are suitable for use in association with either *leu2* plasmids of *his3* plasmids. The double point mutations ensure that revertants arise at a frequency of less than 10^{-10}. Several transformable strains are available from the Yeast Genetic Stock Center.

The choice of host is dictated by the choice of plasmid one wishes to introduce: the host should have a mutation resulting in a defect in the same gene that is being used on the plasmid as a selectable marker. If a dominant selectable marker such as *cup1* (encoding copper resistance) is being used on the plasmid, there is considerable choice of host (haploid, diploid or even an uncharacterized brewers yeast) provided only that the host is copper sensitive, as many yeast strains are.

Many investigators have found it useful to incorporate a *pep4* mutation in the host strain. The most commonly used is the *pep4-3*. Incorporation of this mutation in the host strain does not of itself result in enhanced expression of the foreign protein of interest. It reduces proteolytic degradation of cytoplasmically expressed proteins in cell-free extracts and reduces the degradation of secreted proteins that may occur through cell lysis. The *pep4* mutation can be crossed into the host strain by standard genetical crosses. Tetrad dissection is described in Section 2.2.4, and a method to distinguish *pep4* plus and minus colonies is included in *Table 1*.

Table I. Identification of *pep4−* and *pep4+* haploid segregants from a genetic cross.

1.	Grow colonies on YEPD agar plates.
2.	Mix 3 ml of 0.6% agar (melted and held at 50°C) with 2 ml of 3 mg/ml *N*-acetyl DL-phenylalanine β-naphthyl ester (Sigma) dissolved in DMF (dimethylformamide) in a glass tube.
3.	Pour the mixture over colonies and allow it to solidify.
4.	Gently pour over the surface 4 ml of a solution containing 5 mg/ml Fast Garnet B.C. in 0.1 M Tris-HCl pH 7.3. This dye is obtainable from Sigma, but it should be used with great care as it is a carcinogen.
5.	When the colonies begin to turn red pour off the dye solution and rinse gently with distilled water.
6.	*pep4−* colonies turn red more slowly than wild type colonies and in fact never turn as red: they remain yellowish.

Table 2. Maintenance of yeast stocks

1	Aliquot 2 ml of 30% glycerol into 1 dram vials. Loosely cap.
2.	Autoclave for 20 min. Allow to cool before tightening the caps.
3.	Store at room temperature.
4.	Grow a 3 ml culture of the yeast strain in YEPD[a] (or in the appropriate selective media) overnight.
5.	Add 2 ml of the overnight culture to the vial. Cap and vortex.
6.	Store at −80°C. These are good for 5 years.
7.	To use:
	a) Thaw on ice
	b) Streak a loopful of the glycerol stock onto the appropriate media. Incubate at 30°C (25°C for temperature sensitive strains).
	c) Re-freeze the vial at −80°C.

[a]YEPD medium contains 1% yeast extract, 2% bactopeptone and 2% glucose.

2.1 **Maintenance of yeast stocks**

Yeast stocks can be maintained temporarily at 4°C. It is, however, a sensible precaution to maintain glycerol stocks at −80°C. These can include transformed yeast cells, although it is preferable to retransform yeast cells with stored plasmid DNA. Preparation of yeast glycerol stocks is described in *Table 2*.

2.2 **Strain construction**

Strain construction is often an intimidating task for newcomers to yeast because of an impression that the physical separation of haploid spores by micromanipulation is difficult and requires one who is skilled in witchcraft. This is certainly not the case, but it does require some practice. Media that are required are described in *Table 3*.

2.2.1 *Diploid construction*

When two haploid yeast cells carry individual genes that one wishes to combine in the same haploid cell, it is necessary to mate the cells to form a diploid and then recover and analyse haploid spores after meiosis and sporulation.

Table 3. Media used in strain construction.

YEPD agar:

　1% yeast extract
　2% bactopeptone
　2% glucose
　2% agar

Synthetic complete medium[a]:

　0.67% Difco yeast nitrogen base without amino acids
　2% glucose
　2% agar
　10 μg/ml each adenine and methionine
　20 μg/ml each arginine, histidine, leucine and tryptophan
　10 μg/ml each uracil and lysine
　50 μg/ml each tyrosine, threonine[b] and leucine
　60 μg/ml each phenylalanine and isoleucine

Presporulation agar:

　0.8% yeast extract
　0.3% bactopeptone
　10% glucose
　2% agar

Sporulation agar:

　1% potassium acetate
　0.1% yeast extract
　0.05% glucose
　2% agar

[a]Leucine or any other amino acid can be omitted from this medium to make what are termed drop out plates.
[b]Filter sterilized and added after autoclaving.

It is usual to work with two strains of opposite mating type that have complementary auxotrophic markers. Small amounts of each strain (previously grown on agar plates) are mixed on the surface of a YEPD agar plate and incubated overnight at 30°C.

Alternatively intersecting lines can be drawn with the strains. Cells are then replicaplated onto a medium that lacks the amino acids for which the two haploids are auxotrophic. Only diploids can grow on this medium. You will note growth only at the intersects.

2.2.2 *Preparation of haploid spores for tetrad dissection*

(i)   Streak the cells on the selective media to separate diploids from contaminating haploids and incubate for two days at 30°C.

(ii)   Transfer to a pre-sporulation agar plate using a sterile loop or stab (or a toothpick) and incubate for two days at 30°C.

(iii)   Transfer cells to a sporulation plate and incubate for four or more days at 30°C. Check for sporulation by transferring a portion of the culture to a drop of water on the slide. A sporulating culture will have asci which contain four spores — a tetrad. Some asci may appear to only have three spores but changing the depth of focus should reveal a fourth.

(iv)   Remove a small amount of culture and suspend in a 1 in 40 dilution of filter sterilized glusulase (Endo Labs Garden City, NY). Leave at 30°C for an hour with shaking. An alternative to glusulase is Suc d'Helix pomatia (L'Industri Biologique Francaise, Genevilliers, France). Both enzyme preparations digest the ascus sac without dissociating the four spores from the ascus. Strains can vary in the length of time it takes to digest the ascus.

2.2.3 *Tetrad dissection*

Dissection of the ascus is done upside down in the USA, with the ascus on the lower surface of an agar slab and, in general, the right way up in Europe. The European approach interposes the micromanipulating needle between the objective and the agar and therefore a long working distance objective (often 20×) is vital. An overall magnification of between 150 and 300 is ideal. Doing the dissection upside down should mean that the agar has less contaminating microorganisms but contamination does not seem to be a major problem in Europe.

There are several sorts of micromanipulators and these are reviewed by Sherman (27). The Singer Micromanipulator (Singer Instrument Company Ltd., Reading, Berkshire, UK) the de Fonbrune Series A Micromanipulator (*Figure 5*) distributed by Beaudoin, Paris, France and the micromanipulator manufactured by Lawrence Precision Machine (1616 Winton Avenue, Hayward, CA, USA) are all convenient, if somewhat different.

The micromanipulator needle can be prepared in a microforge but it is possible to do it by hand.

(i)   Heat a 2 mm glass rod in a small flame, such as the pilot light of a bunsen burner and draw it out to a fine tip.

(ii)   For upside down dissecting, bend the tip at right angles (for direct dissection a right angle would obscure the tip in the microscope). The length from the right

Figure 5. The de Fonbrune Series A micromanipulator. The control joystick is on the right and transmits pneumatic signals to the micromanipulator on the left. The microneedle can be seen emanating from the micromanipulator and disappearing into the dissertion chamber on the microscope stage.

angle to the tip is a few millimetres and may vary depending on the height of the dissecting chamber (see below).

(iii) Break the tip between a glass slide and the edge of a cover slip. It should have a diameter of $10-100$ μm.

Sherman (27) has described a simple dissection chamber. It consists of a ⊔ shaped metal frame having outside dimensions of 3×1.5 inches and a depth of 0.375 inches. The bottom of the frame is attached to a 3×1.5 inch glass slide by epoxy glue. An all-glass construction can be substituted.

(i) Pour a plate of dissecting agar (10 ml/plate) while the asci are being treated with glusulase. Allow the agar to dry for about 30 min at 37°C. It is easier to lift and deposit spores if the plates are neither too wet nor too dry.

(ii) Flame a glass slide (3×1.5 inches) dipped in ethanol and place it in an empty sterile Petri dish.

(iii) Using a sterile scalpel, cut a rectangle (2×5 cm) of agar and place it on the glass slide, taking care not to trap air bubbles.

(iv) Streak a loopful of glusulase-treated yeast cells along one long edge of the agar slab.

(v) Place the slide (agar side down) on the dissection chamber. Vaseline is often used to anchor the slide to the chamber. The dissecting needle enters the chamber through the open end. Take care not to break the fragile needle tip.

(vi)   Focus the microscope on the surface of the agar and move the stage until the yeast suspension is visible. Select a cluster of four spores (an ascus).

(vii) Pick up the spores with the microneedle. This can be accomplished by maneouvering the needle such that it is placed on the agar surface close to the ascus. Surface tension will assist in picking up the ascus. You will see the ascus slide towards the needle.

(viii) Lower the needle away from the agar surface. You should not see the ascus anymore. If part of the ascus remains (i.e. one or more spores), do not use it. This is to avoid picking up false spores or cells. Remove the spores adhering to the needle by touching the needle to the agar.

(ix)   Once an ascus is picked up, move the chamber to the opposite edge and deposit all four spores. Note the coordinates on the stage. Pick up three spores and move the chamber 3 mm back toward the streaked yeast suspension. Deposit three spores and pick up two of them. Move the chamber 3 mm closer to the streak. Repeat the process until all four spores have been deposited.

(x)   Move 3 mm along the yeast suspension, locate another ascus and begin again. This process can be repeated until about 15 asci have been dissected. (The regular array is useful once the colonies grow since irregularly spaced colonies are indicative of error and should not be included in any analysis.)

(xi)   Remove the chamber from the stage. Do not break the needle!

(xii) Use a flamed spatula to transfer the agar slab spores-up to the surface of a YEPD plate.

(xiii) Incubate at 30°C until spores are large enough to be able to transfer with a stab or sterile toothpick (2−3 days).

(xiv) Transfer to a master plate, keeping each tetrad separate.

(xv)   Analyse genetic markers by replica plating onto the appropriate plates.

3. YEAST TRANSFORMATION

Intact yeast cells can be transformed with exogenous DNA in a process somewhat similar to bacterial transformation (28). Greater transformation efficiency can be achieved after the removal of the yeast cell wall and the generation of spheroplasts (5,6). This can be accomplished by incubation of yeasts in an osmotic stabilizer with enzymes that degrade the cell wall. These can include such bizarre preparations as the extract of the gut of a French snail or an enzyme preparation that was originally designed to be a dentifrice. Spheroplasts are incubated with DNA in the presence of calcium ions and polyethylene glycol (PEG). The PEG causes protoplast clumping, localized membrane fusion and uptake of DNA. Yeast spheroplasts cannot regenerate a cell wall in liquid media, therefore, putative transformants are mixed in molten agar and plated in Petri dishes where they regenerate cell walls when embedded in agar. The composition of the regeneration media can be designed such that only yeast transformants grow. For instance, if the yeast host is defective for an amino acid biosynthetic pathway gene and the equivalent wild type copy of the gene is carried on the plasmid, then transformants can be selected on regeneration media that lacks the pertinent amino acid. The detailed protocol given in *Table 4* assumes that the *leucine 2* gene is being used. A

Table 4. Yeast transformation: the spheroplast method.

A. *Reagents*

1. YEPD: 1% yeast extract, 2% peptone, 2% glucose (dextrose).
2. SED[a]: 1 M sorbitol[b], 25 mM disodium EDTA pH 8, 6.7 mg/ml dithiothreitol.
3. SCE: 1 M sorbitol[b], 0.1 M sodium citrate, 10 mM disodium EDTA. Adjust to pH 5.8 with HCl.
4. Glusulase: a crude preparation of digestive enzymes from the snail *Helix pomatia* (available from Endo Labs, Garden City, NY).
5. Lysis buffer: 3% (w/v) sarkosyl, 0.5 M Tris-HCl pH 9, 0.2 M EDTA.
6. CaS: 1 M sorbitol, 10 mM $CaCl_2$, 10 mM Tris pH 7.5.
7. Calf thymus DNA: 1 mg/ml in sterile distilled water.
8. PEG[a]: 20% (w/v) polyethylene glycol 4000, 10 mM $CaCl_2$, 10 mM Tris, pH 7.5.
9. SOS[a]: 1 M Sorbitol, 33% (v/v) YEPD, 6.7 mM $CaCl_2$, 14 μg/ml leucine.
10. 1 M Sorbitol[b].
11. −leu top agar: 1 M sorbitol, 2.5% agar, 2% glucose, 0.67% Difco yeast nitrogen base without amino acids, 10 μg/ml each adenine and methionine, 20 μg/ml each histidine, arginine, and tryptophan, 40 μg/ml each uracil and lysine, 50 μg/ml each tyrosine and threonine, 60 μg/ml each phenylalanine and isoleucine.
12. −leu + sorb plates: As in 11 (above) but with 2% agar.
13. −leu agar: As in 12 (above) but without sorbitol.

B. *Protocol*

Day 1: Late afternoon or evening, inoculate 5 ml of YEPD with the strain to be transformed. Incubate on a rotating wheel at 30°C.

Day 2:

1. First thing in the morning, dilute the 'fresh stationary' culture 1:50 into fresh YEPD (20 ml for 1−2 plasmids, 50 ml for 3−5 plasmids, 100 ml for 6−10 plasmids). Incubate at 30°C on a shaker at 200−250 r.p.m. for three generations (4.5−6 h).
2. When culture density reaches $2-4 \times 10^7$ cells/ml (OD600 = 1.5−3), pellet the cells by centrifugation and resuspend them in 1/10 volume (2 ml) of SED at 30°C for 10 min.
3. Pellet the cells by centrifugation and resuspend them in 2 ml SCE + 20 μl glusulase at 30°C for 20 min or longer. Monitor spheroplasting by diluting 5 μl of cell suspension into 45 μl lysis buffer and checking by phase contrast microscopy for the approximate percentage of lysed cells. (90% is probably optimal, 50−60% is certainly good enough, and 100% may be too much. You only want to loosen the thick rigid cell wall and membrane to get the DNA in. 'Over-spheroplasting' reduces the regeneration efficiency.)
4. Pellet the spheroplasts by centrifugation *in round bottomed tubes* and resuspend in 2 ml CaS. Repellet down, drain slightly, and resuspend the spheroplasts in 0.2 ml CaS.
5. Aliquot 0.1 ml into each tube; add 0.75−1 μg of plasmid DNA to each tube, and nothing to one of the tubes (−DNA control). The addition of 10 μg of carrier DNA (for example, calf thymus DNA) enhances transformation efficiency but is not absolutely necessary. Keep at room temperature for 15 min.
6. Add 1 ml (10 volumes) of PEG solution and mix. Leave at room temperature for 15 min.
7. Pellet the cells by centrifugation and resuspend in SOS; incubate at 30°C for 20 min.
8. Add 6 ml of −leu top agar (melted and held at 45°C), mix briefly and pour immediately onto a −leu + sorb plate. Spheroplasts should be exposed to 45°C for as short a time as possible. Let the top agar solidify and incubate the plates at 30°C. If you want to determine transformation efficiency or regeneration efficiency, serially dilute the aliquots of the samples from step 7 in 1 M sorbitol and plate the dilutions with +leu top agar on +leu plus sorb plates (20 μg/ml leucine).
9. Transformants are usually visible in 2−3 days (but can take much longer) and should be picked to −leu plates.

[a]This should be filter sterilized and made fresh every time or kept refrigerated or frozen for a brief period. All other media can be autoclaved and stored long term. YEPD should be autoclaved for 25 min, everything else for no longer than 15 min.
[b]Make up 1 M sorbitol fresh, or keep it frozen. Do not store it at 4°C.

similar protocol has been described by Rothstein in Chapter 3 of Volume II of this series. The minor variations between these protocols reflect the practice of different laboratories. One is not necessarily better than the other and we include *Table 4* to show the method used at Zymogenetics.

Whereas *E. coli* transformants grow on the surface of agar plates and, therefore, can be replica plated, yeast transformants are embedded in agar, making it necessary to recover them individually. Sterilized toothpicks are often used for this purpose as a cheap alternative to disposable loops or stabs. Transformants can be purified by streaking to single colonies on medium that selects for plasmid retention; medium lacking leucine, for example. In expression studies it is advisable to examine the levels of expression in a number of transformants as not all transformants exhibit the same expression levels.

The length of time that elapses before the appearance of transformants can vary from three days to greater than eleven days. The length of time is dependent on the protein being expressed. As a general rule, the longer the time it takes for transformants to appear, the lower the expression level that will be obtained. Some proteins appear to be toxic to a yeast cell and cause considerably lengthened mass doubling times. Such proteins appear to be expressed only at low levels in yeast. The reasons for these phenomena are not well understood but are discussed in some detail by Piggott *et al.* (17). In some instances, the toxicity can be so severe that no transformants grow. In such cases, an attempt to transform yeasts with an integrating vector may be rewarded with success. Ironically, a lower copy number of the expression unit can sometimes give greater expression levels than those possible from multicopy plasmids (14).

It is inadvisable to repeatedly transfer colonies serially by re-streaking on plates. This favours the selection of cells with reduced expression, and consequently, faster growth

Table 5. Yeast transformation: the lithium acetate method.

Day 1: Late afternoon or evening inoculate 5 ml of YEPD with the strain to be transformed. Inoculate at 30°C on a rotating wheel or shaker.

Day 2:

1. First thing in the morning, dilute 1 ml of this 'fresh stationary' phase culture into 80 ml of YEPD and incubate at 30°C at 200−250 r.p.m. on a shaker until the OD600 reaches 0.5−1.0 (4.5−6 h).
2. Divide the culture into two centrifuge bottles and pellet the cells by centrifugation at room temperature, at 8000 r.p.m. for 5 min in a Sorval HB4 rotor for example.
3. Wash the cells once in distilled water.
4. Resuspend the cells in 100 mM lithium acetate and incubate for 30−60 min at 30°C.
5. Pellet the cells by centrifugation and resuspend in 0.4 ml of 100 mM lithium acetate.
6. Place 50 μl of cell suspension in a microcentrifuge tube and add >1 μg DNA. Incubate for 30 min at 30°C.
7. Gently vortex to resuspend the cells and add 0.6 ml of 10 mM Tris-HCl pH 7.5 containing 40% polyethylene glycol-4000.
8. Incubate for 60 min at 30°C and transfer to 42°C for 5 min.
9. Centrifuge the cells for 10 sec in a microcentrifuge.
10. Wash the cell pellet in distilled water and resuspend the cells in 0.1 ml distilled water.
11. Inoculate an agar plate that is selective for transformants such as −leucine plates. Transformants will appear in 2−3 days at 30°C but can take longer depending on the structural gene being expressed.

Table 6. Transferring plasmids directly from *E. coli* to yeast.

1.	Grow a 10 ml overnight culture of *E. coli* transformants in broth at 37°C with appropriate antibiotic selection.
2.	Pellet the *E. coli* cells by centrifugation and resuspend them in 0.5 ml of 1 M sorbitol containing 20 mM EDTA pH 8 and add 50 μl of a 10 mg/ml lysozyme solution.
3.	Place on ice for 10 min and then centrifuge in a microcentrifuge for 5 min.
4.	Resuspend the pellet in 0.1 ml CaS (see *Table 4*) and use in place of DNA in the transformation protocol of *Table 4*.

rates. Re-transformation with stored plasmid is preferred, although yeast transformants can be stored at −80°C (see *Table 2*).

The alternative procedure for yeast transformation, uses lithium ions, and is given in *Table 5*. Once again a similar protocol is described by Rothstein in Chapter 3 of Volume II of this series. The method presented in *Table 5* is the one that we follow at Zymogenetics, and it is included to give an idea of variations upon basic protocols that are followed in different laboratories.

The spheroplast method is the most commonly used and gives a higher transformation efficiency. This is particularly important if one is screening a library transformed into yeast cells, but it may not be a factor if the objective is to isolate a few transformants from a given plasmid. Advantages of the lithium acetate method are (i) preparation of the host for transformation is as simple as the preparation of competent bacteria; (ii) there are no problems with cell fusion during transformation; and (iii) cells are spread directly on the agar surface rather than embedded in agar. The lithium acetate method does give a high frequency of petites (respiratory deficient cells); these can be avoided by picking the rather larger colonies that are respiratory competent (grande).

Although we have not tried it, plasmids can be transferred directly from *E. coli* to yeast. A protocol is given in *Table 6*.

4. ANALYSIS OF TRANSFORMANTS

It is usually important to analyse the prospective transformants and we have detailed several appropriate methods. It is obviously important to determine whether the colonies that are selected after transformation are in fact transformants or revertants. Analyses of transformants can entail colony hybridization or recovery and analysis of the plasmid DNA. In addition, in any examination of foreign gene expression in yeast plasmid copy number is one important factor that affects expression levels.

Where transformants are selected by the ability of colonies to grow on medium minus leucine, there is a possibility that growth results not from transformation but is due to revertants of the *leucine 2* mutation. This phenomenon can be readily checked when one is dealing with plasmids designed to express foreign genes because one can determine whether the suspected leucine plus phenotype is unstable when the cells are grown in non-selective media. Transformants can be suspended in water and spread on YEPD agar such that there are 100−200 colonies per plate. Once they have formed colonies, they can be replica plated to a −leucine plate (0.67% Difco yeast nitrogen base without amino acids, 2% glucose, plus multiple nutritional supplements except leucine, 2%

Table 7. Yeast colony hybridization.

1.	Streak or replica plate cells onto nitrocellulose filters placed on the surface of YEPD agar in a Petri dish.
2.	Incubate overnight at 30°C.
3.	Remove the filters and allow them to dry.
4.	The filters are then transferred to a series of solutions that are used to saturate 3 MM paper. The filter is placed colony-side uppermost on papers impregnated with the following solutions:

    (i)   1 M sorbitol, 20 mM EDTA, 50 mM dithiothreitol.

    (ii)   1 M sorbitol, 20 mM EDTA plus 1 mg/ml zymolyase 60 000 at 37°C for 2 – 3 h. This step needs to be done in a covered dish or the liquid will evaporate. The progress of spheroplasting can be followed as described in the protocol for yeast transformation. The time given is only an estimate of the time necessary for spheroplasting. It is not sacrosanct.

    (iii)   0.5 M NaOH for 7 min at room temperature.

    (iv)   0.5 M Tris-HCl pH 7.0, 10 × SSC[a] for 4 min.

    (v)   0.5 M Tris-HCl pH 7.5, 10 × SSC for 4 min.

    (vi)   Twice with 5 × SSC for 2 min.

5.	Dry the filters on absorbent paper for 30 min.
6.	Bake the filters in a vacuum oven 80°C for 1 – 2 h.

[a]SSC is 0.15 M NaCl, 0.015 M sodium citrate.

Table 8. Quick yeast plasmid isolation.

1.	Grow 10 ml yeast cultures to stationary phase overnight in synthetic − leucine media. 5 ml cultures grown in YEPD liquid media are an acceptable substitute for all but the most unstable plasmids.
2.	Pellet the cells by centrifugation, resuspend them in 1 ml distilled water and transfer to a 1.5 ml microcentrifuge tube.
3.	Pellet the cells by centrifugation for approximately 30 sec in a microcentrifuge. Resuspend the pellet in 0.6 ml of 1 M sorbitol, 0.1 M sodium acetate pH 5.8, 10 mM EDTA, 0.1 M 2-mercaptoethanol, 0.1 mg Zymolyase 60 000 (Miles) per ml.
4.	Incubate for 30 min at 37°C. Check periodically for 'spheroplasting' by microscopic examination.
5.	Add 0.2 ml of 50 mM Tris-HCl pH 8.0, 50 mM EDTA.
6.	Incubate with 2 ml of diethylpyrocarbonate at 65°C for 30 min.
7.	Transfer to ice, add 0.1 M of 5 M potassium acetate and leave for 60 min.
8.	Eat lunch.
9.	Centrifuge for 5 min in a microcentrifuge. Remove the supernatant and add 2 ml of 95% ethanol. Place at −70°C for 30 – 60 min.
10.	Pellet the nucleic acids by centrifugation and resuspend the pellet in 10 mM Tris-HCl pH 8.0, 1 mM EDTA, 0.2 M NaCl.
11.	Reprecipitate the nucleic acids with ethanol as described above and resuspend the final pellet in 10 mM Tris-HCl pH 8.0, 1 mM EDTA.

agar). The plates can be compared to see if any colonies failed to grow on −leucine medium because of plasmid loss.

It is possible to look for specific nucleic acid sequences in yeast strains by colony hybridization. Sample preparation is somewhat different in yeast than in *E. coli*: once the nitrocellulose filter with DNA has been prepared, the protocols are similar to those adaptable with *E. coli*. A detailed protocol is given in *Table 7*. A similar protocol is also described by Rothstein in Chapter 3 of Volume II.

The plasmid preparations from yeast can be used for restriction enzyme digests or can be used to transform *E. coli* cells to amplify the amount of DNA. A protocol for such preparations is given in *Table 8*.

A variety of techniques can be used to measure plasmid copy number, but all require the isolation of total yeast DNA from a transformed strain, followed by a determination of the ratio of the amount of plasmid DNA relative to total genomic DNA. A relatively simple way to get an estimate of the copy number of a high copy number plasmid is to compare the intensity of ethidium bromide staining of a plasmid specific restriction fragment and a fragment corresponding to the repeated ribosomal DNA sequences in total genomic DNA. When total DNA from a transformed yeast is cut with a restriction endonuclease that produces restriction fragments from within the plasmid and the ribosomal DNA repeat, they can be visualized as ethidium bromide staining bands after electrophoresis on agarose gels. The bands stand out against a background staining of random genomic DNA fragments. There are approximately 140 ribosomal DNA repeats in a haploid yeast cell and thus the amount of plasmid DNA can be calculated after quantitation by densitometer scans of photographic negatives of gels. Staining intensity must be normalized for the size of fragments; it is sensible to choose a restriction endonuclease that liberates similarly-sized fragments from both plasmid and ribosomal DNA repeat. A restriction map of the ribosomal DNA repeat is given by Bell *et al.* (29).

$$\text{Copy number} = \frac{\text{(area under plasmid peak) (length of rDNA fragment)}}{\text{(area under rDNA peak) (length of plasmid fragment)}} \times 140$$

An alternative method to determine copy number is by Southern analysis. Total DNA is restricted and fragments separated on a gel. The DNA is transferred to nitrocellulose and hybridized with a probe that is represented (usually once) in the host genome and also on the plasmid. An absolute value for copy number can be determined from densitometer tracings of the autoradiogram. Consideration should also be given to the relative lengths of the fragments and the extent to which fragments are covered by the labelled probe.

5. GROWTH OF CELLS FOR EXPRESSION AND SECRETION STUDIES

Cells can be grown in defined media or complex media. If the expression plasmid has a copy of the *leucine 2* gene and the yeast host is *leucine 2* defective, it is common for transformed cells to be grown in a defined medium which contains all of the essential nutrients with the exception of leucine. Growth in this medium is only possible so long as the cells retain the plasmid.

In small scale cultures (less than 100 ml), it is often possible to grow yeast cells on complex media such as 1% yeast extract, 2% bactopeptone (both from Difco) and 2% of a carbon source. The carbon source is generally glucose when a glycolytic promoter is being used or 1% ethanol plus 3% glycerol when a respiratory promoter, such as that of iso-1-cytochrome-*c*, is used on the expression plasmid. It may be useful to buffer the medium to pH 7.0 and the addition of 0.01% bovine serum albumin (BSA) may protect a secreted recombinant protein from degradation in some instances.

Transformed yeast cells growing as colonies on solid agar can be inoculated directly into liquid media. Yeast cells can be grown at a variety of temperatures and grow well up to 37°C. However, it is usual for cells to be grown at 25° or 30°C unless the use of temperature-sensitive mutants dictate a lower temperature.

Growth can be monitored by a change in optical density at 600 nm or by an alteration in cell numbers using a Coulter Counter (Coulter Electronics, Hialeh, FL). Yeast cells will grow with a doubling time of about 2.5 h at 25 °C in complex medium and 3 h in defined medium. Yeast cells transformed with a plasmid expressing certain mammalian proteins grow at much reduced growth rates. The reduction in growth rate may vary from protein to protein: yeast cells seem capable of expressing alpha-interferon with little effect on growth rate but even closely-related proteins such as beta-interferon can result in a doubling or more of the generation time. It is not possible to predict beforehand whether or not the gene one is wishing to express in yeast will be toxic to a yeast cell.

Samples can be withdrawn at intervals from the culture using a pipette.

6. PREPARATION OF SAMPLES FOR ANALYSIS

Harvested samples can be centrifuged or filtered to separate the culture media from the cells. If only small samples are being processed, a 2 min spin in a microcentrifuge will suffice; for somewhat larger samples ($>$ 100 ml), centrifugation at 8000 r.p.m. for 5 min in a Sorvall HB4 rotor, for example, will separate yeast cells from the culture media. Filtration through millipore filters (pore diameter 0.45 μm) is an adequate alternative.

Where secretion is being investigated, it is necessary in some instances to concentrate the protein in the medium. This procedure can be accomplished using Amicon filtration.

Yeast cells must be broken to recover cytoplasmically expressed proteins. There are a variety of ways this can be done. We detail here a simple method suitable for small volumes of cells ($<$ 100 ml).

(i)   Separate cells from culture filtrate by centrifugation or filtration as described above.

(ii)   Wash cells with appropriate buffer such as phosphate-buffered saline containing 0.01% BSA or a buffer such as 50 mM KH_2PO_4, 2 mM EDTA pH 8.0, 1 mM PMSF (protease inhibitor). Add β-mercaptoethanol to a final concentration of 2 mM.

(iii)   Resuspend the cells in buffer using 1 ml of buffer for every 20 ml of culture prior to harvesting.

(iv)   Transfer samples that are suspended in a small amount of buffer (0.5 ml) to a microcentrifuge tube (1.5 ml volume). Add acid washed 40 μm mesh glass beads (BDH) until there is the barest miniscus of free liquid at the surface.

(v)   Hold the microcentrifuge tube on a vortex mixer (turn the mixer to full speed). Try to hold in such a way that a vortex forms in the tube. This will require some trial and error.

(vi)   Different yeast strains and even the same strain expressing different recombinant proteins can vary in the length of time that it takes to achieve cell breakage by this method. If it takes longer than 5 min, you have a problem. Vortexing should be in 1 min pulses with cooling in an ice bath between pulses.

(vii)   Monitor the efficiency of all breakage by light microscopic examination of a small amount of liquor removed using an eppendorf tip and transferred to a microscope slide. Use approximately 400 $\times$ or greater magnification. It is sometimes possible to underestimate cell breakage because the yeast can maintain an appearance of morphological integrity even though the cell wall has broken and the contents extruded. Such cells can be distinguished from unbroken cells under phase-contrast. Agitation with glass beads will eventually lead to destruction of the wall and only debris can be observed by light microscopy.

(viii)   Remove the broken cell mixture from the beads by placing a 1 ml eppendorf pipette to the bottom of the tube and withdrawing the liquor by suction. A pasteur pipette is a suitable substitute.

(ix)   Place the sample in a microcentrifuge tube and centrifuge for 5 min at 4°C to sediment all debris.

(x)   Remove and save the supernatant. Repeat the centrifugation. Recover the supernatant and treat as a cell-free extract.

For larger samples a round-bottomed test tube can be substituted for a microcentrifuge tube. The size of the test tube is dependent on the size of the sample. If the liquid spills over the top of the test tube when a vortex forms, it is too small. If a vortex does not form, try a larger and possibly wider tube.

7. ANALYSIS OF YEAST EXPRESSION

It is possible to examine expression of foreign proteins in yeast by the detection of a protein band on a gel. If the protein is reasonably well-expressed, a band on a gel can be visualized by Coomassie Blue or silver stain. For poorly-expressed protein, Western blotting using an antibody to the recombinant protein is necessary to visualize the protein of interest. A biological assay is important to determine that the protein being made by yeast has the activity expected. Occasionally proteins that are produced cytoplasmically in yeast do not have the appropriate biological activity. In these instances, secretion into the medium may well correct the problem.

Analysis of the recombinant product involves techniques such as detection on gels by Coomassie stain, Western blotting, ELISA assay, etc. that are in common use and do not need special adaption for yeast, therefore they will not be described here.

Yeast, unlike *E. coli*, has the capacity to glycosylate proteins and it is important to determine the extent of glycosylation of the foreign protein of interest. Glycoproteins can be visualized on gels (30) or after transfer to nitrocellulose (31).

8. PURIFICATION OF YEAST-DERIVED RECOMBINANT PROTEINS

Recombinant proteins can be purified in the same way as any other protein in a cell-free extract. Methods for yeast do not differ from those used for *E. coli* (see Chapter 4). A general rule with yeast, however, is that you do not have to worry about renaturation of denatured protein. In particular, we know of no example of secreted proteins from yeast that did not have the proper biological activity. On a smaller scale, purification of secreted proteins via immunoaffinity chromatography is the prejudice of at least the first author.

9. ACKNOWLEDGEMENTS

Bruce L.A.Carter would like to thank A.R.Goodey for teaching him how to do ligations without adding magnesium.

10. REFERENCES

1. Hall,M.N., Hereford,L. and Herskowitz,I. (1984) *Cell*, **36**, 1057.
2. Guarente,L., Yocum,R.R. and Gifford,P.(1982) *Proc. Natl. Acad. Sci. USA*, **73**, 7410.
3. Emr,S.D., Schauer,L., Hansen,W., Esmon,P. and Schekman,R. (1984) *Mol. Cell. Biol.*, **4**, 2347.
4. Kelly,J.D., Raines,E.W., Ross,R. and Murray,M.J. (1985) *EMBO J.*, **4**, 3399.
5. Beggs,J.D. (1978) *Nature*, **275**, 104.
6. Hinnen,A.J., Hicks,J. and Fink,G. (1978) *Proc. Natl. Acad. Sci. USA*, **75**, 1929.
7. Hagen,F.S., Gray,C.L., O'Hara,P., Grant,F.J., Saari,G.C., Woodbury,R.G., Hart,C.E., Insley,M., Kisiel,W., Kurachi,K. and Davie,E.W. (1986) *Proc. Natl. Acad. Sci. USA*, **83**, 2412.
8. Maniatis,T., Fritsch,E.F. and Sambrook,J. (1982) *Molecular Cloning*, Cold Spring Harbor Laboratory, Cold Spring Harbor, New York.
9. Davis,R.W., Botstein,D. and Roth,J.R. (1980) *Advanced Bacterial Genetics*, Cold Spring Harbor Laboratory, Cold Spring Harbor, New York.
10. Prescott,D.M. (ed.) (1975) *Methods in Cell Biology*. Volumes 11 and 12. Academic Press, New York.
11. Sherman,F., Fink,G.R. and Hicks,J.B. (1982) *Methods in Yeast Genetics*, Cold Spring Harbor Laboratory, Cold Spring Harbor, New York.
12. Wu,R., Grossman,L. and Muldave,K. (eds) (1983) *Methods in Enzymology, Volume 101*, Academic Press, New York.
13. Broach,J.R. (1983) In *Methods in Enzymology*, Wu,R., Grossman,L. and Moldave,K. (eds), Academic Press, New York, Vol. 101, p. 307.
14. Smith,R.A., Duncan,M. and Moir,D.J. (1985) *Science*, **229**, 1219.
15. Bitter,G.A. and Egan,K.M. (1984) *Gene*, **32**, 263.
16. Schaber,M.D., DeChiara,T.M. and Kramer,R.A. (1986) In *Methods in Enzymology*, Pestka,S. (ed.), Academic Press, New York, Vol. 119, p. 416.
17. Piggott,J.R., Watson,M.M., Doel,S.D., Goodey,A.R. and Carter,B.L.A. (1987) In *Yeast Biotechnology*, Spencer,F. (ed.), Academic Press, New York.
18. Hartwell,L.H. (1973) *Exp. Cell Res.*, **76**, 111.
19. Kurjan,J. and Herskowitz,I. (1983) *Cell*, **30**, 933.
20. Julius,D., Blair,L., Brake,A., Sprague,G. and Thorner,J. (1983) *Cell*, **32**, 839.
21. Julius,D., Schekman,R. and Thorner,J. (1984) *Cell*, **36**, 309.
22. Julius,D., Brake,A., Blair,L., Kunisawa,R. and Thorner,J. (1984) *Cell*, **37**, 1075.
23. Brake,A.J., Merryweather,J.P., Cuit,D.G. and Herbelein,J.A. (1984) *Proc. Natl. Acad. Sci. USA*, **81**, 4642.
24. Thim,L., Hansen,M.T., Norris,K., Hoegh,I., Boel,E., Forstrom,J., Ammerer,G. and Fiil,N.P. (1986) *Proc. Natl. Acad. Sci. USA*, **83**, 6766.
25. Shaw,A.R.E., Bleakley,R.C., Merryweather,J.P. and Barr,P.J. (1985) *Cell Immunol.*, **91**, 193.
26. Ammerer,G. (1983) In *Methods in Enzymology*, Wu,R., Grossman,L. and Moldave,K. (eds), Academic Press, New York, Vol. 101, p. 192.
27. Sherman,F. (1975) In *Methods in Cell Biology*. Prescott,D.M. (ed.), Academic Press, New York, vol. 11, p. 189.
28. Ito,H., Fukuda,Y., Murata,K. and Kimura,A. (1983) *J. Bacteriol.*, **153**, 163.

10. REFERENCES

CHAPTER 8

The use of vectors based on gene amplification for the expression of cloned genes in mammalian cells

CHRISTOPHER R.BEBBINGTON and CHRISTOPHER C.G.HENTSCHEL

1. INTRODUCTION

1.1 Strategies for expression of cloned genes in mammalian cells

The ability of cloned genes to function when introduced into mammalian tissue culture cells has proved to be invaluable in studies of gene expression. It also provides a means of obtaining, in large quantities, proteins which are otherwise scarce or which are the completely novel products of gene manipulation. The great advantage in obtaining such proteins from mammalian cells is that they are generally correctly folded, appropriately modified and completely functional, in marked contrast to the results of expression in bacteria.

For many studies of mammalian gene expression, analysis of transient expression, which occurs in a proportion of cells within a few hours of introduction of DNA, is most appropriate. In other cases, when larger amounts of product are needed, it is necessary to identify cell clones in which the vector sequences are retained during cell proliferation. Such stable vector maintenance can be achieved in one of two ways; either by the use of a viral replicon such as bovine papillomavirus (BPV) as described in DNA Cloning Volume II, Chapter 8, or as a consequence of integration of the vector into the host cell's DNA. Any foreign DNA can integrate, at a low frequency, in apparently random sites in the host chromosomes and the resultant clones can be identified by the use of a suitable selectable marker gene. Various selectable vectors and methods for introducing them into tissue culture cells have already been described in DNA Cloning Volume II, Chapter 6. In this chapter, we describe methods for obtaining increased efficiency of gene expression from integrating vectors in stable transfected cell lines.

Genes expressed in eukaryotic vectors can consist of genomic sequences containing natural promoter elements and RNA processing signals, or alternatively, cDNAs can be used provided that they are equipped with a heterologous promoter and polyadenylation signal. Some of the most efficient transcription units can be constructed using viral regulatory signals, many of which function in a variety of host cell types. However, efficient transcription units on their own rarely provide the maximum possible levels of expression: higher levels are generally obtained if the vector copy number can be increased.

The use of viral vectors such as BPV for this purpose has the advantage that a high copy number (up to several hundred copies per cell) is established rapidly and as a result, BPV vectors have been used successfully to express many proteins very efficiently (1). Viral vectors are however restricted in the cell types in which they will replicate and expression levels and episomal maintenance can also be influenced by the particular DNA sequences inserted into them. The alternative means of increasing vector copy number, described here, is to select for amplification of vector sequences after integration into host cell DNA. In principal, this approach is not restricted to particular cell types. Thus, a cell line can be chosen with any required characteristic, such as the ability to carry out particular post-translational modifications or the ability to recognize particular regulatory DNA sequences.

The methodology exploits the phenomenon of gene amplification which is described in the next section.

1.2 Gene amplification

When cultured cells are subjected to appropriate concentrations of certain toxic drugs, variant clones can often be selected which are more resistant to the drug than are wild type cells. One common mechanism by which such variants arise is by overproduction of an essential enzyme whose activity the drug inhibits. The overproduction of enzyme most commonly results from increased levels of its particular mRNA, which in turn is frequently caused by an increase in the number of copies of its structural gene in each cell.

The first gene found to 'amplify' in this way was the dihydrofolate reductase (DHFR) gene, in variants of hamster and mouse cell lines which arose after selection for resistance to the specific inhibitor of DHFR, methotrexate (MTX; see review in ref. 2). When the DHFR gene was subsequently cloned and re-introduced into a cell line which lacked endogenous DHFR activity, the cloned gene was shown to be capable of amplification as well. Since then, at least 12 other genes have been shown to be amplifiable when selected with a specific inhibitor (3). Those for which a full length coding sequence has been cloned are listed in *Table 1*. In all cases tested so far, both genomic DNAs and cDNAs encoding such enzymes are amplifiable when transferred into tissue culture cells in an expression vector (e.g. 6,7,8,9,11,12). Thus, it is unlikely that any particular sequence within these genes is responsible for the mechanism of amplification. Although the mechanism is not fully understood, it appears that the selection protocol serves merely to identify random amplification events occurring with characteristic frequencies in all proliferating cell populations. One plausible theory suggests that these events are associated with errors in DNA replication (2). Consistent with this theory, it is a general feature of gene amplification that the region of chromosomal DNA amplified is much greater than the enzyme's coding sequence (often more than 1000 kb

Table 1. Amplifiable genes cloned and expressed in mammalian cells.

Gene		Selective agent		Ref
Adenosine deaminase	ADA	Deoxycoformycin	dCF	4
Aspartate transcarbamylase	CAD	N(phosphonacetyl)-L-aspartate	PALA	5
Dihydrofolate reductase	DHFR	Methotrexate	MTX	6
Glutamine synthetase	GS	Methionine sulphoximine	MSX	7
Metallothionein-I	MT-1	Heavy metals e.g. Cd^{2+}		8
Thymidine kinase (defective)	TK	−		9
Multi-drug resistance	*mdr*	Adriamycin (and others)	ADM	10

of DNA is amplified intact). As a consequence of this, when transfected genes are selected for amplification, other sequences on the vector also show increased copy number; that is, they are co-amplified.

1.3 **Co-amplification and its uses**

The ability to select for gene amplification can be a powerful tool in a number of circumstances. For instance it can be used to facilitate cloning of amplifiable genes and analysis of their gene and chromatin structure. Here, though, we are interested in the use of amplification to over-express protein products. In this case, the practical consequence of the fact that vector sequences are co-amplified after selection for an amplifiable marker gene is that levels of expression of introduced genes can be increased dramatically. The increase in levels of protein production is frequently found to be roughly proportional to the increase in gene copy number after amplification, at least until a plateau of protein production is approached. DHFR genes have usually been used for this purpose in a mutant CHO cell line which lacks endogenous DHFR activity.

Using selection for DHFR amplification as part of an expression system, some of the highest reported levels of protein production have been achieved for a number of secreted products (1). However, any of the cloned genes listed in *Table 1* could potentially be used as a marker for vector amplification. As described in Section 1.4, some of these genes can be useful in extending the application of the system to a variety of different cell lines.

1.4 **General features of amplifiable vectors**

The vector constructions which can be used are very variable and are discussed in more detail in Section 3, but a typical vector will have the following.
(i)   Bacterial plasmid sequences containing an origin of replication for propagation in *E. coli* and a bacterial selectable marker.
(ii)   A selectable marker gene which functions in mammalian cells.
(iii)   An amplifiable gene.
(iv)   An expression cassette with a convenient cloning site for the insertion of the gene of interest.

It is most convenient if the amplifiable marker also acts as the selectable marker. This is because transfected DNA is liable to re-arrangement and mutation so that not all clones selected for expression of one genetic marker will also express the amplifiable gene. One circumstance in which the amplifiable gene can be used for selection occurs if a cell line is used which is deficient in the enzyme activity of the amplifiable marker gene; this is the case in the example described above in which mutant CHO cells are used which lack DHFR activity. A transfected DHFR gene can thus confer a DHFR$^+$ phenotype on this cell line (characterized by the ability to grow without nucleosides and glycine).

Alternatively, the amplifiable gene may be able to be used as a 'dominant' selectable marker in cell lines which already possess endogenous enzyme activity. In such cases a level of the toxic drug is chosen which kills wild-type cells but allows transfected cells to survive because of their higher levels of expression of the enzyme. Not all dominant selectable markers are amplifiable by selection; the bacterial markers *neo* and *gpt* (see DNA Cloning Volume II, Chapter 6) for instance, cannot be used to select for amplification because there is no inhibitor available which binds stoichiometrically to either of these enzymes. However, all of the mammalian genes in *Table 1* are at least potentially dominant, amplifiable markers.

The features of an ideal amplifiable marker may be summarized as follows:

(i)   The gene is small enough to facilitate vector construction.

(ii)   The gene acts as a dominant selectable marker in a wide variety of cell types.

(iii)   Resistance to the drug is exclusively caused by amplification of the transfected gene.

(iv)   Amplification is achieved using convenient levels of toxic drug (in terms of solubility and cost).

(v)   High level expression of the enzyme should not be deleterious to the cell.

(vi)   The levels of drug used should not cause toxicity by any other means.

The DHFR gene has been most widely used although current DHFR vectors are not ideal. The original DHFR vectors were designed for use in *dhfr⁻* CHO cells in which they are very effective, attaining copy numbers of for example approximately 2000 per cell (12). However, to act as dominant selectable markers in cell lines which contain active *dhfr* genes, the transfected gene must confer resistance to a high enough level of MTX not only to kill wild-type cells but also to inhibit the growth of variants which arise due to amplification of the endogenous genes. Vectors able to be used in this way have been constructed, using either a very strong promoter for efficient expression of DHFR (13) or a cDNA containing a mutant DHFR coding sequence which expresses an enzyme having a lower binding affinity for MTX (14). However, such high levels of MTX are needed for amplification of these vectors in the cell lines tested that they are of limited value since the solubility of the drug becomes limiting. It should be noted though that one of the vectors designed for use in *dhfr⁻* cells, pSV2.dhfr (*Figure 1*) has been used successfully as a dominant marker in mouse fibroblasts (15).

A further disadvantage associated with DHFR-mediated co-amplification is that methotrexate resistance is not exclusively due to amplification (13,16).

Adenosine deaminase (ADA) and glutamine synthetase (GS) have both been used successfully as dominant selectable markers in certain cell lines and can also be subsequently amplified; for instance up to 500 copies/cell in one ADA-transformed cell line, (4) and several thousand copies in one case using GS (17). The usefulness of either of these two markers in any particular circumstance will depend to some extent on the levels of endogenous enzyme in different cell types and on the frequencies of endogenous gene amplification. GS has the advantage that its inhibitor methionine sulphoximine (MSX) is cheap and readily available but the success of the selection protocol is dependent on the ability of the cell to take up glutamic acid from the medium (see Section 2.3). Some cell lines may be defective in this transport step. ADA on the other hand requires the use of compounds which are not commercially available and suffers from the drawback that resistance to dCF can arise by mechanisms other than increased ADA levels (4,18). However, a selection protocol has been devised which can circumvent this problem (see Section 2.4).

The other amplifiable marker described in detail in this chapter is the metallothionein gene. One of two mouse genes, mMT-1, has been studied extensively. The mMT-1

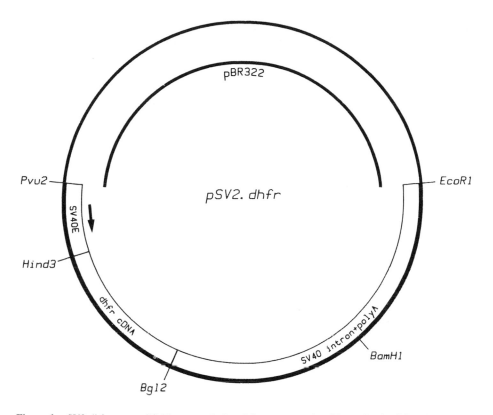

Figure 1. pSV2.dhfr, an amplifiable vector designed for use as a selectable marker in *dhfr*-deficient CHO cells (6). The plasmid is 5.0 kb in length and consists of the following: the 323 bp *Pvu*II-*Hin*dIII fragment of SV40, spanning the origin of replication, orientated so that the SV40 Early promoter directs transcription of the DHFR gene; a 735 bp DHFR cDNA; an intron from SV40 (SV40 nucleotides 4099−4710); a *Bcl*I-*Eco*RI fragment of SV40 (nucleotides 2770−1782) containing the early-region polyadenylation signal; the *Pvu*II-*Eco*RI fragment of pBR322 (2295 bp) containing the origin of replication and the β-lactamase gene, which confers resistence to ampicillin.

gene is small enough for genomic DNA to be conveniently cloned in plasmid vectors (8). It has not been used successfully as a dominant selectable marker (except in BPV vectors, 19) and so an additional marker gene is required for initial selection. However, the simple, cheap selection protocol required for mMT-1 amplification may make this system attractive in some circumstances. It should be noted though that copy numbers in excess of 100 have not been achieved with this system.

Two other genes which have been shown to act as amplifiable markers are not described in detail here, namely CAD and TK. CAD genomic DNA expressed in a cosmid vector can act as a dominant selectable marker in CHO cells (5) but the large size of this gene renders it very cumbersome for vector manipulation. An interesting variation is the use of a bacterial aspartate transcarbamylase to complement a CAD-defective CHO cell line (20). This enzyme is also amplifiable, by selection in PALA, and so could perhaps be used as a selectable, amplifiable marker but is likely to be restricted to this particular mutant cell line.

A defective TK gene has also been shown to be amplifiable (9) but its use is restricted to TK⁻ cells and the copy numbers reported are limited, so it is not described here.

1.5 Methods described in this chapter

In Section 2, protocols are given for initial selection and subsequent gene amplification in cells containing vectors using DHFR, ADA, GS and mMT-1 genes. Section 3 describes some factors which should be taken into consideration in designing an amplification strategy. In Section 4, techniques are provided for the analysis of gene amplification.

2. PROTOCOLS FOR SELECTION FOR GENE AMPLIFICATION

2.1 Dihydrofolate reductase

2.1.1 *Selection in DHFR⁻ CHO cells*

The DHFR gene has been by far the most widely used selection system for co-amplification. Typically, a *dhfr⁻* variant of the CHO-K1 cell line is used, called DUKX B11 (21), since in this cell line a transfected DHFR transcription unit can act

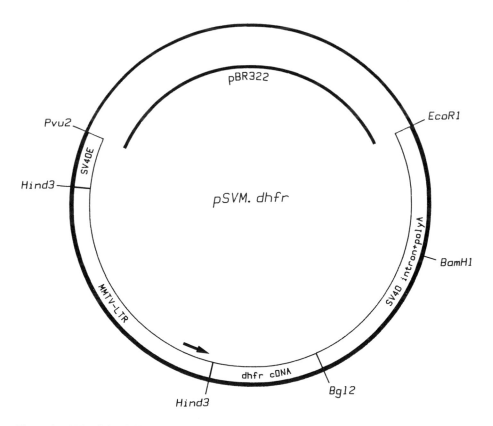

Figure 2. pSVM.dhfr, (6.45 kb) an alternative selectable vector for *dhfr*-deficient cells (22). A regulatable promoter provided by the 5′ long terminal repeat of mouse mammary tumour virus (MMTV-LTR) is inserted into pSV2.dhfr to direct expression of the DHFR cDNA.

Table 2. Media for DHFR selection.

Two alternative sets of media are given: 1. based on Dulbecco's modified Eagle's medium (DMEM) and 2. based on MEM-Alpha medium.

A.   *Stock solutions*

   For non-selective medium:
   1.   Ham's F12 nutrient mixture (Flow: 12−432[a]) *or*
   2.   Alternatively MEM Alpha medium with nucleosides (GIBCO: 041−2571[a]).

   For selective medium:
   1.   Dulbecco's modified Eagle medium (GIBCO: 041−1885[a]) *or*
   2.   Alternatively MEM Alpha medium without nucleosides (GIBCO: 041−2561[a]).

   200 mM L-glutamine (GIBCO). Store at −20°C in 5 ml aliquots.
   Non-essential amino acids (NEAA; GIBCO), for DMEM only.
   Penicillin−streptomycin (P/S; GIBCO: 043−5070[a]). Store at −20°C in 5 ml aliquots.
   Fetal calf-serum (FCS): heat inactivate at 56°C for 30 min and store at −20°C.
   Dialysed FCS (GIBCO: 063−6300[a]) heat inactivated and stored as above.

B.   *Media preparation*

   1.   (i) non-selective medium
          Ham's F12   500 ml
          FCS   50 ml
          L-glutamine   5 ml
          P/S   5 ml
          (ii) selective medium
          DMEM   500 ml
          dialysed FCS   50 ml
          P/S   5 ml

   or

   2.   (i) non-selective medium
          MEM-Alpha with nucleosides   500 ml
          FCS   50 ml
          P/S   5 ml

          (ii) selective medium
          MEM-Alpha without nucleosides 500 ml
          dialysed FCS   50 ml
          P/S   5 ml

[a]Manufacturers' catalogue numbers listed are only to serve as a guide for reference. The products of alternative manufacturers may be adequate or preferable.

as a selectable marker. The cell line requires exogenous nucleosides and glycine for survival as well as proline (because the CHO-K1 parent is incidentally *pro*⁻). A variety of different vectors containing DHFR coding sequences can transform the cells to a *dhfr*⁺ phenotype, thus allowing them to grow without added nucleosides and glycine. Vectors containing a DHFR cDNA under the control of SV40 promoters (6), the MMTV-LTR promoter (22) and the adenovirus major late promoter (23) have all been used successfully in this cell line as have *dhfr* minigenes containing *dhfr* 5′ flanking sequences (12). The frequencies of transformation vary between 2×10^{-5} and 10^{-3} colonies using $1-10$ μg DNA for transfection, depending on the vector and procedure used. However, since the reversion frequency of the cell line is extremely low, ($< 10^{-7}$) any such vectors can be used as selectable markers in this cell line.

Two useful DHFR vectors are shown in *Figures 1* and *2*. Both yield high frequencies of

Table 3. Examples of dhfr-mediated co-amplification.

	pSVM.dhfr	pSV2.dhfr
Number of transfectants/plate	~ 100	~ 100
Number secreting tPA	20	50
Maximum tPA secretion (units/10^6 cells/day)	150	100
Maximum MTX concentration yielding colonies (nM)	20	500
Maximum tPA secretion after 1 round of amplification (units/10^6 cells/day)	1300	1500

A gene encoding tissue plasminogen activator (tPA) was cloned in pSV2.dhfr (*Figure 1*) and pSVM.dhfr (*Figure 2*). About 10^6 DUKX-B11 cells were transfected with 5 μg each plasmid.

transfection in DUKX B11 cells, as shown in the example results given in *Table 3*. Two alternative media for selection of *dhfr*$^+$ clones are given in *Table 2*.

2.1.2 *Protocol for transfection of DHFR$^-$ CHO cells*

(i)   Plate cells at a density of approximately 10^6 cells per 9 cm Petri dish the day before transfection, in non-selective medium (see *Table 2*).

(ii)   Transfect with 10 μg plasmid using the CaPO$_4$ method given in DNA Cloning Volume II, Chapter 6 and then allow the cells to recover in non-selective medium. At this stage, the actual number of cells transfected can be measured from a non-transfected dish. (Methods for counting adherent cells are described in DNA Cloning Volume II, Chapter 6). Also treat some dishes of cells with CaPO$_4$ but without DNA to act as controls.

(iii)   Remove the medium and replace with the selective medium after 24 −48 h (see *Table 2*). Change the medium again after 3−4 days when substantial cell death should be apparent. (The dead cells float off the bottom of the Petri dish).

(iv)   Change the medium again every 3−4 days. After 7−8 days, many small colonies may appear but wait until 10−12 days after transfection before scoring the number of stably transformed colonies as many colonies survive for only a few days due to transient expression of the introduced DHFR genes.

(v)   The transfection frequency with either of the vectors shown in *Figures 1* and 2 should be $1-2 \times 10^{-4}$ transfected cells/10 μg DNA. Cell lines can be established from individual colonies and assayed for expression of the gene of interest.

2.1.3 *Amplification with methotrexate*

The concentration of MTX needed for amplification of a *dhfr* gene depends on the efficiency with which the gene is expressed, which is in part determined by the vector chosen. For instance, in CHO cells, the SV40 early promoter in pSV2.dhfr is a stronger promoter than the MMTV-LTR in pSVM.dhfr. Therefore, clones transfected with pSV2.dhfr are on average more resistant to MTX than clones transfected with pSVM.dhfr. There is however, also variability between individual transfected clones. Therefore cells from each clone to be amplified should be selected using a range of MTX concentrations, using the following protocol.

(i)   Prepare a sterile stock solution of 100 μM MTX in water. This can be stored at $-20°$C.

(ii)   Set up several Petri dishes with approximately 10^6 cells per dish in selective medium and add MTX to final concentrations of 10, 20, 50, 100, 200 and 500 nM.

(iii)   After 10 days, examine the plates for surviving colonies. Clones resistant to the highest concentration of MTX can be analysed individually or can be pooled and subjected to a second round of selection at for instance 500 nM and higher concentrations of MTX.

Gene amplification can be up to 10-fold in the first round of amplification, as measured by gene copy number or expression of a linked gene (see Section 4 for methods of analysis). In subsequent rounds of amplification, gene copy number is often roughly proportional to MTX-resistance and up to 2000 copies have been reported after three or more rounds of selection. Secretion of a co-expressed protein can exceed 3×10^8 molecules/cell/day in highly resistant clones (1).

2.2 Metallothionein

Metallothioneins are small, cysteine-rich proteins which bind to a variety of heavy metals and are important in their detoxification. One of two mouse metallothionein genes (mMT-1) has been cloned and shown to be amplifiable by selection with Cd^{2+} ions (8). There are two important differences when compared with the DHFR gene. Firstly, binding of heavy metals to metallothionein is not toxic to the cell *per se*, but instead prevents other toxic interactions. The phenotypic effect of overexpression of metallothionein is thus indirect. Secondly, the mMT-1 promoter is itself regulated by heavy metals so that gene transcription is increased in response to Cd^{2+}. Probably as a consequence of both of these facts, the copy numbers achievable by selection for mMT-1 amplification are not as great as those obtained using DHFR amplification. In CHO-K1 cells, the mMT-1 gene cannot itself be used as a selectable marker (our unpublished results). Therefore a dominant selectable marker gene such as *neo* or *gpt* must be included in the vector. This has the limitation that not all transfectants will have an active mMT-1 gene and so many will not be amplifiable.

A useful vector from which to obtain the mMT-1 gene is shown in *Figure 3*. A protocol for selecting and amplifying vectors containing a *neo* gene and mMT-1 gene in CHO-K1 cells is as follows.

(i)   Transfect the cells using $CaPO_4$ co-precipitation as described in DNA Cloning Volume II, Chapter 6 in any suitable medium such as Ham's F12 (*Table 2*).

(ii)   After 24 h, add the drug required for selection of the *neo* gene, G418, to a final concentration of 0.8 mg/ml.

(iii)   Change the selective medium again after 3−4 days.

(iv)   Surviving colonies should be visible after 7−10 days These can be allowed to grow together as a pool or can be picked individually and grown as separate cell lines.

(v)   Apply Cd^{2+} selection to the G418-resistant cell lines. $CdCl_2$ can be stored at room temperature as a sterile 10 mM stock solution in water. Suggested final concentrations for selection are 3 μM, 4 μM and 5 μM. Non-transfected CHO-K1 cells should also be plated at the same cell density in these concentrations of $CdCl_2$ to determine the frequency of amplification of endogenous MT genes. The frequency may become significant at or below 3 μM Cd^{2+}.

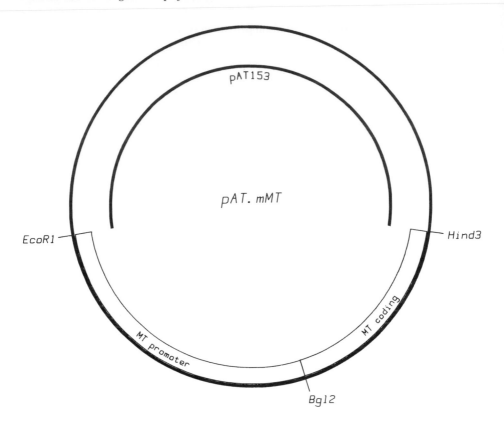

Figure 3. pAT mMT (6.6 kb P.Stephens, unpublished) consists of the 3.3 kb *Eco*RI-*Hind*III fragment containing the entire mMT-1 gene (8) cloned in pAT153.

Table 4. Example of mMT-1 mediated amplification.

	Clone 1	*Clone 2*	*Clone 1* *20 μM*	*Clone 2* *20 μM*
Vector copy number/cell	1−3	3	30	20
tPA secreted (units/10^6 cells/day)	240	260	2400	1800

A cDNA encoding tissue-type plasminogen-activator (tPA) under the control of the mMT-1 promoter was cloned in a vector containing a *neo* gene and an mMT-1 gene. The DNA was transfected into CHO-K1 cells and two clones were chosen for amplification. Cell pools resistant to 5 μM CdCl$_2$ were selected in the first step. These cells were subjected to a second round of amplification and cell pools resistant to 20 μM CdCl$_2$ were assayed for tPA production. (M.Bendig and CRB, unpublished results).

(vi) Clones resistant to Cd^{2+} can be analysed for gene amplification as described in Section 4 or can be subjected to a second round of selection at Cd^{2+} concentrations between 5 and 50 μM.

The increase in gene copy number is generally not as great as observed using DHFR co-amplification. An example of the results which may be obtained is shown in *Table 4*.

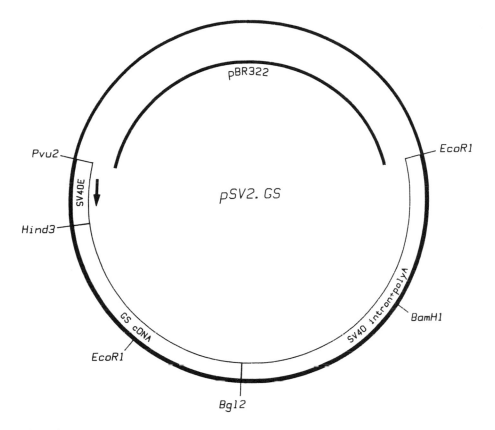

Figure 4. pSV2.GS is 5.5 kb in length (17) and contains a 1.2 kb GS cDNA cloned in place of the *dhfr* sequence in pSV2.dhfr (see *Figure 1*).

2.3 **Glutamine synthetase**

We have recently developed a vector amplification system based on GS (17). Glutamine is a key metabolite in a number of biosynthetic and catabolic pathways and must either be provided as a component of the medium or must be synthesized from glutamate and ammonia by means of GS. Although some cell lines are available which are GS-deficient and so cannot grow in the absence of glutamine, many cultured cell lines, including CHO-K1 do not require glutamine, provided that sufficient glutamate is present in the medium. Under these conditions, therefore, GS is an essential enzyme for cell survival and inhibition by the specific inhibitor (MSX) is lethal.

Two expression vectors which have been used to introduce a functional cloned GS gene into cultured cells are shown in *Figures 4* and *5*. In CHO-K1 cells, the expression levels from either vector are sufficient for them to act as dominant selectable markers by conferring resistance to MSX.

A medium suitable for CHO-K1 cells in which GS activity is required for cell growth is GMEM-S, described in *Table 5*. The high level of glutamine typically present in

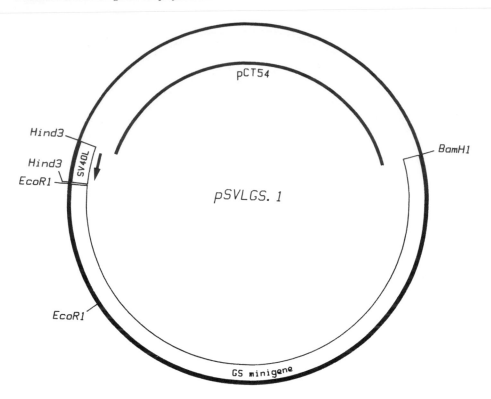

Figure 5. pSVLGS.1 (8.5 kb) contains the 323 bp *Pvu*II-*Hin*dIII fragment of SV40 spanning the origin of replication cloned at the *Hin*dIII site of pCT54 (29) such that the SV40 late promoter directs transcription of a 4.75 kb a GS minigene cloned between the *Eco*RI and *Bam*HI sites of pCT54. The GS minigene consists of 0.94 kb *Eco*RI of cDNA and a genomic fragment which contains a single GS intron, the 3′ end of the coding sequence and includes approximately 1.5 kb of 3′ flanking sequence (17).

tissue culture media (e.g. 2 mM) is replaced by an elevated concentration of glutamate (500 μM compared with 100 μM in most media). The metabolic requirement for glutamine is reduced (though not eliminated) by the addition of nucleosides and an elevated level of asparagine compared with most media. A high level of glucose and sodium pyruvate are provided as alternative carbon sources.

CHO-K1 cells grow well in this medium and MSX is toxic at concentrations above 3 μM. However, for some purposes, the alternative medium in *Table 5*, 'GMEM-met' (Wilson, unpublished) is useful. In this medium, the methionine concentration is increased. MSX is partially detoxified via the methionine catabolism pathway and raising the methionine concentration to saturate this pathway has the effect of increasing the toxicity of MSX. CHO-K1 cells grow less well in this medium than in GMEM-S but the medium is useful in reducing the amount of MSX required to maintain selection of cells with very high GS activity, as described in the following sections.

2.3.1 *Protocol for selection of GS expression vectors*

(i)   Plate the cells at 10^6 cells per 9 cm Petri dish in GMEM-S medium (*Table 5*) and leave overnight. (NB The cells should first be passaged in GMEM-S medium

Table 5. Media for GS selection.

A. *Stock solutions.*

1. Double distilled water autoclaved in 400 ml aliquots
2. 10 × Glasgow MEM w/o glutamine (GIBCO: 042−2541). Store at 4°C
3. 7.5% sodium bicarbonate (GIBCO). Store at 4°C
4. 100 × non-essential amino acids (NEAA). Store at 4°C
5. 100 × Glutamate + Asparagine (G + A): add 600 mg glutamic acid and 600 mg asparagine. Make up to 100 ml in distilled water and sterilize by passing through a sterile 2 μM filter (Nalgene). Store at 4°C
6. 100 × sodium pyruvate (GIBCO)
7. 50 × nucleosides: 35 mg adenosine
                35 mg guanosine
                35 mg cytidine
                35 mg uridine
                12 mg thymidine
    make up to 100 ml with water, filter sterilize and store at −20°C in 10 ml aliquots.
8. 100 × methionine: 600 mg methionine in 100 ml water. Filter sterilize and store at 4°C
9. Dialysed FCS (GIBCO). Heat inactivate at 56°C for 30 min and store at −20°C
10. Penicillin−streptomycin /5000 units/ml (P/S; GIBCO)
11. 100 mM MSX (Sigma): prepare 18 mg/ml solution in tissue-culture medium. Filter sterilize and store at −20°C.

B. *Medium preparation*

Add the following in the order given using aseptic technique.

(a) *GMEM-S*

1.	Water	400 ml
2.	10 × GMEM	50 ml
3.	Sodium bicarbonate	18.5 ml
4.	NEAA	5 ml
5.	G + A	5 ml
6.	Sodium pyruvate	5 ml
7	Nucleosides	10 ml
8.	Dialysed FCS	50 ml
9.	Penicillin-streptomycin	5 ml

GMEM-S contains the non-essential amino acids, alanine, aspartate, glycine, proline and serine (100 μM) glutamate and asparagine (500 μM) and adenosine, guanosine, cytidine and uridine (30 μM) and thymidine (10 μM)

(b) *GMEM-met*

1.	Water	410 ml
2.	10 × GMEM	50 ml
3.	Sodium bicarbonate	18.5 ml
4.	NEAA	5 ml
5.	Sodium pyruvate	5 ml
6.	Methionine	5 ml
7.	Dialysed FCS	50 ml
8.	Penicillin−streptomycin	5 ml

In GMEM-met, the glutamate and asparagine concentrations are reduced to 100 μM each, nucleosides are omitted and the methonine concentration is increased to 500 μM.

    to confirm that the medium supports the growth of the particular cell line chosen).

(ii) Transfect and allow the cells to recover overnight, as described in Section 2.1.2. Also treat at least three plates with $CaPO_4$ precipitate without added DNA to act as controls.

Table 6. Transfection of GS vectors into CHO-K1 cells.

Vector	Number of colonies/10^6 cells at different MSX concentrations				
	15 μM	*20 μM*	*25 μM*	*30 μM*	*100 μM*
pSVLGS.1	13.6	9.2	5.6	2.4	0.24
pSV2.GS	26.4	18	12	12	1.4
'Mock'	0.47	0.24	0	0	0

About 4×10^6 cells were transfected with 10 μg of each plasmid.

(iii)   One day after transfection, add MSX to final concentrations of, for example, 15 μM, 20 μM and 25 μM to transfected and control plates.

(iv)   After a further 2–3 days replace the medium with fresh MSX-containing medium.

(v)   Count the number of colonies 10–14 days after transfection.

Scoring the frequency of colony formation on mock-transfected control plates is important because treatment with MSX could also select for cells which have undergone amplification of the endogeneous gene. The success of pSV2.GS (*Figure 4*) and pSVLGS.1 (*Figure 5*) as dominant selectable markers is due to the fact that expression in these vectors can lead to higher levels of GS than can be attained in one-step amplification of the endogeneous gene. This is illustrated by the results of a representative transfection given in *Table 6*. When selected with 15 μM or 20 μM MSX, endogeneous amplification leads to a barely detectable frequency of colony formation while the apparent transfection frequency is at least 20 times higher, greater than 10^{-5} for both vectors. When selected at higher concentrations of MSX, the background due to endogenous amplification is undetectable but the frequency with which transfected colonies survive is also diminished.

2.3.2 *Amplification of GS vectors*

Cell lines transfected by GS vectors can be subjected to further rounds of MSX selection by the same strategy as has been described for DHFR (see Section 2.1.3). Using either vector, some cell lines derived by transfection of CHO-K1 cells can lead to the formation of colonies resistant to 500 μM MSX in the first round of selection and up to 10 mM after three rounds of selection. However there are marked differences between the two vectors in the copy numbers ultimately achieved. Highly MSX resistant cell lines derived using pSV2.GS contain only at most 10 copies of the vector per cell, whereas up to several thousand copies per cell have been achieved using pSVLGS.1 without concomitant amplification of endogenous genes (17).

In these highly MSX-resistant cell lines, the amount of MSX required to maintain selection can be markedly reduced (e.g. 10-fold) by changing to GMEM-Met medium (see *Table 5*).

2.4 **Adenosine deaminase**

Another gene which can be used for vector amplification is ADA (4). An ADA-deficient mutant CHO cell line is available but ADA expression vectors can also act as dominant selectable markers in a variety of cell types.

Table 7. ADA selection.

The following selections were devised for human choriocarcinoma cells (18) and mouse fibroblasts (25). Slightly different components are added for *dhfr⁻* CHO cells (4).

A. *Medium for Xyl A Selection (18)*

> DMEM (See *Table 2*)
> horse serum 15%[a]
> Xyl A[c] 4μM
> dCF[6]

B. *Medium for 11AAU Selection (25)*

> DMEM
> horse serum 15%[a]
> adenosine (Sigma) 1.1 mM
> alanosine[c] 0.05 mM
> uridine (Sigma) 1 mM
> dCF[b]

[a]Horse serum is used because FCS contains ADA activity which can deplete the medium of xyl A or adenosine during storage. If dialysed FCS is used instead, it should be added immediately prior to use. Serum is treated as in *Table 2*.
[b]dCF is used to inhibit endogenous ADA activity. See text for details.
[c]dCF, alanosine and xyl A can be obtained from the Division of Cancer Treatment, National Cancer Institute, USA (18,25).

ADA is an enzyme of purine nucleoside metabolism, catalysing the conversion of various adenine nucleosides to their inosine analogues. The enzyme is present at varying levels in almost all tissues and cell lines but is not normally an essential enzyme for cells in culture. There are, however, two methods available for making ADA essential for cell growth, so that the specific inhibitor deoxycoformycin (dCF) can be used as a selective agent (4). The first is to supply cells with a toxic analogue of adenosine such as 9-D xyloguanosyl adenine (xyl A). ADA is then required to convert xyl A to its non-toxic inosine analogue. The second method involves increasing the adenosine concentration. Excess adenosine is itself toxic and so ADA is required in this case to reduce the intracellular adenosine concentration. This protocol is termed 11AAU selection. The preparation of two particular media based on these strategies is shown in *Table 7*, after Yeung *et al.* (18,25).

Two different ADA expression vectors have been described and these are shown in *Figures 6* and *7*. Both are reported to yield similar transfection frequencies of up to 10^{-4} transfected cells in the DUKX B11 CHO cell line (4).

The amount of dCF used to select transfectants depends on the cell line and also on the medium used. For instance, the xyl A medium requires less dCF to achieve toxicity than the 11AAU medium. There is also some variability in the tolerance of different cell lines for 11AAU medium (4); hence the xyl A medium is preferred for initial selection. However, further amplification is reported to be difficult to achieve in this medium, probably because of the high frequency with which adenosine kinase-deficient mutants arise (4). Such mutations render ADA dispensable in this medium (18) thus providing an alternate means of attaining resistance to dCF. Therefore, in the following protocol (adapted from refs 4, 18 and 25), the xyl A medium is used for initial selection and the 11AAU medium for amplification.

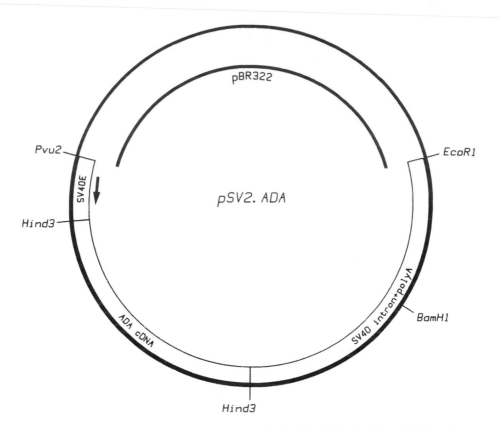

Figure 6. pSV2.ADA (28) contains approximately 1.2 kb of ADA cDNA cloned in a pSV2 based vector. The rest of the sequences are as in *Figure 1*. The plasmid is approximately 5.5 kb in length, and has been used as a dominant selectable marker (4).

2.4.1 *Protocol for ADA selection*

(i)   Transfect cells and allow them to recover for 24−48 h as described in Section 2.1.2 but using xyl A medium (See *Table 7*). Note that the ability of this medium to support growth of the cell line chosen should first be confirmed.

(ii)   Apply dCF selection. The optimum concentration should be determined for each cell line but is typically in the range 3−30 nM.

(iii)   Once dCF-resistant colonies have become established, change the medium to 11AAU for amplification. In this medium, the cells may be resistant to 10× the initial dCF concentration so test for amplification in concentrations of dCF higher than this.

(iv)   Additional amplification steps can be performed on either cell pools or cloned lines.

Such a protocol has been reported to give rise to cells containing about 500 copies of the vector per cell in cell lines resistant to 100 μM dCF (4). As with GS mediated vector-amplification, no increase in copy number of the endogenous genes was detected.

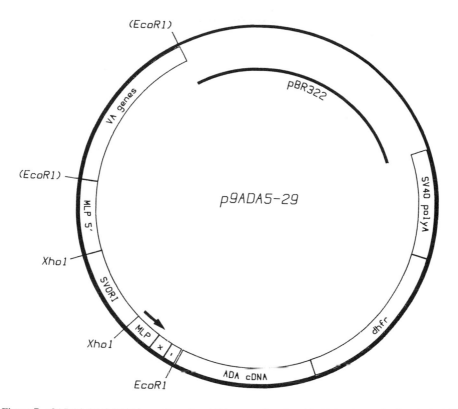

Figure 7. p9ADA5-29 (9.2 kb) is an alternative ADA expression plasmid which acts as a dominant selectable marker in a variety of cell types (4). Transcription of ADA is under the control of the adenovirus major late promoter (MLP) and the SV40 enhancer provided by a 682 bp *Ava*II fragment spanning the SV40 origin of replication (SVORI) cloned at a *Xho*I site in MLP. Interaction between the VA gene products (VA-RNAs) and the tripartite leader of adenovirus (x) provide efficient translation. A 3' splice site from an immunoglobulin gene is also provided (:). A *dhfr* cDNA enhances mRNA stability (4) and a 900 bp *Bcl*1-*Pst*1 sequence from SV40 provides a polyadenylation signal (SV40 poly A). The pBR322 sequences are derived from a derivative of pBR322 containing a deletion of approximately 1.2 kb and contain the tetracycline resistance gene and origin of replication.

3. PLANNING A STRATEGY FOR GENE AMPLIFICATION

The development of a variety of different amplifiable vectors described in Section 2 has extended the use of gene amplification techniques beyond the original *dhfr⁻* CHO cell line, DUKX-B11. This presents the investigator with a choice as to which cell line and vector system to use. As a general rule, it may be best to consider the DHFR system first since the selection system in *dhfr⁻* CHO cells yields high frequencies of transfection, and vector amplification has been extensively studied in this cell line.

There may be, however, several constraints on the cell line chosen imposed by the particular use to which the system is to be put, which are outside the scope of this chapter. For instance major considerations in some circumstances may be the post-translational modifications which the cell line is able to carry out, or the ability of the cell line to respond correctly to particular introduced regulatory sequences. In this case one of the alternative amplification systems can be used. Although DHFR, GS and ADA have all been used to provide dominant selectable markers in certain cell lines, the particular vectors containing GS and ADA genes described here may be generally applicable in many different cell lines. However an additional factor to consider is that access to certain reagents may be limited. For example certain compounds required for the ADA protocols are not widely available.

Here we will consider in detail only factors which may be of general importance in planning a strategy for gene expression: the stability of the amplified sequences in the absence of selection, the design of the vector, and the frequencies of gene amplification.

3.1 Stability of gene amplification

In some cases highly amplified arrays of vector sequences can be retained in the absence of the selective agent (at least for several weeks in culture) while in other cases, the amplified sequences are lost very rapidly if the selection is removed. Whether the sequences are 'stable' or 'unstable' correlates with the state of the vector sequences in the genome (reviewed in ref. 2). In stable cell lines, the amplified genes can be shown by *in situ* hybridization (described in Section 4) to have remained integrated in one or more of the host chromosomes. Because the region of chromosome involved in amplification is often very large, it can be detected as an altered staining pattern by chromosome banding techniques, forming homogeneously staining regions (HSRs). Unstable amplified sequences on the other hand are frequently associated with small acentric chromosome fragments called double minutes (DMs). Because DMs have no centromeres, unequal assortment of DMs at mitosis together with more rapid growth of the cells which retain fewer DMs will lead to loss of the amplified arrays from the cell population.

The presence of DMs or HSRs seems to depend not on the vector used but on the host cell line and perhaps the site of initial integration. The two hamster lines which have been most extensively studied, CHO and BHK-21 tend to show stable gene amplification while in mouse fibroblasts and certain human tumour cell lines, DMs predominate (2). Thus, if stability in the absence of selection is considered important, one of the hamster cell lines which have been used previously may be desirable, although for many purposes it may be acceptable to maintain cells in the presence of the selective agent and the choice of cell line is then much wider.

3.2 Vector design

Vector DNA introduced into a host cell by transfection can frequently become ligated into high molecular weight species so that multiple plasmid molecules ultimately integrate at the same chromosomal location. For this reason, it is not always necessary for the amplifiable gene and the non-selected gene to be on the same vector; instead, two distinct plasmids can be co-transfected. However, single-copy integrations can also occur so it is normally preferable to construct a single vector containing all the required genes. For this purpose, several of the vectors described in Section 2 have a single *Bam*HI restriction site downstream of the amplifiable gene, which forms a suitable site for introducing a complete transcription unit (i.e. see *Figures 1, 2, 4, 5* and *6*).

The orientation and relative positions of the genes in the vector can affect expression levels. Normally it is best for transcription to proceed in the same direction for both genes in the vector but such effects in different constructs can be tested in transient expression experiments (see DNA Cloning Volume II, Chapter 6) provided that a sufficiently sensitive assay for the product of the co-expressed gene is available.

If it is not convenient to construct a single vector, a strategy which selects for integration of two vectors at the same chromosomal site has been described by Kaufman *et al.* (26). This uses a DHFR transcription unit on one vector which lacks a functional transcription-enhancer element. Such a gene yields a low transfection efficiency in *dhfr*⁻ CHO cells (3×10^{-5}) but, when co-transfected with a vector containing a SV40 enhancer, the transformation frequency is 20-fold higher. This is due to integration of the enhancer-containing vector adjacent to the DHFR vector, allowing the enhancer to act to increase the efficiency of DHFR transcription and hence the apparent frequency of transfection.

3.3 The frequency of gene amplification

Several factors can influence the frequency at which colonies resistant to a selective agent can be identified. They include the choice of cell line, the location of the sequence in the genome, the concentration of selective agent (since the degree of amplification and hence resistance achieved varies between individual amplification events) and the cell density. (See ref. 3 for a recent review). However the frequency of amplification at a given locus is typically in the range of $10^{-4}-10^{-6}$, which means that gene amplification is generally readily detectable without recourse to any special techniques for increasing the frequencies. There are however a number of treatments which can enhance the frequency of amplification, either by interfering with DNA synthesis or by activating DNA repair mechanisms. Other agents, which appear to stimulate amplification, may in fact act by enhancing colony formation among cells growing at low cell density. (See ref. 3 for detailed references.)

4. METHODS FOR ANALYSIS OF GENE AMPLIFICATION

Gene amplification can be measured either by DNA hybridization techniques to detect increased copy number of specific DNA sequences and mRNAs or by quantitating expressed proteins. It is often informative to compare all three (DNA, RNA and protein) since the increase in one is sometimes but not always proportional to the degree of amplification of the others. Lastly, it may be useful to localize the amplified sequences by *in situ* hybridization to metaphase chromosome spreads as this can provide information on the likely stability of expressing clones in the absence of selection.

4.1 Measurement of gene copy number

The copy number of a specific DNA sequence can be estimated by probing Southern blots. Methods for preparation of DNA from tissue culture cells have been described in DNA Cloning Volume II, Chapter 6 and the techniques for transfer to nitrocellulose and hybridization with cloned probes are well described elsewhere (27) and so will

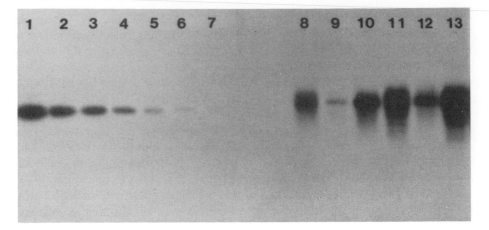

Figure 8. Southern blot analysis of DNA from CHO-K1 cells transfected with pSVLGS.1 to illustrate vector amplification. **Lanes 1–7** contain pSVLGS.1 plasmid DNA (see *Figure 5*), digested with *Bam*HI, to act as a standard for quantitation of vector DNA. **Lane 1** contains 1.25 ng DNA and the subsequent lanes contain 2-fold dilutions of this. **Lanes 8–13** contain 2.5 μg of genomic DNA isolated from transfected cell clones. Three clones are shown, clone 1 (**Lane 8**) isolated by selection for resistance to 20 μM MSX; clone 2 (**Lane 9**) resistant to 20 μM MSX; and clone 3 (**Lane 10**) resistant to 30 μM MSX. **Lane 11** contains DNA from variants of clone 2 resistant to 250 μM MSX; and **Lane 13** represents variants of clone 3 resistant to 500 μM MSX. The Southern blot has been hybridized with a radioactive probe specific for vector DNA. **Lanes 11–13** clearly contain increased numbers of copies of the vector compared with the original transfected clones (**Lanes 8–10**) thus demonstrating amplification.

not be repeated here. The experimental design, however, can be illustrated with reference to *Figure 8* which shows the results of one such experiment.

DNA prepared from transfected cells at different stages of selection for amplification is digested with a suitable restriction enzyme and known amounts of total DNA are electrophoresed and transferred to nitrocellulose. Various amounts of a plasmid DNA containing the sequence of interest (carefully quantitated by measuring the u.v. absorbance; OD 260 nm) are also run on the same gel. Visual inspection or densitometric scanning of the autoradiograph allows an estimate of the amount of cloned sequence per μg of total DNA. If the amount of DNA per cell is assumed to be approximately 6 pg for most diploid mammalian cells, an estimate of the number of molecules per cell can be made.

4.3 **Measurement of levels of RNA**

RNA levels in different cell lines can be compared by Northern blotting experiments which are described elsewhere (27). The experimental design is similar to that for measuring gene copy number. A standard RNA preparation of the specific sequences being analysed can be obtained and quantitated using an SP6 *in vitro* transcription system (as described in Chapter 1 of this volume).

4.4. **Assays for protein expression levels**

If a convenient assay is available for the expression of a protein cloned into an amplifiable vector, this may be used to follow the progress of amplification. In addition, the ex-

Table 8. Preparation of cell extracts for enzyme assays.

1.	Pellet the cells by centrifugation at 1500 r.p.m. in a bench-top centrifuge for 5–10 min.
2.	Wash the cells three times in phosphate-buffered saline (PBS; Flow) by resuspending in PBS using a Pasteur pipette.
3.	Resuspend at a final concentration of about 5×10^7 cells/ml in 0.25 M sucrose, 10 mM Tris-HCl (pH 7.6), 1 mM DTT.
4.	Disrupt the cells by sonication (e.g. using three bursts of 15 sec each).
5.	Centrifuge in an ultracentrifuge at 100 000 g for 45 min at 4°C, or in a microcentrifuge for 10 min.
6.	Remove the supernatant (avoiding lipid material at the surface) and place on ice or store at -20°C until assayed.
7.	Total protein should be estimated using for example the method of Lowry *et al.* (33).

Table 9. Assay for dihydrofolate reductase.

1.	Prepare cell extracts and determine the total protein concentrations as described in *Table 8*.
2.	Prepare the following reagents: 100 mM potassium phosphate buffer (pH 7.9); 5 mM dihydrofolate; 1 mM NADPH.
3.	Set up the reaction mixture in a 1 ml cuvette with a 1 cm path-length as follows: 0.8 ml buffer, 10 μl dihydrofolate, 0.1 ml NADPH, varying amounts of cell extract (up to 0.1 ml) and water to make 1 ml. Also set up a reagent blank with no cell extract.
4.	Incubate at 37°C and measure the absorbance at 340 nm at 1 min intervals.
5.	Enzyme activity can be expressed as nmol dihydrofolate reduced/mg protein/minute calculated from a molar absorbance change of 12 200/M cm.

Table 10. Assay for glutamine synthetase.

A.		*Preparation of Dowex ion exchange columns*
	1.	Add 0.5 M NaOH to some Dowex-1-Cl (8% cross-linked, 200–400 Mesh) in the bottle.
	2.	Aspirate off the fines and wash several times with distilled water.
	3.	Wash with 0.5 M HCl until the pH is below 2.
	4.	Wash several times with distilled water.
	5.	Adjust the supernatant of pH 7 by adding solid imidazole.
	6.	Make standard size (e.g. 0.8 ml) columns in 1 ml plastic pipette tips (e.g. the blue tips suitable for a Gilson P1000 Pipetman). The end of the tip can be cut off and plugged with cotton wool before filling with the Dowex beads.
	7.	Rinse the columns with several millilitres of distilled water.
B.		*Enzyme Assay*
	1.	The reagents required are: 0.5 M sodium tricine pH 7.6, 100 mM ATP pH 7.0, 80 mM NH_4Cl, 400 mM $MgCl_2$, 100 mM [^{14}C]glutamate (4 μCi/mmol).
	2.	Prepare the cell extracts as described in *Table 8*.
	3.	Set up 50 μl reaction mixtures as follows: 5 μl sodium tricine, 7.5 μl ATP, 2.5 μl NH_4Cl, 2.5 μl $MgCl_2$, up to 25 μl enzyme, water to make up to 45 μl, and 5 μl [^{14}C]glutamate.
	4.	Incubate at 37°C for various times, e.g. 5, 10, 15, 20 and 30 min.
	5.	Stop the reaction by adding 200 μl ice-cold distilled water and place on ice.
	6.	Add the total sample to a Dowex column and discard the eluate.
	7.	Elute with two distilled water washes of 0.5 ml each, collecting both eluates. Glutamine is eluted and glutamate retained on the column.
	8.	Add 10 ml scintillation fluid (e.g. Biofluor) and count in a scintillation counter.
	9.	Also count a 'dummy' reaction mixture without added cell extract and calculate the percentage converted by the enzyme per minute.
	10.	Calculate the nmol of glutamate converted/min from the specific activity of the [^{14}C]glutamate and the percent conversion.

Table 11. Assay for adenosine deaminase.

1.	Prepare the cell extract and determine the total protein concentration as described in *Table 8*.
2.	Prepare the following reagents: 50 mM potassium phosphate buffer pH 7.4; 10 mM adenosine.
3.	Set up the reaction mixture in a 1 ml cuvette with a path-length of 1 cm as follows: 0.9 ml buffer; 10 μl adenosine (0.1 μmol) varying amounts of cell extract up to 100 μl and water to make 1 ml. Also set up a reagent blank without any cell extract.
4.	Incubate at 30°C and measure the absorbance at 265 nm of 1 min intervals.
5.	Calculate the amount of enzyme present: one unit of ADA catalyses the deamination of 1 μmol adenosine per minute. (A = 8.6/min/ml under these assay conditions).

Table 12. Reagents for preparation of metaphase chromosome spreads.

1.		PBS. Obtain tablets (e.g. from Flow) and make up according to the manufacturers instructions, Autoclave and store at 4°C.
2.		Colcemid (10 μg/ml). Dissolve 5 mg of colcemid in 5 ml of water. Dilute 1/100 with PBS and filter through a 0.2 μm sterile filter. Store at 4°C.
3.		Actinomycin D (15 μg/ml). Dissolve actinomycin at 5 mg/ml in ethanol. Dilute 1/1000 in water.
4.		0.5% potassium chloride. Dissolve 0.5 g of KCl in 100 ml of water and autoclave.
5.		Fixative. 3:1 methanol:acetic acid
6.		45% acetic acid. Made up in water.
7.		Microscope slides. These are treated as follows:
	(i)	Soak in 1% 'decon' overnight.
	(ii)	Rinse in distilled water.
	(iii)	Soak in dilute HCl for 1 h.
	(iv)	Rinse in distilled water.
	(v)	Soak in ethanol until use.
	(vi)	Just before use, remove from ethanol and air dry.

pression of the amplifiable marker protein can often be assayed since rapid and simple assays for DHFR, GS and ADA are available. These may be particularly useful when using a cell line whose endogenous enzyme activity is currently not known.

A method for preparing cell extracts suitable for all three enzyme assays is given in *Table 8* adapted from refs 30, 31 and 32. An assay for DHFR is given in *Table 9*. The assay uses a spectrophotometric method in which the conversion of NADPH and dihydrofolate to NADP and tetrahydrofolate is detected by a decrease in absorption at 340 nm and is adapted from ref. 30. A radiometric assay for GS is given in *Table 10*. The assay follows the conversion of [14C]glutamate to glutamine, the two amino acids being separated by ion exchange chromatography (31 and Wilson, unpublished). The spectrophotometric assay for ADA of Agarwal and Parks (32) is given in *Table 11*. In this assay, the activity is determined by measuring the decrease in absorbance at 265 nm resulting from the conversion of adenosine to inosine.

4.5 In situ hybridization to metaphase chromosomes

The following protocols can be used to prepare metaphase chromosome preparations

Table 13. Procedure for metaphase spreads.

This protocol utilizes reagents listed in *Table 12*.

1. Pour medium off the cells.
2. Add 20 ml of growth medium containing 0.2 ml of colcemid and 0.5 ml of actinomycin D.
3. Incubate the cells at 37°C for about 75 min. (The optimum time should be determined empirically for each cell type; for longer incubation times, actinomycin D should only be added for the last hour of the incubation).
4. Tap the flask vigorously to dislodge mitotic cells.
5. Take off the supernatant containing the mitotic cells and transfer to a centrifuge tube.
6. Centrifuge at 1200 r.p.m. for 8 min in a bench top centrifuge to pellet the cells.
7. Decant all but 0.5 ml of the supernatant, and resuspend the cell pellet by gently flicking the tube.
8. Add 10 ml of 0.5% KCl dropwise with gentle mixing, and leave at room temperature for 12.5 min.
9. Centrifuge the cells at 1200 r.p.m. for 8 min.
10. Decant all but 0.5 ml of the supernatant and resuspend the cell pellet.
11. Add cold fixative very carefully, dropwise and with gentle mixing, to a final volume of 5 ml. The fixative must be added very slowly at first; once 1 ml has been added it can be added a little more quickly. The fixative and cells must be kept cold at all times (0−4°C).
12. Place at 4°C for 5 min.
13. Centrifuge the cells at 1200 r.p.m. for 8 min.
14. Repeat steps 10−13 twice more.
15. Decant all but 0.5 ml of the supernatant, and resuspend the cell pellets in 1 ml fixative. Store at 4°C.
16. The fixed preparations should be used to make slides the same day.
17. Remove cleaned slides from ethanol and allow to dry.
18. Drop the fixed cell suspension onto the slides and allow the drop to spread out. The spreading is sometimes assisted by first dropping 45% acetic acid onto the slides, followed by the fixed preparation.
19. Allow slides to dry and examine the chromosomes using phase contrast microscopy. The slides are now ready to be used for *in situ* hybridization and should be stored at room temperature, away from dust, until use. The existence of any Double Minute chromosomes can be detected at this stage.

from anchorage dependent cells and subsequently perform *in situ* hybridizations. Cells in culture are first treated with colcemid to inhibit spindle formation and so cause cells to accumulate in metaphase. The metaphase cells are more rounded and less firmly attached to the plastic than the rest of the population and so can be enriched by knocking them off the flask. The mitotic cells are then treated in a hypotonic solution to cause them to swell and are fixed in methanol/acetic acid. When the fixed cell suspension is dropped onto a glass slide, the cells burst and chromosomes are spread on the slide as the fixative evaporates. The reagents for this procedure are listed in *Table 12*, and the procedure itself in *Table 13*.

The metaphase chromosomes are next treated with RNAse, to prevent hybridization of probe to chromosomal RNA, and with acetic anhydride, to acetylate chromosomal proteins and hence further reduce non-specific binding of the probe. Chromosomal DNA is then denatured by heat and hybridized with a DNA probe labelled with $[^{125}I]CTP$. Excess probe is removed by washing in low-salt buffers and the slides are coated in photographic emulsion. After exposure, silver grains are deposited over the sites of probe binding and hence the site of gene amplification. The reagents required are listed in *Table 14* and the procedure in *Table 15*.

Table 14. Reagents for *in situ* hybridization.

A.	*Reagents that may be prepared before the day of the experiment*
1.	20 × SSC: Dissolve

sodium chloride	175.3 g
sodium citrate	88.2g
in water	

Adjust to pH 7.0 with HCl or NaOH and make up to 1 l.

2.   RNase 100 μg/ml in 2 × SSC: Boil for 10 min, cool slowly. Aliquot and store at $-20°C$.

3.   Ethanol (AR)

4.   Formamide (AR): De-ionize by passing over an ion-exchange resin (BioRad AG501-X8) until the pH is neutral. Aliquot and store at $-20°C$.

5.   0.25 M EDTA: Dissolve EDTA 93 g in water. Adjust pH to 8.0 with NaOH and make up to 1 l. Autoclave.

6.   0.1 M triethanolamine, pH 8.0: Mix

triethanolamine	13.3 ml
water	800 ml.

Adjust to pH 8.0 with HCl and make up to 1 l with water.

7.   Acetic anhydride (AR)

8.   100 × Denhardts solution: Dissolve

Ficoll	21 g
Polyvinylpyrrolidone	21 g
Bovine serum albumin (Pentax Fraction V)	21 g
in water and make up to	100 ml
Store in small aliquots at $-20°C$.	

9.   20 × SSPE: Dissolve

NaCl	174 g
$NaH_2PO_4.H_2O$	27.6 g
EDTA	7.4 g
in water	800 ml

Adjust pH to 7.4 with NaOH and make up to 1 l. Autoclave.

10.   50% Dextran sulphate: Dissolve 500 g of Dextran sulphate in water. Make up to 1 l and autoclave.

11.   10 mg/ml Salmon Sperm DNA: Boil for 10 min. Chill on ice and store at $-20°C$.

12.   [^{125}I]CTP (Amersham or alternative supplier) 1500 Ci/mmol or greater.

13.   Ilford Nuclear Emulsion L4 (or equivalent).

14.   D19 developer (Kodak or alternative supplier).

15.   1% Glacial acetic acid.

16.   Photographic Fixative (Kodak Kodafix or alternative).

17.   Giemsa stain (BDH-Gurr).

18.   pH 6.8 buffer (obtained as tablets from BDH or alternative supplier; prepare according to manufacturer's instructions).

19.   Rubber solution glue (Dunlop or alternative).

B.   *The following solutions should be prepared on the day of experiment*

1.   2 × SSC^a (dilute 20 × SSC stock solution 1 in 10)

2.   Ethanol at the following dilutions:

         10% Ethanol: Dilute ethanol in water 10 ml in 1 l

         50% Ethanol: Dilute ethanol in water 500 ml in 1 l

         75% Ethanol: Dilute ethanol in water 750 ml in 1 l

         95% Ethanol: Dilute ethanol in water 950 ml in 1 l

         100% Ethanol.

3.   Denaturation solution (70% formamide, 1mM EDTA, 2 × SSC)

For 500 ml:

formamide	350 ml
EDTA	0.2 ml
20 × SSC	50 ml
water	100 ml

4. Acetic anhydride solution (0.25% acetic anhydride in 0.1 M triethanolamine pH 8.0).
   For 500 ml:
acetic anhydride	1.25 ml
0.1 M triethanolamine buffer	499 ml
5. Hybridization solution (50% formamide, 5 × Denhardt's solution, 5 × SSPE, 10% dextran sulphate, 200 μg/ml salmon sperm DNA).
   For 1 ml:
formamide	500 μl
100 × Denhardt's	50 μl
20 × SSPE	250 μl

[a]SSC is 0.3 M NaCl, 0.03 M sodium citrate.

Table 15. Procedure for *in situ* hybridization.

1. Nick translate 50−100 ng of probe DNA according to standard techniques (27), but using 40 μCi [^{125}I]CTP as the labelled nucleotide.
2. Lyophilize the DNA in a dessicator and resuspend in 300 μl of hybridization solution (*Table 14*).
3. Add 20 μl of RNase solution to each slide under a cover slip. Incubate in a moist chamber at 37°C for 1.5 h.
4. Wash the slides by carefully dipping into troughs containing 2 × SSC. Repeat with four changes of 2 × SSC. Keep the slides vertical so that the cover slips fall off in the wash buffer of their own accord.
5. Dehydrate the slides by immersion for 1 min each in 10, 50, 75, 95 and 100% ethanol. Air dry and store in a dessicator.
6. Denature the chromosomal DNA in denaturing solution at 65°C for 4 min.
7. Wash, dehydrate and store in a dessicator as in 4 and 5 above.
8. Immerse the slides in 0.25% acetic anhydride solution for 15 min at room temperature.
9. Wash, dehydrate and store in a dessicator.
10. Denature the probe suspended in hybridization buffer by incubating the tube in a boiling water bath for 3 min. Place on ice immediately.
11. Add 30 μl of hybridization mix per slide and place a cover slip over the drop of solution. Make sure that there are no air bubbles and that the drop spreads to the edge of the cover slip. This is achieved by lowering the cover slip gently with a pair of forceps.
12. Seal with rubber solution.
13. Place in a moist chamber at 45°C overnight.
14. Carefully remove the cover slips with the slide immersed in 5 × SSC. This is done by holding the cover slip down with one pair of forceps while peeling away the rubber solution with a second pair of forceps. Allow the cover slip to slide off under its own weight.
15. Incubate the slides in 2 × SSC at room temperature for 1−2 h.
16. Wash in 0.5 × SSC at 60°C for 1 h.
17. Wash in 0.1 × SSC at 65°C for 1 h.
18. Dehydrate and store in a dessicator.
19. Emulsion Dip. Warm the emulsion to 55°C in complete darkness in a dark room.
20. Dilute 1:1 with distilled water.
21. Dip the slides, one at a time into the emulsion. (It is advisable to dip a test slide first to check that the emulsion film is uniform and free from bubbles). Draw the slide out slowly with one edge against the side of the bottle.
22. Stand the slides vertically in the dark for 30 min to allow the emulsion to harden.
23. Store in a light-proof slide box with dessicant at 4°C to expose (usually 1−10 days).
24. Develop the slides as follows. Warm the slides to room temperature for 1 h.
25. Develop in D19 at 20°C for 5 min in a coplin jar.
26. Rinse in 1% acetic acid 'stop' bath.
27. Fix in Kodafix (diluted 1:4) for 5 min.
28. Wash in gently running water for 30 min.
29. Stain in Giemsa diluted 1/10 in pH 6.8 buffer for 10−20 min. (Diluted stain should be made up fresh).
30. Air dry and examine under a microscope.

5. ACKNOWLEDGEMENTS

We wish to thank Richard Wilson, Paul Stephens and Mary Bendig for allowing us to include unpublished results. We are also grateful to Richard Wilson and our colleagues at Celltech for comments and to Gill Alcock for typing the manuscript.

6. REFERENCES

1. Bebbington,C.R. and Hentschel,C.C.G. (1985) *Trends Biotechnol.*, **3**, 314.
2. Stark,G.R. and Wahl,G.M. (1984) *Annu. Rev. Biochem.*, **53**, 447.
3. Stark,G.R. (1986) *Cancer Surveys*, **5**, 1.
4. Kaufman,R.J., Murtha,P., Ingolia,D.E., Yeung,C.-Y. and Kellems,R.E. (1986) *Proc. Natl. Acad. Sci. USA*, **83**, 3136.
5. de Saint Vincent,B.R., Delbruck,S., Eckhart,W., Meirloth,J., Vitto,L. and Wahl,G. (1981) *Cell*, **27**, 267.
6. Subramani,S., Mulligan,R. and Berg,P. (1981) *Mol. Cell. Biol.*, **1**, 854.
7. Hayward,B.E., Hussain,A., Wilson,R.H., Woodcock,V., McIntosh,B. and Harris,T.J.R. (1986) *Nucleic Acids Res.*, **14**, 999.
8. Hamer,D.H. and Walling,M.J. (1982) *J. Mol. Appl. Genet.*, **1**, 273.
9. Roberts,J.M. and Axel,R. (1982) in *Gene Amplification*. Schimke,R. (ed.) Cold Spring Harbor Laboratory Press, Cold Spring Harbor, NY.
10. Gros,P., Heriah,Y.B., Croop,J.M. and Housman,D.E. (1986) *Nature*, **323**, 728.
11. Milbrandt,J.D., Azizkahn,J.C. and Hamlin,J.L. (1983) *Mol. Cell. Biol.*, **3**, 1274.
12. Crouse,G.F., McEwan,R.N. and Pearson,M.L. (1983) *Mol. Cell. Biol.*, **3**, 257.
13. Murray,M.J., Kaufman,R.J., Latt,S.A. and Weinberg,R.A. (1983) *Mol. Cell. Biol.*, **3**, 32.
14. O'Hare,K., Benoist,D. and Breathnach,R. (1981) *Proc. Natl. Acad. Sci. USA*, **78**, 1527.
15. Deschatrette,J., Fougere-Deschatrette,C., Corcos,L. and Schimke,R.T. (1985) *Proc. Natl. Acad. Sci. USA*, **82**, 765.
16. Simonsen,C. and Levinson,A.D. (1983) *Proc. Natl. Acad. Sci. USA*, **80**, 2495.
17. Bebbington,C.R. and Hentschel,C.C.G. (1987) submitted.
18. Yeung,C.-Y., Riser,M.E., Kellems,R.E. and Siciliano,M.J. (1983) *J. Biol. Chem.*, **258**, 8330.
19. Pavlakis,G.N. and Hamer,D.H. (1983) *Recent Progress in Hormone Research*, **39**, 353.
20. Ruis,J.C. and Wahl,G.M. (1986) *Mol. Cell. Biol.*, **6**, 3050.
21. Urlaub,G. and Chasin,L.A. (1980) *Proc. Natl. Acad. Sci. USA*, **77**, 4216.
22. Lee,F., Mulligan,R., Berg,P. and Ringold,G. (1981) *Nature*, **294**, 228.
23. Kaufman,R.J. and Sharp,P.A. (1982) *Mol. Cell. Biol.*, **2**, 1304.
24. Sanders,P.G. and Wilson,R.H. (1984) *EMBO J.*, **3**, 65.
25. Yeung,C.-Y., Ingolia,D.E., Bobonis,C., Dunbar,B.S., Riser,M.E., Siciliano,M.J. and Kellems,R.E. (1983) *J. Biol. Chem.*, **258**, 8338.
26. Kaufman,R.J., Wasley,L.C., Spiliotes,A.J., Gossels,S.D., Latt,S.A., Larsen,G.R. and Kay,R.M. (1985) *Mol. Cell. Biol.*, **5**, 1750.
27. Maniatis,T., Fritsch,E.F. and Sambrook,J. eds (1982) *Molecular Cloning*. Cold Spring Harbor Laboratory Press, Cold Spring Harbor, NY.
28. Orkin,S.H., Goff,S.C., Kelley,W.N. and Daddona,P.E. (1985) *Mol. Cell. Biol.*, **5**, 762.
29. Emtage,J.S., Angal,S., Doel,M.T., Harris,T.J.R., Jenkins,B., Lilley,G. and Lowe,P.A. (1983) *Proc. Natl. Acad. Sci. USA*, **80**, 3671.
30. Flintoff,W.F., Davidson,S.V. and Siminovitch,L. (1976) *Somat. Cell Genet.*, **3**, 245.
31. Tiemeier,D.E. and Milman,G. (1972) *J. Biol. Chem.*, **247**, 2272.
32. Agarwal,R.P. and Parks,R.E. (1978) In *Methods Enzymol.* Academic Press, NY, Vol. 51, p. 502. 51, p. 502.
33. Lowry,O.H., Rosebrough,N.J., Farr,A.L. and Randall,R.J. (1951) *J. Biol. Chem.*, **193**, 265.

CHAPTER 9

Retroviral vectors

ANTHONY M.C.BROWN and MICHAEL R.D.SCOTT

1. INTRODUCTION

1.1 Why retroviruses?

The exploitation of retroviruses as vectors in recent years has provided an important and versatile new method of introducing and expressing cloned genes in eukaryotic cells. Many features of retroviruses favour their choice for this purpose, as an alternative to DNA-mediated gene transfer methods or other potential viral vector systems. Firstly, the relatively small genomes of retroviruses can easily be manipulated for the introduction of foreign genes in such a way that any resulting defects in viral replication can be complemented *in trans*. Secondly, the viruses can easily be grown to high titres in culture. The efficiency of infection of susceptible cells is extremely high, which, together with high titre virus stocks, can permit infection of close to 100% of the target cells in a culture. Moreover, after infection a single copy of retroviral DNA becomes stably integrated in the host cell genome in a precisely defined manner, such that virtually all the infected cells can express the genes carried by the virus. In addition, retroviruses carry powerful transcriptional enhancer elements that can ensure high levels of expression in a wide range of cell types.

Although the use of retroviral vectors requires that the gene to be expressed is inserted in the correct manner in an appropriate vector (a proviso which normally limits their application to well characterized sequences), once the correct recombinant virus is constructed the subsequent handling of virus stocks and infection of target cells are technically quite simple.

1.2 Applications of retroviral vectors

The most widespread use of retroviral vectors is as general purpose expression vectors for experimentation in eukaryotic cell culture. In addition, however, retroviral vectors have several more specialized applications in molecular biology, genetics, developmental biology, and possibly in medicine. Some of these are listed below.

(i)   As well as providing an efficient means of expressing cloned genes in cultured cells, retrovirus vectors can be used to infect cells *in vivo* directly, for example by intraperitoneal injection of neonatal mice (1).

(ii) By retroviral infection of hemopoietic stem cells in bone marrow cultures, and subsequent transplantation into irradiated mice, an animal's entire hemopoietic tissue can be reconstituted with cells containing a retrovirus vector (2). Techniques of this sort may make it possible to treat certain hereditary defects by gene therapy (3).

(iii) Retroviruses can also be used to introduce DNA into germ cells, by infecting either whole pre-implantation embryos or pluripotent embryonic stem cells. Subsequent transplantations of these provide effective methods of generating transgenic animals (4,5).

(iv) Infection of pluripotential stem cells with retrovirus vectors can provide easily identifiable markers for cell lineage studies, either during tissue differentiation (6,7), or in embryonic development after infection of pre-implantation embryos (8).

(v) Since retroviral infection usually results in integration of a single copy of viral DNA within the host cell genome, retroviral vectors carrying a foreign gene can be useful as unique genetic markers for individual chromosomes in somatic cell hybrids, chromosome-mediated gene transfer experiments, and recombination studies (9).

(vi) Retroviral vectors can also be used as insertional mutagens, either in cultured cells or in transgenic animals. Incorporation of a marker gene in the vector which is easily selectable in *E. coli* can greatly facilitate subsequent recovery of sequences from the mutated locus (10).

(vii) Since retroviral genomic RNA is susceptible to splicing, intron sequences introduced into a retroviral vector may be accurately excised from the viral genome. Consequently, by cloning proviral DNA after infection, retroviral vectors can be used to generate full-length cDNA copies of moderately sized genes (11,12).

The purpose of this chapter is to provide a practical guide to the use of retroviruses as general purpose expression vectors, and to describe the methods of virus production, testing, and infection, which are common to most of the applications described above. Further details of the more specialised applications will not be presented here. The majority of retrovirus vectors described to date have been derived either from avian retroviruses or from the murine leukaemia viruses (MLV). This chapter will concentrate on MLV-based vectors and the techniques associated with their use.

The next section outlines some of the fundamental aspects of retrovirus biology which underlie the use of these viruses as vectors, and Section 3 presents a guide to different designs of retroviral vector now available. Sections 4−6 describe methods of virus production, infection of cells, and testing of virus stocks, while Section 7 considers some examples of practical problems that may be encountered in the use of these vectors.

2. RETROVIRUS BIOLOGY

2.1 The retrovirus life-cycle

Retroviruses comprise a family of RNA viruses whose replication cycle is distinguished by the conversion of their RNA genome into a DNA form by a virus-encoded reverse transcriptase function. The life-cycle of a typical retrovirus such as the murine leukaemia virus MLV is illustrated in simplified form in *Figure 1*. The virus particles, each of which contain two copies of a single-stranded RNA genome, are composed of a central nucleoprotein core surrounded by a membrane coat which bears specific viral 'envelope' glycoproteins on its outer surface. Infection of target cells is initiated by the interaction

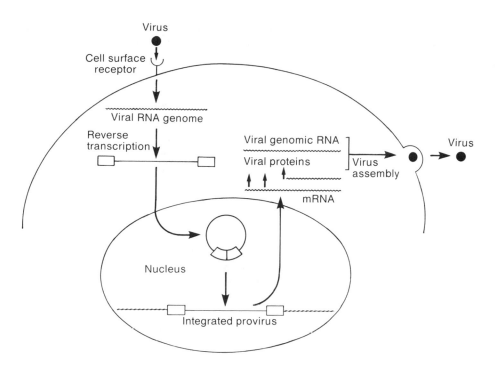

Figure 1. The retrovirus life-cycle (see Section 2.1).

of these glycoproteins with specific cell surface receptors. In most cases, these receptors remain poorly characterized. After entry into the cell, the viral genome is converted into a linear double-stranded DNA form by reverse transcriptase molecules present in the infecting particles. This involves a complex series of steps that includes site-specific binding of primers for reverse transcription, and serial transfers of the nascent DNA strands between templates (13). The linear DNA then enters the nucleus and is converted into a circular form which is probably the substrate for integration into the host cell genome. A single infecting virus particle gives rise to only one integrated copy of viral DNA and this copy is usually stably maintained. Apart from a possible preference for transcriptionally active regions, retroviral insertion shows little or no apparent specificity for particular sites within the target cell DNA and for most purposes may be considered to occur at random locations.

The integrated linear DNA form of the retrovirus genome is known as a provirus and has a characteristic structure with long terminal repeats (LTRs) at either end (see Section 2.2). It is this DNA structure that can be manipulated *in vitro* to make retroviral vectors. A wild-type provirus contains three structural genes, *gag, pol*, and *env*, which encode the core proteins, reverse transcriptase, and envelope proteins, respectively. The promoter in the 5′ LTR drives transcription of the integrated provirus, while the 3′ LTR provides a signal for polyadenylation of the transcripts. In the case of MLV, and many other retroviruses, two distinct RNAs are produced in approximately equal proportions: a full-length 'genomic' transcript, and a smaller sub-genomic mRNA which has undergone splicing and serves as a template for translation of the *env* gene products. The genomic length transcripts direct translation of the *gag* and *pol* gene products, but a proportion of them also serve as RNA genomes and are packaged into viral particles. The nascent viral particles, which contain molecules of reverse transcriptase, now form by budding of the plasma membrane and are released from the cell surface. (See ref. 13 for a more detailed summary of retrovirus replication.)

2.2 Structure of the retroviral genome and provirus

All retroviruses have a similar genetic organization, exemplified here by MLV. The structure of an MLV provirus is shown in *Figure 2*, together with the viral RNA genome and spliced sub-genomic RNA. The principle features of the provirus are as follows (14).

(i)   An LTR at each end of the provirus, containing sequences for the initiation and termination of transcription, reverse transcription of the viral RNA, and integration into the host chromosome. The LTR itself has a tripartite structure containing sequences derived from the 5' end of viral RNA (U5), the 3' end of viral RNA (U3), and a short repeated sequence (R) which is found at the ends of viral RNA.

(ii)   Short sequences [labelled PB(−) and PB(+) in *Figure 2*] required for priming of negative and positive strand synthesis of viral DNA by reverse transcription.

(iii) The packaging sequence ψ, which is necessary for efficient packaging of the viral RNA into virions.

(iv)   The *trans*-acting viral structural genes *gag, pol,* and *env* (see Section 2.1).

(v)   The viral splice donor and acceptor sequences (S_D and S_A) which are used for the production of sub-genomic *env* RNA.

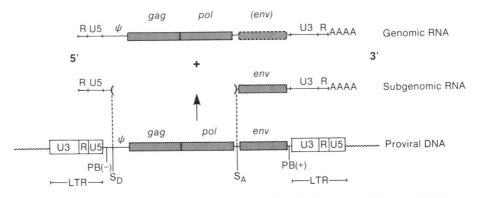

Figure 2. Structure of a retroviral provirus and its relationship to viral transcripts. (Not to scale.) The provirus is composed of two LTRs flanking a central region that contains the three structural genes *gag, pol,* and *env*. The primer binding sites for reverse transcription of viral RNA, PB(−) and PB(+), are located adjacent to the LTRs. Each LTR is composed of sequences derived from the 3' (U3) and 5' (U5) ends of genomic RNA, linked by a copy of a short sequence (R) which is found at both ends of genomic RNA. The U3 sequences contain promoter and enhancer elements. Transcription initiates within the 5' LTR and RNA terminates at a polyadenylation site in the 3' LTR. The full length 'genomic' transcript serves both as the viral RNA genome and as the template for translation of the *gag* and *pol* genes. The *env* gene is translated from a sub-genomic RNA formed by splicing of the primary transcript between the splice donor (S_D) and splice acceptor (S_A) sites. Note that only the genomic length RNA contains the packaging signal (ψ) required for incorporation into virions. A comprehensive map and complete nucleotide sequence of Mo-MLV can be found in ref. 42.

2.3 Receptors, tropism and immunity

A few aspects of the retrovirus life-cycle merit further consideration here because of their relevance to the host-range of retroviral vectors. The host range of a wild-type retrovirus can be limited at either the extracellular or intracellular stages of its life-cycle (15). Of these, the extracellular stage, involving the interaction of viral envelope proteins with their receptors, is the most important.

The envelope proteins of MLV-related viruses can be divided into different classes based on the particular cell-surface receptors with which they interact, and the host-range or 'tropism' of the viruses is accordingly limited to those host species which express the appropriate receptor. Thus an 'ecotropic' murine retrovirus such as Moloney-MLV is limited to infecting mouse and rat cells, while an 'amphotropic' MLV has a much broader host range since its envelope proteins interact with receptors present in a variety of species from birds to humans. Although most MLV-based vectors are derived from Moloney-MLV, their host range can easily be extended beyond its normal limits by pseudotyping (15), i.e. by packaging the vector genome in a virion particle bearing envelope proteins from an amphotropic virus.

In addition to these species-dependent tropisms, retroviral host-range may also be limited by tissue-specific expression of the appropriate cell surface receptors in a given species. In general, most fibroblasts, lymphoid cells, and many others are susceptible to MLV infection, but no extensive survey of cell types has been performed.

Even if a target cell expresses the correct receptors for a particular retrovirus, it should be appreciated that those receptors will be blocked if the cell is already expressing the relevant viral envelope protein (15). Thus a cell that is productively infected with a replication-competent retrovirus will often be immune to superinfection by a virus with the same tropism.

3. CHOOSING A VECTOR

3.1 Principles of vector design

Retroviruses are natural vectors for the transmission and expression of foreign genes. Acutely oncogenic retroviruses will rapidly and efficiently cause tumours in animals, and in most cases will transform appropriate cells in culture. With one exception (see Section 3.3) such viruses are replication defective, having oncogene sequences of cellular origin substituted for viral sequences that encode *trans*-acting functions (16). Viral products essential for the replication and integration of these defective viruses in nature are supplied in *trans* by a non-transforming replication-competent helper virus. The most logical approach to retrovirus vector design is to follow the precedent set by nature and to employ replication-defective vectors which require *trans*-complementation of viral functions. These functions can be supplied either by a helper virus, or by helper cells (also known as 'packaging' cells) harbouring a mutant provirus that cannot itself be packaged into mature virions (17).

The *cis*-acting viral sequences that must be retained by a vector if it is to replicate efficiently are the two LTRs, the priming sites for reverse transcription (adjacent to the LTRs), and the packaging signal sequence close to the 5' LTR (14; see *Figure 2*). All the remaining sequences are dispensable, as their loss can be complemented in *trans*. The structure of the provirus is readily adapted for vector construction since the *cis*-

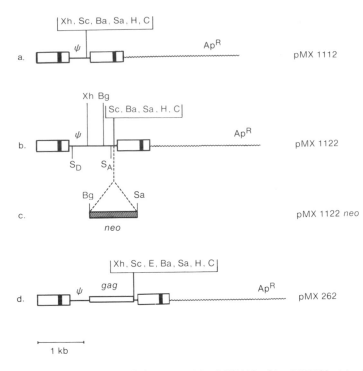

Figure 3. Maps of MLV-based retroviral vectors: (**a**), pMX1112; (**b**), pMX1122; (**c**), pMX1122*neo*; (**d**), pMX262. Each is drawn to scale in linearized form. The positions of unique restriction enzyme sites suitable for use in construction of recombinants are shown, as well as the packaging signal (ψ), and the splicing sites (S_D and S_A) in pMX1122. To construct pMX1122*neo*, a 1.1 kb *BglI – SalI* fragment carring the *neo* gene was inserted between the *Bam*HI and *Sal*I sites of pMX1122. Note that the initiator ATG codon for the *gag* gene is absent from pMX1112 and pMX1122 but is present in pMX262 together with 939 bp of the *gag* open reading frame. Each vector plasmid includes a 2.6 kb fragment (shown as a wavy line) which contains a pBR322 plasmid replication origin and ampicillin resistance gene (Ap^R). These plasmid sequences are not present in viral genomes derived from the vector DNA. Restriction sites: Xh, *Xho*I; Sc, *Sac*II; E, *Eco*RI; Ba, *Bam*HI; Sa, *Sal*I; H, *Hind*III; C, *Cla*I; Bg, *Bgl*II.

acting sequences required for replication are clustered at the ends of the provirus and are segregated from the *trans*-acting sequences in between. This organization makes it easy to insert foreign sequences in the middle of the genome, in place of the viral structural genes.

Section 3.2 will describe the principal different types of replication-defective vectors available. An alternative strategy, in which sequences are inserted into replication-competent vectors, will be dealt with briefly in Section 3.3.

3.2 Replication defective vectors

3.2.1 *Single gene vectors*

In the simplest retroviral vectors, the *trans*-acting viral structural genes are deleted and replaced with one or more restriction enzyme sites for the insertion of new sequences. Several vectors of this sort have been described (e.g. 18, 19). An example of a single gene vector, based on the Moloney murine leukaemia virus (Mo-MLV) and designated pMX1112, is depicted in *Figure 3a*. In this case a polylinker with multiple cloning sites has been substituted for the viral genes *gag, pol* and *env*. A foreign gene inserted here is efficiently expressed from the promoter in the 5′ viral LTR, and the retention of *cis*-acting viral sequences allows production of infectious particles from this vector in the presence of suitable helper functions. Such single gene vectors have the advantage of simplicity over other types of vectors, and in our experience have consistently produced high titre virus stocks that successfully express the gene inserted. More sophisticated vectors may be more versatile but are more often prone to problems of instability and/or poor expression.

The major disadvantage of single gene vectors is the lack of a suitable selection for the presence and expression of the recombinant virus. The production of high titre stocks can often compensate for this (since all the cells in a dish can be infected), but in general this type of vector is limited in its applications, being best employed to transmit genes which elicit a clearly distinguishable phenotype.

3.2.2 *Double gene vectors*

Genes for which no convenient selection exists, and which produce no easily scored phenotype in cultured cells, pose the problem of how to identify transfected or infected cells harbouring the recombinant provirus. The solution has been to install a second gene in the same construction, which encodes a selectable phenotype. Several selectable markers have been used for this purpose, including the genes encoding neomycin phosphotransferase (*neo*), thymidine kinase (*tk*), guanosine phosphoribosyl transferase (*gpt*), hygromycin phosphotransferase B (*hgr*), and dihydrofolate reductase (*dhfr*) (14,20,21).

Vectors carrying *dhfr* have the advantage that the proviral sequences may be amplified in copy number by methotrexate selection, resulting in increased expression and higher virus titres (21). The most widely applicable dominant marker genes, however, are those encoding a selectable drug resistance, such as *neo* or *hgr*: these have the advantage that they may be employed in a wide variety of cell types and do not require special media for selection. In all examples of double gene vectors the gene proximal to the 5′ LTR is expressed from the genomic length viral RNA. Two different strategies have been adopted to express the more distal gene: either it is expressed from a separate subgenomic mRNA formed by splicing of the viral RNA, or it is expressed from an internal promoter inserted within the vector.

(i) *Splicing vectors*. The most natural approach to construction of double-gene vectors is to mimic the mechanism employed by the parental retroviruses and to use the viral splice donor and acceptor sites to form a separate subgenomic RNA analogous to *env* RNA (*Figure 2*). This then becomes the template for translation of the distal gene. The proximal gene is installed in place of the *gag* and *pol* reading frames and is translated from unspliced RNA. An example of such a splicing vector, pMX1122, is shown in *Figure 3b*. This vector has cloning sites for *Xho*I and *Bgl*II in the '*gag*' position, and a multiple cloning site with targets for *Sac*II, *Bam*HI, *Sal*I, *Hind*III and *Cla*I in the '*env*' position immediately following the MLV splice acceptor. In order to provide a selectable marker for this particular vector, a neomycin phosphotransferase gene (*neo*), which confers resistance to the antibiotic G418, was inserted in the '*env*' position, creating the vector MX1122*neo* (*Figure 3c*). A second gene may now be installed in the '*gag*' position and should be co-expressed with *neo*. [An example of the successful use of this vector is described by Brown *et al.* (12).]

Cepko *et al.* (22) created a set of splicing vectors similar to pMX1122 in which *neo* was installed in either the *gag* or *env* position. One of these, pZIP-Neo SV(X)1, which has the *neo* gene in the *env* position and a *Bam*HI site for insertions at the *gag* position, has been widely used in many laboratories.

The most common problem encountered in the use of double gene 'splicing' vectors of this sort is that the efficiency of viral splicing is sometimes severely altered, leading to poor expression of one or other of the two genes carried. This problem is discussed further in Section 7.

(ii) *Double gene vectors with internal promoters.* The splicing vectors described in the previous section are designed to express both inserted genes from the promoter in the 5' LTR. An alternative strategy is to use an additional promoter inserted within the vector in such a position as to drive expression of the more distal gene, while the proximal gene is again expressed from the viral LTR. Thus each gene has its own independent promoter. As with the splicing vectors above, one of the two inserted genes is typically a selectable marker such as *neo*.

Internal promoters have been inserted in retroviral vectors in either orientation relative to transcription from the viral LTR. When the internal promoter is 'backwards', virus production may be impaired to some degree as a result of transcriptional interference from the opposing promoters, and potentially by an effect of anti-sense RNA, although in some cases these problems seem to be minimal (14). A slight advantage of this configuration is that the inserted DNA can retain its polyadenylation signal without affecting virus production. In contrast, when the inserted DNA is transcribed in the same orientation as viral RNA, the presence of a polyadenylation signal may severely inhibit virus production by causing premature polyadenylation of the viral genomic transcript (14). This can simply be avoided, however, by removal of the polyadenylation signal from the insert.

Internal promoter vectors avoid the problems of inadequate or excessive splicing which sometimes impair the performance of splicing vectors (see Section 7). Naturally occurring retroviruses do not contain internal promoters, however, and a possible disadvantage of this type of vector is that interactions between the two promoters (even when in the same orientation) may result in poor expression of one or other of the genes (23,24). Nevertheless, in practice, vectors with internal promoters have been successfully exploited on several occasions, and are becoming increasingly popular.

Internal promoter vectors of this sort have been constructed in many laboratories (e.g. 7,23,25,26). One example, pMV7, described by Kirschmeier *et al.* (26), is shown in *Figure 4*. pMV-7 is based on Moloney sarcoma virus (Mo-MSV), a close relative of Mo-MLV whose RNA is efficiently packaged by MLV helpers or packaging lines. The internal promoter in the pMV-7 vector is derived from the herpes simplex *tk* gene, and is in the same orientation as the viral LTRs (26).

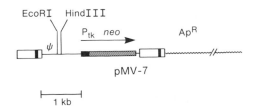

Figure 4. Linear map of the internal promoter vector pMV-7 (26). pMV-7 is derived from Mo-MSV and contains unique restriction sites for *Eco*RI and *Hin*dIII that can be used for the insertion of cloned genes. The *neo* gene, driven by a herpes simplex *tk* promoter (P_{tk}) provides a selectable marker. The wavy line indicates the ampicillin resistance gene (Ap^R) and other plasmid sequences not present in viral genomes derived from the vector DNA.

3.2.3 *Fusion vectors*

Many naturally occurring oncogenic retroviruses express hybrid proteins resulting from fusion of the N-terminal part of a viral *gag* or *env* gene to oncogene sequences derived from host cell DNA. This configuration allows very efficient expression of the hybrid proteins since the signals affecting their translation are those which normally ensure copious production of viral gene products in infected cells. A further consequence is that the resulting proteins may be affected by specific subcellular localization signals in the *gag* or *env* sequences.

When optimal expression of a particular gene product is paramount, and possible constraints in subcellular localization are either acceptable or desired, it may be appropriate to express the gene from a retroviral vector tailored for gene fusion. The vector pMX262 (*Figure 3d*) contains a multiple cloning site inserted after the *Xho*I site in the *gag* gene of Mo-MLV, readily allowing construction of recombinant viruses which express hybrid *gag* fusion proteins. These proteins may be directed to the inner surface of the plasma membrane because of myristylation of their *gag*-derived amino terminus (27). Naturally, the main caveat applying to this approach is that, as with any gene fusion system, the resulting proteins may be unstable and/or biologically inactive.

3.2.4 *Shuttle vectors*

As described in Section 6.3, it is sometimes desirable to be able to recover proviral sequences rapidly from mammalian cells by molecular cloning, for example to analyse the structure of transduced sequences when a retroviral vector has been exploited to process out introns from a genomic DNA insert (19). A 'shuttle' vector system that facilitates the transfer of recombinants between animal and bacterial cells is particularly useful for this purpose. Such vectors contain a eukaryotic origin of replication, either from SV40 (22) or polyoma virus (28), which allows high copy number extra-chromosomal replication in appropriate cells. A pBR322 plasmid replication origin is also present within the provirus so that the circular replicating DNA can easily be recovered by transformation of *E. coli*. Selection of the correct transformants is accomplished by the ability of a *neo* gene in the vector to confer resistance both to G418 in animal cells and to kanamycin or neomycin in bacteria (see Section 6.3). A commonly used retroviral shuttle vector is the double gene 'splicing' vector pZIP Neo SV(X)1 [22; see Section 3.2.2(i)].

3.2.5 *Self-inactivating vectors*

Self-inactivating or 'suicide' vectors are designed to eliminate effects of viral promoter and enhancer sequences upon the regulation and expression of a gene under the control of an internal promoter (29). The vectors are designed such that during reverse transcription and integration, those regions of the viral genome which contain the promoter and enhancer elements become deleted. The proviral LTRs in infected cells are thus transcriptionally inactive, clearing the way for normal expression of internally promoted genes and eliminating potentially undesirable effects of proviral insertion such as transcriptional activation of adjacent genes (13). Although the titre of virus generated so far using these vectors has been low [10^4 c.f.u./ml (29)], self-inactivating vectors are the leading candidates for potential use in human gene therapy (3).

3.3 **Replication competent vectors**

No general purpose replication-competent murine retroviral vectors have yet been constructed, either because of the lack of suitable sites for insertion of foreign genes in MLV without disrupting essential viral sequences or because of size limitations on the viral genome (4). One successful strategy, however, has been to insert short sequences into the viral LTR. This has been used to produce replication-competent MLV carrying the *E. coli* suppressor tRNA gene (*supF*) (30), which has proved useful as a genetic and developmental marker, as well as a tool for facilitated cloning of adjacent sequences after proviral insertion. Nevertheless, it remains to be seen whether protein-coding sequences could be inserted into viral LTRs and efficiently expressed.

A more broadly applicable replication-competent vector is available for avian cells. This is based on the Rous sarcoma virus (RSV), which is unique among acutely transforming retroviruses in being replication-competent. The organization of RSV is unusual because the oncogene *src* is expressed from its own subgenomic RNA formed by additional splicing of the viral RNA, while the viral genes are expressed in the normal fashion (16). Vectors based on RSV have the *src*-coding sequences replaced with a site for insertion of foreign DNA (14,31). This system provides an extremely efficient means of introducing and expressing foreign sequences, and the virus can be grown to very high titres. Unfortunately the constraint of being limited to avian cells precludes its widespread use. Also, for many applications (e.g. gene therapy, ref. 3) it is undesirable to use replication-competent vectors as they have the potential to perpetuate virus spread.

3.4 **Preparation of insert sequences**

The best rule of thumb governing sequences to be inserted into a retrovirus vector is to reduce them to the minimum length required for protein expression, and so avoid unforseen problems of expression or instability. In any case the insert must be small enough that the total size of the viral genomic RNA to be packaged does not exceed $10-11$ kb (14). The ideal arrangement is to use a fragment that encompasses the entire open reading frame with the 5′ and 3′ flanking sequences as short as conveniently possible. Particular attention should be paid to the elimination of sequences affecting transcription or processing of RNA, such as promoters or polyadenylation signals. Additional AUG codons upstream of the intended translation start site should also be avoided since they may interfere with translational efficiency.

To avoid possible complications caused by splicing, a cDNA insert, if available, is preferable to sequences containing introns. Although retrovirus vectors can accurately remove introns from genomic sequences and so be used to generate cDNA copies of cloned genes, this process is not always efficient (14).

4. GENERATION OF RECOMBINANT VIRUS STOCKS

4.1 Production of helper-free stocks

In order to derive a virus stock from a replication-defective recombinant retroviral vector, plasmid DNA containing the proviral form of the recombinant must be introduced into cells which will package retroviral RNA into virus particles. Fibroblast cell lines productively infected with an appropriate helper virus can be used for this purpose, in which case a virus stock is generated that contains a mixture of recombinant and helper viral genomes (see Section 4.2). Alternatively, a retroviral packaging cell line may be used to produce a 'helper-free' virus stock.

Packaging cell lines contain proviral DNA of a helper virus whose packaging signal is deleted, so that its own RNA transcripts cannot be packaged into viral particles. This defect is only *cis*-acting, however, so the helper provirus still produces all the viral proteins required *in trans* for encapsidation of suitable RNA genomes into virions. Consequently, when a recombinant provirus is introduced into packaging cells, its transcripts form the major class of packagable molecules, and the cells produce viral particles that contain almost exclusively RNA genomes of the recombinant vector. Such virus stocks are termed 'helper-free', although in practice they may sometimes contain low titres of replication-competent helpers (32).

Although helper-free virus stocks are replication-defective, they are nevertheless fully infectious. By virtue of viral protein products packaged within the virion, such viruses will efficiently infect susceptible target cells, undergo a round of reverse-transcription, and integrate their proviral DNA in the recipient cell genome (17). From this point transcription will occur from the viral LTR, as well as from internal promoter elements if present in the vector, but in the absence of helper viral gene products no further virus particles will be produced.

Several different packaging cell lines have been described for the production of helper-free stocks of MLV-based retrovirus vectors (17,19,21,32). Of these, the most useful are probably the ψ2 line (17), which packages viral RNA into ecotropic particles (i.e. which have the capacity to infect mouse and rat cells only), and PA317 (32), which will produce broad host range amphotropic stocks free of detectable helper virus. A packaging cell line for avian retroviral vectors is also available (33).

4.1.1 *Transfection of packaging cell lines*

Since all the MLV packaging cell lines so far described have been derived from either

Table 1. Virus production by transient transfection of packaging cells.

1.	Plate packaging cells at a density of 4×10^5 per 6 cm dish one day before transfection.
2.	Dissolve $10-20$ μg of vector DNA in 0.5 ml of sterile 250 mM $CaCl_2$. Add this dropwise with continuous mixing to 0.5 ml of sterile $2\times$ HBS[a]. Leave at room temperature for 15 min for precipitate to form.
3.	Apply 0.5 ml of the $CaPO_4$-DNA precipitate per dish adding it dropwise to the culture medium.
4.	Leave for $8-12$ h and then change the medium.
5.	Harvest the virus $24-72$ h later (see Section 4.3). The optimal time for virus harvest should be determined empirically by harvesting at $12-24$ h intervals and determining the titre of each stock (Section 6.1).

$2\times$ HBS: 1 litre contains 16 g NaCl, 0.74 g KCl, 0.39 g $Na_2HPO_4.7H_2O$, 1 g Dextrose, 5 g HEPES, adjusted to pH 7.05 with NaOH.

Table 2. Production of stably transfected G418 resistant cells.

1.	Transfect the cells as in *Table 1*, but use only 0.5 μg of vector DNA per dish, together with 10 μg of salmon sperm carrier DNA. If the vector itself does not carry a *neo* marker, include 0.1 μg of a *neo*-bearing plasmid in the precipitate.
2.	$24-48$ h after transfection, and before the cells reach confluence, split the cells from each 6 cm dish into two 10 cm dishes containing G418 (Geneticin, Gibco) in the medium. The appropriate G418 concentration for each cell line should be determined empirically, but for most NIH3T3 derivatives is around 400 μg/ml (net). The G418 should stop the cells growing within 24 h and lead to cell death within about a week.
3.	Once cell death is evident the medium can be changed to a G418 concentration of 200 μg/ml and dishes left until G418 resistant colonies are visible.

NIH3T3 or BALB/c 3T3 cells, recombinant retroviral DNA can readily be introduced by transfection using a standard calcium phosphate co-precipitation method (34). A short-term, or transient, transfection can be sufficient to give rise to a low titre virus stock (typically 10^1-10^3 per ml), but for higher titre stocks stably transfected lines must be obtained using a dominant selectable marker. These will often yield stocks of up to 10^5-10^6 infectious units per ml. The virus titre harvested from transient transfections can also be improved by using a retroviral vector on a plasmid that contains the entire early region of polyoma virus and so undergoes multicopy extrachromosomal replication in the packaging cells (35).

A protocol for transient transfection of packaging cells is given in *Table 1*, and details regarding the formation of the calcium phosphate-DNA co-precipitate can be found in the chapter by Gorman in DNA Cloning, volume II (34). The titre of virus ultimately obtained by this procedure will be dependent upon the parameters normally affecting transfection frequencies (purity of DNA used, intrinsic 'transfectability' of the cells, etc.), and also on the properties of the particular vector construct used. Some retroviral constructs repeatedly give lower titres than others, and may give very low or undetectable titres after transient transfection.

To obtain stably transfected packaging cell lines, a standard calcium phosphate transfection procedure is again employed, followed by selection for a dominant marker carried either on the retroviral vector plasmid itself or on a separate co-transfected plasmid. The bacterial *neo* gene, which confers resistance to the neomycin analogue

G418 in mammalian cells, is typically used for this purpose. Transfection of cells with selection for G418 resistance is described in *Table 2*.

4.1.2 *Infection of packaging cell lines*

A more elaborate, but often more satisfactory, procedure for generating a helper-free virus stock involves the sequential use of two different packaging lines, such that virus produced by transfection of the first cell line is used to infect the second (36; *Figure* 5). This usually requires that the vector in question carries a marker that can be used for selection of the infected cells. To circumvent the packaging cells' intrinsic immunity to infection with virus of the same tropism, the virus is passed from an amphotropic packaging line to an ecotropic one, or vice-versa. If it is undesirable, for reasons of biological containment, to handle amphotropic stocks of a particular recombinant, the resistance of $\psi2$ cells to infection with ecotropic virus can be partially overcome by treatment with sub-lethal doses of tunicamycin (36).

The advantages of this two-step procedure over single-step transfection of a packaging line are three-fold.

(i)   Proviral DNA introduced into a cell as a result of retroviral infection is usually expressed at a much higher level than is the identical DNA introduced by transfection (37). The reasons for this are not understood, but as a consequence of the increased abundance of viral RNA the titre of virus from an infected packaging line is often much higher (by as much as 100-fold) than that obtained by transfection.

(ii)   If cells derived from individual infected colonies are used as the source of virus the resulting stock is likely to be more genetically uniform than one originating from transfected cells. This is because transfected cells often contain multiple integrated copies of the transfected DNA, some of which may be rearranged or otherwise mutated, but all of which may contribute to the virus stock. Cells from an infected colony, on the other hand, will contain only individual copies of the proviral DNA integrated in a precisely defined manner.

(iii)   This method offers the opportunity to examine the structure of the proviral DNA from which all the viral genomes are immediately derived, by Southern blot analysis of DNA from single colonies of infected packaging cells. This may be particularly important when the DNA originally inserted in the retroviral vector contained introns, and one wishes to determine whether these have been correctly spliced from the viral genome before using the virus stock for subsequent experiments (see *Figure* 5).

4.1.3 *Transfection of packaging DNA*

Rather than introduce retroviral vector DNA into a packaging cell line, an alternative means of generating a helper-free virus stock is to start with any cell containing the recombinant proviral DNA and introduce by transfection an MLV helper genome whose packaging signal is deleted. This effectively converts the starting cells into a packaging line. The approach is particularly useful for rescuing a recombinant vector as virus from cells already harbouring the proviral DNA.

Table 3. Production of MLV helper virus stocks.

1.	Make a CaPO$_4$ precipitate containing 2 μg pZAP plasmid DNA and 20 μg of salmon sperm carrier DNA per ml of suspension (see *Table 1*).
2.	Apply 0.5 ml of the suspension dropwise to the medium of to 2 $\times$ 10^5 NIH 3T3 cells in a 5 cm dish. Leave for 8–12 h.
3.	Aspirate the dishes and apply fresh medium.
4.	When the cells reach confluence, split them 1:10 into new dishes.
5.	Split the cells 1:25 at confluence and continue to passage in this manner for two weeks.
6.	Harvest the virus stock as described in Section 4.3.
7.	Freeze the cells for future use as a source of helper virus.

4.2 Production of replication-competent virus stocks

4.2.1 *Making a helper virus stock*

A stock of helper virus is made simply by transfecting appropriate cells with cloned DNA of a replication-competent virus in its proviral form. The transfected population is then passaged several times to allow spread of the virus until all the cells in the culture are infected. A suitable proviral clone for generating Moloney MLV helper virus is pZAP (38). For producing high titre stocks, NIH 3T3 cells work well as host cells, as will most rapidly dividing mouse fibroblast lines. Alternatively, to avoid possible recombination with endogenous mouse retroviruses, Rat-1 cells, or their relatives, may be used. A protocol for producing MLV helper stocks is given in *Table 3*.

4.2.2 *Making a mixed stock of helper and recombinant virus*

This can be achieved by either of two methods. In the first method, helper virus stock can be used to infect a cell line that already contains the replication-defective recombinant provirus (introduced either by transfection or infection), so that the recombinant is 'rescued' in a virus stock. (See Section 5 for infection protocols.) Alternatively, DNA of the helper and recombinant proviruses can be co-transfected into suitable host cells, and the viruses subsequently allowed to spread throughout the culture. This second route usually results in an overall higher titre of recombinant virus than the first, as well as a higher ratio of recombinant to helper virus in the mixture. The procedure for this second method is given below.

(i)   Transfect NIH 3T3 cells as described in *Table 2*, using a mixture of recombinant proviral plasmid DNA and cloned helper proviral DNA in a ten to one molar ratio.

(ii)   After transfection, passage the cells for at least ten days to allow virus spread.

(iii)   If the recombinant provirus carries a selectable maker, such as *neo*, split the cells into selective medium at this stage and wait for resistant colonies to grow.

(iv)   Grow the pooled colonies as a mass culture and harvest the virus stock as described below (Section 4.3).

4.3 Harvesting and storage of the virus; optimizing the titre

Retrovirus stocks are obtained from packaging cell lines or productively infected cells by simply harvesting the culture medium in which the cells have been growing. Floating cells and other debris should be removed by centrifugation at 5000 *g* for 5 min.

Infected cells release virus at a maximum rate when growing exponentially. The maximum titre of virus per ml is therefore obtained just before growth of the cells is arrested at confluence. Fresh culture medium is applied when the cells are 80−90% confluent and left for 12−24 h prior to harvesting the virus. A second harvest over the next 12−24 h period may also yield high titres. Use of a minimal volume of medium for harvesting will result in a proportionate increase in virus titre. Virus stocks can be concentrated by centrifuging at 30 000 g for 12−16 h at 4°C and resuspending the pellet in a smaller volume of medium containing 10% serum. A 100-fold concentration will result in less than a 100-fold increase in functional titre, however, as some biological activity will be lost during pelleting.

In order to obtain the maximum possible titre of a particular virus it is preferable to work with clonal lines derived from single colonies of producer cells. This is particularly important if virus is sought from cells transfected with the proviral DNA: individual clonal lines from such a population will often show differences of 10- to 100-fold in virus titre. If the initial transfection is followed by selection for a selectable marker, individual colonies of transfected cells should be picked with cloning cylinders, grown up separately in multi-well dishes, and assayed for virus titre as described in Section 6.1. Those lines producing the highest titres are then retained for further use.

Retrovirus stocks should be stored frozen at −70°C in medium containing 10% serum. There will be a slight drop in titre due to freezing and thawing, so it is advisable to store important stocks in several small aliquots. By checking the titre of an aliquot after thawing, a more accurate measure of the working titre can be obtained.

5. INFECTION OF TARGET CELLS

5.1 Infection with virus stocks

The brevity of this section testifies to the ease with which retrovirus vectors can be used to introduce cloned sequences into target cells, once a functional stock of virus is in hand. For fibroblasts, and many other cell types that express appropriate cell surface receptors, the efficiency of infection should be close to 100% by the following method.

(i)   Plate cells at approximately 4×10^5 per 6 cm dish one day before infection.
(ii)   Make a stock solution of polybrene (Aldrich) at 8 mg/ml in double distilled water; sterilize by filtration and store at 4°C.
(iii)   Draw off the culture medium and replace with 2 ml per dish of fresh medium containing appropriate quantities of virus and 8 μg/ml polybrene. (Polybrene is a polycation that promotes virus binding to the cells.)
(iv)   Return the dishes to the incubator for 2 h.
(v)   Draw off the polybrene-containing medium and replace with 5 ml of fresh medium. Leave the cells at 37°C for at least twenty-four hours (or one cell-division cycle, if longer) before passaging.
(vi)   If the virus carries a selectable marker the cells can now be split into selective medium.

5.2 Infection by co-cultivation

An alternative means of achieving retroviral infection is to co-cultivate the target cells with cells that actively produce the relevant virus. This method is particularly appropriate when the efficiency of infection of the target cells is low, or when multiple infectious events in each cell are required. To prevent subsequent contamination of the target cell culture with donor cells, the latter can be killed by prior exposure to Mitomycin C and will still produce virus for several days. A typical co-cultivation protocol is given below.

(i)   Plate approximately 10^6 virus-producing 'donor' cells in a 10 cm dish.

(ii)   Kill the cells by adding 10 μg/ml Mitomycin C to the culture medium for 1 h, then rinse the dish with PBS and change the medium.

(iii)   Plate 10^6 target cells in the same dish and at the same time add 8 μg/ml polybrene to the medium. (The polybrene treatment can be reduced if the cells show intolerance to this compound.)

(iv)   Leave for $2-3$ days until confluent, then split the infected target cells into fresh medium in a new dish.

6. CHECKING THE VIRUS STOCK

6.1 Titration of the virus

6.1.1 *Viral RNA dot-blot assay*

Virus titres in harvested cell culture medium can be estimated by a choice of methods that rely on physical, biochemical, or biological assays. The most widely applicable method is to determine the quantity of viral genomic RNA in the culture medium by hybridization with ^{32}P-labelled DNA probe. This is conveniently done by a standard RNA dot-blot procedure after concentrating the virus, as described in *Table 4*. Quantitative determinations are achieved by comparing hybridization intensities with those

Table 4. Viral RNA dot-blot assay.

1.	Clarify the virus-containing medium by centrifuging at 10 000 g for 10 min at 4°C.
2.	Pellet the virus from the supernatant by spinning at 200 000 g for 1 h at 4°C. Drain the pellet well.
3.	To each tube add 10 μl of 5 mg/ml yeast tRNA carrier and thoroughly resuspend the virus in 0.4 ml of STE[a] containing 5 μg/ml proteinase K and 0.2% SDS (pre-incubated for 15 min at 37°C).
4.	Transfer each sample to a 1.5 ml snap-cap tube and incubate at 37°C for 30 min. Extract once with an equal volume of phenol:chloroform (1:1). Separate the phases by centrifugation and re-extract the aqueous phase with chloroform. To the final aqueous phase add 0.1 volumes of 3 M sodium acetate and 2 volumes of ethanol. Chill to -70°C.
5.	Pellet the RNA by centrifugation in a microcentrifuge. Drain and allow the pellets to air dry. Take up the RNA pellets in 20 μl of TE[b] and make a series of 5-fold dilutions.
6.	Wet a small sheet of nitrocellulose (or nylon) filter in water, soak in 20 × SSC[c], blot briefly, and place on a sheet of filter paper.
7.	Incubate the RNA samples at 65°C for 5 min and spot 5 μl aliquots onto the filter. (Alternatively, a Schleicher and Schuell 'mini-fold' dot-blot apparatus can be used at this stage.)
8.	Dry the filter under a heat lamp, then bake for one hour under vacuum.
9.	Hybridize by standard procedures with a nick-translated probe (39).
10.	To control for non-specific hybridization, 10 μg/ml RNase A can be added to a duplicate sample before step 7.

[a]STE is 100 mM NaCl, 10 mM Tris-HCl pH 7.5, 1 mM EDTA.
[b]TE is 10 mM Tris-HCl pH 7.5, 1 mM EDTA.
[c]SSC is 0.3 M NaCl, 0.03 M sodium citrate.

Table 5. Reverse transcriptase assay.

The following stock solutions will be required:

      1 M Tris-HCl pH 8.1
      1 M $MgCl_2$
      1 mM DTT
      10% NP40
      10 mg/ml poly(C) (Boehringer Mannheim)
      1 mg/ml oligo(dG)$_{12-18}$ (Collaborative Research)
      1 mCi/ml [^{3}H]dGTP[a](Amersham, 37 Ci/mmol).

1.   Prepare a 2× reaction buffer containing 100 mM Tris-HCl pH 8.1, 20 mM $MgCl_2$, 20 mM DTT, 0.1% NP40.
2.   To 250 µl of the 2× reaction buffer on ice (enough for 10 assays), add 24 µg poly(C), 6 µg oligo(dG), and 10 µCi [^{3}H]dGTP[a].
3.   Add 25 µl of this cocktail to 25 µl of virus-containing medium, or concentrated virus suspension, and incubate at 37°C for 2−4 h.
4.   Spot the entire reaction volume onto a 2 × 2 cm square of DEAE paper (Whatman, DE-81) and allow to dry.
5.   Wash the DEAE squares in 0.5 M Na_2HPO_4 at room temperature for a total of 30 min with five changes of buffer.
6.   Rinse briefly with water twice, and then twice with 95% ethanol. Dry under heat lamp.
7.   Transfer each square to a scintillation vial and count with scintillant.

[a]A variation on this procedure, particularly applicable to screening large numbers of samples, is to substitute ^{32}P-labelled dGTP for the ^{3}H-labelled substrate. The reaction samples are spotted in an array onto a single sheet of DEAE paper which, after washing, is exposed to X-ray film. 0.1−0.5 µCi of [^{32}P]dGTP is used per reaction, and cold dGTP should be added to give a final concentration of 10 µM. For full details see Goff *et al.* (40).

obtained from an accurately titred control virus (Section 6.1.3) or from known quantities of purified RNA or DNA on the filter. By using different DNA probes one can estimate the titres of individual components of a mixed virus stock, and determine directly whether the viruses contain particular sequences of interest.

6.1.2 *Reverse transcriptase assay*

Since retrovirus particles contain an RNA-directed DNA polymerase, an assay of reverse transcriptase activity provides an estimate of the virus titre. This assay is usually not applicable to helper-free stocks, however, since untransfected packaging cell lines spontaneously release significant titres of polymerase-containing particles (17). For stocks containing helper virus, reverse transcriptase assay is the simplest method for qualitative screening of multiple samples. For quantitative titrations, a series of known standards must be used to determine the linear range of the assay.

A protocol for reverse transcriptase assays is given in *Table 5*. The viral polymerase is made accessible by gentle detergent lysis of the virions and is then challenged with a poly(C) template primed with oligo(dG). The incorporation of ^{3}H from labelled dGTP into nucleic acid polymers provides a measure of enzyme activity present, and hence the titre of virus. Cell culture medium containing high titres of virus ($> 10^3$/ml) can be assayed directly. For lower titre stocks the virus must first be concentrated from the medium by pelleting as described in steps 1 and 2 of *Table 4*, and then resuspended thoroughly in 100 μl of viral dilution buffer, on ice. [Viral dilution buffer is 50 mM Tris-HCl pH 8.1, 10 mM dithiothreitol (DTT), 10 mM $MgCl_2$, 100 μg/ml bovine serum albumin.]

6.1.3 *Titration by marker transduction*

Both of the above methods for determining approximate virus titres suffer from a need to start with accurately titred standards for quantitative results, and from their inability to distinguish between defective viruses and functional infectious particles. Clearly the most informative measures of virus titre are those which determine the number of infectious particles by biological assay. For replication-competent MLV this can be achieved by a plaque assay using overlays of XC cells (15), but this is usually unnecessary for routine purposes. Stocks of recombinant viruses carrying a selectable marker gene such as *neo*, however, can easily be titred accurately by determining the frequency of marker transduction upon infection of susceptible target cells with different dilutions of virus. This is calculated from the number of *neo* resistant colonies obtained after infection, taking into account the ratio in which the infected cells were split into selective medium. The titre is then expressed in colony forming units (c.f.u.) per ml of virus. Also, the titre of viruses carring a gene that confers a recognizable, though not selectable, phenotype (e.g. a transforming oncogene) can be determined in a similar manner.

6.2 Checking the structure and expression of the recombinant virus

In view of the unpredictable behaviour of certain novel retroviral constructions (see Section 7), it is usually prudent to check or confirm the structure and expression of recombinant retroviruses by DNA and RNA analysis and by direct monitoring of the expression of foreign proteins, if applicable. For vectors without an identifiable phenotype, some molecular analysis of this sort becomes essential.

The best method of determining the structure of viral genomic RNA is by inference from the proviral DNA form of the virus in infected cells. This is examined by Southern blot analysis of the cellular DNA (39). *Figure 5* shows an example of this demonstrating the removal of introns from a gene cloned in a retrovirus vector. As in *Figure 5*, it is usually convenient to digest the cellular DNA with restriction enzymes that cut within each viral LTR but not within the internal sequences: for vectors based on Moloney MLV the enzymes *Xba*I and *Sac*I can often be used for this purpose. Note that if the infected cells are of murine origin the probe for these blots should not contain MLV sequences as these will hybridize to a complex pattern of MLV-related endogenous proviruses. If necessary, fine structure mapping or DNA sequencing of a recombinant provirus can be accomplished after recovering the proviral DNA from infected cells by cloning (see Section 6.3).

Expression of viral RNA transcripts is analysed by standard Northern blotting procedures using either poly(A)-selected, or total, RNA from infected cells (39).

6.3 Recovering a provirus by cloning

For some purposes it is desirable to have a means of easily recovering recombinant

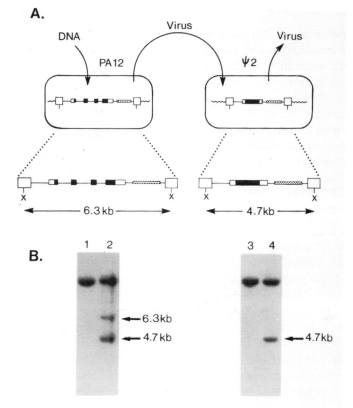

Figure 5. Use of a retroviral vector to remove introns from a cloned gene, and production of virus by using two packaging cell lines sequentially. (Reproduced from ref. 12 with permission, copyright Cell Press). **A**. Generation of virus stocks (Section 4.1.2). A retroviral vector pMX1122*int*-1.*neo* (Section 3.2.2), carrying the mouse mammary oncogene *int*-1 in the *gag* position and *neo* in the *env* position, was introduced into the amphotropic packaging line PA12 (21) by CaPO$_4$ transfection and G418^R colonies were selected. Helper-free amphotropic virus from the pooled colonies was used to infect ψ2 cells, again with selection for G418^R. Individual infected ψ2 colonies were grown as separate lines, analysed by Southern blotting, and used as a source of helper-free virus for subsequent experiments (12). The four exons of the *int*-1 gene are indicated by boxes (with coding regions in black) and the *neo* gene is represented by a stippled box. The expected structures of the proviral DNAs integrated after transfection or infection are shown, the latter having lost the introns of *int*-1, together with the predicted sizes of the LTR-LTR *Xba*I (X) fragments. **B**. Southern blot analysis of proviral DNA in transfected and infected cells, showing loss of the introns of *int*-1 from the retroviral genome. Total cellular DNA was digested with *Xba*I, separated by agarose gel electrophoresis, transferred to nitrocellulose, and probed with ^{32}P-labelled *int*-1 cDNA. **Lanes 1** and **3**, DNA of untransfected PA12 and uninfected ψ2 cells, respectively, showing the endogenous genomic *int*-1 fragment; **lane 2**, DNA from pooled PA12 cells transfected with pMX1122*int*-1.*neo*; **lane 4**, DNA from a single colony of ψ2 cells infected with virus from the transfected PA12 cells. Arrows indicate the 6.3 kb and 4.7 kb proviral fragments corresponding to those diagrammed in panel A. [The 4.7 kb band in **lane 2** probably resulted from infection of the PA12 cells with virus that they themselves produced, as this line is only weakly resistant to superinfection (36).]

proviruses from infected cells by molecular cloning. This is particularly relevant to the use of retrovirus vectors for removal of introns, as cloning of the provirus after a round of infection may allow recovery of a cDNA copy of the inserted gene. Moreover, cloning of a provirus provides the best opportunity for rigorous examination or confirmation of the genetic structure of any retroviral construction after it has been through a cycle of viral replication. Such proviruses can be cloned by conventional methods involving construction of a genomic library and screening by hybridization, but this is particularly laborious since there is usually only one copy of the desired provirus per diploid genome.

Two simplified procedures have been described for the cloning of *neo*-containing proviruses from cellular DNA, both of which involve selection of the desired clones in *E. coli* by virtue of their resistance to kanamycin. The first is a modification of previous marker rescue techniques and involves cloning the provirus directly into a plasmid vector. The second method, which is much more efficient, requires the use of a special retrovirus 'shuttle' vector, as described in Section 3.2.4.

6.3.1 *Cloning the provirus directly into a plasmid vector*

This procedure is described here in outline only, but is applicable to all retroviral vectors carrying a *neo* gene. Genomic DNA is prepared from infected cells, digested with an enzyme such as *Xba*I which cuts only in the proviral LTRs, and then fractionated by preparative gel electrophoresis to obtain a sample enriched for the desired proviral DNA fragment. This sample is ligated to an *Xba*I-digested plasmid vector (or self-ligated if the provirus contains a pBR322 replication origin), and introduced into *E. coli* by transformation. The bacteria are then divided into aliquots, diluted 20-fold, and selected in broth containing kanamycin ($7.5-50$ µg/ml). Each aliquot that grows to saturation density should contain an independent clone of the *neo*-containing proviral DNA fragment. This cloning procedure requires competent bacteria with a transformation efficiency of at least 2×10^7 per µg, in sufficient quantities to generate 2×10^7 transformants, but the powerful kanamycin selection in liquid medium makes the recovery of the desired clones relatively easy. For details of the method see Brown *et al.* (12).

6.3.2 *The cos cell fusion method*

The so-called retroviral 'shuttle' vectors, of which the prototype is pZIP-Neo SV(X)1 (22), are designed specifically to facilitate the cloning of their proviral DNA. As described in Section 3.2.4, the usefulness of pZIP-Neo SV(X)1 as a shuttle vector results from a combination of three relevant components of its construction: an SV40 replication origin, a pBR322 replication origin, and a *neo* gene.

Cepko *et al.* (22) have described an efficient method of recovering plasmid clones of pZIP-Neo SV(X)1 proviruses from infected cells, which is generally applicable to other similar shuttle vectors. The infected cells are first fused with *cos* cells, a monkey cell line expressing SV40 T antigen. In the presence of T antigen, DNA replication is repeatedly triggered from the SV40 origin within the integrated provirus, and recombination leads to excision of numerous closed circular DNA molecules carrying proviral sequences. These circular plasmids are isolated in a Hirt supernatant, and are recovered by transforming competent *E. coli* with selection for kanamycin resistant clones. Details of this cloning procedure are given in *Table 6*.

Table 6. Cloning proviral DNA by *cos* cell fusion and marker rescue (22).

1.	Mix equal quantities of vector-containing cells and *cos* cells by splitting a confluent dish of each 1:2 into a fresh 10 cm dish.
2.	The following day heat some polyethylene glycol 1000 (Baker) until just molten and cool to 40°C. Dilute it 1:1 with serum-free medium and sterilize by filtration.
3.	Wash the cells three times with serum-free medium and drain thoroughly.
4.	Fuse cells by carefully pipetting 2 ml of the 50% PEG medium onto the dish and leave at room temperature for one minute. (The optimum time may vary for different batches of PEG, and too long may be fatal for the cells.)
5.	Gently, but quickly, wash the cells with 10 ml of serum-free medium. Repeat, and then wash twice with medium containing 10% fetal calf serum. Leave the cells in this medium.
6.	Incubate at 37°C for 1–3 days, changing the medium every day.
7.	Wash the cells twice in PBS. Prepare a Hirt supernatant by lysing the cells in 2 ml of 10 mM Tris-HCl pH 7.4, 10 mM EDTA, 2% SDS. Scrape into an Oak Ridge tube and add NaCl from a 5 M stock to give a final concentraton of 1.25 M.
8.	Incubate at 4°C for 6 h and then spin at 38 000 g for 45 min.
9.	Extract once with phenol/chloroform, once with chloroform as in *Table 4* step 4, but precipitate nucleic acids from the final aqueous phase with two volumes of isopropanol. Incubate at −20°C for at least 2 h and pellet the nucleic acids by centrifugation. Resuspend the pellet in TE[a]. Add sodium acetate to 0.3 M and precipitate again with two volumes of isopropanol, as before.
10.	Resuspend the pellet in 200 μl TE containing 100 mM NaCl. Add RNase A (boiled) to 1 μg/ml and incubate at 37°C for 30 min. Cool to room temperature.
11.	Now add spermine to a concentration of 5 mM and leave at room temperature for 10 min. Centrifuge for 10 min in a microcentrifuge and drain the pellet. Rinse gently but thoroughly in 0.5 ml of 75% ethanol, 0.3 M sodium acetate, 10 mM magnesium acetate. Centrifuge again for 10 min and drain the pellet.
12.	Resuspend the DNA in 50 μl TE containing 100 mM NaCl and transform *E. coli* HB101. Select the transformant with 50 μg/ml kanamycin sulphate.

[a]TE is 10 mM Tris-HCl pH 7.5, 1 mM EDTA.

A typical cloning efficiency from this method is around 10^3 kanamycin resistant bacterial colonies from 10^7 mammalian cells. Cepko *et al.* (22) found that the majority of the recovered clones had the expected structure (a proviral DNA circle with a single LTR), although 20% had suffered DNA rearrangements as a result of recombination.

7. POTENTIAL PROBLEMS

While the principles governing the use of retroviruses as vectors are founded on a vast knowledge of the biology of naturally occurring retroviruses, there are still substantial aspects of retrovirus replication and expression which are not understood. Moreover, in some cases the extent of these gaps in our understanding has been only too well revealed by the failure of certain retroviral vector constructs to behave as predicted. Some of the potential problems resulting from the inclusion of promoters, polyadenylation signals, or premature translational starts in the inserted sequences have already been alluded to in Section 3.2.2. and 3.4. Other, less predictable, problems that may be encountered with retroviral vectors will be discussed in this section. This is not meant

Table 7. Transfection and transduction efficiencies of retroviral vectors, showing inhibition of *neo* expression (see Sections 7.1 and 7.2).

Vector	$G418^R$ transfection efficiency[a] colonies per µg DNA	$G418^R$ transduction efficiency[b] c.f.u. per ml
pMX1122*neo*	1.3×10^3	2.5×10^5
pMX1122*myc.neo*	70	3.0×10^5

[a]Transfection efficiency was determined by transfection of NIH3T3 cells with selection for $G418^R$ and is expressed as the $G418^R$ colonies obtained per µg of input vector DNA.
[b]Transduction efficiency was determined in a parallel experiment in which NIH3T3 cells were co-transfected with vector DNA and a 2-fold excess of replication-competent helper (pZAP) DNA. The transducing virus produced by pools of these $G418^R$ transfected colonies was titred by infection of NIH3T3 cells and is expressed as the number of $G418^R$ colony forming units per ml of culture supernatant.

to discourage the reader, since successful examples of the use of retrovirus vectors are already widespread in the literature. The experimenter should be aware of the possible problems, however, and appreciate that a particular vector may behave quite differently when different sequences are inserted.

7.1 Inadequate dual expression

A problem sometimes encountered with double gene vectors is failure to transmit and express both of the markers simultaneously. This seems particularly common with splicing vectors (Section 3.2.2), which depend on a viral RNA splicing efficiency of close to 50% for good expression of both inserted genes. Unfortunately, the rules that govern splicing of retroviral RNA are poorly understood. We and others have observed that sequences installed in the upstream cloning site may affect formation of the subgenomic RNA from which the downstream gene is expressed (20,25). This was seen, for example, in experiments using the vector pMX1122*neo* (*Figure 3c*) with the proto-oncogene c-*myc* inserted in the '*gag*' position. When expression of c-*myc* from this construct was selected (by its ability to co-operate with EJ-*ras* in co-transfection of primary fibroblasts), transformed cells were produced which expressed *myc* protein but contained no detectable sub-genomic *neo* RNA (M.Scott and H.Varmus, unpublished). Moreover, when pMX1122*myc.neo* DNA was transfected into NIH3T3 cells, expression of the downstream *neo* gene was severely inhibited. This was evident from the very low efficiency of transfection to $G418^R$ compared to that obtained with the parental pMX1122*neo* vector (*Table 7*), and inefficient formation of subgenomic *neo* RNA was again observed (M.Scott and H.Varmus, unpublished). Similarly, insertion of c-*myc* upstream of v-*ras* in pMX1122 inhibited splicing of the viral RNA. In contrast, when the oncogene *int*-1 was inserted in the *gag* site of pMX1122*neo*, efficient expression of sub-genomic *neo* RNA was observed (12), indicating that the inhibition of viral RNA splicing can be caused by some inserts but not others.

Double gene vectors with internal promoters do not require the use of viral splice sites, but they too may sometimes give problems of inadequate dual expression. Apart from occasional explanations based on the inability of the LTR or internal promoter to function efficiently in the particular cell type infected, the expression of either marker may be affected by an inhibitory effect exerted between the two promoters. Emerman and Temin (23), working with an avian internal promoter vector, found that selection for expression of the 5' gene caused epigenetic suppression of the 3' promoter, and vice-versa. While this effect depends on the particular combination of promoters used and appears to be more severe in avian vectors, it can also apply to MLV-based vectors to some extent (24).

7.2 **Genetic instability**

Of major concern with all retroviral vectors is their genetic instability. This can be manifested in the form of gross deletions, which can be revealed by Southern blotting, or as point mutations which are harder to detect and thus more insidious. There is apparently no proof-reading activity associated with the RNA polymerase and reverse transcriptase reactions which replicate the viral genome, and the spontaneous mutation rate in retroviruses is unusually high (14,20). It has been estimated that the mutation frequency in retrovirus vectors can be as high as 0.5% per cycle of replication (20).

One potential cause of deletions in retroviral genomes is aberrant splicing of the viral RNA. Although in MLV-based vectors the packaging signal lies downstream of the viral splice donor site so that molecules undergoing splicing from this site will not be packaged, cryptic splice sites within the insert RNA may potentially cause problems. Deletions and rearrangements might also occur as a result of recombination with endogenous murine retroviral sequences, recombination during transfection, or errors in reverse transcription and integration (14). Moreover, deletions may sometimes be inadvertently selected when expression of a particular marker gene is demanded. An example of this was seen in the experiment described in *Table 7*, involving the double gene 'splicing' vector pMX1122*myc.neo*, in which the presence of c-*myc* sequences inhibited splicing of the viral RNA (see Section 7.1). Despite the low efficiency of transfection to G418 resistance by pMX1122*myc.neo*, high titre stocks of *neo* transducing virus could be obtained from transfected colonies (*Table 7*). However, subsequent analysis indicated that these viruses had suffered deletion of c-*myc* (M.Scott and H.Varmus, unpublished). Thus selection for efficient expression of the *neo* gene resulted in loss of the c-*myc* sequences responsible for inhibiting production of sub-genomic *neo* mRNA. A high frequency of deletions that gave improved expression of a selected marker has also been described for an internal promoter vector, but so far only in avian cells (41).

8. ACKNOWLEDGEMENTS

We wish to thank many of our colleagues for helpful advice and discussions, and in particular Harold Varmus, in whose laboratory most of our own experiments with retroviral vectors have been performed. We are also grateful to Connie Cepko for the provirus cloning protocol, and to P.Kirschmeier and B.Weinstein for allowing us to describe the pMV7 vector. A.M.C.B. is a Special Fellow of the Leukemia Society of America.

9. REFERENCES

1. Brightman,B.K., Pattengale,P.K. and Fan,H. (1986) *J. Virol.*, **60**, 68.
2. Williams,D.A., Lemischka,I.R., Nathan,D.G. and Mulligan,R.C. (1984) *Nature*, **310**, 476.
3. Anderson,W.F. (1984) *Science*, **226**, 401.

4. Jahner,D., Haase,K., Mulligan,R.C. and Jaenisch,R. (1985) *Proc. Natl. Acad. Sci. USA*, **82**, 6927.
5. Robertson,E., Bradley,A., Kuehn,M. and Evans,M. (1986) *Nature*, **323**, 445.
6. Dick,J.E., Magli,M.C., Huszar,D., Phillips,R.A. and Bernstein,A. (1985) *Cell*, **42**, 71.
7. Price,J., Turner,D. and Cepko,C. (1987) *Proc. Natl. Acad. Sci. USA*, **84**, 156.
8. Soriano,P. and Jaenisch,R. (1986) *Cell*, **46**, 19.
9. Weis,J.H., Nelson,D.L., Przyborski,M.J., Chaplin,D.D., Mulligan,R.C., Housman,D.E. and Seidman,J.G. (1984) *Proc. Natl. Acad. Sci. USA*, **81**, 4879.
10. King,W., Patel,M.D., Lobel,L.I., Goff,S.P. and Nguyen-Huu,M.C. (1985) *Science*, **228**, 554.
11. Shimotohno,K. and Temin,H. (1982) *Nature*, **299**, 265.
12. Brown,A.M.C., Wildin,R.S., Prendergast,T.J. and Varmus,H.E. (1986) *Cell*, **46**, 1001.
13. Varmus,H.E. (1982) *Science*, **216**, 812.
14. Coffin,J. (1984) In *RNA Tumor Viruses*. Weiss,R., Teich,N., Varmus,H. and Coffin,J. (eds), Cold Spring Harbor Laboratory, Cold Spring Harbor, New York, Vol.2, p.36.
15. Weiss,R. (1982) In *RNA Tumor Viruses*. Weiss,R., Teich,N., Varmus,H. and Coffin,J. (eds), Cold Spring Harbor Laboratory, Cold Spring Harbor, New York, Vol.1, p. 209.
16. Bishop,J.M. and Varmus,H.E. (1982) In *RNA Tumor Viruses*. Weiss,R., Teich,N., Varmus,H. and Coffin,J. (eds), Cold Spring Harbor Laboratory, Cold Spring Harbor, New York, Vol.1, p. 999.
17. Mann,R., Mulligan,R.C. and Baltimore,D. (1983) *Cell*, **33**, 153.
18. Kriegler,M., Perez,C.F., Hardy,C. and Botchan,M. (1984) *Cell*, **38**, 483.
19. Sorge,J., Wright,D., Erdman,V.D. and Cutting,A.E. (1984) *Mol. Cell. Biol.*, **4**, 1730.
20. Dougherty,J.P. and Temin,H.M. (1986) *Mol. Cell. Biol.*, **7**, 4387.
21. Miller,A.D., Law,M.F. and Verma,I.M. (1985) *Mol. Cell. Biol.*, **5**, 431.
22. Cepko,C.L., Roberts,B.E. and Mulligan,R.C. (1984) *Cell*, **37**, 1053.
23. Emerman,M. and Temin,H.M. (1984a) *Cell*, **39**, 459.
24. Emerman,M. and Temin,H.M. (1986) *Nucleic Acids Res.*, **14**, 9381.
25. Gilboa,E., Eglitis,M.A., Kantoff,P.W. and Anderson,W.F. (1986) *Biotechniques*, **4**, 504.
26. Kirschmeier,P.T., Housey,G.M., Johnson,M.D., Perkins,A.S. and Weinstein,I.B., submitted for publication.
27. Dickson,C., Eisenman,R. and Fan,H. (1984) In *RNA Tumor Viruses*. Weiss,R., Teich,N., Varmus,H. and Coffin,J. (eds), Cold Spring Harbor Laboratory, Cold Spring Harbor, New York, Vol. 2, p. 135.
28. Berger,S.A. and Bernstein,A. (1985) *Mol. Cell. Biol.*, **5**, 305.
29. Yu,S.F., von Ruden,T., Kantoff,P.W., Garber,C., Sieberg,M., Ruther,U., Anderson,W.F., Wagner,E. and Gilboa,E. (1986) *Proc. Natl. Acad. Sci. USA*, **83**, 2566.
30. Reik,W., Weiber,H. and Jaenisch,R. (1985) *Proc. Natl. Acad. Sci. USA*, **82**, 1141.
31. Hughes,S. and Kosik,E. (1984) *Virology*, **136**, 89.
32. Miller,A.D. and Buttimore,C. (1986) *Mol. Cell. Biol.*, **6**, 2895.
33. Watanabe,S. and Temin,H.M. (1983) *Mol. Cell. Biol.*, **3**, 2241.
34. Gorman,C. (1985) In *DNA Cloning − A Practical Approach*. Glover,D.M. (ed.), IRL Press, Oxford, Vol. II, p. 143.
35. Korman,A.J., Frantz,J.D., Strominger,J.L. and Mulligan,R.C. (1987) *Proc. Natl. Acad. Sci. USA*, in press.
36. Miller,A.D., Trauber,D.R. and Buttimore,C. (1986) *Somatic Cell Mol. Genet.*, **12**, 175.
37. Hwang,L.S. and Gilboa,E. (1984) *J. Virol.*, **50**, 417.
38. Hoffmann,J.W., Steffen,D., Gusella,J., Tabin,C., Bird,S., Lowing,D. and Weinberg,R.A. (1982) *J. Virol.*, **44**, 144.
39. Maniatis,T., Fritsch,E.F. and Sambrook,J. (1982) *Molecular Cloning*, Cold Spring Harbor Laboratory, Cold Spring Harbor, New York.
40. Goff,S., Traktman,P. and Baltimore,D. (1981) *J. Virol.*, **38**, 239.
41. Emerman,M. and Temin,H.M. (1984b) *J. Virol.*, **50**, 42.
42. Appendix B in *RNA Tumor Viruses* (1985) Weiss,R., Teich,N., Varmus,H. and Coffin,J. (eds), Cold Spring Harbor Laboratory, Cold Spring Harbor, New York, Vol. 2, p. 766.

CHAPTER 10

The production of transgenic mice by the microinjection of cloned DNA into fertilized one-cell eggs

DAVID MURPHY and JENNIFER HANSON

1. INTRODUCTION

1.1 Transgenic animals

The past decade has seen the molecular cloning and structural characterization of a large number of mammalian genes. The function and regulation of these genes is now being studied in gene transfer experiments. Wild-type constructs and mutated derivatives can be transfected into tissue culture cells (1) in order to identify *cis* acting regulatory elements and to investigate the physiological consequences of the expression of gene products. However, even if appropriate tissue culture systems exist for the gene of interest, only limited perspectives on gene expression can be derived from such *in vitro* experiments. Ultimately, gene function and expression must be studied from within the complexities of the whole organism. A number of techniques have been developed that allow the introduction of defined DNA sequences into the germline of mice and other mammals. Once inserted, these sequences − termed transgenes − are stably transmitted from generation to generation. Of fundamental importance is the observation that transgenes are often expressed, and subject to correct developmental, tissue specific and physiological regulation. It is therefore now possible to analyse the role and regulation of specific cloned genes within the whole organism − the transgenic organism.

1.2 Routes to the germline

There are three basic methodologies available for making transgenic mice, all of which involve intervention at the pre-implantation stages of development (*Figure 1*). These techniques are:

(i)   The infection of pre-implantation embryos with recombinant retroviruses.
(ii)   The manipulation of embryonal stem cells (ES or EK cells).
(iii) The microinjection of fertilized one-cell eggs with DNA.

1.2.1 Retroviruses

The infection of pre-implantation embryos with recombinant retroviruses is an easy technique that does not require any expensive equipment. However, each gene of interest must first be recloned into a viral vector which is then transfected into a cell line that

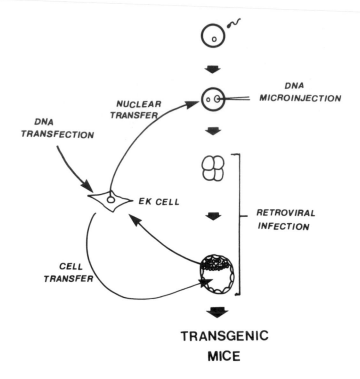

Figure 1. Routes into the germ line. Intervention at various stages from fertilization to implantation can result in the acquisition of novel gene sequences by mammalian organisms. See Section 1.2.

produces specific infectious recombinant virus particles. However, there is a limit to the size of insert that a recombinant virus can accommodate (∼10 kb) and the DNA of interest may contain splicing or termination signals that could interfere with viral function and viability. To infect embryos, eight-cell stage morulae are stripped of their zonae pellucida and placed in tissue culture dishes containing fibroblasts that are producing the recombinant virus. Following infection, the embryos, which have developed as far as the blastocyst stage, are returned to the uterus of a pseudopregnant foster mother. A proportion of the embryos will continue normal development and give rise to transgenic pups. Retroviral integration occurs via a precise mechanism that results in the insertion of a single, intact copy of the provirus containing the gene of interest, flanked by retroviral long terminal repeats (LTRs). This precision, resulting in single copy inserts, is the distinct advantage of the method over its rivals. However, whilst each integration event is single copy, multiple events can occur in a single cell and multiple insertions can be found in each cell of the embryo. This results in a founder animal which is mosaic for a large number of insertions. Extensive outbreeding is required in order to establish pure lines suitable for the study of gene expression. Some transgenes have been expressed in mice containing recombinant retroviruses (2,3). However, the effect of the strong viral regulatory elements contained within the flanking LTRs upon the specificity of the expression of the transgene remains to be fully determined.

1.2.2 *Embryonal stem cells*

ES or EK cells are pluripotent embryonic stem cells derived from the blastocyst (4,5). ES cells can be cultured and manipulated *in vitro* then returned to the living organism by injection into the blastocyst. The ES cells will colonize the embryo and participate in normal development, contributing to all somatic tissues and sometimes to the germ line (6). ES cells can be transfected with cloned genes (7) or infected with recombinant retroviruses (8) prior to being injected into the blastocyst. The practical advantage of this technique is that it may be possible to select or screen transformed ES cells for some desirable property, for example transgene copy number, chromosomal location or expression. All founder animals are mosaics of transgene positive and transgene negative cells and consequently must be bred in order to produce pure transgenic lines. However, ES cells often fail to colonize the germline presumably because of the accumulation of chromosomal abnormalities during *in vitro* cultivation and selection.

The problem of mosaicism in founder animals could be overcome by using transformed and selected ES cells as donors of nuclei. The pronuclei of one-cell fertilized eggs can be removed and replaced in transplantation experiments by donor nuclei, usually derived from other eggs (9). ES cell nuclei carrying a transgene may be able to colonize an enucleated egg, which may then proceed with normal development. The resulting founder animal would carry the transgene in all its cells.

In the future it may be possible to direct mutations to specific genes in the mouse by targeting *in vitro* mutagenized constructs into ES cells using homologous recombination (10,11).

1.2.3 *Microinjection*

This remains the most popular and successful method for the production of transgenic mice, despite the fact that it demands precise technical skill and expensive equipment. The advantages of speed and reliability of the technique far outweigh any of its disadvantages.

(i) *Summary of the microinjection method.* The process of making transgenic mice by microinjection is summarized in flow diagram form in *Figure 2*. The method is outlined below, with reference to the appropriate sections of the rest of this chapter.

(1)   Donor female mice are superovulated (Section 2.3.4) and mated with stud male mice.

(2)   About 12 h p.c. (post coitum) the oviducts of the donor females are removed and the fertilized one-cell eggs are harvested (Section 2.3.6) and placed into culture (Section 2.3.5).

(3)   The eggs are then microinjected (Section 3) with purified cloned DNA fragments (Section 4.1).

(4)   Eggs that survive injection are returned by oviduct transfer (Section 2.3.7) to the natural environment provided by a 0.5 day p.c. pseudopregnant recipient surrogate mother. Pseudopregnant recipients are produced by mating sexually mature females with vasectomized males (Section 2.3.3).

(5)   A proportion of the transplanted eggs will survive to term and will either be

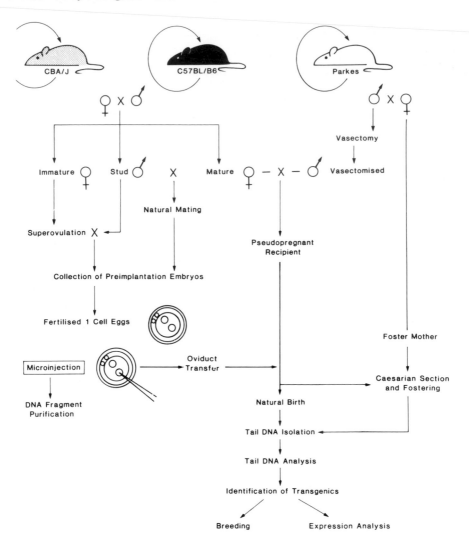

Figure 2. Flow diagram of the process of making transgenic mice by the microinjection of fertilized one-cell eggs with cloned DNA.

delivered naturally, or by caesarian section (Section 2.3.8).

(6) Transgenic animals in a litter are identified by hybridization analysis of high molecular weight genomic DNA isolated from tail tissue (Section 4.2).

(7) Transgenic animals are then bred to produce a line, and are analysed for trans-gene expression (Section 5).

(ii) *The state and organization of the exogenous DNA incorporated into the genome following microinjection.* The mechanism by which injected DNA integrates into host chromosomes is unknown, but some ideas about the nature of the process have been inferred from a study of the state and organization of the inserts found in transgenic mice (12). About 70% of transgenic mice carry exogenous DNA in all of their somatic and germ cells, indicating that integration usually occurs prior to the first round of DNA replication. The remaining 30% of transgenic mice show some degree of mosaicism and in these animals integration must have occurred at some stage after the first round of DNA replication. The copy number of the transgene can vary considerably − from one to several thousand. However, within a particular founder animal there is usually only one insert site. Multiple copies of a transgene are usually arranged in a head to tail tandem array within a single locus. The insert site within the host genome is probably determined randomly. Integration events have been observed on many different autosomes (13), on the X chromosome (14) and on the Y chromosome (D.M., J.H. and Brigid Hogan, unpublished observations).

(iii) *The efficiency of the microinjection method.* The efficiency of producing trans-genic mice by microinjection varies considerably between experiments. However, under optimum conditions, 60−80% of eggs survive injection. Of these, 10−30% implant in the pseudopregnant recipient, proceed through normal development and are born. 10−30% of pups born are transgenic. Some of the variables governing the efficiency are somewhat intangible, for example, experimental dexterity. However, both the condition of the DNA used to inject the eggs (Section 4.1) and the choice of mouse strain (Section 2.2.1) can have a profound effect on the overall efficiency of the technique, and both can be carefully controlled.

The rest of this chapter describes detailed protocols for the production, maintenance and analysis of transgenic mice. This will include animal husbandry and manipulation; microinjection; DNA manipulations; and the analysis of gene expression in transgenic mice.

2. ANIMAL HUSBANDRY AND MANIPULATION

This section describes techniques directly involving live animals and should only be referred to as a guide to learning by the novice. All manipulations involving animals should be taught directly to the novice by a skilled and experienced operative. Two of the methods described below, vasectomy and oviduct transfer, are surgical procedures carried out on live mice and it is imperative that the novice learns these techniques under careful direction. It is recommended that the novice gains skill and confidence on cadavers before moving on to live, anaesthetized subjects. If a live mouse being operated on appears to be in any distress or discomfort then the operator, novice or skilled, should immediately kill the animal by cervical dislocation (see Section 2.3.1).

2.1 Animal welfare and legal requirements

The production and maintenance of transgenic mice necessitates that the investigator is responsible for the care of hundreds, and maybe thousands, of animals. As such, only scientists working in institutions with the necessary facilities and experience can carry out transgenic experiments. A suitable animal facility must be able to provide:

(i)   spacious caging;
(ii)   cage washing (and preferably, cage sterilization);

(iii)   a regular change of clean, comfortable bedding;
(iv)   ventilation;
(v)   a food and water supply;
(vi)   environmental control (i.e. temperature, light and humidity);
(vii)   access to veterinary care.

In Britain, the conditions under which laboratory animals are maintained are strictly defined under the Animals (Scientific Procedures) Act 1986. Institutions at which procedures involving animals can be carried out are termed 'designated' establishments, having received a 'designation' certificate under the Act. The conduct of scientific procedures involving animals is also strictly regulated by governments and institutions. The 1986 Act requires investigators to obtain a Personal Licence permitting them to work with animals. Personal Licence holders must then work within the limits of a specific Project Licence. Full details of the legal framework regulating laboratory animal welfare in Britain can be obtained from The Home Office, Queen Anne's Gate, London SW1H 9AT. Investigators in other countries should consult with the relevant governmental or institutional authorities before embarking upon studies using transgenic animals. Legal requirements aside, it should be the general rule of scientists that the welfare of the animals in their charge should override all other considerations.

2.2 Animal and equipment requirements

2.2.1 *Animal requirements*

An extensive animal colony is required if transgenic mice are to be produced and maintained successfully. As can be seen from *Figure 2*, a number of different types of animal are required for different purposes. These different requirements are dealt with separately.

(i) *Mice needed to produce fertilized one-cell eggs.* Fertilized one-cell eggs for micro-injection are produced as a consequence of a mating between a donor female and a stud male. The choice of the strain of the mice used is very important. Brinster *et al.* (15) compared the efficiency of transgenic mouse production following manipulation of C57Bl/6 inbred mouse eggs and C57Bl/6 × CBA/J hybrid eggs. A number of parameters were shown to be strain dependent, including yield of eggs from the donor female and the survival of eggs following injection. Overall, the experiments on the hybrid eggs were 8-fold more efficient than those on the inbred eggs. Inbred zygotes should only be used when the genetic background of the host animal needs to be carefully controlled.

The microinjection of F2 zygotes resulting from matings between CBA/J × C57Bl/6 or 10 F1 hybrid males and superovulated females results in excellent efficiencies. Such a protocol demands the maintenance of the following animals.

(1)   At least 20 F1 hybrid stud males caged individually. Sexually mature males will act as good studs for between eight months and a year. An individual male should only be presented with a female on every alternate day. A record of the individual animal's plugging record (see Section 2.3.4) should be kept, and the male should be replaced if it suffers from repeated poor performance.

Table 1. Surgical[a] and dissection requirements.

1.	37°C tissue culture incubator gassed with 5% CO_2
2.	Animal balance
3.	70% ethanol in a squeeze bottle
4.	Paper tissues
5.	Dissection scissors (large and small)
6.	Two pairs of sharpened 5 watchmaker's forceps
7.	Surgical silk suture (size 5.0)
8.	Curved surgical needles (size 10, triangular, pointed)
9.	Alcohol burner
10.	Fibre optic illumination (e.g. Schott KL 1500)
11.	Stereo dissecting microscope (e.g. Nikon SMZ-10TD)
12.	9 mm autoclips and applicator (Clay Adams[b])
13.	1 pair of fine blunt forceps
14.	Artery clip (1 1/2″)
15.	Sterile disposable 1 ml syringes
16.	Sterile disposable 0.1 × 16 mm needles
17.	9 cm Petri dish lid
18.	35 mm sterile tissue culture dishes
19.	Hard glass capillaries 1.5 mm o.d. (BDH, catalogue number 32124)

[a]Surgical and dissecting instruments are available from Holborn Surgical and Veterinary Instruments Ltd., Dolphin Works, Margate Road, Broadstairs, Kent, UK.
[b]Available from Arnold R.Horwell Ltd., 73 Maygrove Road, West Hampstead, London NW6 2BP, UK.

Table 2. Identification of ovulating female mice.

Stage of oestrous cycle	Vaginal characteristics
A. Dioestrous	Opening small Tissues blue and moist
B. Prooestrous	Opening gaping Tissues red-pink and moist Dorsal and ventral surface folds
C. Oestrous (Ovulating)	Opening gaping Tissues pink and moist Pronounced folds
D. Metoestrous	Tissues pale and dry White cell debris

(2)   A supply of immature (12 – 14 g) F1 hybrid females. These are superovulated, mated with the F1 hybrid males and sacrificed to supply the fertilized one-cell eggs. The number of females required will depend upon the number of micro-injection experiments that are carried out. Ten immature females will supply at least 250 injectable eggs.

(3)   Large colonies of CBA/J mice and C57/B16 or 10 mice need to be maintained in order to supply the F1 hybrid donor females by inter-strain crosses. Alternatively, it is often easier and cheaper to purchase immature F1 hybrid females from a reputable commercial or institutional supplier.

(ii) *Mice needed to act as recipients for microinjected eggs.* Pseudopregnant recipient females (0.5 day p.c.) are used as surrogate mothers to nurture surviving microinjected eggs to birth. Oestrous females are made pseudopregnant by mating them with vasectomized males (see Section 2.3.3 for details of the vasectomy operation). The vasectomized male can be of any strain, but Parkes males are particularly suitable because of their good performance. Vasectomized males are caged individually. 20−30 vasectomized males, mated on alternate days with females analysed for their stage in the oestrous cycle (see Section 2.3.4 and *Table 2*), should be able to supply at least five pseudopregnant recipients per day. Females can be of any strain with good maternal characteristics, but need to be sexually mature and greater than 19 g in weight.

(iii) *Mice needed to act as foster mothers.* A larger animal unit may be able to supply suitable foster mothers, when needed, to receive pups delivered by caesarian section (see Section 2.3.8). Whilst such a facility is desirable, it is not an absolute requirement.

2.2.2 *Equipment requirements*

Table 1 lists the general equipment needed to undertake the surgical and dissection procedures described in this chapter. Specific chemicals and reagents are described in the appropriate section.

2.2.3 *Egg transfer pipettes*

Two types of egg transfer pipettes need to be prepared in advance; general transfer pipettes and oviduct transfer pipettes (*Figure 3B*). Both are made from BDH hard glass capillaries and are assembled into a mouth operated system made up of a mouthpiece, a rubber tube and a pipette holder. Methods for preparing the pipettes are detailed in *Table 3*.

2.3 **Animal manipulations**

2.3.1 *Killing a mouse*

The recommended method for killing mice is to break the neck. Dislocating the neck is quick and causes the animal the minimum of distress. Pick the animal up by the tail then place it on top of a cage. Still holding it by the tail, allow the mouse to run away such that it is stretched out with its hind legs almost in the air and its fore limbs gripping the cage bars firmly. Apply firm pressure at the base of the skull either with a spatula blade or by pinching with thumb and forefinger. At the same time pull on the tail. It is this stretching action that breaks the neck, the pressure at the base of the spine defining the point of dislocation.

2.3.2 *Anaesthetizing a mouse*

(i)   Make a 100% Avertin stock by mixing 10 g of tribromoethyl alcohol (Fluka, catalogue number 90710) with 10 ml of tertiary amyl alcohol (BDH, catalogue number 27214). Store at 4°C, protected from light.

(ii)   To make the working solution, dilute to 2.5% in sterile water. Store at 4°C, protected from light.

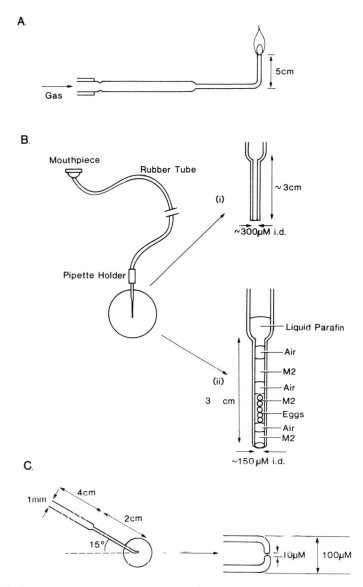

Figure 3. A. Structure of a gas microflame constructed out of a Pasteur pipette. **B.** Design and assembly of a mouth operated pipette holder containing (i) a general egg transfer pipette and (ii) an oviduct transfer pipette. **C.** Design of an egg holding pipette.

(iii)   Use between 15 μl and 17 μl per gram of body weight. The exact dose required varies between batches and should be redetermined everytime a 100% stock is made.

(iv)   The anaesthetic is introduced intraperitoneally. First weigh the animal and determine the dose required. Load the 2.5% avertin into a sterile 1 ml disposable syringe fitted with a 0.5 × 16 mm needle. Exclude any air bubbles. Restrain

Table 3. Preparation of transfer pipettes.

A. *Preparation of general transfer pipettes (Figure 3Bi)*

1. Set up a glass microflame burner made from a Pasteur pipette as shown in *Figure 3A*. The flame should be 1 cm high.

2. Soften the middle of a BDH hard glass capillary in the microflame. Withdraw from the heat and pull sharply on the ends. Pull until the two halves snap apart. If the pipettes are too long (>5 cm) or too narrow (<200 μM), score with a diamond pencil and gently snap off the excess glass.

3. The internal diameter of the pipette should be around 300 μM and the end should be flush with no jagged edges.

B. *Oviduct transfer pipettes (Figure 3Bii)*

1. Follow the procedure for making general transfer pipettes described above, except aim to make pipettes with internal diameters of around 150 μM.

2. Flame polish the end by gently touching the end of the pipette into the edge of a microflame. As soon as a yellow sodium flame is observed, withdraw the pipette. Ensure that the opening of the pipette is large enough to accommodate a mouse egg (>120 μM).

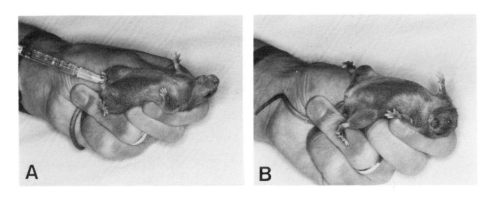

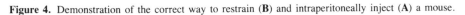

Figure 4. Demonstration of the correct way to restrain (**B**) and intraperitoneally inject (**A**) a mouse.

the animal with one hand as shown in *Figure 4B*. With the other hand, introduce the needle into the abdomen of the mouse, as shown in *Figure 4A*. Avoid the bladder and the diaphragm. Inject the anaesthetic, then wait momentarily before withdrawing the needle. Accidental subcutaneous injection is revealed by leakage of blebs of avertin through the skin.

(v) The animal will remain fully anaesthetized for 30−60 min − sufficient time to perform the surgical task. Following the operation the animal should be left undisturbed to recover in a quiet, warm place.

2.3.3 *Vasectomizing a male mouse*

Sexually mature mice are sterilized by vasectomy, and used to engender pseudo-pregnancy in sexually mature females. Any strain of mouse with a good sexual performance can be used (for example, Parkes).

(i) The vasectomy operation should be performed on young, healthy, sexually mature (around 2 months of age) male.

(ii) Anaesthetize the subject as described in Section 2.3.2. Place the animal abdomen side up on the lid of a 9 cm glass or plastic Petri dish.

(iii) Spray the lower abdomen with 70% ethanol. Comb the hair away from the incision site with a pair of fine forceps. The 1.5 cm transverse incision will be made at a point level with the top of the hind limbs (see *Figures 5A* and *B*).

(iv) Lift the skin away from the body wall at the incision point with a pair of forceps. Cut the skin with a large pair of dissecting scissors (*Figure 5A*). Stretch the incision with the outer edges of a pair of scissors to prevent bleeding.

(v) Cut the body wall (*Figure 5B*). Stretch the incision to prevent bleeding.

(vi) Introduce a single stitch through the body wall to one side of the incision and leave the silk suture in place (*Figure 5C*).

(vii) Pull out the fat pad on one side of the animal and with it the testis, epididymis and vas deferens (*Figure 5D*).

(viii) Identify the vas deferens located underneath the testis and free it of the membranes holding it (*Figure 5E*).

(ix) Hold the vas deferens in a loop with one pair of forceps. Heat a large pair of blunt forceps until glowing red. Grip the vas deferens loop with the red hot forceps tips. This will burn away the vas deferens and cauterize the ends (*Figure 5F*).

(x) Separate the cauterized ends (*Figure 5G*).

(xi) Return the organs to the inside of the body wall using a blunt pair of forceps (*Figure 5H*).

(xii) Repeat on the other side of the animal.

(xiii) Sew up the body wall with at least two stitches (*Figure 5I*).

(xiv) Clip the skin together with Autoclips (*Figure 5J*).

(xv) Cage the vasectomized males individually. Wait for a few weeks after the operation before using the animal to produce pseudopregnant surrogate mothers.

2.3.4 *Mating mice*

For most purposes, for example maintaining stocks of normal or transgenic strains, mice can be allowed to mate and breed with the minimum of intervention. Breeding is controlled by the careful regulation of the transfer of males and females between cages. However, 'timed matings', where the timing of ovulation, copulation and fertilization are controlled, are required for two purposes:

(i) to provide a supply of fertilized F2 hybrid one-cell eggs for microinjection;

(ii) to prepare pseudopregnant F1 hybrid females to act as surrogate mothers for the microinjected eggs.

Matings can be timed either by environmental conditions (natural matings) or by superovulating the female mouse by the administration of gonadotrophins. Natural matings between sexually mature but young (6 weeks to 4 months old) F1 hybrid females and stud F1 hybrid males can be used to provide a supply of fertilized eggs for microinjection. However, it is better to use matings between F1 stud males and superovulated immature females. Superovulation results in a much greater yield of eggs per female than natural matings (around 30 per mouse, compared to around 10) and consequently the number of animals required to supply the necessary number of eggs

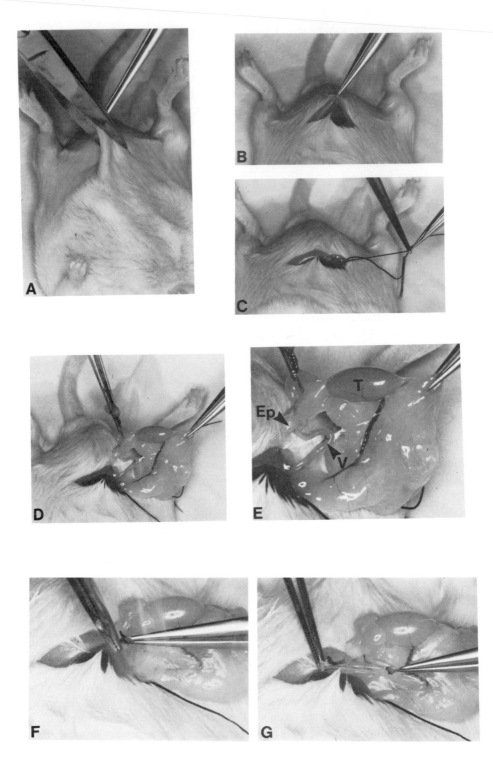

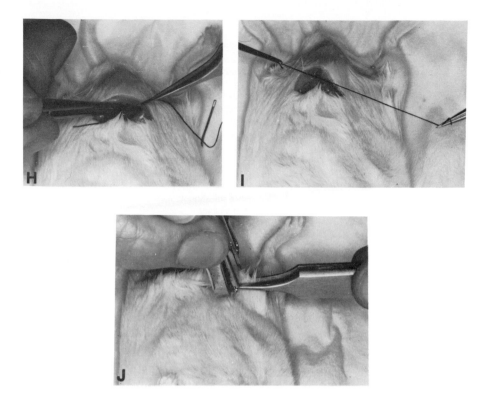

Figure 5. Vasectomizing a male mouse. Refer to Section 2.3.3 for details. Key: T, testis; Ep, epididymis; V, vas deferens.

is greatly reduced. Natural matings between mature F1 hybrid females and vasectomized or otherwise sterile males are required to provide 0.5 day p.c. pseudopregnant recipient female mice.

The regime for natural matings is as follows:

(i)   Maintain stud male, vasectomized male and sexually mature female mice on constant light – dark cycle. The mice are in the dark between the hours of 17.00 and 06.00 and in the light between 06.00 and 17.00 Females maintained on such a cycle will ovulate every 4 days, 5 h after the onset of darkness, at around midnight. Males will copulate with ovulating females in the middle of the dark period (around 00.30) and fertilization will take place between 30 min and 2 h later. Such a programme will give fertilized eggs that can be harvested at around 12.00 of the day following copulation and that are suitable for microinjection until around midnight. Pseudopregnant recipient mice can be implanted with fertile microinjected eggs anytime on the day following an infertile mating.

(ii)   Between the hours of 16.00 and 18.00 of the day before the female mice are required, place one female in the cage of a stud or vasectomized male. If sufficient female stocks are available, it is possible to randomly pair the females in the knowledge that, on average, one in four will be in oestrous and will consequently

Table 4. Superovulated females for mating.

---

1. Prepare stocks of the gonadotrophin follicle stimulating hormone (FSH) and human chorionic gonadotrophin (hCG)[a].

2. At around 12.00 hours inject each of 5 − 10 sexually immature F1 hybrid females (12.5 − 14 g; 4 − 5 weeks old) with 5 IU of FSH (i.e. 100 μl of the 50 IU/ml stock). Restrain the animal with one hand (*Figure 4B*) and inject the hormone intraperitoneally (*Figure 4A*). Avoid the diaphragm and the bladder.

3. 46 − 48 h later, inject each of the females intraperitoneally with 5 IU of hCG (i.e. 100 μl of the 50 IU/ml stock). Immediately place each of the females with a stud male.

4. The following morning, check for successful mating by identifying the copulatory plug [see Section 2.3.4(i)]. 80 − 100% of superovulated females should be impregnated.

---

[a]FSH (trade name Folligon) and hCG (trade name Chorulon) are supplied by Intervet Laboratories Ltd., Science Park, Milton Road, Cambridge CB4 4BH, UK. Both hormones are made up to a concentration of 50 IU/ml in sterile water or 0.9% NaCl, divided into 1 ml aliquots and stored at −70°C.

mate. However, it is preferable to pre-select the females on the basis of their stage in the oestrous cycle, which is gauged by the state of the vagina (*Table 2*). Between 50% and 80% of females that are visually determined to be in oestrous will be impregnated.

(iii)   In the morning, examine the females for a copulatory plug. This is evidence that a successful mating has occurred and consists of a white mass of coagulated protein blocking the vagina. In most instances, the plug is easily seen, but it sometimes lies deep in the vagina, and the mice should be examined carefully with the aid of a smooth, blunt probe. The plug will have dissolved away by the afternoon.

The procedure for mating superovulated females is given in *Table 4*.

2.3.5 *Culture of fertilized one-cell mouse eggs*

For the purpose of making transgenic mice, fertilized one-cell eggs need to be maintained outside of their natural environment for between 3 and 36 h. Fertilized eggs are collected at approximately 12 h p.c. and are injected at some point during the following 12 h. The eggs must then be returned to the natural environment of a pseudopregnant surrogate mother by oviduct transfer (Section 2.3.7). This can either be done soon after injection, whilst the eggs are still at the one-cell stage, or the eggs can be cultured overnight and transferred at the two-cell stage (*Figure 10C*). In either case the eggs are introduced into 0.5 day p.c. pseudopregnant females.

Eggs at the one- and two-cell stages are maintained in M16 microdrop cultures in a 37°C tissue culture incubator gassed with 5% CO_2. Microdrops are made up of small drops of M16 medium (20 − 40 μl) arranged in an array in a 35 mm tissue culture dish and covered with liquid paraffin to prevent evaporation. When eggs are being handled outside the incubator, for example when they are being collected or microinjected, they are maintained in M2 medium. The pH of M2 medium is maintained by the addition of Hepes buffer. Detailed methods for the preparation of M2 and M16 media are presented in *Table 5*.

Both M2 and M16 media contain bovine serum albumin (BSA). BSA reduces the stickiness of the eggs, provides trace requirements and mops up low level poisons.

Table 5. Preparation of M2 and M16 culture media.

All stocks should be made up using sterile disposable plastic containers and pipettes. Washed glass items can be contaminated with detergents that are toxic to eggs.

A.   *Concentrated component stocks*

1.   10 × A.   For 100 ml.   5.534 g NaCl
                                                                    0.356 g KCl
                                                                    0.162 g KH$_2$PO$_4$
                                                                    0.293 g MgSO$_4$.7H$_2$O
                                                                    2.61   g sodium lactate
                                                                    1.0   g glucose
                                                                    0.06   g penicillin
                                                                    0.05   g streptomycin

Weigh out the components (except for the sodium lactate) into a 100 ml volumetric flask. Weigh out the sodium lactate into a beaker and add to the volumetric flask. Rinse the beaker with double distilled water and use this wash to make up the A stock to 100 ml.

2.   10 × B.   For 100 ml.   2.101 g NaHCO$_3$
                                                                    0.01   g phenol red

3.   100 × C.   For 10 ml.   0.036 g Na pyruvate

4.   100 × D.   For 10 ml.   0.252 g CaCl$_2$.2H$_2$O

Weigh out the components in to 10 or 100 ml volumetric flasks and make up with double distilled water.

5.   10 × E.   For 100 ml.   5.958 g Hepes
                                                                    0.010 g phenol red

Weigh out the components into a beaker and dissolve in 50 ml of double distilled water. Adjust to pH 7.4 with 0.2 M NaOH, then transfer to a 100 ml volumetric flask. Make up to 100 ml with washings rinsed from the beaker.

Filter all concentrated stocks through 0.45 μm Millipore filters into sterile plastic tubes. Store frozen at −20°C. Working stocks can be kept at 4°C. At 4°C, A, D and E will keep for 3 months, but B and C should be changed every 2 weeks.

B.   *Preparation of M2 and M16 media from concentrated stocks*

Stock	M2	M16
10× A	10 ml	10 ml
10 × B	1.6 ml	10 ml
100 × C	1.0 ml	1.0 ml
100 × D	1.0 ml	1.0 ml
10 × E	8.4 ml	−
double distilled water	78 ml	78 ml
bovine serum albumin (BSA)	400 mg	400 mg
Total	100 ml	100 ml

1.   Measure the double distilled water into a flask.
2.   Aliquot the concentrated stocks into the water, then carefully rinse the pipette by sucking the liquid up and down.
3.   Add the BSA and mix gently until dissolved.
4.   Force through a 0.45 μM Millipore filter using a large sterile disposable syringe, aliquoting into sterile containers.
5.   Store at 4°C. Prepare fresh every week.

However, some batches of BSA will not sustain egg development. Each new stock of BSA should therefore be tested for its ability to sustain eggs through several cleavage divisions before being used to culture microinjected eggs.

2.3.6 *Collection of fertilized one-cell eggs*

(i)   At least one hour before collecting the eggs, set up two 35 mm tissue culture dishes containing M16 medium and two 35 mm tissue culture dishes containing M16 microdrop cultures. Allow these to equilibrate in a 37°C incubator gassed with 5% CO_2. At the same time prepare four 35 mm tissue culture dishes containing M2 medium and leave at room temperature.

(ii)   Kill the plugged donor female as described in Section 2.3.1.

(iii)   Lay the animal on its back and soak the abdomen with 70% ethanol from a squeeze bottle.

(iv)   Skin the lower half of the animal, cut the body wall, and enter the abdominal cavity to reveal one arm of the reproductive tract as shown in *Figure 6A*. Identify the coiled oviduct, which is to be found between the ovary and the uterus.

(v)   Gripping the uterus with a pair of fine forceps, pull the reproductive tract away from the rest of the animal. Use a pair of fine scissors to puncture the membrane (the mesometrium) that joins the reproductive tract to the body wall. Trim the mesometrium away from the oviduct (*Figure 6A*).

(vi)   Cut between the ovary and the oviduct (*Figure 6B*).

(vii)   Carefully hold the oviduct with a pair of sharp watchmaker's forceps, then cut between the uterus and the oviduct (*Figure 6C*).

(viii) Place the oviduct into one of the dishes of M2 prepared earlier.

(ix)   Dissect out the oviduct from the other horn of the reproductive tract and then from the rest of the donor females. Place all the oviducts into the same dish of M2.

(x)   View the oviducts under $10-20 \times$ magnification using a stereo dissecting microscope. Identify the swollen ampulla containing the cumulus mass (the fertilized eggs surrounded by cumulus cells; *Figure 6D*).

(xi)   Using two pairs of sharp watchmaker's forceps, tear the ampulla. The cumulus mass should spill out of the hole (*Figure 6E*). Sometimes it is necessary to tease the eggs out of the ampulla with forceps. Remove the emptied oviduct from tissue culture dish. Repeat with the rest of the oviducts.

(xii)   Using a general egg transfer pipette (Section 2.2.3) collect all the cumulus masses and any individual eggs, and disperse them in a fresh dish of M2.

(xiii) Mix the cumulus masses with around 50 μl of 10 mg/ml hyaluronidase (Sigma, catalogue number H3884) in M2. Digestion with hyaluronidase for a few minutes will release the eggs from the cumulus cells. Pipetting the eggs up and down will speed the process.

(xiv)   Harvest the eggs then rinse twice in a fresh dish of M2 to wash away traces of enzyme. Each time the eggs are washed, try to leave behind the cumulus cells.

(xv)   Wash the eggs twice in one of the dishes of equilibrated M16 prepared earlier, then transfer them to microdrop culture.

(xvi)   Incubate at 37°C in 5% CO_2 until required for microinjection.

2.3.7 *Oviduct transfer*

(i)   Anaesthetize a 0.5 day p.c. pseudopregnant recipient female as described in Section 2.3.2.

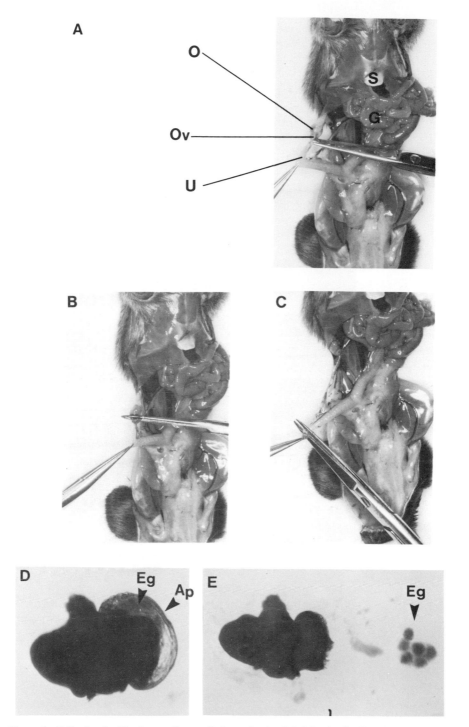

Figure 6. Collecting fertilized one-cell eggs. Refer to Section 2.3.6 for details. Key: S, sternum; G, gut; O, ovary; Ov, oviduct; U, uterus; Eg, eggs; A, ampulla.

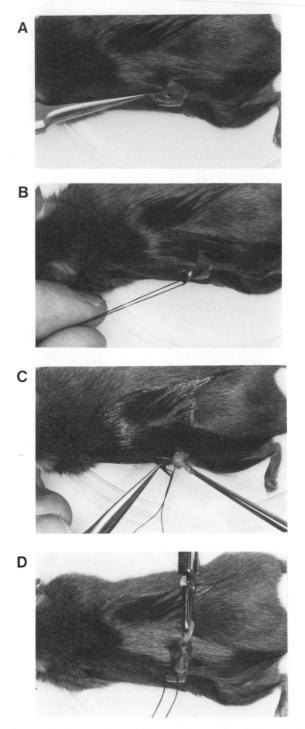

Figure 7. Exposing the reproductive tract for an oviduct transfer operation. Refer to Section 2.3.7 for details.

(ii)   Place the animal abdomen side down on the lid of a 9 cm Petri dish. Spray the back with 70% ethanol.

(iii)   Comb away the hair from the incision site using a fine pair of forceps. The skin is cut transversely 1 cm down from the spine at a point level with the last rib (*Figure 7A*).

(iv)   Make a 1 cm cut through the skin with a large, sharp pair of scissors. Stretch the incision to prevent bleeding.

(v)   Locate the orange coloured ovary beneath the body wall. Make a 3−5 mm cut through the body wall with a fine, sharp pair of scissors at a point a few millimeters away from the ovary (*Figure 7A*). Stretch the incision to prevent bleeding.

(vi)   Introduce a single stitch through the body wall on one side of the incision and leave the silk suture in place (*Figure 7B*).

(vii)   Pull out the fat pad joined to the ovary with a fine but blunt pair of forceps. The ovary, oviduct and uterus will be pulled out with the fat pad (*Figure 7C*).

(viii)   Attach an artery clip to the fat pad, carefully avoiding the ovary. The reproductive tract is held in position over the back of the animal by the artery clip with the coils of the oviduct uppermost (*Figure 7D* and *Figure 8A*).

(ix)   Transport the animal on the Petri dish lid to the stage of a stereo dissecting microscope illuminated with a fibre optic light source. View the oviduct under 10−20 × magnification (*Figure 8A*).

(x)   The opening of the oviduct, the infundibulum, is located in a cavity below the ovary and behind the coils of the oviduct. Gently move the oviduct coils down to reveal the cavity. Sometimes the infundibulum can be seen behind the transparent membrane that covers the ovary, the oviduct and the cavity. Identify an area of the membrane, preferably above the infundibulum, that is free of capillaries. Tear the membrane at this point using watchmaker's forceps. The infundibulum can now be lifted out of the cavity when gently gripped by a sharp pair of watchmaker's forceps (*Figure 8A*).

(xi)   Prepare the eggs for transfer. Remove a maximum of 30 microinjected eggs from microdrop culture and wash them in M2 medium. Load the eggs into an oviduct transfer pipette (Section 2.2.3 and *Figure 3Bii*). First fill the pipette as far as the shoulder with liquid paraffin oil. The viscosity of the oil affords a greater degree of control when transporting eggs. Then take up a small amount of air, then a small amount of M2, then more air. The eggs are then introduced into the pipette in M2 medium. Draw up the eggs in a minimum volume of medium such that they are stacked in a rank. Then introduce another small air bubble and a final column of M2. The arrangement of the oviduct transfer pipette is diagrammed in *Figure 3Bii*.

(xii)   Return to the mouse. Use a paper tissue to mop up any body fluids, blood or blood clots around the oviduct. *Figure 8A−D* are photographs of a demonstration operation performed on a cadaver and consequently the tissue is unnaturally dry and lifeless. *Figure 8E* is a picture of an actual operation being performed on a live mouse. Note the blood and fluid which, unless removed, obscures the oviduct.

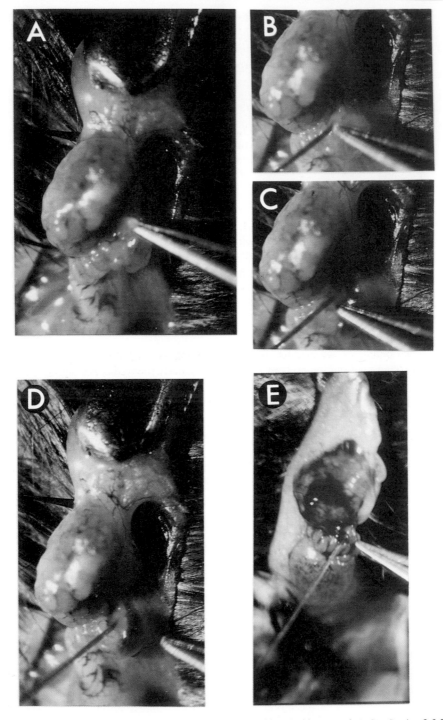

Figure 8. Microsurgical introduction of material into the oviduct (oviduct transfer). See Section 2.3.7 for details.

(xiii) Grip the tip of the infundibulum with a sharp pair of watchmaker's forceps. Pull out the infundibulum from behind the oviduct coils and through the punctured membrane such that the opening can be accessed by the oviduct transfer pipette (*Figure 8A*).

(xiv) Push the tip of the oviduct transfer pipette into the opening of the infundibulum. The opening cannot be seen and is located by gentle prodding with the tip of the pipette. The tissue will 'give' at the opening and the pipette will enter the infundibulum (*Figure 8B*).

(xv) Expel the contents of the pipette and monitor by the appearance of bubbles of air in the ampulla. When three bubbles have appeared, one can be sure that the eggs have been successfully deposited into the ampulla. In *Figure 8B, C* and *D*, blue dye has been used in order to more clearly demonstrate the emptying of the pipette into the ampulla.

(xvi) Withdraw the oviduct transfer pipette. Remove the artery clip and, gripping the fat pad with a blunt pair of forceps, return the reproductive tract to the inside of the body wall. Sew up the body wall with one or two stitches then clip the skin together with an autoclip.

(xvii) Repeat with the other side of the reproductive tract if availability of microinjected eggs allows.

2.3.8 *Caesarian section and fostering*

Often, the number of microinjected eggs developing to term in a surrogate mother is very low. Under such circumstances the embryos are 'over nourished' and grow very large compared to the embryos of a normal sized litter. If the embryos grow too large to be delivered down the birth canal, the pregnancy will proceed beyond the normal gestation period of 19−20 days. By 21−22 days there is a risk that the pups will die in the uterus. It is therefore sometimes necessary to rescue pups by caesarian section and fostered. It may also be necessary to foster valuable unweaned pups born normally to a mother that dies unexpectedly. Foster mothers need to have pups of their own of about the same age as the pups to be fostered and should be of a strain with good maternal characteristics. Parkes females make excellent foster mothers, not only because of their motherly nature, but also because their white pups can easily be distinguished from the agouti or black CBA/C57Bl hybrid fostered pups. The procedures for Caesarian section and fostering are given in *Tables 6* and *7*, respectively.

Table 6. Caesarian section.

1. Kill the mother by neck dislocation (Section 2.3.1).
2. Soak the abdomen in 70% ethanol, skin the lower half of the animal and cut away the body wall revealing the embryos in the uterus. Cut out the uterus.
3. Separate the embryos by cutting the uterus then gently squeeze the embryos free of uterine tissue. Dissect away the membranes surrounding the pups. Cut the umbilical cord.
4. Wipe away any fluid from the mouth and nose area with a paper tissue and gently squeeze the chest with blunt forceps to stimulate breathing.
5. Place the pups on a damp tissue and keep warm until fostered.

Table 7. Fostering.

1.	Remove the foster mother from her own pups.
2.	Quickly mix in the foster pups with the natural babies.
3.	Try and make the foster mother urinate on the babies. Urination can usually be induced by picking the mouse up as shown in *Figure 4B*.
4.	Return the mother to the cage then leave undisturbed for an hour or two.
5.	Remove some of the natural babies to leave a litter of 12 pups at the most. The foster mother will be unable to care for a larger litter.

Table 8. Microinjection equipment.

1.	Inverted microscope (e.g. Nikon Diaphot; see Section 3.1.1)
2.	Right hand Leitz micromanipulator
3.	Left hand Leitz micromanipulator
4.	Two Leitz single instrument holders
5.	Leitz single instrument tubes
6.	Leitz glass capillaries 1 mm o.d. (catalogue number 520119)
7.	Baseplate
8.	Microforge (e.g. DeFondbrune[a])
9.	Pipette puller (e.g. Kopf Model 720[b])
10.	Fluorinert electronic liquid (3M company, FC77)
11.	Light paraffin oil
12.	Injection pipette capillaries (Clark Electromedical Instruments, catalogue number GC 100 TF - 15[b])
13.	Agla micrometer syringe MS01[c].
14.	5 cm long, 26 gauge needle
15.	Glass depression slides
16.	50 cc glass syringe with ground glass plunger
17.	Tygon tubing 3/32 inch i.d., 5/32 inch o.d.
18.	One clamp stand
19.	Diamond pencil
20.	Disposable 1 ml syringes

[a]Available from Microinstruments (Oxford) Ltd., 7 Little Clarendon Street, Oxford OX1 2HP, UK.
[b]Available from Clark Electromedical Instruments, PO Box 8, Pangbourne, Reading RG8 7HU, UK.
[c]Available form Wellcome Reagents Ltd., Wellcome Research Laboratories, Langley Court, Beckenham, Kent BR3 3BS, UK.

3. MICROINJECTION

3.1 Microinjection equipment

Table 8 lists the equipment required for the microinjection of mouse eggs. *Figure 9* shows a Nikon−Leitz microinjection apparatus. A few specific points regarding micro-injection equipment are made below.

3.1.1 *The microscope*

The inverted microscope used for microinjection should have the following features:

(i)   image erected optics;
(ii)   a fixed stage (i.e. the objective lens moves rather than the stage when focusing);
(iii)   a condensor with a long working distance;
(iv)   10 × eyepieces;
(v)   a 4 × objective for low magnification work;

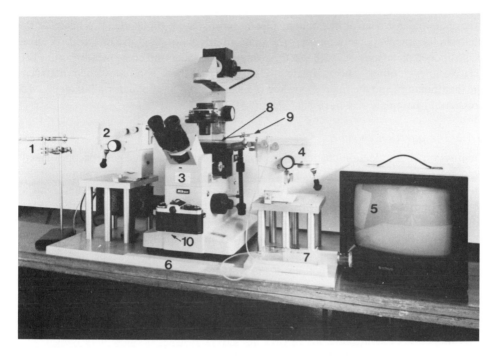

Figure 9. Arrangement of a Nikon−Leitz microinjection apparatus. Key: **1**, Agla micrometer syringe linked by liquid paraffin filled plastic tubing to the egg holding pipette; **2**, left hand Leitz micromanipulator controlling the egg holding pipette; **3**, Nikon Diaphot inverted microscope; **4**, right hand Leitz micromanipulator controlling the microinjection pipette; **5**, video monitor (optional); **6**, baseplate; **7**, 50 ml glass syringe linked by air filled plastic tubing to the microinjection pipette; **8**, glass depression slide containing the injection chamber; **9**, right hand Leitz instrument tube holding the injection pipette (the left hand Leitz instrument tube is obscured by the microscope eyepieces); **10**, camera (optional).

(vi)   a 40 × objective for microinjection;

(vii)   suitable optics.

The best optics for visualizing the internal structure of one-cell eggs are the Nomarski differential interference contrast (DIC) microscopy system. However, DIC optics are very expensive and glass injection chambers are obligatory. Hoffman modulation contrast optics do not give the same resolution as DIC, but are cheaper and are compatible with plastic injection chambers. Bright field optics can be used if Nomarski or Hoffman optics are unavailable and are preferable to phase contrast microscopy.

3.1.2 *Micromanipulation*

Microinjection is achieved by the micromanipulation of fertilized eggs using two pipette types: the holding pipette, which holds the egg in place whilst it is injected; and the injection pipette, which is loaded with DNA solution and actually pierces the egg. Both of these pipettes are controlled using micromanipulators. The most commonly used micromanipulator used is that supplied by Leitz.

The Leitz micromanipulator is easy to use and has the particular advantage of having a convenient joy-stick control for fine horizontal movement in two planes. One micromanipulator is positioned on either side of the microscope (see *Figure 9*). The left hand micromanipulator controls the holding pipette, whilst the right hand micromanipulator controls the microinjection pipette. The micromanipulators and the microscope must be positioned on a baseplate such that these three components are conveniently positioned relative to each other. The baseplate also ensures that there is no movement between the manipulators and the microscope and reduces vibration. A plan for a Nikon−Leitz compatible baseplate has been published (16).

3.1.3 *The injection chamber*

Depression slide injection chambers are compatible with inverted microscopes fitted with any optical system. Siliconize the glass slide by rinsing it in a 3% solution of dichloromethyl silane in chloroform. Wash the slide thoroughly in water and with a standard household detergent. Rinse the slide with ethanol and wipe dry with a paper tissue. Place a flat drop of M2 medium into the centre of the depression. The M2 drop should be no more than 1 cm across. Cover the M2 drop with light paraffin oil to prevent evaporation. Place the injection chamber on the stage of microscope and using a 4 × objective, focus on the bottom of the M2 drop.

3.1.4 *Preparation of holding pipettes*

A holding pipette is shown in *Figure 3C*. One holding pipette should last for a whole microinjection session. Holding pipettes are rarely re-used because they tend to get dirty and clogged with egg debris and liquid paraffin. Large numbers of holding pipettes can be prepared in advance and stored loose in a Petri dish.

(i)   Draw a 1 mm o.d. Leitz hard glass capillary in a microflame. Soften the glass by turning it in the flame then pull on either end of the capillary. At the same time withdraw the glass from the heat. Be careful to obtain straight drawn capillaries.

(ii)   Using a diamond pencil, score the drawn section around 2 cm away from the shoulder and break the capillary at this point. Examine the capillary under a dissecting microscope. The end should be perfectly flush, with no jagged edges and the capillary should be perfectly straight. The external diameter should be no less than 80 μm, and no more than 150 μm. Reject any capillaries that do not conform to these requirements.

(iii)   Mount a suitable drawn capillary in the vertical position in a Defonbrune microforge. Using a 4 × objective, focus on the tip of the capillary. Bring the filament of the microforge close up to, but not touching, the capillary tip. Heat the filament and observe the melting of the tip. When the internal diameter of the tip reaches 10−15 μM, turn off the current to the filament.

(iv)   Carefully move the capillary to the horizontal position. Locate the filament below the capillary, 1−2 mm from the tip. Move the filament up to the capillary until they are very close, but not touching. Heat the filament and allow the capillary to bend. Turn off the current to the filament when the capillary has bent by 15° to the horizontal. This process can be monitored either by eye or by using low power magnification. Carefully remove the holding pipette from the microforge.

(v)   The holding pipette is now ready for assembly into the micromanipulation system. Connect a Leitz instrument tube to an Agla micrometer syringe via one meter of Tygon tubing. Fill the whole system with light paraffin oil. Ensure that all air bubbles have been excluded.

(vi) Fill the holding pipette with Flourinert electronic liquid using a 5 cm long, 26 gauge needle connected to a 1 ml disposable syringe. Insert the holding pipette into the oil filled Leitz instrument tube and tighten the ring to hold it in place. Carefully clamp the instrument tube into the instrument tube holder of the left hand micromanipulator. Adjust the Agla syringe until fluid stops flowing out of the holding pipette, but do not allow air to flow into the pipette.

(vii) By adjusting the instrument tube and the controls of the instrument tube holder, position the tip of the holding pipette above the injection chamber such that it is horizontal. The shadow of the holding pipette should be visible through the microscope when using a 4 × objective. Using the fine controls of the micromanipulator, lower the holding pipette into the injection chamber. Ensure that the holding pipette is free to move in the horizontal plane throughout the field of view when controlled by the joy-stick, and does not catch on the bottom of the chamber.

(viii) Adjust the Agla syringe until the meniscus between the Fluorinert and the M2 medium is close to the tip of the holding pipette.

3.1.5 *Preparation of microinjection pipettes*

Microinjection pipettes are prepared using thin walled glass tubing with an outside diameter of 1 mm. Capillaries with internal filaments are particularly useful because they allow the injection pipette to be filled with DNA from the end distal to the point by capillary action. Pipettes are made on a mechanical pipette puller. The appropriate temperature and mechanical pull settings will have to be worked out by trial and error. A good pipette will have an opening of around 1 μM. Smaller openings will tend to clog easily, whilst larger openings are more likely to burst the egg. Pipettes should be prepared as required.

The microinjection pipette is operated by the right hand micromanipulator. A Leitz instrument tube is connected by a 1 metre length of Tygon tubing to a 50 ml syringe with a ground glass plunger. The plunger may require lubricating with a small amount of light paraffin oil. The system is air filled. The injection pipette is loaded with DNA solution by capillary action. As soon as liquid can be seen at the tip then the pipette is loaded sufficiently. Avoid contaminating the DNA stock solution with, for example, talcum powder dust from disposable gloves or enzymes from the exposed hand. Assemble the pipette into the instrument tube. Clamp the instrument tube onto the instrument tube holder of the micromanipulator. Using the instrument tube holder controls, position the tip of the injection pipette above the injection chamber. Then, using the fine vertical control of the micromanipulator, lower the pipette tip into the M2 medium drop, all the time monitoring the position of the tip by viewing down the microscope with a 4 × objective. Ensure that the injection pipette can be freely moved in the vertical plane when operated by the micromanipulator joy-stick.

3.2 **Microinjection of fertilized one-cell mouse eggs**

(i) Assemble the microinjection apparatus as described in Section 3.1. Remove around 20 fertilized eggs from storage in M16 at 37°C using a general egg transfer pipette. Wash the eggs twice in M2, then load them in as small a volume as possible into a transfer pipette and discharge them into the injection chamber. Observe the entry of the eggs into the injection chamber using a 4 × objective. Try to keep the eggs in a group positioned below the holding and injection pipettes. Ensure that no air bubbles are released into the chamber with the eggs. Air bubbles will completely disrupt the chamber. Not only is it likely that the eggs will be lost, but also the chamber may have to be re-assembled.

(ii)   Re-adjust the vertical position of the holding and injection pipettes such that they are in the same plane as the eggs and are consequently able to readily manipulate the eggs. Bring the tip of the holding pipette up to an egg and by adjusting the Agla syringe, apply light suction such that the egg is held onto the end of the pipette.

(iii)   Bring the egg to the centre of the field of view. Switch to the 40 × DIC objective and focus on the egg. By focusing up and down, locate the position of the larger of the two pronuclei (usually the male). By adjusting the Agla syringe, the holding pipette and the injection needle, move the egg until the larger pronucleus is in a position central to, but away from, the holding pipette (*Figure 10A*). Ensure that the egg is tightly held by the holding pipette by applying slightly more suction. However, although the zona pellucida may be deformed, do not allow the egg itself to be pulled into the holding pipette.

(iv)   Focus on the pronucleus to be injected. Bring the tip of the injection pipette up to the zona pellucida of the egg. Adjust the fine vertical micromanipulator control to place the tip of the injection pipette in the same focal plane as the targeted pronucleus.

(v)   Inject the egg. The zona pellucida is easily pierced by the injection needle. When the injection needle appears to be inside the nucleus, squeeze on the injection syringe. One of three things will then happen: (1) the egg nucleus may swell. This is indicative of a successful injection. Continue to apply pressure until the nucleus has reached roughly twice its normal volume (*Figure 10B*) then quickly withdraw the injection pipette; (2) a small, clear bubble may appear at the end of the injection needle and the zona pellucida may swell. This indicates that the egg membrane, which can be very elastic, has not yet been pierced. To penetrate the membrane, continue to push the pipette through to the far side of the nucleus, pull back until the tip is again in the nucleus and then squeeze on the injection syringe again; (3) nothing. This is probably due to the injection needle being blocked. Change the needle and, if necessary, the DNA stock.

(vi)   Following injection, cytoplasmic granules may be seen to flow out into the peri-vitelline space. This is indicative of egg lysis. If eggs lyse on two or three successive injections, then change the injection needle. The injection needle should also be changed if it appears to be getting dirty or clogged.

(vii)   Following injection, return to the 4 × objective and place the egg above the holding and injection pipettes, well away from the uninjected eggs. The post-injection eggs should be divided into two groups − those that have survived injection and those that have not.

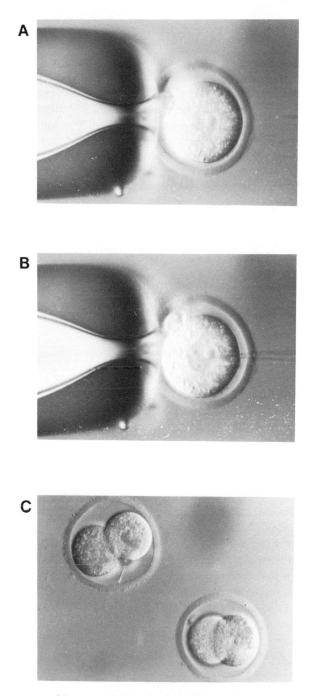

Figure 10. A. Arrangement of the microinjection chamber at high power magnification (×400) using DIC optics. The holding pipette is on the left, gripping the zona pellucida of the egg. The microinjection needle is on the right. The large male pronucleus, containing numerous nucleoli, is clearly visible in the middle of the egg. **B**. Microinjection and consequent swelling of the male pronucleus. **C**. Two-cell stage eggs viewed under DIC at ×400 magnification.

(viii) Eggs should be maintained in M2 medium for a maximum of 15 min. A skilled operative should be able to inject between 15 and 40 eggs in such a time. Once all the eggs in a batch have been injected, those that have survived are removed from the injection chamber, washed twice in M16, and returned to M16 microdrop culture until transferred to the oviduct of a 0.5 day p.c. pseudopregnant female (see Section 2.3.7). Eggs that have not survived injection are discarded. Eggs can be transferred to a pseudopregnant recipient that same day, or following culture overnight by which time the eggs have reached the two cell stage (*Figure 10C*).

4. DNA MANIPULATIONS

4.1 **DNA for microinjection**

One of the advantages of the microinjection method of producing transgenic mice over rival techniques is that any cloned DNA (derived from lambda, plasmid or cosmid vectors) can be introduced into a zygote and will integrate and contribute to the germ line. Additional manipulations, such as recloning into special vectors and virus preparation, are not required. The efficiency of the microinjection process is, however, affected by the properties and quality of the DNA used (15). These factors are considered in this section.

4.1.1 *Physical state of the DNA*

Cloned DNA of any size, including lambda clones of up to 50 kb (17), can be introduced into mice by microinjection. Linear DNA integrates 5-fold more efficiently than super-coiled DNA (15) but the structure of the fragment ends created by different restriction enzymes has little effect (15,18).

4.1.2 *The DNA solution*

Microinjection DNA is dissolved in a buffer of 10 mM Tris-HCl pH 7.4, 0.1−0.25 mM EDTA. Higher concentrations of EDTA and low concentrations of $MgCl_2$ are toxic to eggs. There is no correlation between the concentration of the microinjected DNA and the resulting copy number of the transgene. Excessively high concentrations of DNA are however toxic to the egg (15). It is estimated that around 1−2 pl of DNA solution is injected into the pronucleus by microinjection. Most investigators use DNA concentrations of between 1 and 5 μg/ml and are therefore microinjecting around 500 copies of the DNA fragment, depending upon its size. Some workers make dilutions of the injection DNA stock (for example, 1, 2.5 and 5 μg/ml) and rotate between these solutions during an injection session as the microinjection pipettes are changed.

4.1.3 *Procaryotic DNA sequences*

DNA sequences derived from procaryotic or eucaryotic species can be microinjected and both will contribute to the germ line with equal efficiency. The presence of contiguous vector derived procaryotic DNA sequences in a fragment of injected DNA can, however, severely inhibit the expression of some eucaryotic transgenes, for example

Table 9. Method for the preparation of plasmid DNA.

1.	Inoculate a 5 ml culture with a single bacterial colony and incubate overnight. Use this culture to seed a 100 ml culture which is vigorously shaken overnight at 37°C.
2.	Pellet the bacteria by centrifugation for example at 7000 r.p.m. for 5 min in a Sorvall SS34 or HB4 rotors. Drain off the supernatant from the pellet very well.
3.	Resuspend the bacteria in 5 ml of 50 mM glucose, 25 mM Tris-HCl pH 8.0, 10 mM EDTA, then add 10 ml of fresh 0.2 M NaOH, 1.0% SDS. Swirl and place on ice for 5 min.
4.	Add 5 ml of ice cold 5 M potassium acetate pH 8[a], mix well and place on ice for 5 min. Centrifuge at 8000 r.p.m. for 5 min.
5.	Transfer the supernatant to a fresh tube and mix with 0.6 volume (12 ml) isopropanol. Centrifuge at 8000 r.p.m. for 5 min.
6.	Pour off the supernatant and resuspend the pellet in 2 ml of TE[b]. Add 2 ml of ice cold 5 M LiCl, mix and centrifuge at 10 000 r.p.m. for 5 min.
7.	Transfer the supernatant to a fresh tube and mix with 8 ml of ethanol. Incubate at −70°C for 30 min, then collect the precipitate by centrifugation at 10 000 r.p.m. for 10 min.
8.	Pour off the supernatant and resuspend the pellet in 0.5 ml of TE containing 40 μg/ml RNase A[c]. Incubate at 37°C for 15 min.
9.	Mix with 0.5 ml of 2.5 M NaCl containing 20% PEG 6000. Incubate overnight at 4°C. Centrifuge at 10 000 r.p.m. for 5 min, drain the pellet and resuspend in 0.5 ml of TE.
10.	Add 0.5 ml of chloroform, mix by vortexing, centrifuge at 10 000 r.p.m. for 1 min then transfer the aqueous phase (top layer) to a fresh tube. Repeat the chloroform extraction.
11.	Add 0.5 ml of phenol[d] to the aqueous phase, vortex to mix and centrifuge at 10 000 r.p.m. for 2 min. Transfer the aqueous phase (top layer) to a fresh tube containing 50 μl of 3 M sodium acetate. Add 550 μl of isopropanol and mix.
12.	Incubate at −70°C for at least 15 min, then centrifuge at 10 000 r.p.m. for 5 min. Add 1 ml of cold 70% ethanol to the pellet and vortex well. Repellet by centrifugation at 10 000 r.pm. for 2 min.
13.	Dry the plasmid DNA pellet under vacuum and resuspend in 0.5 ml of TE.

[a]5 M potassium acetate pH 8 is made by mixing equal volumes of 3 M potassium acetate and 2 M acetic acid.
[b]TE is 10 mM Tris-HCl pH 7.5, 1 mM EDTA.
[c]RNase A (Sigma, catalogue number R 5125) is dissolved in TE and incubated in a boiling waterbath for 10 min to destroy any contaminating DNase.
[d]Phenol (redistilled, nucleic acid grade; Gibco - BRL, catalogue number 5509UA) is equilibrated with TE before use.

globin (19,20,21), alpha fetoprotein (AFP; 22) and actin (23). Chada *et al.* (19) reported that the tissue specific expression of an exogenous β-globin gene could only be elicited in the absence of plasmid sequences. Similarly, Townes *et al.* (21) were able to increase the expression of a human β-globin transgene by up to 1000-fold by removing plasmid sequences. In some circumstances, bacterial coding sequences (for example chloramphenicol acetyl transferase, CAT) are incorporated into hybrid genes and used to report on expression directed by eucaryotic promoter elements. Unlike some vector sequences, CAT sequences do not seem to inhibit the use of contiguous eucaryotic regulatory elements. CAT has been used to report on the expression of both the αA-crystallin promoter (24) and the Rous sarcoma virus long terminal repeat (25). Any inhibitory effect of procaryote derived DNA may therefore be specific to sequences contained within the commonly used lambda and pBR322 derived vectors. As a general rule therefore, investigators now remove all vector sequences prior to injecting cloned eucaryotic genes in order to maximize the quality, quantity and reproducibility of transgene expression.

Table 10. Purification of DNA for microinjection using glass beads.

A. *Preparation of the glass beads*

1. Mix 250 ml of powdered glass flint[a] with 500 ml of sterile water[b]. Allow to settle for 1 h. Discard the settled glass and recover the fines by centrifugation.
2. Resuspend the fines in 200 ml of water. Add 200 ml concentrated nitric acid and bring to the boil. Carry out this step in a fume hood.
3. Allow to cool, then centrifuge to recover the glass beads. Wash away the acid by resuspending the pellet in water and then centrifuge to recover the glass. Repeat until the water has a neutral pH.
4. Store the glass at room temperature as a 50% slurry in sterile water.

B. *Recovery and purification of DNA fragments from agarose gels*

1. Digest the DNA using appropriate restriction enzymes according to the manufacturers instructions.
2. Fractionate the restricted DNA in an agarose gel using TAE buffer[c] containing 50 μg/ml ethidium bromide. Visualize the DNA under long wave u.v. light and excise the desired fragment into a pre-weighed 1.5 ml Eppendorf type tube in as small a volume as possible.
3. Weigh the gel and estimate the volume. Add 2 volumes of 6 M NaI[d]. Incubate at 37°C, vortexing occasionally, until the gel dissolves.
4. Reform the glass bead slurry by vortexing. To the solubilized gel, add 1 μl of glass suspension for every 2 μg of DNA present. Chill on ice for one hour with occasional agitation.
5. Centrifuge the glass powder. To ensure a loose pellet, spin at low speed for a brief period (1 – 2 sec in a microcentrifuge).
6. Discard the supernatant and disperse the glass pellet in 0.5 original gel volumes of 6 M NaI. Pellet the glass beads (1 – 2 sec in a microcentrifuge).
7. Disperse the pellet in 0.5 original gel volumes of ethanol wash solution[e]. Centrifuge to pellet glass and repeat.
8. Remove as much of the supernatant as possible without allowing the pellet to dry. Add 10 mM Tris-HCl pH 7.4, 0.2 mM EDTA (>50 μl) immediately. Elute the DNA by incubating at 37°C for 15 min.
9. Spin out the glass and transfer the supernatant containing the DNA to a fresh tube[f].
10. To further remove impurities, pass the DNA through a Sephadex G-50 column equilibrated in 10 mM Tris-HCl pH 7.4, 0.2 mM EDTA and filter through a small 0.45 μM Millipore filter[g].
11. Assay the DNA by spectrophotometry or comparative ethidium bromide staining.

[a]Powdered flint glass is obtained from glass supply companies (e.g., Eagle Ceramics Inc., 12267 Wilkins Avenue, Rockville, Maryland, MD 20852, USA).
[b]Use sterile materials throughout as bacteria can grow in the glass bead slurry.
[c]20 × TAE buffer is 0.8 M Tris-HCl pH 8.0, 0.4 M sodium acetate, 0.02 M EDTA.
[d]6 M NaI is made by dissolving 90.8 g of NaI and 0.5 g of Na_2SO_3 in water to a final volume of 100 ml. This solution is filtered through a 0.45 μM Nalgene filter. A few Na_2SO_3 crystals are added to the filtrate. The Na_2SO_3 does not dissolve fully. Store at 4°C and protect from light.
[e]Ethanol wash solution is 50% ethanol, 0.1 M NaCl, 10 mM Tris-HCl pH 7.5, 1 mM EDTA. Store at −20°C.
[f]Subsequent to this point, all tubes and tips should be rinsed with filtered water prior to use.
[g]Millipore type HV, catalogue number SJHVOO4NS.

4.1.4 *Preparation and purification of microinjection DNA*

DNA for microinjection can be isolated from cosmid or plasmid clones by any of the standard techniques of lysozyme/Triton X-100 lysis or lysozyme/alkaline lysis followed by banding of supercoiled molecules in ethidium bromide/CsCl gradients (26). A method for the preparation of good quality plasmid DNA that does not demand an ultracentrifugation step (27) is given in *Table 9*.

Vector free DNA fragments are isolated by restriction enzyme digestion followed by preparative agarose gel electrophoresis. Microinjection DNA fragments must be

Table 11. Isolation of genomic DNA from mouse tails.

1.	While restraining the animal with one hand (see Figure 4B), use a sharp pair of scissors to cut off around 1 cm of tail. Place the piece of tail in 700 μl of 50 mM Tris-HCl pH 8.0, 100 mM EDTA, 100 mM NaCl, 1% SDS containing 100 μg/ml Proteinase K[a]. Before releasing the animal, mark it by ear or toe clipping so that it can be identified.
2.	Mince the tail with a pair of sharp, fine scissors. Incubate at 50°C overnight, preferably with agitation.
3.	In the morning, add 5 μl of 1 mg/ml RNase A[b]. Incubate at 37°C for at least 1 h.
4.	Add 700 μl of TE equilibrated phenol. Gently mix with the digested tail solution until homogeneous (this could take up to 20 min).
5.	Separate the phases by centrifugation at 10 000 r.p.m. in a microcentrifuge for 10 min. Transfer the viscous aqueous phase (top layer) and the interphase to a fresh tube.
6.	Add 700 μl of phenol−chloroform[c] and gently mix the phases. Separate again by centrifugation at 10 000 r.p.m. in a microcentrifuge. Transfer the upper aqueous layer to a fresh tube. This time, avoid any interphase.
7.	Add 800−1000 μl of 100% ethanol and gently mix. A large, white, stringy precipitate should appear. Pellet this by centrifugation in a microcentrifuge for 2 min.
8.	Discard the supernatant and rinse the pellet with 1 ml of cold 70% ethanol. Repellet the DNA by microcentrifugation for 1 min. Remove as much of the supernatant as possible and dry the pellet under vacuum.
9.	Resuspend the DNA by adding 250 μl of TE. Incubate at 37°C for a few hours to allow the DNA to dissolve.
10.	Assay the DNA by spectrophotometry.

[a]Sigma, catalogue number P-0390.
[b]Sigma, catalogue number R-5125. RNase should be made up in TE and incubated in a boiling waterbath for 10 min before use to destroy any contaminating DNase.
[c]Phenol−chloroform is TE equilibrated phenol mixed with an equal volume of chloroform and a 1/50th volume of *iso*-amylalcohol.

free of all contaminants that may be toxic to the eggs and free of all particulate matter that could clog the injection pipette. A method for achieving such standards of purity is presented in *Table 10*.

4.2 **Identification of transgenic mice**

Transgenic animals are identified by hybridization analysis of high molecular weight genomic DNA isolated from tail tissue. A method for the isolation of tail DNA is given in *Table 11*.

The method used to analyse the DNA depends upon the nature of the transgene. If the transgene has a homologue within the mouse genome then Southern hybridization analysis (26,28) must be undertaken. If the transgene is wholly or partially non-homologous to any part of the mouse genome then dot blot (or slot blot) analysis (29) can be used.

4.2.1 *Southern analysis*

A foreign gene integrated in the mouse genome can be distinguished from an endogenous homologue by differing restriction endonuclease cleavage patterns. Even if the transgene is identical to the endogenous gene it will be flanked by different restriction enzyme sites and can be distinguished accordingly. Alternatively, if the transgene is derived from another species it may be possible to distinguish it from the homologous mouse counterpart by virtue of different internal restriction enzyme sites. An example of such

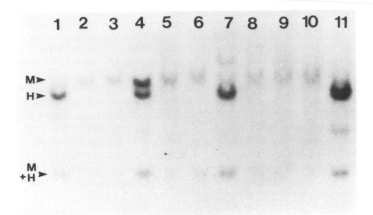

Figure 11. A Southern hybridization analysis of high molecular weight DNA isolated from mouse tail tissue. Genomic DNA was isolated from tail biopsies from eleven mice resulting from the injection of fertilized one-cell eggs with a fragment of the human c-*fos* gene. The DNA was cleaved with the *Pst*I restriction endonuclease, fractionated through a 0.8% agarose gel, transferred to nitrocellulose and hybridized with a c-*fos* probe. Endogenous mouse (M) and exogenous human (H) fragments are detected.

an analysis is shown in *Figure 11*. Eleven pups have been born to a surrogate mother impregnated with eggs microinjected with a fragment of the human c-*fos* gene (D.M., J.H., Richard Treissman and Brigid Hogan, unpublished data). Southern hybridization of *Pst*I-cleaved tail DNA reveals that the exogenous DNA, which has a different pattern of internal *Pst*I sites than the endogenous gene, is present only in mice 1, 4, 7 and 11. The endogenous bands provide controls for the quantity and quality of the tail DNA preparation.

4.2.2 *Slot or dot blotting*

Slot or dot blotting is a quick and easy method of tail DNA analysis, but it can only be applied to mice bearing a transgene with no homology to mouse DNA (for example, a hybrid gene with a viral or procaryotic reporter element). A method is described in *Table 12* and an example result is shown in *Figure 12*.

Slot or dot blot analyses should be performed in duplicate with one filter being analysed with a transgene probe and the other with an endogenous mouse gene probe. This is because tail DNA is difficult to quantitate due to contamination with RNA. Hybridization to an endogenous mouse probe ensures that false negatives are avoided and affords a degree of comparative quantitation.

4.2.3 *Identification of homozygous transgenic mice*

Mice homozygous for a transgene are derived as a result of a cross between two heterozygotes. Homozygous, heterozygous and negative mice are produced from such a cross in the ratio of 1:2:1. Homozygotes are identified by virtue of their having twice as many copies of the transgene DNA as their heterozygous parents and littermates. Homozygosity is then confirmed genetically. Slot or Southern blot analysis can be used to identify homozygotes. The choice of method depends upon whether the transgene

Table 12. Slot or dot blotting of genomic DNA.

1.	Adjust 10 μg of DNA to 0.3 M with NaOH.
2.	Incubate in a boiling waterbath for 10 min. Quench on ice.
3.	Stand the DNA at room temperature for 5 min, then adjust to 2 M with ammonium acetate.
4.	Soak a pre-cut nitrocellulose sheet[a] in 20 × SSC[b] for at least 5 min, and then assemble the slot[c] or dot blot[d] apparatus according to the manufacturers instructions.
5.	Apply the DNA to the slot or dot blot apparatus.
6.	Remove the nitrocellulose sheet from the apparatus and allow to dry at room temperature.
7.	Bake the filter at 80°C for 2 h.
8.	Prehybridize the filter overnight at 42°C in 50% deionized formamide[e], 5 × SSC, 5 × Denhart's solution[f], 0.1% SDS, 50 mM sodium phosphate buffer pH 7.5, 200 μg/ml sheared salmon sperm DNA[g] in a sealed plastic bag.
9.	Add the probe[h] to a concentration of less than 25 ng/ml. Incubate at 42°C overnight, preferably with agitation.
10.	Wash the filter with constant agitation at 65°C twice for 30 min with 2 × SSC, 0.1% SDS and twice for 30 min with 0.1 × SSC, 0.1% SDS.
11.	Autoradiograph the filter.

[a]Schleicher and Schüll, 0.45 μM, BA85.
[b]20 × SSC is 3 M NaCl, 0.3 M sodium citrate.
[c]For example, Schleicher and Schüll, Minifold II Slot-Blotter (catalogue number, SRC 072/0).
[d]For example, Schleicher and Schüll, Micro Sample Filtration Manifold (catalogue number, SRC-96).
[e]Formamide is deionized by stirring with Dowex XG8 mixed bed resin for 1 h followed by filtration through Whatman 1MM paper. Fluka formamide 47670 does not require deionization.
[f]50 × Denhardt's solution is 1% Ficoll, 1% BSA (fraction V), 1% polyvinylpyrrolidone.
[g]Salmon sperm DNA (Sigma, catalogue number D-1626) is prepared by dissolving the solid at 10 mg/ml then sonicating, or shearing by passing the viscous solution through an 18 gauge needle. Some investigators clean up the solution by phenol−chloroform extraction and ethanol precipitation. The DNA is denatured by incubation in a boiling waterbath for 10 min.
[h]Double-stranded DNA probes must be denatured before use.

has homology with an endogenous mouse gene or not (see above). In either case, quantitation is crucial and this is achieved by comparing the hybridization signal of the transgene probe with that of an endogenous mouse probe. A slot blot analysis of a line of mice containing Simian Virus 40 (SV40) transgene sequences, which have no homology to mouse DNA, is illustrated in *Figure 12*. Two genetically obligate heterozygote animals were mated and their offspring (A, B and C) analysed. Duplicate filters bearing tail DNA were probed with either radiolabelled SV40 DNA, to detect the transgene, or a mouse gene − in this case c-*fos*. The equality of hybridization of the c-*fos* probe confirms that the three DNA samples were loaded in equal amounts. However the levels of hybridization to the SV40 probe revealed that mouse A contains more transgene DNA than either B and C. Quantitative densitometer scanning of the autoradiograph, or scintillation counting of the hybridized slots demonstrated that mouse A had twice as much viral DNA as mice B and C and is therefore probably homozygous. This was confirmed by genetic analysis. Mouse A, a male, was mated with a normal F1 female and the resulting pups were analysed by slot blotting. As all 10 pups were heterozygous for the transgene, it was concluded that mouse A, the father, was a homozygote.

5. TRANSGENIC MICE − BREEDING AND GENE EXPRESSION ANALYSIS

5.1 Breeding transgenic lines

As soon as a founder animal has been identified as being transgenic (Section 4.2) it

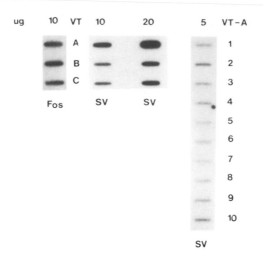

Figure 12. Slot blot analysis of genomic DNA isolated from tail tissue. See Section 4.2.3 for details.

is necessary to mate the animal in order to establish a line. The line must, of course, be established before the founder is sacrificed for analysis. This is easier if the founder is male. A male founder can be very quickly mated with a large number of females, whereas it is necessary for a female founder to produce and wean at least one litter before she can be sacrificed. It is best to positively identify first generation transgenics by hybridization analysis before the founder is sacrificed.

In most cases, 50% of the offspring resulting from a mating between a founder animal and a wild-type mate are transgenic — both founder and first generation animals are obligate heterozygotes for the transgene. However, it should be noted that some founder transgenic mice are germline mosaics and consequently a smaller proportion of first generation offspring are transgene positive. It is necessary to screen all pups by tail DNA analysis until a homozygous line is established (see Section 4.2.3). Some transgenic lines cannot be maintained as homozygotes because between 5% and 15% of transgene insertion events result in homozygous lethal mutations.

5.2 The expression of genes in transgenic mice

A large amount of data on the expression of exogenous DNA in transgenic mice has accumulated over the past few years and it is not possible to review all of this information in this chapter. Rather, the reader is referred to the review by Palmiter and Brinster (12). Only a few general principles will be enunciated here.

Around half of all transgenic mouse lines do not express their transgenes. This is thought to be either due to the presence of inhibitory sequences within the transgene (for example, procaryotic sequences — Section 4.1) or to the site of integration of the transgene. The exogenous DNA may be integrated into a chromosomal location that is transcriptionally inactive. Most transgenic mice that express their transgenes do so in a manner that is appropriate to the regulatory elements present. However, the adjacent cellular DNA can influence the expression of a transgene. Some transgenic mice express their foreign DNA in an inappropriate manner and this is thought to be due to insertion effects such as the juxtaposition of the transgene and an endogenous enhancer element.

The extent and location of sequences required to elicit appropriate expression varies from gene to gene. Some genes, for example insulin (30), elastase (31,32) and αA-crystallin (24,25), only require a few hundred base pairs of upstream 5' sequences. Other genes, for example AFP, require up to 10 kb of 5' DNA (22). But, some genes, for example the human globin genes (33), also require sequences 3' to the transcription initiation site, as well as 5' upstream elements.

5.3 The application of transgenic technology

The benefits of transgenic technology will initially be in areas of basic science. Studies on transgenic mice will contribute to most areas of mammalian biology in the following, not mutually exclusive, ways.

(i) The analysis of the *cis* acting regulatory sequences that mediate the tissue specific, developmental and physiological regulation of gene expression.

(ii) The analysis of the physiological consequences to the whole organism of the inappropriate or altered expression of normal or mutated gene products, including oncogenes.

(iii) Transgenic mice will be used to isolate novel mutants. Recessive mutants often arise in transgenic mice as a consequence of the insertion of a transgene into a functional gene. The mutated gene can then be readily cloned using the transgene tag as a probe (34). In the future, it may be possible to direct mutations to specific genes by introducing antisense constructs into mice, as has been achieved for plants (35).

Out of such fundamental studies will emerge the potential for a more practical application of transgenic technology, to biotechnology and agriculture. Already transgenic pigs, sheep and rabbits have been constructed (36), but it will be a long time before the agriculturalist can seriously consider transgenic technology as a new tool in animal breeding.

6. ACKNOWLEDGEMENTS

We would like to thank the Graphics and Photography Departments at NIMR for their help in the preparation of the figures. The work of D.M. and J.H. has been funded by the Medical Research Council. We would like to thank Brigid Hogan for teaching us so much and for allowing us to pursue speculative research projects in her laboratory.

7. REFERENCES

1. Gorman,C. (1985) High efficiency gene transfer into mammalian cells. In *DNA Cloning — A Practical Approach*. Glover,D.M. (ed.), IRL Press, Oxford, Vol. II, p. 143 – 190.
2. Jahner,D., Haase,K., Mulligan,R. and Jaenisch,R. (1985) *Proc. Natl. Acad. Sci. USA*, **82**, 6927.
3. van der Putten,H., Botteri,F.M., Miller,A.D., Rosenfeld,M.G., Fan,H., Evans,R.M. and Verma,I.M. (1985) *Proc. Natl. Acad. Sci. USA*, **82**, 6148.
4. Evans,M.J. and Kaufman,M.H. (1981) *Nature*, **292**, 154.
5. Martin,G.R. (1981) *Proc. Natl. Acad. Sci. USA*, **78**, 7634.
6. Bradley,A., Evans,M.H., Kaufman,M.H. and Robertson,E. (1984) *Nature*, **309**, 255.
7. Lovell-Badge,R.H., Bygrave,A.E., Bradley,A., Robertson,E., Evans,M.J. and Cheah,K.S.E. (1985) *Cold Spring Harbor Symp. Quant. Biol.*, **50**, 707.

8. Robertson,E., Bradley,A., Kuehn,M. and Evans,M. (1986) *Nature*, **323**, 445.
9. McGrath,J. and Solter,D. (1983) *Science*, **220**, 1300.
10. Smithies,O., Gregg,R.G., Boggs,S.S., Koralewski,M.A. and Kucherlapati,R.S. (1985) *Nature*, **317**, 230.
11. Thomas,K.R., Folger,K.R. and Capecchi,M.R. (1986) *Cell*, **44**, 4189.
12. Palmiter,R.D. and Brinster,R.E. (1987) *Annu. Rev. Genet.*, in press.
13. Lacy,E., Roberts,S., Evans,E.P., Burtenshaw,M.D. and Constantini,F. (1983) *Cell*, **34**, 343.
14. Krumlauf,R., Chapman,V.M., Hammer,R.E., Brinster,R.L. and Tilghman,S.M. (1985) *Nature*, **319**, 224.
15. Brinster,R.L., Chen,H.Y., Trumbauer,M.E., Yagle,M.K. and Palmiter,R.D. (1985) *Proc. Natl. Acad. Sci. USA*, **82**, 4438.
16. Hogan,B., Constantini,F. and Lacy,E. (1986) *Manipulating the Mouse Embryo — A Laboratory Manual*. Cold Spring Harbor, New York.
17. Constantini,F. and Lacy,E. (1981) *Nature*, **294**, 92.
18. Grosschedl,R., Weaver,D., Baltimore,D. and Constantini,F. (1984) *Cell*, **38**, 647.
19. Chada,K., Magram,J., Raphael,K., Radice,G., Lacy,E. and Constantini,F. (1985) *Nature*, **314**, 377.
20. Magram,J., Chada,K. and Constantini,F. (1985) *Nature*, **315**, 338.
21. Townes,T.M., Lingrel,J.B., Chen,H.Y., Brinster,R.L. and Palmiter,R.D. (1985) *EMBO J.*, **4**, 1715.
22. Krumlauf,R., Hammer,R.E., Tilghman,S.M. and Brinster,R.L. (1985) *Cold Spring Harbor Symp. Quant. Biol.*, **50**, 371.
23. Shani,M. (1986) *Mol. Cell Biol.*, **6**, 2642.
24. Overbeek,P.A., Chepelinsky,A., Khillan,J.S., Piatgorsky,J. and Westphal,M. (1985) *Proc. Natl. Acad. Sci. USA*, **82**, 7815.
25. Overbeek,P.A., Lai,S.-P., van Quill,K.R. and Westphal,H. (1986) *Science*, **231**, 1574.
26. Maniatis,T., Fritsch,E.F. and Sambrook,J. (1982) *Molecular Cloning: A Laboratory Manual*. Cold Spring Harbor, New York.
27. Treissman,R. (1985) *Cell*, **43**, 889.
28. Southern,E. (1974) *J. Mol. Biol.*, **98**, 503.
29. Kafatos,F.C., Jones,W.C. and Efstratiados,A. (1979) *Nucleic Acids Res.*, **7**, 1541.
30. Hanahan,D. (1985) *Nature*, **315**, 115.
31. Ornitz,D.M., Palmiter,R.D., Hammer,R.E,, Brinster,R.L., Swift,G. and MacDonald,R.J. (1985) *Nature*, **313**, 600.
32. Ornitz,D.M., Palmiter,R.D., Messing,A., Hammer,R.E., Pinkert,C.A. and Brinster,R.L. (1985) *Cold Spring Harbor Symp. Quant. Biol.*, **50**, 399.
33. Kollias,G., Wrighton,N., Hurst,J. and Grosveld,F. (1986) *Cell*, **46**, 89.
34. Woychik,R.P., Stewart,T.A., Davis,L.G., D'Eustachhio,P. and Leder,P. (1985) *Nature*, **318**, 36.
35. Ecker,J.A. and Davis,R.W. (1986) *Proc. Natl. Acad. Sci. USA*, **83**, 5372.
36. Hammer,R.E., Pursel,V.G., Rexroad,C.E., Wall,R.J., Bolt,D.J., Ebert,K.M., Palmiter,R.D. and Brinster,R.L. (1985) *Nature*, **315**, 680.

INDEX

Also available from IRL Press

DNA Cloning Volume I

Contents:

The use of phage lambda replacement vectors in the construction of representative genomic DNA libraries   *K.Kaiser and N.E.Murray*

Constructing and screening cDNA libraries in λgt 10 and λgt 11   *T.V.Huynh, R.A.Young and R.W.Davis*

An alternative procedure for the synthesis of double stranded cDNA for cloning in phage and plasmid vectors   *C.J.Watson and J.F.Jackson*

Immunological detection of chimeric β-galactosidases expressed by plasmid vectors   *M.Koenen, H.-W.Griesser and B.Müller-Hill*

The pEMBL family of single-stranded vectors   *L.Dente, M.Sollazzo, C.Baldari, G.Cesareni and R.Cortese*

Techniques for transformation of *E. coli*   *D.Hanahan*

The use of genetic markers for the selection and allelic exchange of *in vitro* induced mutations that do not have a phenotype in *E. coli*   *G.Cesareno, C.Traboni, G.Ciliberto, L.Dente and R.Cortese*

The oligonucleotide-directed construction of mutations in recombinant filamentous phage   *H.-J.Fritz*

Broad host range cloning vectors for Gram-negative bacteria   *F.C.H.Franklin*

DNA Cloning Volume II

Contents:

Bacillus cloning methods   *K G Hardy*

Gene cloning in *Streptomyces*   *I S Hunter*

Cloning in yeast   *R Rothstein*

Genetic engineering of plants   *C Lichtenstein and J Draper*

P element mediated germ line transformation of *Drosophila*   *R E Karess*

High efficiency gene transfer into mammalian cells   *C Gorman*

The construction and characterisation of vaccinia virus recombinants expressing foreign genes   *M Mackett, G L Smith and B Moss*

Bovine papillomavirus DNA: a eukaryotic cloning vector   *M S Campo*